T0399035

Modern Character

Modern Character

1888–1905

JULIAN MURPHET

OXFORD
UNIVERSITY PRESS

Great Clarendon Street, Oxford, OX2 6DP,
United Kingdom

Oxford University Press is a department of the University of Oxford.
It furthers the University's objective of excellence in research, scholarship,
and education by publishing worldwide. Oxford is a registered trade mark of
Oxford University Press in the UK and in certain other countries

Published in the United States of America by Oxford University Press
198 Madison Avenue, New York, NY 10016, United States of America

British Library Cataloguing in Publication Data

Data available

Library of Congress Control Number: 2023946457

ISBN 9780192863126

DOI: 10.1093/oso/9780192863126.001.0001

Printed and bound by
CPI Group (UK) Ltd, Croydon, CR0 4YY

For Laura Marcus

in memoriam

Preface

It is a question as old as the Seven Hills of Athens. Is character multiple or singular? In Book X of *The Republic*, Socrates and Glaucon discuss imitative poetry once more, and hit upon a fundamental misgiving with the Homeric and tragic traditions of narrative representation. Reflecting on the optimal constitution of the soul, Socrates proposes that a stoical, impersonal mastery of one's emotional turmoil is far preferable to the variable moods and affects that cast one's character to the breeze. The 'best part of us' is supposed to master and subdue 'the hurt part' that gives rise to the compulsive dissolutions of lamentation, grief, and sorrow. And herein lies the problem of mimetic poetry.

> Now, this excitable character admits of many multicolored imitations. But a rational and quiet character, which always remains pretty well the same, is neither easy to imitate nor easy to understand when imitated, especially not by a crowd consisting of all sorts of people gathered together at a theater festival . . .[1]

Literary representation feeds upon and amplifies the 'irrational, idle' forces in our souls, refracting them into clearly recognizable but dissociated passions, and so contributes to the undoing of our sober selves. The 'rational and quiet character', not being distinguished by any notable traits or identifying marks, eludes representation; it is, indeed, not susceptible to representation, much as Kant would later stipulate for consciousness, since, as what all representation is referred to, it is subtracted from the field as the eye from what it surveys.[2] Plato, auguring the age of reason, makes a case for the 'reasoning character' (the *ratio*) as immune to mimesis.

> Clearly, then, an imitative poet isn't by nature related to the part of the soul that rules in such a character, and, if he's to attain a good reputation with the majority of people, his cleverness isn't directed to pleasing it. Instead, he's related to the excitable and multicolored character, since it is easy to imitate.[3]

[1] Plato, *Republic* X, 604d–e, trans. G. M. A. Grube and C. D. C. Reeve, in John M. Cooper, ed., *Plato: Complete Works* (Indianapolis: Hackett, 1997), 1209.

[2] See Fredric Jameson, *A Singular Modernity: Essay on the Ontology of the Present* (London: Verso, 2002), 44–54.

[3] Plato, *Republic* X, 605a, Cooper, ed., *Plato*, 1209.

Successful literature, then, undoes the rational consistency and singularity of a noble character by exposing it to the appetites of the plebs: 'an imitative poet puts a bad constitution in the soul of each individual by making images that are far removed from the truth and by gratifying the irrational part' (*Republic* X, 605b–c, 1209–10). A good reason to ban it from the ideal city.

Theoretical reflection on 'character' has always turned in the gyre created by atmospheric tensions between the One and the Many, and Plato reminds us palpably of the class struggles implicit in such tensions. The 'best part' of the soul is noble, singular, regulatory, cool, implacable; the 'irrational part' is open to the various complications, multiplicities, colorations, and excitations that emanate from the crowd, the unruly multitude of a theatre-going populace. The One is incapable of representation; the Many are the stock in trade of *mimēsis*. As it is in the *polis*, so it is in *ēthos* and *kharaktēr*. Whatever the multifarious distinctive traits and marks that define an individual or a people, there is one occult, unrepresentable essence—of reasoning, impersonal sovereignty—that presides over its ever-shifting complexion of tones and shades. Without it, multiplicity descends into anarchy: decadence. With it, a sound will can be translated into effects and the good may yet prevail. Such an aristocratic, monarchic conception of character will fluctuate in literary speculation over the next two and half millennia, making room for republican and democratic currents of thought without ever fully being deposed—apart from one brief interlude which is the topic of this book.

Outside of mainstream literary theory, ancient concerns intersect with contemporary theory in more suggestive ways. Here, the monarchic conception of character has been under siege for a century or more. Neuroscience proposes that what I took for a self, a 'sovereign nation' of self-consistent, organized integrity, turns out to be a fort besieged by a 'riot of free agents', making 'me' 'a blind head of state, barricaded in the presidential suite, listening only to handpicked advisors as the country reels through ad hoc mobilizations'.[4] Where 'I' was, there 'they' go: 'Too many parts for [my] brain to remember. Even a part named the unnamed substance. And they all had a mind of their own, each haggling to be heard above the others' (439). What could be more provisional, fictional, than the 'one' I took myself to be? It is a question already provoked, and extensively explored, by Freud a century before, only now cast in a new aesthetic form:

> What do we find in the brain? Billions of neurons (around twenty billion in humans) connected in a network of innumerable links, the synapses. 'The human brain', says Changeux, 'makes one think of a gigantic assembly of tens of billions of interlacing neuronal "spider's webs" in which myriads of electrical impulses flash by, relayed from time to time by a rich array of chemical signals.' These

[4] Richard Powers, *The Echo Maker* (London: Vintage, 2007), 439, 460.

'spider's webs', neuronal connections also called 'arborizations', are constituted progressively over the course of an individual's development.[5]

For Nietzsche and the materialist psychologists of the 1880s, all of this was already obvious.

> However far a man may go in self-knowledge, nothing . . . can be more incomplete than his image of the totality of *drives* which constitute his being. He can scarcely name even the cruder ones: their number and strength, their ebb and flood, their play and counterplay among one another and above all the laws of their *nutriment* remain wholly unknown to him.[6]

The naturalistic sense of the 'soul as a society constructed out of drives and affects' ran throughout psychological speculation before Freud.[7] Ribot wrote of the 'sum of conscious, sub-conscious, and unconscious (purely physical) states which at the [given] moment constitute the person, the ego'.[8] Henry Maudsley thought that 'What we call the ego, is in reality an abstraction in which are contained the residua of all former feelings, thoughts, volitions,—a combination which is continually becoming more and more complex.'[9]

So much for psychology. What, then, of the social self? Writing about class composition in the new millennium, McKenzie Wark suggests that, as a relational category, class connects 'not individuals but . . . *dividuals*, units of being smaller than an individual. It turns out that individuals can indeed be further divided.'[10] Gerald Raunig ties this breaking apart of the older individual to contemporary developments in 'Big-Data-Knowledge-Complexes', and claims that 'machinic capitalism' 'arranges the molecular level of dividual desiring into new compliant assemblages'.[11] Negt and Kluge, in their *History and Obstinacy*, present a human being constituted, not by regularity and integrity, but by internal differentiation and subdivision. 'Crack open the psyche, and you find a multiplicity of vying voices and impulses, an elaborate dialectical configuration of forces and

[5] Catherine Malabou, *What Should We Do with Our Brain?*, trans. Sebastian Rand (New York: Fordham University Press, 2008), 17–18.

[6] Friedrich Nietzsche, *Daybreak*, II, 119, ed. Maudemarie Clark and Brian Leiter, trans. R. J. Hollingdale (Cambridge: Cambridge University Press, 1997), 74.

[7] Friedrich Nietzsche, *Beyond Good and Evil: Prelude to a Philosophy of the Future*, 12, ed. Rolf-Peter Horstmann and Judith Norman, trans. Judith Norman (Cambridge: Cambridge University Press, 2002), 14.

[8] Théodule Ribot, *Diseases of the Will*, trans. Merwin Snell (Chicago: Open Court, 1894 [c.1883]), 21.

[9] Henry Maudsley, *The Physiology and Pathology of the Mind* (1867), qtd. in *The Westminster Review* (January & April 1868), 62 [37–64].

[10] McKenzie Wark, *Capital is Dead*, Ebook edition (London and New York: Verso, 2019), Kindle Locations 1513–16.

[11] Gerald Raunig, *Dividuum: Machinic Capitalism and Molecular Revolution*, trans. Aileen Derieg (Pasadena: Semiotext(e), 2016), 90.

counterforces arranged with a sense for equilibrium.'[12] Richard Sennett established a profound relationship between the disintegration of basic moral and psychological unities, and the relentless assault by the economy on traditional forms of life. What he calls the 'corrosion of character' under late capitalism amounts to a pulverization of the stable ego by new 'flexible' work regimes and the 24/7 world clock of grinding accumulation. 'A pliant self, a collage of fragments unceasing in its becoming, ever open to new experience—these are just the psychological conditions suited to short-term work experience, flexible institutions, and constant risk-taking.'[13] The similarity of this minor-key description to the major-key account of a 'schizo' selfhood in Deleuze and Guattari's *Anti-Oedipus* is striking, and chimes with that text's interest in 'pure multiplicity', the plethora of 'desiring-machines' plugged into a body without organs: 'There is no sort of evolution of drives that would cause these drives and their objects to progress in the direction of an integrated whole, any more than there is an original totality from which they can be derived.'[14] Drives *are*; they intersect and diverge, passing through the individuals whom they cleave and dissociate *en route* to other assemblages.

The term 'dividual' derives from the ruminations of Bertolt Brecht on metapsychology: 'What should be stressed about the individual is precisely his divisibility (as he belongs to several collectives).'[15]

> The individual appeared to us more and more as a contradictory complex in constant development. Seen from outside, it may behave as a unity, and still it is a multitude full of fights, in which the most different tendencies gain the upper hand, so that the eventual action only represents the compromise. (22.2: 691)

As 'the individual is a "dividual"', 'an abstraction, concealing the fact that the human subject really is a superimposition of many different characters',[16] so multiplicity separates the pliant stuff of personhood into fragments of a lost whole. '[The human being] falls apart, he loses his breath. He turns into something else, he is nameless, he no longer has any face, he escapes from his overstretched state into

[12] Devin Fore, Introduction to Alexander Kluge and Oskar Negt, *History and Obstinacy*, trans. Richard Langston et al., ed. Devin Fore (New York: Zone Books, 2014), 44.

[13] Richard Sennett, *The Corrosion of Character: The Personal Consequences of Work in the New Capitalism* (New York and London: W. W. Norton, 1998), 133.

[14] Gilles Deleuze and Félix Guattari, *Anti-Oedipus: Capitalism and Schizophrenia*, trans. Robert Hurley, Mark Seem, and Helen R. Lane (Minneapolis: University of Minnesota Press, 1983), 44.

[15] Bertolt Brecht, *Große kommentierte Berliner und Frankfurter Ausgabe* (Berlin-Weimar-Frankfurt am Main: Suhrkamp, 1989–2000), 21: 359. Partly translated in Wolfgang Haug, 'Philosophizing with Marx, Gramsci and Brecht', *boundary 2* 34.3 (Fall 2007), 150.

[16] Stefan Jonsson, 'Neither Masses nor Individuals: Representations of the Collective in Interwar German Culture', in Kathleen Canning, Kerstin Barndt, and Kristin McGuire, eds., *Weimar Publics / Weimar Subjects: Rethinking the Political Culture of Germany in the 1920s* (New York and Oxford: Berghahn Books, 2010), 291. See also Stefan Jonsson, *Crowds and Democracy: The Idea and Image of the Masses from Revolution to Fascism* (New York: Columbia University Press, 2013), 160.

his smallest proportion—from his dispensability into nothingness.'[17] The direct equation that Brecht makes between this characterological disassembly and the mass-production processes of the Fordist assembly line—in *Mann ist Mann*—is particularly lucid:

> Tonight you are going to see a man reassembled like a car,
> Leaving all his individual components just as they are.[18]

What I propose in this book is a way of looking at an episode of literary history as a genuine intervention in thought. In brief, the kind of anti-Platonic thinking about character we see elaborated by Nietzsche, Brecht, Freud, Deleuze, Sennett, Kluge, and others in the twentieth century—dethroning the singular 'rational and quiet' seat of character in the name of a swarming multitude of irreconcilable 'dividual' components—can be mapped onto a determinate break from Western models of literary character made by a motley crew of writers at the end of the nineteenth century. These writers, fully accepting Plato's charge that 'the excitable and multicolored character' is easier to represent than the rational subject of Enlightenment, pushed the insight as far as it could go, pursuing their formally audacious depictions of characterological deliquescence and decay as a critical engagement with what Reason was doing to modern life: sapping it of romance, enshrining an empty bureaucratic centre, putting rational means to irrational ends, subduing independence and charisma, paying for inordinate wealth with structural poverty, and shoring up the sovereign Western subject with ubiquitous sexual and racial divisions of labour. It was these literary artists who, defecting on centuries of formal protocols around character presentation, collectively jettisoned the hegemonic 'best part' of the human soul in order to give the 'hurt part' its proper due: creating new chromaticisms of intensifying mood and affect, combining brittle personae into unprecedented group formations, descending into anomie and aimlessness, and discovering rich aesthetic potentiality in the molecular corpuscles of a shattered individuality. This momentous *putsch* against the singular on the part of the multiple is one of the great unsung passages in literary history. It cannot adequately be sung in a single volume, and this work, which covers only the years 1888–1905, is conceived as the first of three consecutive volumes that would take us through to the 1930s and so complete a picture of the most monumental and underappreciated event in characterology since Shakespeare. Whether there is an appetite for that fuller picture remains to be seen.

[17] Bertolt Brecht, '[Notizen über] Individuum und Masse' [1929], in *Gesammelte Werke* (Frankfurt am Main: Suhrkamp, 1967), 60. Translated by Stefan Jonsson.

[18] Bertolt Brecht, *Man Equals Man*, trans. Gerhard Nellhaus, in *Collected Plays: Two*, ed. John Willett and Ralph Mannheim (London: Methuen, 1979), 38.

Acknowledgements

I am grateful to John Frow in many things, including his support for this project. I thank Regenia Gagnier for her help with Chapter 5, Benjamin Madden for his help with Chapter 6, Madeleine Seys for her help with Chapter 9, and for her help with the Bibliography, Clare Charlesworth. Anonymous readers for Oxford University Press clarified certain methodological issues. I thank them both. At the Press, I am extremely grateful to Jacqueline Norton, who has supported this project from the start, and to the editorial team in literary studies for their exemplary work. At home, I am grateful for the love and support of Tamlyn Avery, who can't be thanked sufficiently. My sons, Felix and Gabriel, and my parents, Mary and Richard, are constant sources of love and care.

This book was chiefly written for Laura Marcus, whose untimely death has left a hole where its chief interlocutor ought to be. Like so many, I benefited in innumerable ways from her generosity and warmth of soul. We are all poorer for her loss.

Acknowledgements

Contents

Introduction

At some point early in the current century, a consensus emerged about the excesses and oversights of a recent movement in literary studies, so-called poststructuralism, which in its methodological zeal had overstated the degree to which textuality was an unstable process woven of multiple codes, at the expense of more commonsense and pragmatic engagements with literary discourse.[1] In no other domain of literary theory has this reaction been more conspicuous than in the contemporary reconsideration of 'character', where all the established axioms of the 1970s and 1980s appear to have been rejected for their antihumanism and indifference to moral philosophy, their perverse refusal to endorse models of literary personhood that cannot be reduced to diagrams, semiotics, and imbricated codes.[2] This reaction against a once-privileged conceptual apparatus has taken two distinct paths in character scholarship: theoretical metalanguage, and literary history. In wide-ranging studies such as Anderson, Felski, and Moi's *Character: Three Inquiries*, Blakey Vermeule's *Why Do We Care about Literary Characters?*, and Marjorie Garber's *Character: The History of a Cultural Obsession*, we find a hostility towards any approach that leaves us 'with nothing to say about characters as objects of identification, sources of emotional response, or agents of moral vision and behavior', in life or literature.[3] Their interest is in showing how irreducible and transhistorical these moral and psychological domains of character have always been, and how

[1] See the discussions in Terry Eagleton, *After Theory* (New York: Basic Books, 2004); Rosi Braidotti, *After Poststructuralism: Transitions and Transformations* (London: Routledge, 2010); David R. Howarth, *Poststructuralism and After: Subjectivity and Power* (Basingstoke: Palgrave Macmillan, 2013); Paul Jay, *The Humanities 'Crisis' and the Future of Literary Studies* (Basingstoke: Palgrave Macmillan, 2014); Galin Tihanov, *The Birth and Death of Literary Theory: Regimes of Relevance in Russia and Beyond* (Stanford: Stanford University Press, 2019); and Benoît Dillet, Iain MacKenzie, and Rob Porter, 'Conclusion: Poststructuralism Today?', in Dillet, MacKenzie, and Porter, eds., *The Edinburgh Companion to Poststructuralism* (Edinburgh: Edinburgh University Press, 2013), 507–26.

[2] The classics of poststructuralist 'character criticism' were Roland Barthes, *S/Z*, trans. Richard Miller (Oxford: Blackwell, 1990); Hélène Cixous, 'The Character of "Character"', *New Literary History* 5 (1974): 383–402; and A. J. Greimas, *On Meaning: Selected Writings in Semiotic Theory*, trans. Paul J. Perron and Frank H. Collins (Minneapolis: University of Minnesota Press, 1987). But see also James H. Maddox Jr., *Joyce's Ulysses and the Assault upon Character* (New Brunswick: Rutgers University Press, 1978); James Naremore, *The World without a Self: Virginia Woolf and the Novel* (New Haven: Yale University Press, 1973); and Thomas Docherty, *Reading (Absent) Character: Towards a Theory of Characterization in Fiction* (Oxford: Clarendon Press, 1983).

[3] Amanda Anderson, Rita Felski, and Toril Moi, *Character: Three Inquiries in Literary Studies* (Chicago and London: University of Chicago Press, 2019), 4. See also Marjorie Garber, *Character: The History of a Cultural Obsession* (New York: Farrar, Straus, and Giroux, 2020); and Blakey Vermeule, *Why Do We Care about Literary Characters?* (Baltimore: Johns Hopkins University Press, 2009).

Modern Character. Julian Murphet, Oxford University Press. © Julian Murphet (2023).
DOI: 10.1093/oso/9780192863126.003.0001

tangled up with the protocols of literary representation they still are.[4] In more historical studies, like the contemporary survey of Marco Carraciolo's *Strange Narrators in Contemporary Fiction*, Sotirios Paraschas' nineteenth-century coverage in *Reappearing Characters in Nineteenth-Century French Literature*, or the eighteenth-century optic brought by Tara Wallace to *Imperial Characters*, the emphasis is also on perduring psychic modes of readerly investment in character, fictional personae's extra-literary cognitive and emotive bases in general social practices—and not on formal constructedness per se.[5] In one way or another, the presiding anti-theoretical intellectual mood has shaped the findings of historical literary inquiry, with the result that a book with the title *Fictional Characters, Real Problems: The Search for Ethical Content in Literature* (a work which never once mentions the names Barthes, Genette, or Greimas) can stand as typical of much work in the field today.[6]

What has happened to the bulk of character scholarship over the last thirty years is a case of reactive transvaluation, where profound shifts in the theoretical landscape have been critically applied to historical case studies. But if theory is only ever a distillation of historical facts, then surely this is putting the cart before the horse. What we want to know is not what 'character' is and must be by virtue of hard-wired cognitive and aesthetic laws, but what it has been capable of becoming in the hands of our most adventurous literary artists, who will have answered that question only in specific social and historical circumstances. The most important contributions to the theory and history of literary character in our recent period have hewed steadfastly to that critical maxim and advanced our knowledge of the topic in ways that 'rise from the abstract to the concrete' through full immersion in the formal characteristics of the historically situated bodies of work under consideration. A string of major monographs leads us from Chaucer and Spenser (in Elizabeth Fowler's *Literary Character*), through Fielding and Sterne (Deirdre Lynch's *The Economy of Character*), through Scott, Hazlitt, and Beddoes (Jonas Cope's *Dissolution of Character*), through Defoe and Hardy (Nicola Lacey's *Women, Crime, and Character*), through Austen, Balzac, and Dickens (Alex Woloch's *The One vs. the Many*), to Emerson and Melville (Susan Manning's *Poetics of Character*)—but then notably breaks from literary history and resumes again in the postmodern period (Elinor Fuchs' *Death of Character*; Murray Smith's

[4] '[F]ictional characters stay the same in one respect: they are the greatest practical-reasoning schemes ever invented. We use them to sort out basic moral problems or to practice new emotional situations.' Vermeule, *Why Do We Care about Literary Characters?*, xii.

[5] See Marco Carraciolo, *Strange Narrators in Contemporary Fiction: Explorations in Readers' Engagement with Characters* (Lincoln: University of Nebraska Press, 2016); Sotirios Paraschas, *Reappearing Characters in Nineteenth-Century French Literature: Authorship, Originality, and Intellectual Property* (London: Palgrave Macmillan, 2018); Tara Ghoshal Wallace, *Imperial Characters: Home and Periphery in Eighteenth-Century Literature* (Lewisburg: Bucknell University Press, 2010).

[6] Garry L. Hagberg, *Fictional Characters, Real Problems: The Search for Ethical Content in Literature* (Oxford: Oxford University Press, 2016).

Engaging Characters; Jeremy Rosen's *Minor Characters Have Their Day*).[7] This contemporary tradition of serious scholarly achievement undertakes a discontinuous and relatively subterranean theoretical initiative that stands aloof from the dominant trend of 'naive' or ethical criticism; but it would be fair to say that the theory of character developed in each of these works is so specific to its period of literary history that it forms a methodological monad with little overt application in any of the others. In that sense, the missing meta-theoretical labour could be said to have been displaced onto the shoulders of John Frow, whose epochal *Character and Person* is our period's summative statement on the matter at hand, gathering not only the latent theoretical consonances across these and other literary-historical works, but all of the major conceptual milestones of the structuralist and poststructuralist moments as well.[8] The only disadvantage of this towering work is, to be sure, its relative abstraction from the historical situations out of which 'character' and 'person' are woven in the first place—something the study was never intended to do, its agenda being entirely theoretical. Placing Frow's work alongside the string of monographs just rehearsed and thinking them together as a complex whole might yet be the best way to theorize the literary history of character today, and to historicize our sustaining theoretical victories over the empirical chaos of the literary record. Yet the historical sequence here—covered by Fowler through Woloch and Rosen—is far from complete. Most conspicuous, of course, is the absence of modernism from this body of work (though it punctuates Frow's book in salutary doses), an absence that is a major motivation behind the conception of the present study, whose ostensible purpose is fill that gap and so complete a provisional record of the major formal developments in literary character from Chaucer to the present day.

The gap in question, however, is more than merely accidental. It is symptomatic and emerges precisely from the anti-Theory impetus that rejects the '"modernist-formalist" alliance' and its supposed hostility towards 'treating characters as if they were real'.[9] What if this hostility stemmed, not from an invidious mandarin disposition, but from determinate historical movements in literary history itself? The

[7] See Elizabeth Fowler, *Literary Character: The Human Figure in Early English Writing* (Ithaca and London: Cornell University Press, 2003); Deirdre Shauna Lynch, *The Economy of Character: Novels, Market Culture, and the Business of Inner Meaning* (Chicago and London: University of Chicago Press, 1998); Jonas Cope, *The Dissolution of Character in Late Romanticism, 1820–1839* (Edinburgh: Edinburgh University Press, 2018); Alex Woloch, *The One vs. the Many: Minor Characters and the Space of the Protagonist in the Novel* (Princeton and Oxford: Princeton University Press, 2003); Nicola Lacey, *Women, Crime, and Character: From Moll Flanders to Tess of the D'Urbervilles* (Oxford and New York: Oxford University Press, 2008); Susan Manning, *Poetics of Character: Transatlantic Encounters 1700–1900* (Cambridge: Cambridge University Press, 2013); Elinor Fuchs, *The Death of Character: Perspectives on Theater after Modernism* (Bloomington and Indianapolis: Indiana University Press, 1996); Murray Smith, *Engaging Characters: Fiction, Emotion, and the Cinema* (Oxford: Clarendon Press, 1995); Jeremy Rosen, *Minor Characters Have Their Day: Genre and the Contemporary Literary Marketplace* (New York: Columbia University Press, 2016).

[8] John Frow, *Character and Person* (Oxford: Oxford University Press, 2014).

[9] See Toril Moi's contribution to Anderson, Felski, and Moi, *Character*, esp. 30–49.

guiding premise of *Modern Character* is that metacommentary on questions of literary form cannot be isolated from the horizon of literary history; and that something very peculiar happened on that horizon between the years of 1888 and 1905 which should have significant repercussions on any subsequent theoretical discussion of literary character (as it did, to be sure, during the heyday of poststructuralism). In brief, I will argue that what happened tended, in a variety of ways, to loosen the conventions of literary character from prevailing norms of comprehension and consumption: 'characters [understood] as objects of identification, sources of emotional response, or agents of moral vision and behavior'.[10] For reasons that are complex and sometimes contradictory, writers at this critical juncture in literary history developed techniques and representational devices that would repel, or at least problematize, these entrenched ethical habits of reading in favour of what I will follow Rancière in calling a more 'aesthetic' approach to character.[11]

As a central component of the apparatus of literary discourse for millennia, character has traditionally served as the principal conductor of that vital readerly activity, identification.[12] But what seems to have happened at the turn of the twentieth century, in any number of distinct locations, is that this conductive node was relatively (and sometimes explicitly) deprivileged along with identification itself, to clear space for other modes of investment in the literary text: pattern recognition, holistic awareness, catching waves of free-floating sensation and affect, sensing distributed resonance, and similar kinds of attentive percipience that were hampered by excessive character identification. The 'common tendency to treat characters as if they were persons' was, all at once, resisted by writers who had learned to resent a number of uncomfortable consequences stemming from it.[13] These included the sense of artistic complicity with an exhausted and compromised model of the individual, a neglect of higher-order spiritual or

[10] Anderson, Felski, and Moi, *Character*, 4.

[11] 'At the end of the nineteenth century, Mallarmé opposed the derisory stage that simply offered the ladies and gentlemen of the audience their counterfeits, and tried to tease out the new power of a form of fiction no longer linked to belief in the existence of a character, but to the "special power of illusion" proper to each art.' Jacques Rancière, *Figures of History*, trans. Julie Rose (Cambridge: Polity, 2014), 55–6. My argument is that Mallarmé sounded the initial shots in a much wider campaign to make this aesthetic shift, with enormous consequences for the category of character.

[12] See Murray Smith, *Engaging Characters: Fiction, Emotion, and the Cinema* (Oxford: Clarendon Press, 1995), 110–16; P. E. Jose and W. F. Brewer, 'Development of Story-Liking: Character Identification, Suspense, and Outcome Resolution', *Developmental Psychology* 20 (1984): 911–24; Fotis Jannidis, *Figur und Person: Beitrag zu einer historischen Narratologie* (Berlin: De Gruyter, 2004), 229–36; K. Oatley and M. Gholamain, 'Emotions and Identification: Connections between Readers and Fiction', in M. Hjort and S. Laver, eds., *Emotion and the Arts* (Oxford: Oxford University Press, 1997), 263–81; Hans Robert Jauß, 'Levels of Identification of Hero and Audience', *New Literary History* 5.2 (1974): 283–317; Simone Winko, 'On the Constitution of Characters in Poetry', in Jens Eder, Fotis Jannidis, and Ralf Schneider, eds., *Characters in Fictional Worlds: Understanding Imaginary Beings in Literature, Film, and Other Media* (Berlin: De Gruyter, 2010), 208–31.

[13] Anderson, Felski, and Moi, *Character*, 12. Here I must note a strong divergence from the assumed models of characterology in modernism presented by Amanda Anderson: 'the glorification of the subjective in Wilde; the will to power and the heroic characterology of Nietzsche (becoming who one is); the more general aggrandizement of the individual in early modernism'. *The Way We Argue Now: A*

aesthetic values, an inculcated blindness to social transformations that tended towards more generic and collective forms of identity,[14] and the widening scope of global encounters fostered by imperialism and free trade. That literary 'character' should be reconsidered and remodelled at this moment is on one level hardly surprising; this is, after all, the beginning of a world-wide artistic revolt against automated forms and values. What is surprising is that contemporary arguments about this critical category have been working hard to downplay the significance of this for theoretical reflection. My case is that literary history must always be allowed to resonate in literary theoretical arguments, and that historical changes in practice, however long their duration, signal the necessity for changes in a conceptual *dispositif.*

Here it seems appropriate to suggest that what the poststructuralists were making of the concept of character in the 1970s was a direct result of their extensive readings in what the generation of modernists had already done to it in writing from the period extending from 1888 through to the end of the 1920s:[15] dismantling its assumed consistency and depth, demonstrating its Humean properties of inner flux and discontinuity, foregrounding its multiple affective and perceptive states, resisting its reduction to simple agency within a plot, allowing its various personae to overlap and contradict one another, forming it into groups, and so on. Theoretical capture tends to reify such achievements as transhistorical concepts, and a set of distributed practices is represented as a set of invariable principles and values. So, the typical 'poststructuralist' reading of character may well have preferred to 'avoid concepts such as the autonomous subject, the human, or reference to reality',[16] in order to focus on textual problems (for example, the social construction of the human, the functions and structures of social subjectivity, or the textual shaping of reality), in a way that took the lessons of the modernists as gospel for a reappraisal of the entire history of literature—overlooking the many precious victories over prejudice and superstition represented by each of those concepts.[17]

Study in the Cultures of Theory (Princeton: Princeton University Press, 2006), 139. This is, indeed, the very opposite of what my study will show to be the case.

[14] 'Most people are other people. Their thoughts are someone else's opinions, their life a mimicry, their passions a quotation [. . .] they borrow their ideas from a sort of circulating library of thought.' Oscar Wilde, *De Profundis and Other Prison Writings*, ed. Colm Tóibín (London: Penguin, 2013), 118, 146.

[15] It is always worth remembering what inveterate readers the leading theoreticians of this school were of the modernists: see Julia Kristeva, *Revolution in Poetic Language*, trans. Margaret Walker (New York: Columbia University Press, 1984); Gilles Deleuze, 'The Exhausted', in *Essays Critical and Clinical*, trans. Daniel W. Smith and Michael A. Greco (Minneapolis: University of Minnesota Press, 1997), 152–74; the essays on Mallarmé, Joyce, and Celan in Jacques Derrida, *Acts of Literature*, ed. and trans. Derek Attridge (New York: Routledge, 1992), 110–26, 253–309, 370–413; as a small sample.

[16] Anderson, Felski, and Moi, *Character*, p. 4.

[17] The literature on the emergence of the 'modern self' is too vast to require much elucidation here, but obviously Charles Taylor, *Sources of the Self: The Making of the Modern Identity* (Cambridge, MA: Harvard University Press, 1989); Erving Goffmann, *The Presentation of Self in Everyday Life* (New York: Doubleday, 1959); Jerrold E. Seigel, *The Idea of the Self: Thought and Experience in Western Europe since the Seventeenth Century* (Cambridge: Cambridge University Press, 2005); and

For instance, Michel Foucault's well-known questions—'under what conditions and through what forms can an entity like the subject appear in the order of discourse; what position does it occupy; what functions does it exhibit; and what rules does it follow in each type of discourse?'—may have tended to sidestep the several advantages 'the subject' betokened at the level of experience, action, and consciousness; and his practical advice—'the subject (and its substitutes) must be stripped of its creative role and analysed as a complex and variable function of discourse'—flown in the face of some extraordinary advances in narrative technique across the eighteenth and nineteenth centuries.[18] And yet, it remains the case that, for two or three generations over the turn of the twentieth century, many of the world's most significant literary artists agreed that it might indeed be productive to proceed as if 'the subject' and its cognate categories, well-established and now conventional characterological notions, were effectively 'under erasure' or at least pushed to the margins of their literary enterprise. That is the central claim of this book, along with the corollary claim that theory ignores this episode of literary history at considerable peril.

We can now begin thinking these problems through in a practical application. A relatively straightforward example of how an incipient new tendency works its way stealthily through established formal conventions can be found in Anton Chekhov's momentous 'A Boring Story' (Скучная история; 1889), which appears on the very threshold of the literary history being examined here. The story is an obvious derivation from the model pioneered by Lev Tolstoy in his novella 'The Death of Ivan Ilych' (Смерть Ивана Ильича; 1886): an old pedant nearing the end of his life confronts the fact that he is alienated from those nearest to him. But Chekhov resists Tolstoy's efforts in the direction of reconciliation to concentrate on the gap separating his protagonist—Nikolai Stepanovich—from his colleagues, his loved ones, and himself. If Tolstoy's character study moves towards introspective discovery and spiritual illumination, Chekhov's remains adamantly in the mode of sceptical alienation. The difference is apparent in Chekhov's formal decision to keep all but the final episode of his tale in the 'iterative' present tense of generic, repetitive temporality, as against Tolstoy's more conventional narrative preterite. 'A Boring Story' proceeds in the iterative to underscore its diegetic narrator's generic condition: what happens to him daily has always happened, nothing is new under the sun, and his 'character' is a kind of life sentence in the suffocating temporality of the always-already. There is a subjective misgiving at the heart of this novella, an internal resistance that only one other character—the narrator's beloved, adopted Katya—can detect and sympathize with; and it is a resistance with nowhere narratively to go.

Gilles Deleuze, *Empiricism and Subjectivity: An Essay on Hume's Theory of Human Nature* (New York: Columbia University Press, 2001), can stand as lodestars for any contemporary survey of the field.

[18] Michel Foucault, 'What Is an Author?', in *Language, Counter-Memory, Practice: Selected Essays and Interviews*, ed. Donald F. Bouchard (Ithaca: Cornell University Press, 1977), 137 [113–38].

Into this intriguing mutation of the Tolstoyan frame there then intrude indications that something momentous and consequential is happening to the category of character; portents, I suggest, of things to come. In the first place, there is the explicit excision of the protagonist's patronymic, a denomination seized upon by the narrator as a way of prying open a new kind of negative capability. If, as John Frow writes, '[f]ictional characters are identified above all (but not necessarily) by a name'—'a kind of hook on which properties are hung'—and if, furthermore, the patronym is the chief authenticating suture between a person and a social role in a patriarchy (say, a scientist-professor in the Russian state), then withholding one is a blow to that crucial 'imputation of identity' in the fictional persona and to the mechanics of identification that flow from it.[19] The narrator who bears a famous name but refrains from mentioning it reflects on its aura:

> This name of mine is popular. In Russia it is known to every literate person, and abroad it is mentioned from podiums with the addition of well-known and esteemed. It is one of those few fortunate names which it is considered bad tone to abuse or take in vain, in public or in print. And so it should be. For my name is closely connected with the notion of a man who is famous, richly endowed, and unquestionably useful. [. . .] Generally, there is not a single blot on my learned name, and it has nothing to complain of. It is happy.[20]

Clearly, however, there has been a delamination of this happy name from its increasingly miserable bearer, and this separation functions as a kind of permanent irony—'As my name is brilliant and beautiful, so I myself am dull and ugly' (56)—which has its figural precedents in the grotesque allegories of Gogol. As with the nose or overcoat in a Gogol story, the name here seems to have a life of its own. In the story's final sequence, in Kharkov, 'Nikolai Stepanovich So-and-so' [Николай Степанович такой-то] reads about his arrival in the city in a local paper: 'Evidently, great names are created so as to live by themselves, apart from their bearers. Now my name is peacefully going about Kharkov . . .' (105). Name and person have fatefully gone their separate ways. The decision to withhold the patronymic from the story's discourse is in the service of a structural irony that underscores the encroaching anonymity of the protagonist, his falling out of the frame his illustrious name continues to occupy, into a region of blank and generic old age.

This is only the beginning of the immense risks taken in this tale; for alongside the problem of the proper name another problem emerges, concerning the consistency of the person orphaned by his name, his very coherence and integrity. And it transpires that the true 'event' of the story is the far more radical abandonment

[19] Frow, *Character and Person*, 187.

[20] Anton Chekhov, *Stories*, trans. Richard Pevear and Larissa Volokhonsky (New York: Bantam Books, 2000), 55–6.

of the de-nominated person by 'the general idea or the god of the living man', the perduring core of character as such:

> And however much I think, however widely my thought ranges, it's clear to me that my wishes lack some chief thing, some very important thing. In my predilection for science, in my wish to live, in this sitting on a strange bed and trying to know myself, in all the thoughts, feelings, and conceptions I form about everything, something general is lacking that would unite it all into a single whole. Each feeling and thought lives separately in me, and in all my opinions about science, the theatre, literature, students, and in all the pictures drawn by my imagination, even the most skillful analyst would be unable to find what is known as a general idea or the god of the living man.
>
> And if there isn't that, there's nothing.
>
> (104–5)

Corresponding to the absence of that 'hook' of a name on which to hang characteristic properties, is this desertion of the inner 'god' that holds a personality together, gives it ethical coherence. The resultant sense of inner multiplicity, a swarm of irreconcilable percepts and affects, 'a fragmentation of experience that calls our ordinary notions of identity into question',[21] lacks any informing substance, and even the most 'skillful analyst' of all—the literary artist, or novelist—cannot discover what has ceased to exist. Character undergoes a dissolution in the maelstrom of residual and unmoored psychic part-objects. What results from this is what much of the following study attempts to chart: it is called 'modern character', and from it various theoretical lessons can be learned.

First, a character is not always fixed to a name. Second, a character need not even have a character. Third, a story need be about nothing but these 'not havings'. And fourth, the result—the title simply calls it 'dreary' or 'boring' [Скучная], but that is obviously a placeholder for something else—is an affect otherwise inaccessible to more conventionally named and integrated fictional personae. As a transitional text, positioned on the border between one literary order of things and another, Chekhov's tale is not yet divorced from readerly, ethical habits of engagement. Readers can continue to identify with and understand this old man, appreciate his vexatious condition, see him in the round; he belongs to a long history of protagonists who are exhausted or worn out by the world. And yet, something has happened within the conventional frame that signals deep and historic tectonic shifts. There is a loosening of discourse from moral expectation; an acceptance of psychic fragmentation as a permanent condition; an abandonment of narrative intrigue or even interest; and a refusal to resolve any of the aesthetic ruptures on

[21] Lindsay Waters, Introduction to Paul de Man, *Critical Writings, 1953–1978* (Minneapolis: University of Minnesota Press, 1989), xxxii.

display. All of this is located in the very narratological place where a voice fails to coincide with a name, and where a person fails to coincide with a role—that is to say, it is entirely a matter of characterization. Chekhov has seized an opportunity lying dormant in the Tolstoyan form and forced a break in literary history—the break we will be calling *modern character.*

The person responsible for nominating 'modern character' as such was a contemporary of Chekhov, and another of the key figures in the story that follows: August Strindberg. In his preface to *Miss Julie* (1888), written as a calling card for Émile Zola, we detect several prefigurations of the poststructuralist critique of character:

> As modern characters, living in an age of transition more urgently hysterical than the one that preceded it, I have depicted the figures in my play as more split and vacillating, a mixture of the old and the new [...]. My souls (characters) are conglomerates of past and present stages of culture, bits out of books and newspapers, scraps of humanity, torn shreds of once fine clothing now turned to rags, exactly as the human soul is patched together [...]. Miss Julie is a modern character.[22]

Strindberg, steeped as he was in Naturalism at the time, related his aesthetic decisions about characterological fragmentation and anachronistic conglomeration to recent sociological developments in the life of the 'human soul'; but the discovery being articulated here is about much more than current trends in psychology and determinism. Essentially, Strindberg is announcing the same kind of artistic breakthrough that Chekhov's Nikolai Stepanovich discovers when he looks into himself and finds that every 'feeling and thought lives separately in me'—namely, that character is now not so much an identity as a field of contention between radically separated elements, a jerry-rigged assemblage of disparate phenomena and powers lacking any integrating master component. And very different things can be done with such a character than the usual business of delegating to it the responsibility of carrying out a sequence of actions while allowing it the luxury of expressing its innermost 'soul'. To be a modern character like Miss Julie or Nikolai Stepanovich is to be delivered (relatively speaking) from the compulsions of a plot and the injunctions of a moral substance, free to perform a very different set of functions.

The poststructuralist critique of character made similar arguments on a theoretical level. The inaugural separation of the 'agential' from the other, more discursive aspects of character, stemming ultimately from Aristotle, entailed a methodological predisposition not to 'see character solely as a function of action', as has been charged,[23] but merely to sequester this dimension of character from the fact that

[22] August Strindberg, 'Preface' to *Miss Julie* in Michael Robinson, ed. and trans., *Miss Julie and Other Plays* (Oxford: Oxford University Press, 1998), 59–60. See much more in Chapter 3, below.

[23] Anderson, Felski, and Moi, *Character*, 3.

these agents 'must necessarily [also] have their distinctive qualities both of character and thought'.[24] This partition allowed analysis to pursue two distinct paths that intermittently interrelated: character as a function of plot, and character as that nimbus of qualities and ideations that give rise to an illusion of individuality. With this methodological rift in place, it became possible to show how artificial and constructed each aspect of character truly was. Agency was purely a formal category dictated by the concerns of the plot, and (with Greimas and Propp) able to be analysed into multiple foci or shared by any number of fictional personae. Meanwhile, Roland Barthes would follow Todorov, who wrote that 'the grammatical subject is always without internal properties; these can come only from its momentary conjunction with a predicate', and insisted that the same was true for narrative character.[25] 'The seme (or the signified of connotation, strictly speaking) is a connotator of persons, places, objects, of which the signified is a *character*. Character is an adjective, an attribute, a predicate (for example: *unnatural, shadowy, star, composite, excessive, impious*, etc.).'[26] The classical realist text is thus one engineered around an 'ideology of the person' which the proliferation and concentration of semes under the proper name cements in form and function.

> As soon as a Name exists (even a pronoun) to flow toward and fasten onto, the semes become predicates, indictors of truth, and the Name becomes a subject: we can say that what is proper to narrative is not action but the character as Proper Name: the semic raw material (corresponding to a certain moment in our history of the narrative) *completes* what is proper to being, *fills* the name with adjectives. (190–1)

My point here is that this separation was a major part of the purpose of 'modern character' in the first place, which led to a greater degree of deliquescence of both characterological agency and consistent quality than in any previous period in literary history. As we will see in the various chapters of this book, there arose in the 1890s a marked suspicion and hostility towards the very idea of a plot, and an awareness that action had falsely dominated the repertoire of character representation in fiction and drama for too long. This gave rise to a related tendency to fashion works that demoted action to test what 'distinctive qualities both of character and thought' might look like when spared the trials of agency. For Aristotle, character was simply 'what makes us ascribe certain qualities to the agents', and qualities were for Aristotle secondary, epiphenomenal things, since it

[24] Aristotle, *The Poetics*, §6, in *The Complete Works of Aristotle, Vol. 2*, ed. and trans. Jonathan Barnes, Bollingen Series LXXI: 2 (Princeton: Princeton University Press, 1984), 2320.

[25] Tzvetan Todorov, *Grammaire du Décaméron*, quoted and translated in Jonathan Culler, *Structuralist Poetics: Structuralism, Linguistics, and the Study of Literature* (Ithaca: Cornell University Press, 1975), 235.

[26] Barthes, *S/Z*, 190.

is 'in our actions that we are happy or the reverse'.[27] But 'modern character' was a widespread effort to reverse this entrenched hierarchy. Liberated (relatively) from the dictates of plot mechanics, characters attracted ever-proliferating adjectives which rapidly became semi-autonomous, like Nikolai Stepanovich's multifarious feelings and thoughts and Miss Julie's patchwork quilt of impulses and notions, or those nebulous, nameless states we will call affects.[28] Around the turn of the twentieth century, it became important and necessary to play with the hypothesis that literary characters are not there particularly to be 'identified' with; that they can be presented precisely to be *seen through* as lures of identification, and tarried with for ends other than ethical or sympathetic. Formal means were thus engineered for them to transfer our literary perceptions and affections from the domain of the *ethical* to the level of the *aesthetic* itself.

This particularly matters because the effort, while not always political in explicit orientation, tallies with a gathering impatience with that 'ideology of the person' which Barthes later nominated as the target of this approach to character.[29] As early as 1848, we find two strident critics of contemporary bourgeois society inveighing against one of its ideological lynchpins: the notion of the 'individual'. '[T]he work of the proletarians has lost all individual character, and, consequently, all charm for the workman', they write; and 'capital is independent and has individuality, while the living person is dependent and has no individuality'.[30] Factory conditions of labour (deskilling, erosion of handicraft, 'cooperation' in its invidious aspect) have dispelled all claims of the individual over his product and the nature of his work, while commodification and the wage relation have abrogated social individuality from without. Their call for an 'abolition of bourgeois individuality, bourgeois independence, and bourgeois freedom' (225) is thus a cry on behalf of real individuality. To their enemies, they cry:

> You must, therefore, confess that by 'individual' you mean no other person than the bourgeois, than the middle-class owner of property. This person must, indeed, be swept out of the way, and made impossible.
>
> (225)

[27] Aristotle, *The Poetics*, 2320.

[28] Much of my subsequent discussion of this fashionable topic will not take the typical, transhistorical route promoted by the psychologists, but that suggested by Fredric Jameson in his *The Antinomies of Realism* (London: Verso, 2013). 'The "serious" writer—that is, the one who aspires to the distinction of literature—will keep faith with what alone authentically survives the weakening of all the joints and joists, the bulkheads and loadbearing supports, of narrative as such, of the récit on its points of submersion: namely affect as such, whose triumph over its structural adversary is that bodiliness that alone marks any singularity in the everyday, and which now turns to engage its new literary adversary in lyric and language. Its fate is henceforth the fate of modernism . . .' (184).

[29] Barthes, *S/Z*, 190.

[30] Karl Marx and Friedrich Engels, *Manifesto of the Communist Party*, in Marx, *Economic and Philosophic Manuscripts of 1844* (Amherst, NY: Prometheus Books, 1988), 216.

Propping 'this person' up, in the meantime, was the very institution of literature itself. The evolution of literary form over the eighteenth and nineteenth centuries was specifically engineered to buttress and consolidate this peculiar Western European conception of modern 'personhood', famously summarized by Clifford Geertz as 'a bounded, unique more or less integrated motivational and cognitive universe, a dynamic center of awareness, emotion, judgment, and action organized into a distinctive whole and set contrastively both against other such wholes and against its social and natural background'.[31] W. J. Harvey naturalized this conception—'unique, isolate, discrete', he wrote—in his mimetic account of character in *Character and the Novel*.[32] But this bourgeois notion of bounded, integrated selfhood was historically recent in Europe and quite exceptional with regard to most of the rest of the world, where very different ideas continued to hold sway.

The prevailing Western ideas of character in the nineteenth century were assayed early by Baptist preacher John Foster, whose *Essay on Decision of Character* (1804) went through nine editions by 1830.[33] The pamphlet set out the moral terms on which the Romantics would build their strident ethos and their most successful literary characters: boldness, courage, decisiveness, all the 'commanding' qualities of spirit that sustained one's 'Vigour of Action' through all the 'harassing Alternations of will'.[34] His assault on the 'irresolute mind' cross-sections a generous sample of literary and historical figures in search of its archetype. Milton's Abdiel and Satan, Shakespeare's Macbeth and Lady Macbeth, Richard III, and Prospero, along with Caesar, Cromwell, and Luther, all instance 'that active ardent constancy, which I describe as a capital feature of the decisive character' (46). This encomium for the 'persistent untameable efficacy of soul' (47), grounded in the mimetic theory of character-modelling, echoes far across the subsequent century: in Carlyle's 'great man' theory of history;[35] in Nietzsche's estimate of character as a styling of the will-to-power; in Samuel Smiles' genial *Self-Help* (1897), with its declaration that the 'chief use of biography consists in the noble models of character in which it abounds'.[36] Literature's place in this bourgeois ecology of character was assured and deeply implicated in its ideological mission: to normalize Aristotle's subjugation of quality to activity, and so to organize the ever-increasing number of characterological qualities—appetites, affects, specialized sense perceptions, shocks, and so on—that a burgeoning commodity culture was normalizing,

[31] Clifford Geertz, '"From the Native's Point of View": On the Nature of Anthropological Understanding', in *Local Knowledge: Further Essays in Interpretive Anthropology* (New York: Basic Books, 1983), 59 [55–71].

[32] W. J. Harvey, *Character and the Novel* (Ithaca: Cornell University Press, 1965), 31.

[33] John Foster, *Essay on Decision of Character* (New York: Printed for booksellers, 1830).

[34] Foster, *Essay on Decision of Character*, 7.

[35] 'The History of the world is but the Biography of great men.' Thomas Carlyle, *On Heroes, Hero-Worship, and the Heroic in History*, ed. David R. Sorenson and Brent E. Kinser (New Haven: Yale University Press, 2013), 30.

[36] Samuel Smiles, *Self-Help: With Illustrations of Character, Conduct, and Perseverance* (1859) (Oxford: Oxford University Press, 2002), 303.

within an available 'aristocratic' conception of self-mastery. The 'ideology of the person' as our later generation of writers encountered it was thus a well-established extra-literary *discipline* (in Foucault's sense) with profound roots in the literary culture of the age: in light fiction as much as serious novels, and on the stage in creaking melodramatic forms, all reinforcing a set of assumptions via strategies of identification with represented individuation.

My claim is that artists began to realize towards the end of this long century of bourgeois hegemony that the available techniques for representing literary character were in lockstep with that integrated, unified model of the social individual that, for one reason or another, was coming into objective crisis.[37] Taking many of their cues from contemporary psychology, but in tune too with economic trends in the division of labour and with new demographic pressures on the ancient idea of 'character' as *ethos* (national, sovereign, individual), these artists began to reject the notion of a rounded, identifiable, consistent literary persona and to explore new ways of organizing literary materials around alternative models of constructed personhood—characterless, dividual, grouped, multiple, inconsistent, minor, insignificant, artificial, riven by unnameable affects, abstract, networked, marionette-like, impulsive, and so on—all of which would serve as blueprints for the major revolutions about to sweep through the arts in the first three decades of the twentieth century. This pioneering cluster of artists is today relatively unsung for the enormity of their achievement in this regard; but without their efforts it is doubtful whether Joyce, Stein, Eliot, Woolf, Brecht, Pirandello, Ionesco, and the rest of that storied company, would have been in any position to undertake their experiments with character in the 1920s. More to the point for this study, it is this earlier generation who should take the lion's share of the credit for doing something theoretically consequential to the very concept of character for the first time in three hundred years. It is they who have made it very difficult, if not impossible, for the presently governing ethical consensus about literary character to assimilate the intransigent series of experiments and developments that characterize this period in literary history, spanning roughly from 1888 to 1930. For it is they who effected the most radical diremption in literary history from the idea that characters are by definition 'sympathetic' and worthy of identification; that character is about empathy and unification; that it has, as a literary category, anything specifically moral about it whatsoever.

Breaking down this systematic assault into its constituent initiatives, I foreshadow here the major *leitmotiven* that play across the volume that follows—several of which we have already noticed in embryo.

[37] For more on this topic, see Michael L. Klein, *Music and the Crises of the Modern Subject* (Bloomington: Indiana University Press, 2015); Saurabh Dube, *Subjects of Modernity* (Manchester: Manchester University Press, 2017); Pal Ahluwalia, 'Specificities: Citizens and Subjects—Citizenship, Subjectivity and the Crisis of Modernity', *Social Identities* 5.3 (1999): 313–29; and the essays collected in Special Issue 'Who Comes after the Subject?', ed. Jean-Luc Nancy, *Topoi* 7.2 (September 1988).

1. The disarticulation of represented persons from narrative plots, and a consequent disabling of our interest in them as agents. Having little or nothing to do, these characters either drift aimlessly or retreat into their own interiority where new depths are sounded and moods explored.
2. An exacerbation of what has been called the 'crisis of protagonicity' in late nineteenth-century literature.[38] The abandonment or attenuation of the function of the 'hero', and an erosion of the salience associated with its central position in characterological space. A character can swell to colonize every corner of a text without for all that being a protagonist.
3. 'The Emotion of Multitude'.[39] Compensating for the collapse of protagonicity is a new accent on group personae and distributed resonance. Conrad's crews, Hauptmann's peasants, Maeterlinck's 'blind', Strindberg's halls of mirrors, Chekhov's groups, James' triads and quadrilaterals: the multiple is a choric fact of modern drama and literature, driving what Ian Watt called 'the requisite impersonal urgency'.[40] But, even more powerfully, it will turn out that the 'individual' has itself been exposed as a multiple—inconsistent, self-antagonizing, and variously composited out of drives, affects, and functions in disarray. The emotion of multitude is internal as well as external.
4. Affective chromaticism. Time and again, what surges up from the interior or gets conducted between the nodes of the multiple, is an uncontrollable discordance of new and nameless affective intensities. At best, with the Decadents, characters can become scientist-connoisseurs of these riptides of inner sensation, but as a rule, they are undone by them, dismantled into the nerve-ends and synapses that conduct them from one place to another.

One last concept can help us come to terms with these strange deformations of characterology at the end of the nineteenth century. This is *stultitia*. Foucault's description of the opposition between the 'Stoic conception of the unity of existence' and 'the plurality of *stultitia*, of the disordered and morbid soul', ties back to Plato's inaugural distinction between the 'rational and quiet character' of reason and the 'excitable character' of multitudinous affects and is a useful way of distinguishing between the bourgeois discipline of 'the ideology of the person' and a growing interest in its dissolution across this period.[41]

[38] Fredric Jameson, *The Antinomies of Realism* (London: Verso, 2013), 95–113.

[39] 'Greek drama has got the emotion of multitude from its chorus', writes Yeats; 'Ibsen and Maeterlinck have [. . .] created a new form, for they get multitude from the wild duck in the attic, or from the crown at the bottom of the fountain, vague symbols that set the mind wandering from idea to idea, emotion to emotion.' W. B. Yeats, *Essays and Introductions* (London: Macmillan, 1961), 215, 216.

[40] Ian Watt, *Essays on Conrad* (Cambridge: Cambridge University Press, 2004), 71.

[41] Michel Foucault, *Discourse and Truth and Parrhesia*, ed. Daniele Lorenzini, Henri-Paul Fruchaud, and Nancy Luxton, trans. Nancy Luxton (Chicago: University of Chicago Press, 2019), 29; Plato, *Republic* X, 604d–e, trans. G. M. A. Grube and C. D. C. Reeve, in John M. Cooper, ed., *Plato: Complete Works* (Indianapolis: Hackett, 1997), 1209.

> The *stultus* is essentially someone who does not will, who does not will himself, who does not want the self, whose will is not directed towards the only object one can freely will, absolutely and always, which is oneself. In *stultitia* there is a disconnection between the will and the self, a nonconnection, a nonbelonging characteristic of *stultitia*, which is both its most manifest effect and deepest root.[42]

Perhaps it should serve as one of the cardinal points of decadence, this account of a person 'not only open to the plurality of the external world but also broken up in time' (132), and consequently unable to amount to a self. But in any event, it is a significant aid in comprehending what is happening to character at this time in literary history. Our interest is formal, not psychological, and what remains to be said is that *stultitia* suggested itself as a technical solution to an objective crisis in narrative and dramatic aesthetics—namely, the final obsolescence of all vestiges of the heroic quest, which rendered protagonicity and much of its established character space redundant.[43] Character itself would become the formal space in which to observe 'the plurality of *stultitia*'—psychic part-objects, fragments of a former unity, separated and flowing their different ways—rather than remain a function of a residual feudal narrative paradigm.

In the first part of this study, I trace the impact of this initiative in the 'little theatres' of the 1890s and 1900s. This crucial institution—enabling the appearance of Strindberg's Scandinavian Experimental Theatre in Copenhagen (1889) and his Intimate Theatre in Stockholm (1907), the fabled Moscow Art Theatre (1898), and Germany's Freie Bühne (1889), not to mention J. T. Grein's Independent Theatre in London (1891) and the Irish National Theatre in Dublin (1902)—triggered the most comprehensive revolution in dramatic art since the Elizabethan theatres of the late sixteenth century. Beginning in Paris with André Antoine's Théâtre-Libre (1887) and Aurélien-Marie Lugné-Poe's breakaway Théâtre de l'Oeuvre (1893), the small theatre movement was in fact the material origin of much of the modernist aesthetic avant-garde, and in it the protocols of dramatic characterization were altered decisively. In the last works of Ibsen, which had an especial affinity with these smaller stages, we will chart (in Chapter 1) the progressive demotion of dramatic action undertaken by the elder statesman of the European stage, and a consequential shift towards an externalized interiority. Allowing the deadweight

[42] Michel Foucault, *Hermeneutics of the Subject: Lectures at the Collège de France, 1981–1982*, ed. Frédéric Gros, trans. Graham Burchell (New York: Palgrave Macmillan, 2005), 133.

[43] 'The nineteenth century, indeed, may be characterized as the era of the triumph of everyday life, and of the hegemony of its categories everywhere, over the rarer and more exceptional moments of heroic deeds and "extreme situations".' Fredric Jameson, *Antinomies of Realism* (London and New York: Verso, 2013), 109. 'One is reminded of the antithesis evoked in the Protestant Ethic between "adventure capitalism" —impulsive, violent, confiding in fortune, and present in almost every epoch, like those narratives that in English are called "romances"—and the sober, predictable, repressed ethos of bureaucratic-rational capitalism, which is instead, like the "novel", a recent European invention.' Franco Moretti, 'Serious Century', in Moretti, ed., *The Novel, Vol. 1: History, Geography, and Culture* (Princeton: Princeton University Press, 2006), 384.

of everyday life to stifle all remaining vestiges of heroic conduct and its associated speech genres, Ibsen proposed a flickering, impalpable characterological presence in the empty prattle of tedious bourgeois conversations: the Unconscious. Maurice Maeterlinck, one of the great forgotten artists of this moment, seized hold of Ibsen's implicit challenge to depict the unseen and enact the inexistent, and took the decay of dramatic action to extreme lengths. As we will see in Chapter 2, his theatre of stasis and androids, of non-events and curious abstractions, made 'character' a virtual impossibility. In its place were the vague outlines and gestures of an exhausted stage tradition, rendered uncanny by the division of the stage into areas populated by weird groups and their transferential, depersonalized moods. Chapter 3 finds August Strindberg in his post-Inferno period, pushing his earlier Naturalism in directions that would take it outside verisimilitude altogether. Dissolving the objective world of his stage into the hallucinated self-representation of a single morbid mind, Strindberg discovered an entirely new theatrical language for the deposition of the modern *stultus*: dramatis personae composed exclusively of fractured manifestations and atavistic avatars of the Ego that is not One. Finally, in the fourth chapter, the astonishing last cycle of plays by Anton Chekhov from *The Seagull* through to *The Cherry Orchard* affords an opportunity to see how the greatest literary artist of the turn of the century turned dramatic character on its head, by deposing the protagonist and clearing its space for the emergence of radically new characterological forms: groups and their distributed affects, henceforth not constrained to individual embodiment, but scrambled across a company of players in a spiritual language never heard before on any stage.

Part Two charts a similar trajectory through the medium of prose over the same period. New forms like the novella and the 'artistic' short story having dethroned the triple-decker novel as the forms of choice for aesthetically innovative work in narrative discourse, we will nonetheless see, in major works by Gabriele D'Annunzio, Henry James, and Joseph Conrad, the 'blow-back' of that innovation (and the innovations tracked in Part One) into the substance of the novel form itself. Chapter 5 turns to consider the Decadent novellas of the 1890s as major stations of the sudden evolution of modern character. The fictions of Huysmans, Stevenson, and Wilde all consecrate a new norm of characterology: the bachelor-machine with his compulsive connoisseurship over his own affective surplus. The abstractions made possible by the relinquishment of the marriage plot and almost all narrative action allow characters to drift free from means-ends rationality into an uncharted realm of infinitely sub-divisible roles and masks, and in the name of a ruthless new quest for experience itself. In Chapter 6, we scrutinize the sadly neglected novelistic corpus of Gabriele D'Annunzio, for evidence of what the leading Nietzschean artist of his time was doing to the literary category of character: allowing it to decompose into its radiant subsidiary elements, as a ferocious and flailing subjective will comes to terms with the unhealthy fact that it is unequal to the henceforth impossible project of unification. Here, the disconnection between the will and the self is so extreme that the will effectively pulverizes and stultifies the 'self' into a molecular cascade of affective intensities. The late work of Henry James is assayed in Chapter 7, where we find a novel solution to the crisis of characterology. Rather than plumbing the psychological depths and excavating a newly rounded model of the individual, James redoubles his attention to the narrative surface, where he elaborates a planar geometry of sides, angles, and areas of influence without any third dimension to speak of. In this rarefied textual space, not morals but aesthetics always govern, and individuals cede to groups, as the various quartets and triangles of his compositions stage complex algebraic solutions to problems arising from the sheer abstraction of the entire undertaking. Chapter 8 turns to the dizzying originality of Knut Hamsun, particularly his *Hunger*, where the sacrifice of plot, action, and 'morale' is so extreme as to force new mutations in the substance of his characters. When your central character is a narrator and a writer who, because he has no pecuniary means of keeping a roof over his head, is unable to finish a single story, the result is a manic projection of pseudo-characters, half-finished but unrealized personae, all over social space; and a radical decomposition of the body and being of the protagonist, who unravels into the world. The 'New Woman' emerged as a social imago at around this time, and in Chapter 9, we see what the woman who called herself 'George Egerton' did with it in two highly experimental collections of short stories. We find that it provided her with a readymade frame on which to construct unprecedented mappings of a very specific modern female subjectivity: inconsistent, subject to impersonal affective vibrations, rootless, itinerant, and open to strange new becomings for which little in the literary record had prepared her readers. The disintegration of personality undertaken by the major novels by Edith Wharton and Kate Chopin in this period are the subject of Chapter 10. Yet again, we find their protagonists withheld from decisive action but subject to internal recalibrations, as their separation as agents from the usual plot mechanics suspends them over vortices of affective possibility and becoming. In each, the outer limit of the social field betokened by working-class and Black 'minor characters' seeps back into the narrative space as a characterological void spinning with new and nameless potentials. Finally, in Chapter 11, we look to the major early works of Joseph Conrad as a further development of many of these same trends out into the world of Empire and global trade via the sea-routes of the merchant marine. In Conrad, we discover that the internal decompositions of the 'self' already charted by the writers considered above can be mapped onto the socio-political fragmentations and racial hierarchies of the world itself in its imperialist phase. The result is a final apotheosis of 'character' into a figment of some prior order of things, a scrap of ideological detritus already comprehensively made over and substituted for by processes and dynamics that have scant use for identity or individuality.

A final word about the origins of 'modern character': they are not metropolitan. Consider the authors surveyed in this volume. An impoverished, uneducated tailor's son from Hamarøy, in Norway's far north, by way of Minneapolis and Copenhagen; a serving-maid's son from the Stockholm suburb of Norrtullsgatan; a serf's grandson and son of a grocery-store manager born on the shores of the Sea of Azov in the Ekaterinoslave Governorate in the old Russian Empire; a wealthy provincial dilletante from Ghent; the daughter of an Irish naval Captain born in Melbourne, Australia, who spent time in New Zealand, Chile, Dublin, and Kristiania; a Louisiana Creole; a precocious Abruzesse from Pescara; a scion of the Polish *szlachta* in Berdychiv; and so on. Modern character may derive a good deal of its social logic from the fragmentations and reifications of industrial capitalism in its Western theatre of specialization, but it achieved a distinctive aesthetic form in the work of writers fetched from the hinterlands, who bore within themselves the living memory of a life less broken.[44] It seems to me a matter of decisive importance that the formal adventure we are about to undertake should be conducted by writers whose experience of the boulevards and *bons marchés* was mediated by styles of life not yet fully subordinated to the 'general equivalent'. Between them, they upheld 'a curious kind of commitment to modernity—not to its central project (the establishment of a global market), but to the difference that project made to the world around it. What [they] expressed was the messy and contradictory stage of modernization in a mixed or unfinished state: the uncanny overlaps in lived experience between rural and urban, metropolitan and colonial, industrial and artisanal modes of life.'[45] It was in this mixed topsoil that modern character sent down tenacious and durable roots; its curious flora now requires extensive analysis.

[44] For more on this interesting topic, see Leonardo Lissi, *Marginal Modernity: The Aesthetics of Dependency from Kierkegaard to Joyce* (New York: Fordham University Press, 2012); Toril Moi, *Henrik Ibsen and the Birth of Modernism* (Oxford: Oxford University Press, 2006); Elisabeth Oxfeldt, *Nordic Orientalism: Paris and the Cosmopolitan Imagination* (Copenhagen: Musuem Tusculanum Press, 2005); Alys Moody and Stephen J. Ross, eds., *Global Modernists on Modernism: An Anthology* (London: Bloomsbury, 2020); Harsha Ram, *The Imperial Sublime: A Russian Poetics of Empire* (Madison: University of Wisconsin Press, 2006); Arnold Weinstein, *Northern Arts: The Breakthrough of Scandinavian Literature and Art, from Ibsen to Bergman* (Princeton: Princeton University Press, 2008).

[45] Julian Murphet, 'On the Market and Uneven Development', *Affirmations* 1.1 (Autumn 2013), 10 [1–20].

PART ONE

1
Ibsen

In the concept of 'Ibsen' are two incommensurable drives struggling for dominance: the one leading us back through the formal carapace of the 'well-made play' to the mid-nineteenth century, with its melodramatic traditions and professionally delineated characters; the other drawing us through uncanny theatrical effects of banality, stasis, and unvoiced expression into the main currents of the twentieth. In both these senses, Ibsen was to have proven perhaps the most instrumental figure in inaugurating the period of the break with which this study is concerned. He stolidly represented everything that was stale and in need of overcoming; and at the same time foreshadowed and stimulated many of the most significant ruptures with what he represented. These internal contradictions of the work provoked Henry James to decry Ibsen's 'massively common and middle-class' preoccupations, and yet to endorse 'his intensity, his vividness, the hard compulsions of his strangely inscrutable art'.[1] Bernard Shaw wrote that in 'Ibsen's works we find the old traditions and the new conditions struggling in the same play, like a gudgeon half swallowed by a pike'; all the 'weariness of the mean dull life in which nothing happens' is contradicted by 'a final catastrophe of the approved fifth-act-blank-verse type. Hedwig and Hedda shoot themselves: Rosmer and Rebecca throw themselves into the mill-race: Solness and Rubeck are dashed to pieces.'[2] The 'last great bourgeois' as Lunacharsky called him, subservient to the dictates of a common form, propelling his characters into unworthy dénouements, Ibsen was also St John the Baptist to both Beckett's 'nothing happens' and those vivid intensities of nameless affect that would remake character altogether between 1888 and 1905.[3]

The Scribean 'well-made play' having colonized the stages of Europe and America by the 1850s, Ibsen long proved unwilling to transcend it despite serious misgivings.[4] It presupposed certain inflexible ideas about characterization—'In it

[1] Henry James, qtd. in Richard Gilman, *The Making of Modern Drama* (New Haven: Yale University Press, 1999), 68.

[2] George Bernard Shaw, 'Against the Well-Made Play', in George W. Brandt, ed., *Modern Theories of Drama: A Selection of Writings on Drama and Theatre, 1840–1990* (Oxford: Oxford University Press, 1998), 100.

[3] Anatoly Lunacharsky, '"The Last Great Bourgeois": On the Plays of Henrik Ibsen' (c.1906), *New Theatre Quarterly* 10.39 (August 1994), 240 [223–41].

[4] 'Technically, he found the *scène à faire* too useful to throw out', and Nora's tarantella in *A Doll's House* was perceived at the time as 'Ibsen's last concession to the old technique'. See J. L. Styan, *Modern Drama in Theory and Practice*, Vol. 1 (Cambridge: Cambridge University Press, 1981), 18, 25. George Steiner called Ibsen's plays 'marvels of construction in the prevailing manner of the late nineteenth-century drawing-room play. The joints are as closely fitted as in the domestic melodramas of Augier

DOI: 10.1093/oso/9780192863126.003.0002

characters too often appear as pure abstractions; to portray contrast (the hobby-horse of French drama) they are usually painted as either angels or devils, seldom as people', as he wrote[5]—which cast a long shadow over the dramatist. For one, characters in a Scribean drama are drawn to maximize the effects of 'tortuous intrigue, overheard conversations, intercepted letters and strained coincidence'[6]—that is, their design is reverse engineered from the plot devices to perform a pattern of secrecy, reversal, and revelation. This accent on suspense makes characters subservient to the mechanics of action-driven narrative organization, but it also presupposes a certain model of depth revealed by dialogue: the crisis precipitates a scene in which all will be laid bare via lengthy discussions whose speech-acts generally present more than the drama was able to demonstrate.[7] Further, these characters tend to be drawn from the ruling or upper classes, amongst whom discretion, linguistic facility, and hidden depths can all be plausibly presupposed. In his string of plays from 1850 through to the early 1870s (thirteen up to *Emperor and Galilean*, 1873), Ibsen ploughed this furrow with remarkable industry, and created, in spite of the convoluted plots that sustained them, 'major characters [. . .] convincingly drawn as rounded individuals'.[8] Ibsen made his early reputation as a master craftsman of the well-made play and his signature contribution to the form consisted in this attainment of 'rounded individuality'—complex states of mind hinging on modulations between public affairs and private intrigues, individuals stamped by their psycho-social situations, sometimes even riven by them. 'Interest in "psychology" was a part of the age's fascination with the philosophy of personality, the investigation of the soul, and profound descriptions of character in terms of existential qualities and moral imperatives—of which Ibsen and Kierkegaard would be the most celebrated exponents in Scandinavia. There was little such psychology in Scribe, and a wealth of it in Shakespeare and Goethe. Interest in the complex and divided mind had caught on in Denmark as early as the late Romantic period.'[9] Though subordinate to a commercial plot, Ibsen's characters were 'personalities' in that very specific Scandinavian sense,

and Dumas.' George Steiner, *The Death of Tragedy* (New York: Alfred A. Knopf, 1961), 290. Yet as early as 1851, Ibsen was writing: 'When a public has grown accustomed, as ours has, year in and year out, to the dramatic candy-floss [*slikkerier*] of Scribe & Co., cautiously seasoned with a suitable admixture of various poetical substitutes, it is very understandable that the solider German fare must strike even the ostrich stomachs of our theatre-goers as somewhat in-digestible.' Review of Karl Gutzkow's *Zopf und Schwert*, 13 April 1851, quoted in Michael Meyer, *Ibsen: A Biography* (Garden City, NY: Doubleday, 1971), 71.

[5] Ibsen, quoted in Meyer, *Ibsen*, 72.

[6] John Orr, *Tragic Drama and Modern Society: A Sociology of Dramatic Form from 1800 to the Present*, 2nd ed. (Basingstoke: Macmillan, 1989), 6.

[7] 'One naturally expects that the hero's character will reveal itself through dramatic action; but our author is of another opinion. Instead of letting his hero do things, he makes him *tell* the audience about his *ennui*, how life has lost its sparkle and everything seems an interminable misery.' Ibsen, review of *Un Homme Blasé*, May 1851, quoted in Meyer, *Ibsen*, 73.

[8] David Thomas, *Henrik Ibsen*, Macmillan Modern Dramatists (London: Macmillan, 1983), 13.

[9] Ivo de Figueiredo, *Henrik Ibsen: The Man and the Mask*, trans. Robert Ferguson (New Haven: Yale University Press, 2019), 100.

'sympathetically unsympathetic' in Shaw's phrase, or 'fissured characters', rendered through histrionic devices and 'the medium of natural stage dialogue'.[10] As he retorted to a review of *Peer Gynt* (1867) that had disparaged the play's thin, allegorical personae, 'And isn't Peer Gynt a personality, finished, individualized? I *know* he is.'[11]

Ibsen's gradually perfected sense of dramatic personality was the very standard against which the break was about to be made. Ibsen's countryman Knut Hamsun would howl it down in 1891, at a public lecture in Bergen, where Ibsen had begun his professional life as writer and director forty years before in Ole Bull's Norwegian Theatre. Having praised the emergence in France of 'an aristocratic, psychological style of literature' that transcended naturalism, Hamsun took aim at his elder:

> Finally he came to Henrik Ibsen, the most famous of them all. Ibsen had, Hamsun railed, been content more than anybody else to produce the most simplistic psychological portrayals. This, Hamsun pronounced, was a result not only of the limitations of dramatic form in conveying the inner life of characters, but also of Ibsen's rigidity and lack of nuance in his understanding of the human psyche.[12]

This historic shift from an outmoded psychology to a distinctive modern one, associated with French decadence, brands Ibsen with simplistic characterological conservatism; yet such a charge misses an immense subterranean movement in the master's work from 1873 onward, gathering pace through the 1880s, and attaining full expression in the great late sequence of plays in the 1890s. Strindberg had detected it in *Rosmersholm* (1886), whose obscurities were 'quite intelligible to someone who has the necessary grounding in modern psychology'. The case of Rebecca West is referred to a 'web of unconscious deceptions' in society where 'dissembling and simulation have penetrated all the pores of human nature', which allows the dramatist to abandon external modes of compulsion in favour of these new phenomena: 'either *Grössenwahn*, the overestimation of the self, or *micromania*, its underestimation', and the resultant 'modern soul murder, or psychic suicide'.[13] From another vantage point, this was also heralded as Ibsen's 'spirit of

[10] George Bernard Shaw, *Bernard Shaw: Collected Letters, Volume I: 1874–1897*, ed. Dan H. Laurence (New York: Viking, 1985), 292; Heinrich Laube quoted in Simon Williams, 'Ibsen and the Theatre', in James McFarlane, ed., *The Cambridge Companion to Ibsen* (Cambridge: Cambridge University Press, 1994), 178 [165–82]; Bjørn Hemmer, 'Ibsen and the Realistic Problem Drama', in *Cambridge Companion to Ibsen*, 75 [68–88].

[11] Quoted in Toril Moi, *Henrik Ibsen and the Birth of Modernism* (Oxford: Oxford University Press, 2006), 34.

[12] Ingar Sletten Kolloen, *Knut Hamsun: Dreamer and Dissenter*, trans. Deborah Dawkin and Erik Skuggevik (New Haven: Yale University Press, 2009), 60–1. Ibsen also takes a battering from Hamsun's eccentric protagonist, Nagel, in *Mysteries* (1892).

[13] August Strindberg, 'Soul Murder (Apropos *Rosmersholm*)', in *Selected Essays*, ed. and trans. Michael Robinson (Cambridge: Cambridge University Press, 1996), 64–70.

wayward boyish beauty' that blew through James Joyce a couple of years later, 'like a keen wind' from the Scandinavian provinces, prompting the young Irishman to defend in public the later Ibsen's commitment to life 'as we see it before our eyes, men and women as we meet them in the real world, not as we apprehend them in the world of faery'.[14] Just so, Ibsen encouraged his actors 'to draw on "real life and real life only" when embodying his characters'[15]—but what real life was this?

On the one hand, 'real life' is simply the category of the ordinary, the banal: 'ordinary, everyday life—no strong emotions, no deep feelings, and, above all, no thoughts isolated from the main subject', as Ibsen described his later work to Georg Brandes.[16] The characters speak 'the genuine plain language spoken in real life'.[17] What Toril Moi calls 'ordinary conversations' come to characterize the plays in ways that openly jar with melodramatic and Scribean traditions, and she proposes that Ibsen 'turns to the ordinary and the everyday, not as something that has to be overcome, exaggerated, or idealized, but as a sphere where we have to take on the task of building meaningful human relationships'.[18] The risks were significant, as Clement Scott's contemporary report on the London premiere of *Ghosts* made clear—'it is all dull, undramatic, uninteresting verbosity—formless, objectless, pointless'—but the rewards of this conquest of the ordinary were to prove immense.[19] Still, the ordinary scarcely exhausts the category of 'real life', and for clues to other dimensions we can look to production history. For his noted performances in *Pillars of Society* (1877), *The Wild Duck* (1884), and *Little Eyolf* (1894), in Vienna in the 1890s, the actor Friedrich Mitterwurzer pinpointed an aspect of his roles (Consul Bernick, Hjalmar Ekdal, Alfred Allmers) that further elucidates Ibsen's notion:

> As Bernick, there was no centre to his character: it was a series of masks that changed depending upon whom he was talking to and the situation in which he found himself. So complete was each transformation and so equally was each mask an expression of Bernick that he did not appear to be a hypocrite, but someone who lacked any identifiable personality. The play therefore appeared to be less the satire that it was normally regarded to be, more a study of the damage

[14] James Joyce, quoted in Richard Ellmann, *James Joyce*, new and revised ed. (Oxford: Oxford University Press, 1982), 54, 72. The British press, meanwhile, had smelled nothing but filth, ordure, and decay in Ibsen's drama: see the extraordinary diatribe against *Ghosts* in the *Daily Telegraph*, 14 March 1891, reprinted in Michael Egan, *Henrik Ibsen: The Critical Heritage* (London: Routledge, 1972), 189–93.

[15] Frode Helland and Julie Holledge, eds., *Ibsen on Theatre* (London: Nick Hern Books, 2018), 123.

[16] Henrik Ibsen, *Letters and Speeches*, ed. and trans. Evert Sprinchorn (New York: Hill & Wang, 1964), 84.

[17] Ibsen quoted in Raymond Williams, *Drama from Ibsen to Brecht* (Harmondsworth: Penguin, 1976), 40.

[18] Moi, *Henrik Ibsen and the Birth of Modernism*, 89.

[19] Notice on *Ghosts* in the *Daily Telegraph*, 14 March 1891, reprinted in Egan, *Henrik Ibsen: The Critical Heritage*, 188 [187–8].

> that can be caused by one who lacks any coherent sense of his own self. [. . .] As Allmers, Mitterwurzer represented the point of crisis where a man's sense of his own identity collapses and the moral crisis which is composed of his search for a new centre.[20]

Here a fissure has led to a shattering of character, a leakage of its substance. 'Real life', in this sense, is the unravelling of fictionalized versions of selfhood. It is what obliges a character to defect from anything like a stable or consistent identity, the selection of masks a name presents to the world. 'The masks which the necessity of hypocrisy has imposed on man are many and various', Strindberg commented.[21] But was this a matter of aggressive interpretation, or was there something in the form of the later plays themselves that elicited this radical performance style?

There are at least four immanent formal factors in the plays that make clear the shift, visible from *The Wild Duck* onward, away from Ibsen's former reliance on the well-made play form and its attendant characterology. These are, first, a reorganization of the plot around a now absent (already completed) core of action; second, a shift to patterns of dialogue including more and more incidental, insignificant speech; third, a relative emancipation of the dramatis personae from their emplotment in an inexorable and logical sequence of events; and fourth, the appearance of 'uncanny visitors [who] are instrumental in disrupting the superficiality of the stage worlds'.[22] These four qualities interpenetrate, to be sure, yet each sheds its own explanatory light on why, in the 1890s, Ibsen's plays should have proven such a seedbed of characterological innovation in various national performance settings, despite the author's reputation for dull and crusty kinds of psychology. Georg Lukács and Peter Szondi both remark that the true peculiarity of Ibsen's late plots is the gene-splicing they effect between a mechanical Scribean economy and the *Oedipus Rex*: a consignment of most of the essential action of the plays to the past, whose gradual uncovering in the present forms the crux of each drama, as in detective fiction.[23] 'For Ibsen, the past dominates instead of the present. The past itself and not a past event is thematised; it is remembered and is still active internally. Thus, the interpersonal is displaced by the intrapersonal.'[24] This gives extra piquancy to Meyerhold's observations that the 'New Drama' *à la* Ibsen

[20] Williams, 'Ibsen and the Theatre', 179.
[21] Strindberg, 'Soul Murder', 71.
[22] Helland and Holledge, eds., *Ibsen on Theatre*, 102.
[23] Georg Lukács, *Studies in European Realism: A Sociological Survey of the Writings of Balzac, Stendhal, Zola, Tolstoy, Gorki, and Others*, trans. Edith Bone (London: Merlin Press, 1972), 133; Peter Szondi, *Theory of the Modern Drama*, Critical Edition, ed. and trans. Michael Hays, Theory and History of Literature 29 (Minneapolis: University of Minnesota Press, 1987), 12–16. See also Brian Johnston, 'Plot and Story in The Master Builder', in Johnston, ed., *Ibsen's Selected Plays* (New York: Norton, 2004), 515–24. It is perhaps worth mentioning that Lukács, who visited the ailing Ibsen in Norway in 1902, had 'struck up a fraternal union with Ibsen's protagonists—Brand, Peer Gynt, Rosmer, Hedda Gabler, Rubek'. Arpad Kadarkay, *The Lukács Reader* (Oxford: Blackwell, 1995), 66.
[24] Szondi, *Theory of Modern Drama*, 45.

(and Wagner) is secretly a movement backward, a rediscovery of the 'precepts of antiquity' in 'Dionysian *catharsis*' where 'the revelation of character, is becoming incidental.'[25] The conjuring of the Sophoclean prototype contributes to a rejection of Scribean protocols of characterization, pulling Ibsen further away from a model of surface and depth, secret and revelation, and towards a 'Dionysian' liquidation of the very boundaries of personhood. Meyerhold's perception of a desire in Ibsen to 'penetrate *behind* the mask, *beyond* the action into the character as perceived by the mind [. . .] to penetrate to the *inner mask*' (173), posits a gap between the superficial stage character with her various social masks, and the mental and emotional '*inner mask*' that she presents to herself. '[T]hey sense within themselves the distance between themselves and their soul', as Lukács remarked; a distance that will prove pivotal to a long tradition of twentieth-century characterization.[26]

Meanwhile, the relative demotion of incident in Ibsen's later work prompted Maurice Maeterlinck to remark in 1894: 'One of the most remarkable characteristics of *The Master-Builder* is that it is a play more or less without action. I mean that it is in fact bereft, or as good as bereft, of psychological action in the accepted sense of the term. And that is one of the reasons why I admire it.'[27] This diminution of 'action' within the space of Scribean drama then allows for a mutation in the form, a deformation of the dialogue. On the one hand, this emphasis on discourse at the expense of action put greater weight on the words exchanged: '[T]he longer they sit and talk, the more crushing are the results of their conversations that they have to face when they continue with their daily lives.'[28] On the other, more dialogue leads to more noise, an escalating amount of empty language for which Maeterlinck coined the apt term 'dialogue "du second degré"', 'a form of dialogue freed from its plot-furthering role':[29] prattle, inconsequential banter, empty chatter, of which Maeterlinck wrote:

> No; there must be something other than externally necessary dialogue. [. . .] It is only the words which seem at first hearing useless that really count in a play. It is in them that the soul of the play is hidden. Alongside the indispensable dialogue, there is almost always another dialogue which seems superfluous. Look closely, and you will see that it is the only one that the soul really listens to, because it is only here that it is being spoken to.[30]

[25] Meyerhold, qtd. in Nils Åke Nilsson, 'Intonation and Rhythm in Chekhov's Plays', in Robert Louis Jackson, ed., *Chekhov: A Collection of Critical Essays* (Englewood Cliffs, NJ: Prentice-Hall 1967), 173 [161–74].

[26] Georg Lukács, *Theory of the Novel*, trans. Anna Bostock (London: Merlin, 1971), 88.

[27] Maeterlinck quoted in Patrick McGuinness, *Maurice Maeterlinck and the Making of Modern Theatre* (Oxford: Oxford University Press, 2000), 242–3.

[28] Dmitry Trubotchkin, '"A Brilliant Failure": *Rosmersholm* at the Moscow Art Theater (1908) and Its First Studio (1918)', in Erika Fischer-Lichte, Barbara Gronau, and Christel Weiler, eds., *Global Ibsen: Performing Multiple Modernities* (London: Routledge, 2011), 247 [243–56].

[29] McGuinness, *Maurice Maeterlinck*, 240.

[30] McGuinness, *Maurice Maeterlinck*, 240–1.

With little to do in terms of furthering the plot (already over and done with), character speech in late Ibsen turns increasingly on 'useless language', dramatically superfluous utterance, untethered to narrative incident, and disconnected, too, from the Scribean mechanics of personal revelation. This second-degree discourse resonates in a space separate from that of the drama and establishes a critical dissonance from within the proscenium, an implicit metatheatricality without which modern character was never going to develop.

There is, writes Jacques Rancière, 'a break with the traditional model of theatrical action to which Ibsen's plays, however "realist" their subjects might be, bear exemplary witness'.[31] This break 'with the causal system implied by a chain of events and the logic of characters distinct to the theatrical tradition' (118) is best exemplified, in Rancière's account, by the encounter in *The Master-Builder* (1892) between the mature and successful builder, Solness, and the young woman, Hilde Wangel. Hilde has come to claim her promised kingdom from Solness ten years after they first met, and their encounter is framed entirely in words, hers to him, as he has forgotten every detail of the earlier meeting. Her described memory of his victorious placing of the wreath on the finished church spire in her small town, followed by his giddy kissing of her (a mere child of nine) and making of the promise, smites the play's machinery of cause and effect with a hammer blow. 'Plot dissolves, being replaced by a mere sequence of static scenes', as Lukács put it.[32] Rancière continues:

> The new drama is above all another use of speech: it must no longer comment on the action. Nor does it have to express the motives for jealousy or revenge, but only the weight of these outside forces that make individuals act beyond all rationality of calculated means and ends. The new economy of speech must be given its own visibility, lending form to the sensible presence of thought. The stage must manifest the visibility that is latent in the music of exchanged words [. . .].
>
> (119)

There is thus another 'static' drama visible through the fissures that run across the surface of Ibsen's well-made play, and a covert lyricism running through the often-leaden language. As one reviewer wrote of Meyerhold's 1906 Petersburg production of *Hedda Gabler*, 'In the rhythm of the monotonously uttered words, behind the outer spoken dialogue, one feels an inner, hidden dialogue of sensation and impression which cannot be expressed by the words.'[33] Behind the characters, another Character; behind their speech, another Speech; within their

[31] Jacques Rancière, *Aisthesis*, trans. Zakir Paul (London and New York: Verso, 2013), 114.
[32] Georg Lukács, 'The Intellectual Physiognomy in Characterization' (c.1955), in *Writer and Critic and Other Essays*, ed. and trans. Arthur D. Kahn (New York: Grosset & Dunlap, 1970), 164 [149–88].
[33] Qtd. in Thomas Eekman, *Anton Čechov, 1860–1960: Some Essays* (Leiden: E. J. Brill, 1960), 180.

silences, a deeper Silence. 'This dialogue expresses not the thoughts, sentiments, and intentions of the characters, but the thought of the "third person" who haunts the dialogue, the confrontation with the Unknown, with the anonymous and meaningless forces of life.'[34] Aspiring to the condition of music, the 'exchanged words' do not say what they say;[35] they flicker with an obscure energy that perforates them from within, pointing the way towards Chekhov's last plays. Chekhov himself expressed little but contempt for Ibsen, and various critics have suggested his preference for Maeterlinck as a confirmation of his anti-Ibsenism.[36] Yet here we see the complex lineage of a 'theatre of stasis' and non-communication, and of those characters proper to it, which springs from Maeterlinck's uncanny appreciation of the Norwegian's later drama.

***

Dramatic character is distinct from novelistic character in any number of ways, but principally in the absence of free indirect discourse or omniscient narratorial commentary on interior psychological states. The stage is predisposed to disclose the objective aspects of character: interactivity, action, and dramatic tests. Fugitive interiority can be revealed on stage via soliloquies (considered passé by the 1880s), revealing dialogue, gestures, or more adventurous 'expressive' dramaturgical devices, none of which had been highly developed by the time Ibsen wrote his final sequence of dramas. In what follows, we will want to examine, briefly, some significant technical steps taken in the direction of modern character by Ibsen in these late works, steps never so revolutionary as those of his more radical successors, but subtle and fine-grained in their observation, betokening the seismic shocks to come. As Rilke eulogized Ibsen's immense discretion:

> you had to determine and note down things that could scarcely be measured: an increase of half a degree in a feeling; the angle, which you read at close quarters, at which a will almost unburdened reacts; the slight cloudiness in a drop of longing; and that infinitesimal change of colour in an atom of trust. For life was now to be found in such processes, our life that had slipped into us and had withdrawn so deep inside that it was hardly possible to conjecture about it any more. With your disposition as one who revealed, a timelessly tragic writer, you were bound

[34] Jacques Rancière, *The Aesthetic Unconscious*, trans. Debra Keates and James Swenson (Cambridge: Polity, 2009), 39.

[35] Ibsen's was 'a lyricism that was informal, hidden, a matter of textures and relationships [...]. Driven down into the depths, beyond the audience's immediate ear, it lay out of the grasp of paraphrase and socially exploitable meanings [...].' Gilman, *The Making of Modern Drama*, 64.

[36] 'Ibsen, then, belongs to the old drama of communication, Chekhov to the new drama of non-communication, which is perhaps why he seems so "modern" to us today. No doubt it was this "head-on" quality in Ibsen that Chekhov found unappealing.' Michael Green, 'The Russian Symbolist Theater: Some Connections', *Pacific Coast Philology* 12 (1977), 6 [5–14].

> of necessity to transform that capillary action at a stroke into the most persuasive gestures, the most commonplace things.[37]

It is here among these almost imperceptible shifts in angle and degree, opacity and coloration, that Ibsen achieved his most durable effects of characterization. Yet they invariably concern what are at the same time very considerable 'ethical' issues in a sociological or political sense; and the great majority of Ibsen criticism has botched its findings about Ibsen's modernism on this score: confounding 'molar' principles of feminism, the erosion of patriarchy, and the collapse of idealism with the nigh-invisible capillary, 'molecular' processes of characterization that Rilke, Maeterlinck, and Strindberg had been so astute in recognizing. The challenge is to keep these two intermingled moments analytically separate in order to resist the temptation to identify form with theme, and to forestall the triumph of ethical criticism. For characters are not what they represent; they are the very representability offered to the theme such that it should take wing and not lapse into mere statement.

The Lady from the Sea [*Fruen fra havet*] (1888), begins by positing some mysterious correspondences between the work of two artists and Ellida Wangel, the woman who lives in the seaside house in Northern Norway where they have gathered. The painter, Ballested, has painted in the setting of fjord and rocks where a lost mermaid will die, but 'it still needs a figure'; and 'It was the lady of the house here who gave me the idea of painting this.'[38] The sculptor, Lyngstrand, is meanwhile about 'to start on a big work. A sort of group, you might say' (47), featuring a confrontation between a drowned man and the woman (like Ellida) who has betrayed their love oath to the sea. Ellida has 'a very special affinity with the sea' (39) (she 'has something of the sea in' her, 101; her 'mind is like the sea. It ebbs and it flows', 122) and this means that she is only loosely set in the stolid naturalist scenography of the play's *terra firma* (she is constantly swimming in the fjord, and feels an irresistible 'undertow', 84). The two projected artworks are efforts to materialize in aesthetic form this undertow: what lies hidden in her past that sets her apart from the others. They thus allegorize the play itself, whose purpose it will be to cure Ellida's curious syndrome by giving form to it: not in plastic or kinetic shapes, but via verbal intercourse. Ellida Wangel, having (like Molly Bloom) refused sexual relations with her husband since the birth of her dead son, is receding from worldly, naturalistic salience into a romantic, fantastical twilight. The true originality of Ibsen's formal approach to this familiar binary struggle

[37] Rainer Maria Rilke, *The Notebooks of Malte Laurids Brigge*, trans. Michael Hulse (London: Penguin, 2009), 54.

[38] Henrik Ibsen, *The Lady from the Sea*, trans. James Walter McFarlane, in McFarlane, ed., *The Oxford Ibsen, Volume VII: The Lady from the Sea, Hedda Gabler, The Master Builder* (Oxford: Oxford University Press, 1966), 30.

between romance and naturalism is to have displaced its dynamic away from the architecture of the plot and onto the topography of Ellida's psyche.

The melodrama of Ellida's attachment to the mysterious sailor, their heathen betrothal, his murder of a ship's captain and flight, their magical affinities and correspondences (including the appearance of his eyes in the doomed child she has with Dr. Wangel seven years later)—all are shunted into a biographical past whose repression has caused it to hollow out a cavity within the 'well-made play' where resound the echoes of an older aesthetic ideology. That cavity is nothing other than Ellida Wangel's 'unconscious', a lumber room of superannuated romantic tropes, which her conversations with her husband haul piecemeal into view. This ingenious modulation of the form means that the thematization of the past renders the character herself in four dimensions: temporality is saturated with personality, and character with time; the chasm between romantic idealism and modern scepticism is experienced as a fold in the character herself. Ellida diagnoses her own malady as 'denne dragende hjemve efter havet' ['this relentless undertow—this homesickness for the sea' (59)], and the play associates this force with a neurotic regression into the interior, 'the undertow of the mind, the deep-seated impulses of the psyche'.[39]

Nothing happens on stage but conversations—and these are everything. Critics have routinely described the many sessions between Ellida and Wangel as prefigurative of the Viennese talking cure.[40] But this is a technical victory for the modern drama before it is an early endorsement of psychoanalytic method. What it means for the plot to consist almost entirely in an interrupted series of interlocutions between husband and wife about her symptoms, her syndrome, and its aetiology, is that the audience is trained to attend to the minor variations in tone, pitch, volume, and affectivity that articulate the stages of a patient's gradual victory over her condition and the past it preserves. There is nothing in any previous drama to compare with this sensitivity to molecular shifts in a character's verbal and gestural self-presentation, on which the play has persuaded us to understand that everything depends. No decisive action, no *deus ex machina*, but only painstaking modulations of a character's self-enactment in language, signs of which Ibsen has written into these scenes' stage directions: *shakes her head*; *brooding, and not listening to him*; *to herself*; *tense*; *vehemently*; *clings passionately to him*—a single page asks all this of Ellida's speech to Wangel. This is a striking demonstration of Ibsen's insistence on the capillary actions of a body-in-language,

[39] Errol Durbach, *Ibsen the Romantic: Analogues of Paradise in the Later Plays* (London: Macmillan, 1982), 157.

[40] See, for instance, Lorraine Markotic, 'Epiphanic Transformations: Lou Andreas-Salomé's Reading of Nora, Rebecca and Ellida', *Modern Drama* 41.3 (Fall 1998): 423–41; H. Zwart, 'The Call from Afar: A Heideggerian-Lacanian Re-reading of Ibsen's *The Lady from the Sea*', *Ibsen Studies* 15 (2015): 172–202; Lata Marina Varghese, 'The Sea Within: Trauma and Recovery in Ibsen's *The Lady from the Sea* and O'Neill's *Anna Christie*', *The Investigator* 2.4 (2016).

the almost imperceptible colorations and refractions that allows the dramatist to reframe 'romance' and aesthetic idealism as symptoms of a soul in anguish, in need of working-through. It is not just, as James McFarlane long ago observed, that *The Lady from the Sea* thus becomes Ibsen's most successful effort 'to externalize this kind of inner drama of the mind', but that it also stands as a powerful metatheatrical manifesto about how to treat the residual elements of a discredited aesthetic ideology.[41] By making what Ellida calls 'all these alluring yet destructive forces' (108) the private burden of a single character around whom the others move delicately, the playwright can continue to wrestle with them as psychological and emotional complexes rather than simply abandoning them. As Toril Moi writes, 'The reason why the [artists'] half-dead mermaid and the unfaithful sailor's wife express Ellida's inner state at the beginning of the play is that, like them, she has remained frozen in a desperate, more or less melodramatic, moment. Perhaps we can see her immobility and stasis as profoundly antitheatrical, as a negative version of the immutable Ideal. Against this, *The Lady from the Sea* posits the idea of acclimatization, adaptability, changeability, and—ultimately—transformation.'[42] A collateral result is that 'the notion of idealistic love is obliterated' as well,[43] delivering the female protagonist over to a new theatrical domain where her own voluntary decisions might reassess the space of the possible.

It would be a mistake, however, to conclude that Ibsen simply sides with the ordinary and the rational against the tidal pull of the fantastical and sublime. 'This cheerful parting from the past is something that Ibsen failed to achieve.'[44] After all, it is these forces that twist Ellida out of the frame of the quotidian and create the dramatic situation to begin with; without them, there is nothing to develop, and they cannot simply be transcended. The banal and superficial world to which she has sworn herself by play's end is a narrow, claustrophobic prison that Ellida's stepdaughters are already chafing against bitterly. Rather, the true secret of Ibsen's discovery that character itself might be the space where the dramatic situation is developed and resolved is that there can be, on this stage, no binding resolution, no climactic hauling out of the bodies. What Wangel calls the 'craving for the unattainable . . . for the limitless, for the infinite' (120) is a fixed psychic lodestar, a veritable drive, that no talking cure can ultimately disable. As he wrote in his own synopsis of the play, Ibsen understood very well that the 'happy, easy' life to which Ellida is resigning herself

[41] James McFarlane, *Ibsen and Meaning: Studies, Essays, & Prefaces* (Norwich: Norvik Press, 1989), 277.
[42] Moi, *Henrik Ibsen and the Birth of Modernism*, 304.
[43] Figueiredo, *Henrik Ibsen*, 528.
[44] Georg Lukács, *Essays on Realism*, ed. Rodney Livingstone, trans. David Fernbach (Cambridge, MA: MIT Press, 1981), 160.

> is a life of shadows. No initiative; no fight for liberty. Only longings and desires. This is how life is lived in the brief light summer. And afterwards—into the darkness. Then longings are roused for the life of the great world outside. But what would be gained from that? [. . .] Everywhere limitation. From this comes melancholy like a subdued song of mourning over the whole of human existence and all the activities of men. One bright summer day with a great darkness thereafter—that is all. [. . .] The sea's power of attraction. The longing for the sea. People akin to the sea. Bound by the sea. Dependent on the sea. Must return to it. [. . .] The great secret is the dependence of the human will upon 'the will-less'.[45]

What Ibsen proposed as 'modern character' is the discovery and affirmation of the will within the 'will-less', what Rancière has called 'this radical identity of *pathos* and *logos* that, in the age of Ibsen, Strindberg, and Wagnerism, became the ultimate truth and the "moral" of the aesthetic unconscious'.[46] The essence of Ellida Wangel is that she is simultaneously a vector of disappearance into the oceanic 'outside', of abysses and Thanatic horror, and a patient, hardworking striver for a new surface normality where men and women sit together and, as equals, talk through their tribulations. The latter alone is not a character, it is a tendentious cipher; but conjoined with the former, it is a deformation in dramatic space capable of engendering a new characterology.

In *Hedda Gabler* (1890), Ibsen intensifies the unresolved contradictions of *Lady from the Sea*. The high-spirited, beautiful Hedda is positioned between the two representative figures of Dr. Jørgen Tesman, her husband, and Ejlert Lövborg, her former lover, who converge around a vacant professorship: 'It is the difference between a research aficionado and a man of spirit; the one keeps purely to registering the facts, while the other is meant to have a view of the future', as Adorno summarized the contention.[47] While Hedda's perception of them matters most to the development of the plot, the divergence between what she sees and what the audience perceives increases as the play progresses, opening a gulf around the central character—generally filled in the critical literature by Freudian speculations about neurosis or some other syndrome.[48] For Hedda, Tesman is a tedious pedant, a pedestrian intellect, while Lövborg is the embodiment of idealism and a dying grandeur—very possibly a genius and a worthy candidate for noble self-sacrifice in a fallen world of petty bureaucratic careerism. A newly married woman who has only recently forgone a libidinal round of pleasures and indulgence, Hedda feels the Tesman home to be the crypt of all her passions and the site of a stultifying

[45] Ibsen, Draft for *The Lady from the Sea*, in McFarlane, ed., *Oxford Ibsen, Vol. VII*, 449–50.

[46] Rancière, *Aesthetic Unconscious*, 79.

[47] Theodor Adorno, *Philosophical Elements of a Theory of Society*, ed. Tobias ten Brink and Marc Phillip Nogueira, trans. Wieland Hoban (Cambridge: Polity, 2019), 19.

[48] The classic instance is Joseph Wood Krutch, *Modernism in Modern Drama: A Definition and an Estimate* (Ithaca: Cornell University Press, 1953), 11.

victory over romance by the everyday; marriage, as the adjacent instance of Mr. and Mrs. Elvsted makes very clear, is a sexless desert of contempt. Unlike Ellida Wangel, however, Hedda refuses all compromise with the powers of convention, remaining a steadfast devotee of 'the idealist cult of noble beauty, glorious heroism, and transcendent self-sacrifice'.[49] She is, in that sense, an unrepentant anachronism on a stage that has abandoned her. As an artist skilled in melodramatic performance (she effectively writes scenes, gives prompts, manipulates props like lost manuscripts and pistols, directs actors, and sets stages), Hedda does everything in her power to override the naturalist transformation of theatrical space around her, to pull it back into conformity with her outsized romantic desires and recreate conditions under which 'life might be livable, in spite of everything'.[50] Yet the results are inevitably otherwise, and Hedda's nomination of 'this farce' (255) is advised. Hedda's character is the complex product of a body trapped in a naturalist play whose soul aspires to an idealist melodrama but achieves only lurid farce; a palimpsest of incompatible personae writhing in a single figure, trapped between positivism and an absconded ideal. Ibsen's depiction of what is 'mean, repulsive and even ridiculous' in Hedda is also his commitment to her magnificence, and this 'unelucidated juxtaposition of mutually exclusive judgements' is the key to what is undeniably modern in this manner of characterization.[51] In her grandeur lies her pettiness.

Little Eyolf (1894), Ibsen's uncanniest play and his most perverse, presents a characterology mired in fathomless reversibility, subject to 'the law of change', as Alfred Allmers likes to say. Allmers' half-sister Asta, who had once dressed in his cast-off clothes and played his imaginary brother 'little Eyolf', brings Alfred together with Rita, who bears him a son, Asta's transvestite namesake, 'little Eyolf'. Eyolf is crippled when his parents leave him on a tabletop to make love, falling to the floor and shattering his bones just as Alfred tells Rita about the incestuous transgender origin of the name 'Eyolf'. Neither parent is able to love him from this point forward: Alfred burying himself in theoretical work on 'Human Responsibility' while Rita descends into neurosis; which means that the disabled little Eyolf is raised by Asta, the elder Eyolf, feeding Rita's jealousy and the little boy's appetite for peasant fables. On the morning of his father's return from a sojourn in the mountains, which has improved his spiritual self-image, a Rat-Wife appears with her little dog to tell stories of her pied-piper magic powers over 'all the little creepie-crawlies' that she leads to their death in the deeps. 'Then it's all as nice and quiet and dark as they had ever wished for', she croons, 'dear little things. Down there they sleep a long sleep—they who are hated and persecuted of men'.[52] Little Eyolf follows her down to the fjord and, unable to swim, sets out upon the waters

[49] Moi, *Henrik Ibsen and the Birth of Modernism*, 96.
[50] Henrik Ibsen, *Hedda Gabler*, trans. Jens Arup, in McFarlane, ed., *Oxford Ibsen, Vol. VII*, 225.
[51] Lukács, *Essays on Realism*, 162.
[52] Henrik Ibsen, *Little Eyolf*, in McFarlane, ed., *Oxford Ibsen, Vol. VII*, 49.

where he drowns, leaving only his crutch as sign of his passing. By the next day, he has become one of the most haunting images in all drama. Having questioned the local boys about what they saw of Eyolf's last moments, Rita reports to her husband:

RITA. They say they saw him lying on the bottom. Deep down in the clear water. [. . .]
ALLMERS. Did they say anything about how he was lying when they saw him?
RITA. Yes. They said he was lying on his back. With his eyes wide open.
ALLMERS. His eyes open. But quite still?
RITA. Yes, quite still. Then something came and took him out to sea. They called it the undercurrent. [. . .]
ALLMERS [in a dull voice]. And no one will ever . . . ever see him again.
RITA [moaning]. Night and day I shall see him lying there.
ALLMERS. With those big open eyes.
RITA [shudders]. With those big open eyes, yes. I can see them! I can see them so clearly! (77)

Before long, though the sister will transpire not to be a sister, incest threatens to hold sway: the elder Eyolf is invited to become little Eyolf once again (96). But in the end, in the greatest transubstantiation of all, little Eyolf's place is filled not by the sister-brother-lover, but by the very barefoot neighbourhood urchins who bore witness to his demise, their rat-like multiple (the 'hated and persecuted of men') filling the void left by the singular boy who was only ever a cipher for a love that dare not speak its name. This extraordinary phantasmagoria, whose deep affinities with *Struwwelpeter* were pointed out by Adorno, represents a creative surrender to those very forces—the deep, the oceanic currents, the undertow—that Ellida Wangel had resisted.[53] It is not only Freud's rat-man who associates rodent vermin with children: Ibsen, too, clinches the association indelibly in this play, which simultaneously tilts the balance away from nuclear familial ideals and genealogies.[54] Reviving the figure of the Stranger in *Lady from the Sea*, the Rat-Wife herself incarnates an ascendant principle of allegorical, non-naturalist characterization, whose appearance early in Act One deforms the characterology of the play entirely. As Raymond Williams put it, *Little Eyolf* 'virtually dispenses with "characters", in the sense in which Ibsen, and the naturalist theatre after him, understood the term'—but his reading is odd.

[53] See Theodor Adorno, *Minima Moralia: Reflections from Damaged Life*, trans. E. F. N. Jephcott (London: Verso, 2005), 91–2.

[54] Sigmund Freud, 'Notes Upon a Case of Obsessional Neurosis' (c.1909), in *The Standard Edition of the Complete Psychological Works of Sigmund Freud, Volume X: Two Case Histories* (1909), trans. James Strachey (London: Hogarth Press, 1955), 215–16 [153–318].

> The main persons of the play are not so much independent portraits, as aspects of a single dramatic concept. This concept is that of Eyolf, the embodiment of remorse. Eyolf is not only the crippled child whose 'calling' is to be a soldier. Eyolf is Asta, the woman with whom Allmers had lived in happiness, and also Allmers himself. Rita, with her 'gold and green forests', comes to be governed by Eyolf, first in her desire to be rid of the child's 'evil eye', and later by the wide-open eyes of the drowned child staring up at her from the depths. The Rat-Wife is a 'helper and server'. Only Borgheim, the faithful roadbuilder, is part of the usual mechanism of character.[55]

Eyolf, however, is hardly the 'embodiment of remorse'. Rather, the name is a perverse, anamorphic stain within the characterological space, emanating from an incestuous blockage and projected wilfully onto an erotic pairing without any project beyond the couplers' will. It is an empty signifier, and all these named aspects of its internal dynamism fail to fulfil the perverse lineaments of its 'character', one of whose two aspects is that of Death itself: 'And when that . . . travelling companion came and took him . . . it was then I felt utter loathing. For him. For the whole thing. For all this life—a life which, even so, we dare not quit. [. . .] It's all empty and barren, whichever way I look' (102). Its other face is, of course, the nameless multitude, the swarms of rat-children, water-babies, the beaten children of the poor, who, lifted from the depths by human responsibility, will now 'live in Eyolf's room. Read his books. Play with his toys. Take turns at sitting in his place at table' (103). The play has created for itself a uniquely transfigurative space where 'characters' are dissolved into moments of a subterranean utopian force, 'all those things lying under . . . and behind . . . the surface' (79), which is simultaneously Death *and* social uplift: partaking of the ocean depths and the mountain peaks. Bottomless disgust with life modulates with that selfless duty towards the other which lifts the face 'Up . . . towards the mountains. Towards the stars. Towards the vast silence', where the good life might finally announce itself (106).

John Gabriel Borkman (1896) yet again stretches its characterology across Ibsen's evolving symbolic dualism between depths and peaks; but substitutes dark mineshafts for the ocean abyss of the previous plays. Much else is distinctly familiar. It is as Franco Moretti has written: 'so many of his characters *are* ghosts: the minor figure of one play returns as the protagonist in another, or the other way around; a wife leaves her home at the end of one play, and stays to the bitter end in the following one . . . It's like a twenty-year-long experiment Ibsen is running: changing a variable here and there, to see what happens in the system.'[56] Here

[55] Raymond Williams, *Drama from Ibsen to Brecht* (New York: Oxford University Press, 1969), 67–8.
[56] Franco Moretti, *The Bourgeois: Between History and Literature* (London: Verso, 2013), 170.

the distinctive variation on *Little Eyolf* is that the figure of the son, in which all was submerged in the previous play, is suffered to mature and commit himself to 'live, live, live',[57] to become banal and so lapse out of Ibsen's interest altogether. The melodramatic tussle between the twin sisters Rentheim over Erhart Borkman's destiny, his duty, and even his name, is finally only a dramatic ruse behind which emerges a far more sinister and metaphysical drama concerning what Lacan called, after *Antigone*, the uncanny interlude 'between two deaths'.[58] This drama concerns only three characters, who form a strange trinity nominated in the play's final moments as 'One dead man and two shadows' (233): John Gabriel Borkman, his estranged wife Gunhild, and her sister Ella Rentheim, each suffering from compounded spiritual and physical disfigurements in a mummified state of non-development, sixteen years after the commercial disgrace that lost Borkman his social position and landed him in prison. Prison is, indeed, the principal dramatic metaphor here, along with the sense of posthumous life that haunts it. The striking division between spatial layers in the Borkman home, ramified in the divisions between first, second, and third acts, allows us first to hear the ruined capitalist John Gabriel Borkman 'like a sick wolf pacing his cage up there in the great room' where he is entombed just above his wife's sitting room (163)[59] and listening to the local musical prodigy playing him the *Danse macabre*; before we visit him in his lair in Act Two, striking his ridiculous superannuated poses and lording it over one of his former subordinates. Permanently 'marooned in some limbo between life and death, present and past [...] jubilant affirmation and the guilt which debilitates it',[60] trapped in the twilit 'grey area' (as Moretti calls it) of his own culpability for the Faustian crime of wanting to tear out of the earth the mineral wherewithal of general wealth and prosperity, and its tawdry financial dénouement, Borkman does not really inhabit the prison constructed for him by fate; rather, he lives in an abstract realm of shapes, forces, and gestures that have nothing to do with naturalist scenography. The remarkable power of Ibsen's penultimate play is how it flickers between the solid, foursquare world we see on stage and the growing, irresistible power of Borkman's own haunted fantasies over the dramaturgy and the disappointing plot about his son.[61] What grandeur remains to him consists only in the fantasmatic supplement to his ruined capitalist dreams; and it is this supplement that takes over the play in the great fourth act. With outstretched arms, ecstatic and visionary, Borkman in the forest clearing atop his mountain hails the

[57] Henrik Ibsen, *John Gabriel Borkman*, in McFarlane, ed., *Oxford Ibsen*, Vol. VII, 215, 217.

[58] See Jacques Lacan, *The Seminar of Jacques Lacan, Book VII: The Ethics of Psychoanalysis, 1959–1960*, ed. Jacques-Alain Miller, trans. Dennis Porter (New York: Norton, 1992), 270–90.

[59] An example of movement momentarily freezing 'into static patterns in space', as Martin Esslin puts it. See Martin Esslin, *The Field of Drama: How the Signs of Drama Create Meaning on Stage and Screen* (London: Methuen, 1987), 68.

[60] Terry Eagleton, *Sweet Violence: The Idea of the Tragic* (Oxford: Blackwell, 2003), 231.

[61] See the discussion in Clayton Hamilton, *The Theory of the Theatre* (New York: Henry Holt, 1913), 123–4.

many 'Factories I would have created', 'the smoke from the great steamships out on the fjord', 'the veins of metal reaching out their twisting, sinuous, beckoning arms to me'—all 'you who lie in a trance of death in the darkness and the deep' (230–1), by whom he does not mean the dead, but instead the *uncreated*, the unrealized, the unborn. Borkman's depths are populated not by those who have gone under, pulled by the undertow, but those who, in Norway's abortive industrial development, were never yet conjured into existence by the magic wand of capital.

> Visionary; despotic; destructive; self-destructive: this is Ibsen's entrepreneur. Borkman renounces love for gold, like Alberich in The Ring; is jailed; imprisons himself at home for eight more years; and in the rapture of his vision, marches into the ice to certain death. That's why the entrepreneur is so important for the late Ibsen: he brings hubris back into the world—and hence tragedy.[62]

But the tragedy is absurd, as the play well knows. And what Borkman cannot and will not see is precisely what *Little Eyolf* has already seen *in nuce*: the innumerable multiplication of the children of the proletarian poor whose labour would have forged Borkman's 'cold dark kingdom' out of his dreams to begin with. The abstraction of character has here reached a new extreme in Ibsen's work, as we progressively attend to the monodrama lurking in the background of the melodrama, and watch one broken man's imaginary life seep into the pores of the well-made play, saturating it to the point that it literally falls away in the final act, where 'space suddenly becomes fluid'.[63] That scene's transubstantiation of one characterology by another, its definitive shift from a family romance plot to a crystalline triad of undead spectres, ranks as one of Ibsen's most profound offerings to the new spirit in drama.

[62] Moretti, *The Bourgeois*, 184.

[63] Benjamin K. Bennett, 'Strindberg and Ibsen: Toward a Cubism of Time in Drama', in Frederick J. Marker and Christopher Innes, eds., *Modernism in European Drama: Ibsen, Strindberg, Pirandello, Beckett* (Toronto: University of Toronto Press, 1998), 73 [69–91].

2
Maeterlinck

His theatre of marionettes, who are at the same time children and spirits, at once more simple and more abstract than real people, is the reaction of the imagination against the wholly prose theatre of Ibsen, into which life comes nakedly, cruelly, subtly, but without distinction, without poetry. Maeterlinck has invented plays which are pictures, in which the crudity of action is subdued into misty outlines.[1]

The first thing that strikes us in the drama of the day is the decay, one might almost say the creeping paralysis, of external action. Next we note a very pronounced desire to penetrate deeper and deeper into human consciousness.[2]

Ibsen shifted the business of character further and further away from the stifling protocols of the well-made play and towards an increasingly abstract space coordinated by *interiority*, on the one hand, and *metaphysics*, on the other. This movement was to prove critical to a thoroughly new apprehension of dramatic character untethered to action, development, or realization, over subsequent decades. But one place where interiority and metaphysics intersect is, of course, perfectly familiar to the conventions of melodrama, and in the line descending from Ibsen one can generally detect the genetic continuity of a preoccupation with characters' deaths, which Shaw's complaint canonizes: 'Hedwig and Hedda shoot themselves: Rosmer and Rebecca throw themselves into the mill-race: Solness and Rubeck are dashed to pieces.'[3] The convenience of a stage death is both that it fixes a character in the retroactive force it confers upon whom it strikes, and that it introduces an enigmatic interval within the established characterology—an absence that ripples through character space and renders it relatively abstract. Happening onstage, death obliges the stage to suffer a disappearance, from which it recovers only when a certain machinery is put to work. Absent that machinery, death's wedge opens cracks in the conventions that tell apart actor from role, character from character, and agent from act. Maurice Maeterlinck was the artist

[1] Arthur Symons, *Plays, Acting and Music: A Book of Theory* (New York: E. P. Dutton, 1909), 77.

[2] Maurice Maeterlinck, *The Double Garden*, trans. Alfred Sutro (New York: Dodd, Mead, 1904), 115.

[3] George Bernard Shaw, 'Against the Well-Made Play', in George W. Brandt, ed., *Modern Theories of Drama: A Selection of Writings on Drama and Theatre, 1840–1990* (Oxford: Oxford University Press, 1998), 100.

Modern Character. Julian Murphet, Oxford University Press. © Julian Murphet (2023).
DOI: 10.1093/oso/9780192863126.003.0003

best situated to sink his art into these cracks and expand them. If Ibsen's stage was pulled laterally by Death's undertow, Maeterlinck allowed some as-yet Unknown entity to stand forth on the stage, sometimes nominated 'Death' (as by Rilke), but never in such a way as to resolve the oppressive mystery of its apparition.[4] More than any other contemporary playwright, Maeterlinck was able to seize the Ibsen-ite discrepancy between *what appears* on stage and *what does not* as an occasion to admit this inexorable guest, who should never be mistaken for a 'character'. As he once observed, 'the higher the point from which humanity is perceived, the more character becomes erased', and his drama was staged as though from this alpine vantage point.[5] In the words of the Old Man in *Intérieur*, intending his fellow dramatis personae, 'I seem to see them from the altitude of another world.'[6] Maeterlinck's early works for theatre allowed for this reverse-telescopic view of the human, erasing all signs of character even as it created a higher-order one: the Unknown.

Maeterlinck had first speculated on this negative presence, 'le *troisième* personnage, *l'Inconnu*', in relation to Ibsen's 'actionless' dramas. This 'plus one' is not one of the dramatis personae but summoned through the fissures appearing in the 'conventional reality' of the characters' roles:

> [Ibsen] builds characters with minutely detailed, clear and individual lives, and he seems to place great importance on these little signs of humanity. But we discover that he does not really care about these things! And uses these small expediencies only to enable the third person, the unknown—the only one who lives a deep and inexhaustive life—to profit from the fake and conventional reality of these secondary beings. This is how he almost always creates the impression of people talking about the weather in the bedroom of a dead man.[7]

Conventional surfaces are established by the playwright only to vanish as 'expediencies' behind the uncanny apparition of something hidden. Ibsen, starving the stage of action and filling it with empty talk, conjured a silent spectre within the quotidian. 'Who is the third who walks always beside you?'[8] One of the

[4] It was Rilke's opinion that 'Das Unbekannte war der eigentliche Handelnde, die Hauptperson in diesen Dramen, und wenn es manches Mal geradezu ›der Tod‹ heißt, wird es dadurch nicht weniger bedrückend und rätselhaft.' Rainer Maria Rilke, 'Das Theater des Maeterlinck' (1901), in *Sämtliche Werke* vol. 5 (Frankfurt: Insel Verlag, 1965), 536.

[5] Maurice Maeterlinck, 'Interview: Conversation with MM (with Jules Huret)', in David Willinger and Daniel Gerould, eds. and trans., *A Maeterlinck Reader: Plays, Poems, Short Fiction, Aphorisms, and Essays*, Belgian Francophone Library (New York: Peter Lang, 2011), 315–16.

[6] Maurice Maeterlinck, 'Interior', trans. William Archer, in *Three Little Dramas* (London: Duckworth & Co., 1899), 78.

[7] Maeterlinck, qtd. in Patrick McGuinness, *Maurice Maeterlinck and the Making of Modern Theatre* (Oxford: Oxford University Press, 2000), 244–5.

[8] T. S. Eliot, 'The Waste Land', l. 359, *The Complete Poems and Plays of T. S. Eliot* (London: Faber & Faber, 1969), 73.

quintessential characterological questions of modernity is first asked here of Hilde and Solness, and it supplies the key to Maeterlinck's dramaturgy.

For Rilke, Maeterlinck's secret as the 'poet of the Unknown' was that he deployed the means of representation to present the unrepresentable: 'the silence is the happening, the word is the delay'; 'in [these plays] the attempt is made to speak in a visible way of this other invisible life and its figures'.[9] If here the play is *not* the thing, if, behind that thing, *another thing* is looming—about which one had best remain silent because it is of the essence of silence—then we are surely in the environs of Symbolism. But Symbolism has been so routinely misunderstood that we need to be clear about what is at stake. For the true Symbolist, nothing is worse than a 'symbol': any conventional association between image and idea. Rather, what is called for is precisely the 'suppression of the difference between symbolic and direct expression', or in other words the omission of that distracting middle term, the metaphor.[10] Artaud grasped this at once about Maeterlinck, his 'way of unifying—by virtue of whatever mysterious analogies—a feeling and an object, putting them on the same mental plane without recourse to a metaphor'.[11] It is never a question of one thing standing for another thing, but of getting a certain element of an assemblage to stand in for the totality, to suggest its dynamic potential or latency. So it is, too, for Ibsen's characters: they do not 'symbolize' the Unknown, they enact its halting emergence through the very banality of their being and doing.

Maeterlinck did not persevere with Ibsen's way of 'not really caring about' character, but instead sacrificed even those 'small expediencies' of a residual naturalism to a dramaturgy of androids, 'steeped in passivity, quietism, and skepticism'.[12] Rilke's description is apt: 'Maeterlinck has written dramas for marionettes, by which he meant not visages but bodies[,] figures which let themselves be bent in a certain, quite primitive but distantly visible manner'.[13] Defacialized, abstracted from any identity, such posable figures default from the Hegelian idea of 'the Self'. As Kandinsky wrote, 'La Princesse Maleine, Les Sept Princesses, Les Aveugles, etc., are not people of past times as are the heroes in Shakespeare. They are merely souls lost in the clouds, threatened by them with death, eternally menaced by some invisible and sombre power'.[14] Like Nietzsche before him (who had inveighed against

[9] '[D]as Schweigen ist das Geschehen, das Wort die Verzögerung.' Rilke, 'Demnächst und gestern' (1898); qtd. and trans. in George C. Schoolfield, *Young Rilke and His Time* (Rochester: Camden House, 2009), 192n.16. '[I]n ihnen ist der Versuch gemacht, von jenem anderen unsichtbaren Leben sichtbar und mit Gestalten zu reden.' Rilke, 'Das Theater des Maeterlink' (1901), 533. See also the discussion in Hans W. Panthel, *Rainer Maria Rilke und Maurice Maeterlinck* (Berlin: Erik Schmidt, 1973), 85–7.

[10] Jacques Rancière, *Aisthesis*, trans. Zakir Paul (London and New York: Verso, 2013), 101.

[11] Antonin Artaud, qtd. in Ronald Hayman, *Artaud and After* (Oxford: Oxford University Press, 1977), 49.

[12] David Krasner, *A History of Modern Drama, Vol. 1* (Oxford: Wiley-Blackwell, 2012), 150.

[13] Rilke qtd. and trans. in Schoolfield, *Young Rilke and His Time*, 145n.4.

[14] Wassily Kandinsky, *Concerning the Spiritual in Art*, trans. Michael Sadler (London: Constable and Co., 1914), 44–5.

'the excessive growth in the *presentation of character* and of psychological refinement in tragedy' after Attic drama[15]), for Maeterlinck the very notion of 'character' was suspect, likely bankrupt: 'isn't what is called a *character study* neither more nor less than one of those very concessions the poet is forever being forced to make? Strictly speaking, character is an inferior mark of humanity; usually a purely external sign; the more it is specified, the more humanity is particularized and narrowed down.'[16] What mattered was to reduce the dramatic potency of character, asphyxiate its semiology, in an asymptotic approach to the *inhuman* within the human: the uncanny marionette, subject to forces beyond the realm of petty human interests. On the one hand, the actor had to be veiled, obscured, 'reduced, almost to nothing', denying 'the human being that he is' any right of appearance on the stage,[17] since 'masterpieces are symbols, and the symbol never withstands the active presence of man.'[18] On the other, the language spoken must drift apart from anything essential, towards Ibsen's *dialogue du second degré*: 'the only words that count in the play are those that at first seemed useless, for it is therein that the essence lies.'[19] For Maeterlinck's puppets, Katherine Worth writes, '"not knowing", "not remembering", "not saying" become vital modes of expression.'[20] The figures on the stage, then, dehumanized as far as possible and denied any particularity of speech or gesture, might well attain 'the symbol': 'If the poem rises to the level of the symbol performance must rise likewise, and might it not do so by becoming more *abstract*?'[21]

Getting in the way of abstraction was a certain *Weltanschauung* in the very form of the well-made play, the degree to which it was, in its melodramatic aspects, still genetically mortgaged to a romance ideology that had outlived its usefulness. That Ibsen had reduced the quotient of romance—action, adventure, intrigue—to a minimum was a great step, but Maeterlinck's aversion from every trace of the theatre's anachronistic dependency on feudal 'murder, outrage and treachery' was intense: 'Indeed, when I go to a theatre, I feel as though I were spending a few hours with my ancestors. [. . .] I am shown a deceived husband killing his wife, a woman poisoning her lover, a son avenging his father, a father slaughtering his children, children putting their father to death, murdered kings,

[15] Friedrich Nietzsche, *The Birth of Tragedy and Other Writings*, ed. Raymond Geuss and Ronald Speirs, trans. Ronald Speirs (Cambridge: Cambridge University Press, 1999), 83.

[16] Maeterlinck qtd. in McGuinness, *Maurice Maeterlinck*, 76.

[17] Maeterlinck qtd. in McGuinness, *Maurice Maeterlinck*, 113, 114.

[18] Maurice Maeterlinck, 'Menus propos – le théâtre', in *La jeune Belgique* (Brussels, 1890), trans. in Henri Dorra, ed., *Symbolist Art Theories: A Critical Anthology* (Berkeley: University of California Press, 1994), 144–5.

[19] Maurice Maeterlinck, *The Treasure of the Humble*, trans. Alfred Sutro (New York: Dodd, Mead & Co., 1902), 111.

[20] Katherine Worth, *The Irish Drama of Europe from Yeats to Beckett* (London: Athlone, 1986), 77.

[21] Patrick McGuinness, 'Mallarmé, Maeterlinck, and the *Via Negativa*', in Alan Ackerman and Martin Puchner, eds., *Against Theatre: Creative Destructions on the Modernist Stage* (Basingstoke: Palgrave Macmillan, 2006), 159 [149–67].

ravished virgins, imprisoned citizens—in a word, all the sublimity of tradition.'[22] This matrix of cliché from which 'the tradition' is conjured forestalls the emergence of the Unknown, drowning silence in noise and tragedy in incident. For 'the true tragic element of life only begins at the moment when so-called adventures, sorrows, and dangers have disappeared' (99). This includes, of course, the agents of such adventures: heroes, villains, helpers, damsels in distress. If bourgeois modernity itself, 'the humble and inevitable reality of daily existence' (171), had swallowed up the 'higher life' and its 'noble thoughts' (without blending with it), then it was philosophically irresponsible and aesthetically retrograde to persist with mechanics of plot and character that evoked the spirit of romance. It was not that 'noble thoughts' (of the Beautiful, the Ideal, the True) had perished; just that their lack of practical articulation with 'the ordinary' had made it impossible to access them directly. Maeterlinck's abstractions suspended the machinery of romance in order to secrete what remained of its promise.

So it was that he explored 'the dramatic possibilities of non-events', using two-dimensional quasi-persons to perform them.[23] In his plays, there 'is sequence but no causality—that is, one event follows another but is not caused by it'—and the reasons for what happens on stage are obscure to characters and audience alike.[24] Maeterlinck's is a static theatre of subtraction, mortification, and minimization, pursued along two formal paths: the pastiche of a five-act romance; and a startling new one-act form. Maeterlinck took these two paths simultaneously, as if unsure which was more likely to succeed. His contemporaries tended to side with the romances, while posterity has shown a marked preference for the one-act plays. In the five-act plays—*La Princesse Maleine* (1889), *Pelléas et Mélisande* (1892), *Alladine et Palomides* (1894), *La Mort de Tintagiles* (1894), *Aglavaine et Sélysette* (1896)—we note a persistence of certain irrevocable features of romantic Shakespearian dramaturgy, filtered through the brothers Grimm: feudal settings, dynastic tensions, internecine strife, blighted landscapes, fair princesses, and much else besides—but all somehow stricken, lacking conviction, decadent. As our interest here is exclusively with the characters of these plays, their constitution and interactions, what immediately strikes the reader is the sheer peculiarity of the names used to identify these interchangeable dramatis personae. If, as John Frow points out, in a typical literary text, 'fictional characters exist as projections from the proper name onto that "semic configuration"' of qualities that clusters around and predicates it over the course of a narration, then in these plays that projection is weakened to the point of collapse.[25] While in many novels, for example, nameless

[22] Maeterlinck, *Treasure of the Humble*, 103, 104.
[23] Marvin Carlson, *Theories of the Theatre: A Historical and Critical Survey, from the Greeks to the Present* (Ithaca: Cornell University Press, 1984), 429.
[24] Bert Cardullo, 'Introduction', in Cardullo, ed., *Theories of the Avant-Garde Theatre: A Casebook from Kleist to Camus* (Lanham: Scarecrow Press, 2013), 5.
[25] John Frow, *Character and Person* (Oxford: Oxford University Press, 2014), 190.

foundlings progress towards a claiming of their lost names, in these plays, named characters are abandoned by their impossible names which, thanks to vacant repetition, suffer total semantic derogation. These absurd three-syllable proper nouns, used eponymously to label the dramas, may have the aroma of medieval romance, but are singular to Maeterlinck's dramas (they name, literally, *nobody*), and that tension between generality and singularity is critical to the characters who bear them—as is what turns out to be the weakness of any relationship between person and name.

The eponymous heroine of *La Princesse Maleine* cannot properly enter the semiotic web of circumstance into which she is cast by the speech of others, because her name will not adhere to her. Whatever actions and intentions their sentences enjoin her to via verbal predication will have missed their mark; the name 'Maleine' floats free of her person. As she drifts aimlessly through her drama, she is ever cast into new roles, roles which supersede her name:

ANNE (INSIDE): Who's there?
MALEINE: Me!
ANNE: Me, who?
MALEINE: Princess Ma . . . The new maid-servant.[26]

Mistaking her for the princess she now serves, her long-lost betrothed provokes the following exchange:

HJALMAR: What are you thinking about, Uglyanne?
MALEINE: I'm thinking about Princess Maleine.
HJALMAR: What did you say?
MALEINE: I'm thinking about Princess Maleine.
HJALMAR: You know Princess Maleine?
MALEINE: I am Princess Maleine.
HJALMAR: What?
MALEINE: I am Princess Maleine.
HJALMAR: You're not Uglyanne?
MALEINE: I am Princess Maleine.
HJALMAR: You're Princess Maleine! You're Princess Maleine! But she's dead.
MALEINE: I am Princess Maleine. (86)

Each reassurance produces the opposite effect. In this echo chamber of repetition and misrecognition, the name fatefully separates from its bearer. Anagnorisis must fail in a character space like this; even Maleine's Narcissus moment is a moment

[26] Maeterlinck, 'Princess Maleine', in *Maeterlinck Reader*, 82.

of non-recognition: '(*leaning over the parapet of a bridge*): When I see myself in the water, I don't know myself anymore!' (76).

This derangement of the privileged relationship between character, name, and face is then amplified across the available spectrum of characterization. As Patrick McGuinness notes, these are 'barely defined, barely conscious characters',[27] about whose avatars in another play Yeats remarked,

> We do not know in what country they were born, or in what period they were born, or how old they are, or what they look like, and we do not always know whether they are brother and sister, or lover and lover, or husband and wife.[28]

Symons called them 'vague people [. . .] disembodied of the more trivial accidents of life', like backgrounds, ages, nationalities, and selves; 'these are no characters, these are no realizable persons; they are a mask of shadows, a dance of silhouettes behind the white sheet'.[29] Maeterlinck's radical diminution of the number of 'semes' that are drawn to and 'traverse' the 'magnetic field' of his unlikely proper names over the course of a five-act play leaves his characters bereft of all personality.[30] Émile Verhaeren observed of *Maleine* that 'Here we have creatures, like sleepwalkers, ghostly, incoherent, creating a tale which seems like a dream.'[31] There is no question of them ever becoming anything other than what they are: will-less automata, creatures sprung from Ellida's ocean in *Lady from the Sea*. As Palomides complains, 'I feel that I never shall be what I had hoped that I might become [. . .]. Fate has stepped out towards me; or I, it may be, have beckoned to Fate.'[32] This is a quintessential Maeterlinck effect: a character giving voice to the impossibility of his amounting to anything, bearing witness to what he will never be able to do. And lest we suppose that, sundered from action, these characters are at least equipped with the wherewithal to reflect existentially on their condition, their language is there to remind us of the opposite. Instead of Hamletesque soliloquys and Schopenhauerian profundities, there is only an endless string of barely articulate banalities and *non sequiturs*; 'incoherence, faltering sentences, pauses, and repetitions make up the dialogue', a conversation riddled with 'repetition, contradiction and echolalia'.[33] There is thus throughout Maeterlinck's plays a concerted movement to erase from his personae all typical marks of characterization,

[27] McGuinness, *Maurice Maeterlinck*, 52.

[28] W. B. Yeats, *Uncollected Prose*, Vol. II, ed. J. P. Frayne and C. Johnson (London: Macmillan, 1975), 52.

[29] Arthur Symons, *The Symbolist Movement in Literature* (New York: E. P. Dutton & Co., 1919), 311; Arthur Symons, *Dramatis Personae* (London: Faber and Gwyer, 1925), 28.

[30] Roland Barthes, *S/Z*, trans. Richard Miller (Oxford: Blackwell, 1990), 68.

[31] Verhaeren, 'La Princesse Maleine' (1889), qtd. in McGuinness, *Maurice Maeterlinck*, 79.

[32] Maeterlinck, 'Alladine and Palomides', trans. Alfred Sutro, in *Three Little Dramas*, 30.

[33] McGuinness, *Maurice Maeterlinck*, 59; Margaret Rose, *The Symbolist Tradition from Maeterlinck and Yeats to Beckett and Pinter* (Milan: Edizione Unicopli, 1989), 62.

a thoroughgoing 'rejection of the human image'.[34] But Maeterlinck prefers to leave ghostly residues of character rather than tipping over into allegory; Palomides does not personify will-lessness, he is the *stultus* of character once will is removed.[35] Maeterlinck's is a theatre of stultification in the radical sense of subtracting all the commanding psychic components of a 'care of the self' that would compose an ethical unity out of these leftover traits and costumes, habits and gestures, from an exhausted stage tradition.

The separation of agency from the plays' agents was first remarked as a deficiency by Édouard Schuré in relation to *Maleine*: 'Maeterlinck's theatre suffers from two crucial shortcomings, an absence of will in the characters and lack of logic in the progression of action.'[36] But this agreement between plot and character is perfectly logical, and of the essence of Maeterlinck's characterology. Doing nothing, retreating from the front of action, is the agents' chief means of acknowledging that, in the transition from scene to scene and act to act, the events of the play (such as they are) fall through the dramaturgical cracks, never occurring on stage. This is perhaps surprising, in that we cannot fail to recognize these works, with Mallarmé, as spectral melodramas.[37] And yet the scenes are never 'scenes', however melodramatic these five-act dramas may seem, but empty vacillations and neutered equivocations. There are no duels, no murders, no rapes. 'The immobility and inactivity of those dramas are notorious. Although all the characters, throughout the course of all the plays, remain in almost one and the same posture, the possibility of action keeps growing in their souls, to burst forth in the last scene as the catastrophe.'[38] In this sense, what Peter Szondi says of the one-act plays is perfectly applicable to the 'major' dramas as well: 'the category "action" is replaced by "situation"'.[39] It is just that the situation is stretched over a decidedly larger frame, thinner and thinner, to the point of vanishing. What results is an acute instance of Villers' 'dramatic literature in which, unusually, intrigue, "characters", and dramatic action are only of secondary interest'[40]—deliberately flouting a five-act melodramatic structure for the purpose. Maeterlinck's formulation (vis-à-vis *Pelléas*) is precise: 'Nothing, or almost nothing, happens; it is hardly more than the drama of a desire. And its action, most of the time, is not only internal, but takes

[34] Elinor Fuchs, *The Death of Character: Perspectives on Theatre after Modernism* (Bloomington: Indiana University Press, 1996), 29.

[35] Michel Foucault, *Hermeneutics of the Subject: Lectures at the Collège de France, 1981–1982*, ed. Frédéric Gros, trans. Graham Burchell (New York: Palgrave Macmillan, 2005), 133.

[36] Schuré (1904), qtd. in McGuinness, *Maurice Maeterlinck*, 82.

[37] '[I]t seems as if the play [*Palléas et Mélisande*] is a superior variation on the good old melodrama.' Mallarmé, *Le Petit Parisien*, 18 May 1893, qtd. in McGuinness, *Maurice Maeterlinck*, 129.

[38] Valery Briusov, 'Realism and Convention on the Stage' (c.1908), trans. Laurence Senelick in Cardullo, ed., *Theories of the Avant-Garde Theatre*, 77 [69–80].

[39] Peter Szondi, *Theory of the Modern Drama*, Critical Edition, ed. and trans. Michael Hays, *Theory and History of Literature 29* (Minneapolis: University of Minnesota Press, 1987), 32.

[40] Villers de L'Isle Adam, 'Une literature dramatique nouvelle' (notes for a lecture on *Axël*, 1884), qtd. in McGuinness, *Maurice Maeterlinck*, 54.

place without the protagonists' knowledge.'[41] Indeed, the 'protagonist' of a five-act Maeterlinck melodrama tends to remain unaware of whatever action it is given her to perform—protagonicity has collapsed into witless automatism. As McGuinness puts it, to 'approach Mélisande as a "character" is to become aware of how inadequate such concepts as "character", "action", and "psychology" are in Maeterlinck's theatre, of how irretrievably *foreign* his characters are to any established dramatic genre' (142).

One reason for this demotion of action, agency, and self-awareness, is the fitness of such an approach to the new theatres of Lugné-Poe and Paul Fort, with their insistence on minimizing the actor's charisma and personality while on stage and deflecting any interest from star players.[42] Another is the admission of an entirely new source of theatrical motivation, namely the *unconscious*. 'I feel myself attracted', wrote Maeterlinck, 'above all, by the unconscious gestures of being, which pass their luminous hands through the loop-holes of this rampart of artifice in which we are confined.'[43] Rather than resort to named emotions from the tradition (revenge, jealousy, ambition, remorse), Maeterlinck prefers to subject his personae to impulses fetched up from what he calls the '*mare tenebrarum*': 'Our soul contains an interior sea, a frightening and veritable *mare tenebrarum* where strange storms of the inarticulate and the inexpressible rage' (295). These nameless and inexpressible moods we will be inclined to call *affects* in order to distinguish them from the noble passions of high drama—they are 'forebodings, unexplained, overlooked, or extinguished faculties and notions, irrational motives, the marvels of death, the mysteries of sleep' (295). Such nameless intensities, and their expressive gestures, can best be presented on the ruins of the older emotions; which is one reason why Maeterlinck perseveres with the five-act tragic structure.[44] It is in the experience of formal disappointment, in failing to recognize conventional plot-turns and motives, that we begin to intuit upsurges of the *mare tenebrarum*. *La Mort de Tintagiles* is full of these 'strange storms': the doomed boy responding to his sister's anxious question, 'Where does it hurt?' with the chilling line, 'I can't tell you, sister Ygraine, it's everywhere'; the 'compulsive clasping' of sibling to sibling—'When you touch one of them, the other two shiver'; and above all the iron grip of Tintagiles' teeth and fingers on his sister's hair.[45] These characters cannot complete a single successful act to ward off fate, but their enactment of gestures springing from the 'interior sea' is intensely stirring. It endows the last

[41] Maeterlinck, letter to Gérard Harry c.1892, qtd. in McGuinness, *Maurice Maeterlinck*, 130.

[42] See the discussion in J. L Styan, *Modern Drama in Theory and Practice*, Vol. 1 (Cambridge: Cambridge University Press, 1981), 12–36.

[43] Maeterlinck, 'Confession of a Poet', *Maeterlinck Reader*, 295.

[44] See, on this historical antagonism between 'affects' and 'named emotions' in the late nineteenth century, Fredric Jameson's *The Antinomies of Realism* (London: Verso, 2013), esp. 27–77.

[45] Maeterlinck, 'The Death of Tintagiles', in *Maeterlinck Reader*, 249, 252, 255 [242–60].

stand of the boy, as the mad Queen descends upon him behind the door, with an arresting heroism: 'She couldn't hold me back. I hit her and hit her. I ran' (258).

The staging of that final scene is illustrative of Maeterlinck's strongest and most original contribution to modern dramaturgy: namely, his insistence on rigid stage divisions and barriers—walls, doors, windows—which sequester one character-group from another. We can see this, freighted with symbolism, in Ibsen's *The Wild Duck*, but in Maeterlinck's hands the conspicuous stage division is the occasion for his most powerful affects, which come not from symbolic representativity, or from psychological interiority, but from literal blockages on sensory perception. What he discovered was the unique power of a physical bar against seeing and hearing, a barrier between parts of the stage or between onstage and offstage space, rendering characters equivocal in their dual status as subjects and objects of a situation. The obstacle turns one character into an object of another character's concern and interest; the only action permitted being the internalization or *subjectification* of the barred other's pain. Time and again, what 'happens' in a Maeterlinck play is simply that one persona becomes acutely susceptible to the suffering of another, behind some barrier or other. This is somewhat more complex than Szondi's 'subject-object separation which turns human beings into objects', or Rose's 'attention to the offstage space in order to create suspense by hinting at those enigmatic realms beyond surface reality'.[46] For what is at stake is in fact the transfer of affect from one place to another, by virtue of sensory deprivation; and so the derangement of any bounded coherence of personhood. The door in *La Mort de Tintagiles*, behind which the boy dies while his sister frantically tries to enter, is a particularly memorable obstacle, but there are others in the five-act plays: the maid-servants in a 'nether hall' of the castle in *Pelléas et Mélisande*, conversing about the discovery of the cursed lovers in front of the great door, as outside, unseen, children play and yell;[47] the acousmatic lovers of *Alladine et Palomides* whom Maeterlinck has lain in separate rooms along a corridor, neither of which we see into, speaking their final *adieus* offstage:

THE VOICE OF PALOMIDES: I suffer no more, but I want to see you . . .
THE VOICE OF ALLADINE: Never again shall we see one another, for the doors are all closed . . .[48]

And it is Pluto the 'Big Black Dog' scratching at the door behind which Maleine dies, again offstage, who first establishes this convention with great force: at key moments we will be situated, with servants and dogs, in the vestibular places just outside where the momentous events transpire. As Mallarmé wrote:

[46] Szondi, *Theory of Modern Drama*, 34; Rose, *Symbolist Tradition*, 59.
[47] Maeterlinck, 'Pelleas and Melisande', in *Maeterlinck Reader*, 232–5.
[48] Maeterlinck, 'Alladine and Palomides', in *Three Little Dramas*, 59.

> The walls, a massive block on all reality, darkness, basalt, in the emptiness of a hall—the walls, or rather, thick and isolated wall hangings, aged in the local rarefaction; so that their faded inhabitants, before becoming the holes there, stretching out, one tragic time, a limb in their ordinary pain, and even smiling, could stammer or drivel, alone, the sentence of their destiny.[49]

There is the additional feature of these striking scenes that the characters onstage are transformed into narrators of what is taking place beyond the veil; they are no longer agents but reporters, and so the mode of representation subtly shifts from dramatic to epic. But as the most arresting examples of this occur in the one-act plays, it is perhaps time to consider these fascinating monodies, 'forms which, more than any other theatre of their day, hold the clue to the shape of twentieth-century drama'.[50] Here, in *Les Aveugles* (1890), *L'Intruse* (1890), and *L'Intérieur* (1894), we are displaced much further along a spectrum of reduction and abstraction: the 'minimally defined'[51] characters no longer have any names to speak of; there is not even the hint of a past life that they have forgotten; and scarcely the shadow of a plot intrudes to interfere with the 'situation' that now announces itself as theatrically paramount. Indeed, so minimized have these plays become that the dramatis personae have nothing further to do but *wait* for the advent of the 'third person' their stunted and vestigial presence will have summoned from the void. Maeterlinck called these remarkable works 'drames d'attente'—dramas of waiting—and their concentrated form perversely seems to stretch the temporal axis of their performance into unendurable lengths of monotony. As a result, André Potvin once wrote, 'the [Maeterlinck] character does not have the strength to dominate the Instant by measuring it'[52]—there is simply nothing to measure it against, and an instant dilates into an eternity. Meanwhile space itself, absolutely localized in one sense, is cleared of every suggestion of significance, every trivial mark of memory, action, or intention, so that (to paraphrase Mallarmé), at last, nothing can take place but the place: the sombre room in a chateau; the clearing in an ancient forest; the garden at the rear of a house. Characters, unmoored from all responsibility, cast into a position of 'immobility, confinement, and inactivity',[53] do not occupy this space; they are occupied by it. It seeps into them, yielding, in their absorption of it, 'space for an entire plot in a single fear'.[54] Rilke writes of Maeterlinck 'employing the stage to unify a mass of people, rather than to differentiate individuals in the name of a more refined enjoyment' (236), and that is

[49] Mallarmé, qtd. and trans. in McGuinness, *Maurice Maeterlinck*, 165.
[50] McGuinness, *Maurice Maeterlinck*, 169.
[51] Rose, *Symbolist Tradition*, 63.
[52] André Potvin, 'Les Paysages de Maeterlinck et Kafka' (154), qtd. and trans. in McGuinness, *Maurice Maeterlinck*, 161.
[53] McGuinness, *Maurice Maeterlinck*, 227.
[54] Rainer Maria Rilke, *Diaries of a Young Poet*, trans. Edward Snow and Michael Winkler (New York: Norton, 1997), 236.

indicative of a whole era's shift of emphasis from figure to ground, from character to group; but it misses what we have described as this artist's most striking technique, namely his use of stage blockages to divide the 'unified mass' anew, not into separate individuals, but into disparate groups.

L'Intruse, which forces the issue through residues of gothic machinery, encloses its familial 'unified mass' within a room with a heavy door on either side, a concealed door leading to the basement, and stained-glass windows at the rear. Until the dénouement, only a maid and three children are able to pass through any door, and none through the door stage left; the sense of claustrophobic entrapment is complete. When the Grandfather wishes he were 'off somewhere else', he is unable to specify where: 'I don't know where—into another room, anywhere! Anywhere!'[55] His blindness, moreover, transforms his spatial fixity into an occasion for desultory descriptions—of sounds, movements, lights, and arrangements, within and without—provided by the Uncle, Father, and three Daughters, to flesh out and erroneously explain away the gathering dread. Behind one door, right, lies a sickly infant, recently delivered of the old man's daughter, now bedridden behind the door at left, whose postpartum life hangs in the balance. 'My girls, tell me what's going on here? Tell me for the love of God, the rest of you who can see. I'm all alone here, trapped in endless darkness' (160). The dialogue, such as it is, is a fitful acquiescence to his request, none of which satisfies his growing anxiety, which takes the form of a conviction that *someone else* has entered the chamber, a seventh person, whom none can see. Thus, an attenuated epic narration subtly supervenes over proceedings, undoing the fundamental dramatic unity of time. *L'Intruse* is clearly meant as a formal realization of Maeterlinck's conviction that 'an old man, seated in his armchair, waiting patiently, with his lamp beside him; giving unconscious ear to all the eternal laws that reign about his house' lives a 'deeper, more human and more universal life than the lover who strangles his mistress, the captain who conquers in battle, or "the husband who avenges his honour"'.[56] In ridding himself of the sentimental trappings of romance, however, Maeterlinck indulged a propinquity between Symbolism and the gothic which tended to ossify his image of that 'universal life' in two dimensions. As Andrei Bely once remarked, 'To indicate the approach of death, [Maeterlinck] makes an old man say, "Is there not someone else among us?" Too glaring a symbol. Isn't this allegory? Too abstract in its expressions.'[57]

More successful is *Les Aveugles*, whose setting in a forest motivates the device of a ring wall of 'tall mournful trees' and pitch darkness to isolate the company of twelve blind asylum inmates from the offstage world, and which further divides the company into two groups, strictly along gender lines, using 'an uprooted tree and

[55] Maeterlinck, 'The Intruder', in *Maeterlinck Reader*, 165–6.
[56] Maeterlinck, *Treasure of the Humble*, 105–6.
[57] Andrei Bely, 'The Cherry Orchard', in Laurence P. Senelick, trans. and ed., *Russian Dramatic Theory from Pushkin to the Symbolists* (Austin: University of Texas Press, 1981), 91.

fragments of shattered boulders': men to the right, and women to the left.[58] Once again, these physical obstacles ramify the blindness of the nameless, deindividuated characters on the stage: what we see is an image of their collective inability to see, a penumbral gloom that justifies their phatic questions and answers. Stichomythia characterizes these verbal stabs in the dark: 'Say something! I need to hear where you are!' 'Here, we're sitting on some stones' (169). The minimal differences that tell one from another—three of the men are 'born blind', one is 'deaf', one woman is 'old', one 'young', another 'mad'—tend to dissipate in this pea soup of banality. If, as Maeterlinck insisted of Ibsen's *Master Builder*, 'the only words that count in the play are those that at first seemed useless, for it is therein that the essence lies',[59] then this whole play is written out of that futility of exchange.

FIFTH BLIND MAN: Take pity on those who can't see!
FIRST BORN BLIND: Who's talking that senseless way?
SECOND BORN BLIND: I think it's the one who can't hear.
FIRST BORN BLIND: Quiet down. This is no time for begging. (172)

These are less individuals than comic limbs of an amoeba-like dodecapod, cloven into two like Aristophanes' Androgyne in *The Symposium*; the gendered division turns this 'unified mass' against itself at the level of the group, not the person. As a result, there is little 'oppositional dynamic' in the play, just waves of distributed affect.[60] Their abandonment by the Priest who lies dead, unperceived, in their midst leads these blind persons towards instinctual and primitive drives—terror, dread, homelessness, aggression—whose knotty complexion they suffer in a networked fashion: rather than individuating them, it tends to amalgamate them in stratigraphic bands. The stage obstacles oblige them to speak narratively and descriptively about their situation, and so to develop an *epic self-relation* which is unique in all drama to this point.

Into this thoroughly original scene, however, Maeterlinck was once again tempted to force the advent of a '*troisième* personage' rather than let it emerge spontaneously from the situation. It is the chronic shortcoming of his art that he misunderstood his own reading of Ibsen, and tended, in his concentrated one-act forms, to suggest quite explicitly an invisible presence through conventional stagecraft. In relation to Ibsen, he had been quite clear. The Unknown, he wrote, feeds on the 'fake and conventional reality' of the common herd of 'secondary beings' that populate the stage; their 'minutely detailed, clear and individual lives', all their 'little signs of humanity', are so much fodder to the canon of a new aesthetics, which liquidates 'these small expediencies' in order to adduce the *third person*.

[58] Maeterlinck, 'The Blind', in *Maeterlinck Reader*, 168.
[59] Maeterlinck, *Treasure of the Humble*, 111.
[60] Fuchs, *The Death of Character*, 105.

But in his own works, by disposing of all 'these small expediencies' of characterization, by sacrificing that inherited 'fake and conventional reality', Maeterlinck leaves nothing for the Unknown to feed on, and so must drag it on to the stage with the clumsiest of devices, 'through sounds off, light, stage and off-stage space'.[61]

Maeterlinck's stated ideal of dramatic production does not, in the end, correlate with much of his work—bar the singular masterpiece, *L'Intérieur*, where it does finally seem fulfilled. As he wrote, the ideal was:

> To put people on-stage in ordinary and humanly possible circumstances (since we will have to go on using ruses for some time to come), but to put them there in such a way as to enable, by some imperceptible displacement of the normal angle of vision, their relations with the unknown to emerge clearly.[62]

In the other work, be it five- or one-act, the 'normal angle of vision' is insufficiently established for the 'imperceptible displacement' to take place. There is nothing 'ordinary' or 'humanly possible' about the circumstances in the mock-romances; and in the shorter works, the 'ordinary' is forced to the margins by an aggressive gothic device. Despite Maeterlinck's considerable success in using stage props and obstacles to conjure flurries of affects from the *mare tenebrarum*—by blocking sense perception and motivating affective displacements—he never really allows his 'people on-stage' to develop a relation to the unknown through those affects, because they are hypostasized as Death. This is one reason why the consensus was with Strindberg's opinion: 'Maeterlinck is best left unperformed.'[63] Only in *Intérieur* does he manage the 'ruse' successfully.

By dividing the stage into two zones, the old garden of a family home and the home itself, seen from the rear through three ground-floor windows, Maeterlinck attains his specific affective ecology through what had been his least utilized medium: glass. In place of heavy doors and walls, these windows no longer block the visible spectrum, but forbid any sound from penetrating into the garden where the Old Man and Stranger arrive to impart the news of a death in the family. The characters on the other side of this glass—Father, Mother, two Daughters, and Child—are thus, as it were, converted into the playwright's ideal performers: Symons' 'shadows, silhouettes behind the white sheet', marionettes, or indeed the flickering two-dimensional images of early cinema. His stage instructions insist on the ontological divide between the house-dwellers and the spectators who assemble in the garden: the former's 'movements appear grave, slow, apart, and as though spiritualized by the distance, the light, and the transparent film of the window

[61] McGuinness, *Maurice Maeterlinck*, 248.

[62] Maeterlinck, quoted in McGuinness, *Maurice Maeterlinck*, 249.

[63] August Strindberg, 'Open Letters to the Intimate Theatre', 14–20 October 1909, in *Strindberg on Drama and Theatre: A Source Book*, trans. and ed. Egil Törnqvist and Birgitta Steene (Amsterdam: Amsterdam University Press, 2007), 167 [158–69].

panes.'[64] It is thus as if, silent and in slow-motion, the family has already been stricken by the news that is about to reach them in the play's only action.

That scene is a sepulchral homage to the final act of Ibsen's *Pillars of Society* (1877), and Rummel's plan of revealing the family of Consul Bernick to a full ceremonial procession in their backyard by raising the curtains on his living quarters. 'When the garden is filled with a host of faces, then the curtains will rise to reveal a surprised and delighted family group. A citizen's home ought to be like a bell jar.'[65] Ibsen's theatrical vision of the 'happy surprised family' through a set of windowpanes is conjured up by Maeterlinck and scenographically inverted to set it in a different key. What follows is the slow delay of the play's only action, as the Old Man chosen to bring the sad tidings meticulously describes what we can already see, a family enclosed in its meaningless everyday inertia—'doing nothing... looking at nothing' (66). That informational redundancy is, however, the very core of the play itself, since, in it, Maeterlinck has discovered a completely unprecedented dramatic principle: if banality is narrated by an onlooker who bears the news that will shatter it, its simultaneous presentation—however minimal, however mute—becomes surcharged with a prodigious melancholy voltage. What we bear witness to, distributed across five unnamed figures, is not grief but the place where grief will discharge itself, the human material on which it will inevitably go to work. In no other work of drama to this point has the *anticipation* of a named emotion spread itself out across a character space in the form of something else, a nameless, unplaceable affect lodged in the debate about how best to break the news, and the description of the dead girl herself. The vestige of Ophelia crowns that description in a redoubtable Pre-Raphaelitism, with strong echoes of Little Eyolf's sad fate: 'I saw her hair, which had floated up almost into a circle round her head, and was swaying hither and thither with the current . . .' (69).[66] But the point of it all is to shift the theatrical apprehension of death away from a simple personification, and towards a staged 'equation' between the fate of a doomed girl and the framed, silent spectacle of her ignorant family behind glass. Death is no longer the uninvited guest, wheeled on with gothic shudders; it is immanent, not imminent.

> They look like lifeless puppets, and all the time so many things are passing in their souls. They do not themselves know what they are. (71)[67]

Simply 'doing nothing' and 'looking at nothing' behind the 'transparent film' of a window makes these characters into nodes of the doom that has overcome their daughter and sister and is secretly 'what they are' already. 'Poor things, they would

[64] Maeterlinck, 'Interior', in *Three Little Dramas*, 65.

[65] Henrik Ibsen, *Pillars of Society*, trans. Rolf Fjelde, in *Ibsen: The Complete Major Prose Plays* (New York: Plume, 1978), 95.

[66] '... j'aperçois sa chevelure qui s'était élevée presque en cercle, au-dessus de sa tête, et qui tournoyait ainsi, selon le courant . . .'

[67] 'Elles ont l'air de poupées immobiles, et tant d'événements se passent dans leur cœur. Elles ne savent pas elles-mêmes ce qu'elles sont.'

see nothing though they looked for a hundred thousand years' (76). And that spectacle, of the Family's not seeing, is shattering. 'I did not know that there was anything so sad in life, or that it could strike such terror to those who look on at it' (78). Here is that 'imperceptible displacement of the normal angle of vision' necessary to transform the quotidian into the extraordinary and usher in the unknown. It is fitting that the agent who finally forces the act, impelling the Old Man to traverse the threshold between inside and outside, and enter the house, is a group character, a Crowd of peasants, bearing the body inexorably hither while the Stranger debates with the Old Man how and when to prepare the blow. Fitting because, like *Les Aveugles*, this is a truly 'post-subjective' drama, neither interested in characterization nor turning on individual agency. 'Seen in the lighted frame, silently moving about their everyday business, unaware that they are being watched from their garden by a messenger bringing tidings of death, the characters of *Interieur* do indeed seem to inhabit some other dimension.'[68] The drama belongs to a 'molar' characterology, the interaction of three groups who converge and align into a compound image of 'what a face looks like when Death is passing into its eyes' (82).[69]

Intérieur thus achieves the ideal of Maeterlinck's so-called 'théâtre statique': the 'tragique quotidienne' presented in all its ordinariness, but non-identical with itself, because transformed by the addition of a spectator who knows more than the unconscious subjects of the tragedy, and indeed ultimately donates their tragedy to them. The spectator therefore becomes a narrator of the event he is about to inflict, and his narration *is the event* itself. His position as spectator/narrator is amplified and distributed, by the end of the play, across a large number of others as nameless as he, which becomes a group figure for the function of the audience, literally represented on stage as observers in a mass formation. Szondi is thus right to say that 'an epic situation' is created inside the drama, and that Maeterlinck effected a 'shift toward the epic within the concept' of drama itself.[70] But this misses the specificity of the 'imperceptible displacement' at stake; for it is literally Maeterlinck's '*troisième* personage'—or better, the '*troisième* personne'—which here appears as the interval between what we see and what we hear in *Intérieur*. This 'third person' is a way of disposing tragic material in the third person, epically. The relationship is grammatical as much as it is characterological: *third* does not simply mean 'plus one' or supernumerary, it also means that *all the other ones* have glazed over into the third person—all the 'I's are now *they*. There can be no protagonists or even 'minor characters' in this proto-epic space. And this remains one of the most convulsive shocks delivered to the logic of literary character in the history of any form.

[68] Katharine Worth, 'Evolution of European "Drama of the Interior": Maeterlinck, Wilde, and Yeats', *Maske und Kothurn: Internationale Beiträge zur Theaterwissenschaft* 25.1–2 (1979), 169 [161–70].

[69] '. . . qu'un visage au moment où la mort va passer dans ses yeux'.

[70] Szondi, *Theory of Modern Drama*, 34, 35.

3
Strindberg

In 1895 Ibsen bought and hung in his study Christian Krogh's imposing oil portrait of his younger contemporary, the Swede August Strindberg, which Ibsen dubbed 'Insanity Emergent'. Claiming to work better with its 'demonic eyes' staring down at him, Ibsen declared, 'He is my mortal enemy, and shall hang there and watch while I write.'[1] It is also said that, pointing to the portrait, Ibsen described its sitter as 'One greater than I'.[2] Such ambivalence was inevitable, considering the extraordinary conflux of radical aesthetic and philosophic ideas taking place between May 1888 and May 1890 amongst Ibsen, Strindberg, and Nietzsche (whom both were reading), with Georg Brandes serving 'as a kind of message centre or synapse'.[3] Strindberg had stubbornly forged his own character as 'the Enemy' in relation to all his contemporaries, and having taken repeated aim at the Norwegian's 'detestable ideas' it was only natural that mutual antipathy should inform their relations.[4] But respect was also in order, as Strindberg's assault on the proscenium arch was more decisive than any member of this generation, drawing the spectator into a kaleidoscopic 'method of presentation through which he shows us his heroes and their fictional world from several changing points of view during the progress of the action'.[5] This allowed him to relinquish the dramatic burdens of his characters' pasts, their guilts and nostalgias, in order to dwell on their inconsistent drives and immitigable antagonisms in the present. Ibsen's recognition of Strindberg's superiority as an artist had little to do with his craftsmanship or architectural designs; it referred to his quicksilver percipience in relation to 'modern character' as such—a new kind of fatalism determined by genes, ideologemes, fixations, appetites, and a radical dividuality incapable of resolution, all of which he ushered onto the stage in extraordinary profusion.[6]

[1] Michael Meyer, *Ibsen: A Biography* (Garden City, NY: Doubleday, 1971), 732.

[2] Claud Field, Introduction to August Strindberg, *The Inferno* (London: William Rider & Son, 1912), 2.

[3] Evert Sprinchorn, 'Strindberg and the Superman', in Göran Stockenström, ed., *Strindberg's Dramaturgy* (Minneapolis: University of Minnesota Press, 1988), 19 [14–26].

[4] See Richard Gilman, *The Making of Modern Drama* (New Haven: Yale University Press, 1999), 95; and the brief essays in I. M. Opperud, ed., 'Ibsen och Strindberg: Giganternas kamp', Special Issue, *Parnass* 16.2 (2009): 3–33.

[5] Freddie Rokem, 'The Camera and the Aesthetics of Repetition', in Stockenström, ed., *Strindberg's Dramaturgy*, 109 [107–28].

[6] For more on 'dividuality', see the Preface of this volume.

Modern Character. Julian Murphet, Oxford University Press. © Julian Murphet (2023).
DOI: 10.1093/oso/9780192863126.003.0004

Strindberg, 'the precursor of all modernity . . . the most modern of moderns',[7] was intensely shaken by Maeterlinck's 'static drama' and turned to it repeatedly as a critical resource in his uncompromising campaign against the norms of middle-class theatre. Though he was resistant on first encounter in the 1890s (being, as he said, 'immersed in materialism'), over the years his own aesthetic trajectory hewed closer and closer to the Belgian's Symbolist 'beauty and profundity'.[8] While it may have been 'difficult to become his disciple', Strindberg frequently 'admit[ted his] ties to the master' (169). It was after the so-called 'Inferno years' of retreat from the arts (1896–9) that this relationship fully developed, in ways that demanded a new theatre entirely: the 'Intimate Theatre' that Strindberg established with August Falck in Stockholm in 1907—and where his chamber plays *The Ghost Sonata* (1907) and *The Pelican* (1907) would premiere. In step with other *fin-de-siècle* 'little theatres', that theatre's goals were to avoid expedients, facile effects, set pieces, star turns. 'No predetermined form is to limit the author, for the motif determines the form. Consequently, freedom in the treatment, constrained only by the unity of the conception and the artistic sense.'[9] All vestiges of the well-made play were *verboten*. And if, 'when actors performed Maeterlinck in the theatre, another type of acting was called for' (167), then that too would shape the style of performance at the Intimate Theatre. When, however, after a straight run of twenty-four Strindberg plays, Falck bravely decided to stage a production of *L'Intruse* at the Intimate Theatre in 1910, that was too much Maeterlinck for the sublime Swedish egotist: the relationship with Falck exploded, and the Theatre collapsed. Yet the connection ran deep. 'Maeterlinck's secret', Strindberg wrote, 'is this: His characters are active on a plane other than the one on which we live' (166–7); and other, we might add, than the one they live on as well. It was this very duality, the allegorical feeling such characters engender, their sense of being 'in communication with a higher world' (167), that would increasingly shape and reshape Strindberg's experiments with dramatic characterology until his death in 1912. As Evert Sprinchorn remarks, 'It remained for Strindberg to cultivate the seeds that Maeterlinck had planted.'[10]

Strindberg's 'Inferno' (a state of nervous and creative collapse documented, quasi-fictionally, in his novel of that name[11]) marked an epoch in several senses, not least the 'epistemological break' between the artist's enthusiastic conscription

[7] Eugene O'Neill, 'Strindberg and Our Theatre', from a playbill for *The Spook (Ghost) Sonata*, in *New York Times*, 6 January 1924, in Oscar Cargill, *O'Neill and His Plays* (New York: New York University Press, 1982), 108.

[8] August Strindberg, 'Open Letters to the Intimate Theatre', 14–20 October 1909, in *Strindberg on Drama and Theatre: A Source Book*, trans. and ed. Egil Törnqvist and Birgitta Steene (Amsterdam: Amsterdam University Press, 2007), 166–7.

[9] Qtd. in *Strindberg on Drama and Theatre*, 19.

[10] Evert Sprinchorn, *Strindberg as Dramatist* (New Haven: Yale University Press, 1982), 76.

[11] See August Strindberg, *Inferno, Alone, and Other Writings*, ed. and trans. Evert Sprinchorn (Garden City, NY: Anchor Books Doubleday, 1968).

to a Naturalist credo and his subsequent rapprochement with Symbolism and chamber drama. This aesthetic transformation can, however, be overstated;[12] and Strindberg himself proclaimed, 'To me falls the task of bridging the gap between naturalism and supra-naturalism. By proclaiming that the latter is only a development of the former.'[13] What interests us here are the implications this has for his characterization and characterology: if Symbolist proto-Expressionism is, in this artist's hands, less a break from than a continuity with Naturalist strategies of representation, then these labels matter less than the artist's provocative insistence, 'It's got to be new. New and different!'[14] All that really mattered was 'to modernize the form'.[15] There is something consistent across the apparent disjuncture between Strindberg's earlier Naturalist fascination with the mechanical psychological materialisms of Nietzsche, Zola, Théodule Ribot, and Henry Maudsley, and his later interest in more avowedly spiritual and religious themes. What that something is will emerge from what follows, but it is worth stressing at once that what is 'new and different' about Strindberg's art of characterization concerns multiplicity: the multiplicity covered and sutured by the 'One' of a singular name, body, face, and voice.[16] Whether he is dramatizing subjective incoherence and the polyphony of motives in a Naturalist manner, or allegorizing the psychological interior via masks and avatars *à la* Symbolism, for Strindberg the key to what he called 'modern character' was the stark impossibility of 'be[ing] at one with one's character',[17] and so of character itself. Strindberg is the first major artist to reject everything that term had canonized in psychology as well as literary theory; what he replaced it with would smash apart two centuries of accumulated faith in bourgeois individualism.

To comprehend the immensity of this achievement in the art of dramatic character construction, it is first necessary to acquaint ourselves with the rudiments of Strindberg's Naturalism. By 1890, Strindberg had arrived at a conception of the human being, not as a unified, three-dimensional figure but a decentred, internally disaggregated, swirling cloud of multiple motivations—hostile, inchoate

[12] 'Strindberg [. . .] confronts us with what appears to be a radical discontinuity between the naturalistic works of the late 1880s and the modernist dramaturgy of his later plays, beginning in 1898.' Michael Robinson, *Studies in Strindberg* (London: Ubiquity Press, 1998), 116. See also Törnqvist, *Strindberg on Drama and Theatre*, 12; Göran Stockenström, 'Crisis and Change: Strindberg the Unconscious Modernist', in Michael Robinson, ed., *The Cambridge Companion to August Strindberg* (Cambridge: Cambridge University Press, 2009), 79–92; Emily H. Raub, 'Muteness and Modern Drama' (PhD dissertation, Rutgers University, 2012).

[13] Strindberg qtd. in J. L. Styan, *Modern Drama in Theory and Practice*, Vol. 1 (Cambridge: Cambridge University Press, 1981), 44.

[14] Qtd. in Gilman, *Making of Modern Drama*, 106. Gilman references Strindberg's essay 'The New Arts! or the Role of Chance in Artistic Creation', but this statement appears to be a paraphrase rather than a direct quotation.

[15] August Strindberg, 'Preface' to *Miss Julie* in *Miss Julie and Other Plays*, ed. and trans. Michael Robinson (Oxford: Oxford University Press, 1998), 56.

[16] See my 'Character and Event', *SubStance* 36.3 (113) (September 2007): 106–25.

[17] August Strindberg, 'Character a Role?' (1894), in *Selected Essays*, ed. and trans. Michael Robinson (Cambridge: Cambridge University Press, 1996), 111.

tendencies corralled behind a façade of identity. *Son of a Servant*, his loosely autobiographical account of early manhood, contains some of Strindberg's more incisive statements on the conservative function of character, both aesthetically and ethically, in a hypocritical bourgeois public sphere:

> A man with a so-called character is often a simple piece of mechanism; [. . .] a man with a character is generally a very ordinary individual, and what may be called a little stupid. 'Character' and automaton seem often synonymous. Dickens's famous characters are puppets, and the characters on the stage must be automata. A well-drawn character is synonymous with a caricature.[18]

In this *reductio ad absurdum* of the steadily reifying nineteenth-century bourgeois theory of character—exemplified by the work of Hippolyte Taine[19]—Strindberg stresses the deadening powers of convention and doxa over the limitless potential of the human being. In a typical Strindbergian move, this is then related to bourgeois aesthetics, where we find that what is most 'charming' and 'original' about Dickens—his delightfully eccentric minor characters—is just his catering to a market for two-dimensional automata, his proliferation of caricatures and thus his betrayal of lived psychological complexity.

> And where is to be found the central 'ego',—the core of character? The 'ego' was a complex of impulses and desires, some of which were to be restrained, and others unfettered. John's individuality was a fairly rich but chaotic complex [. . .].[20]

The 'chaotic complex' can be sourced back to a multitude of incompatible ideological tributaries: 'most of the words he spoke were borrowed from books or from school-fellows, his gestures from teachers and friends, his behaviour from relatives, his temperament from his mother and wet-nurse, his tastes from his father, perhaps from his grandfather' (261). Leaving the inevitable question, 'What, then, had he of his own? Nothing' (261). It is here, in the intimate 'nothing', the open matrix of possibilities prior to characterization—in characterlessness as such—that Strindberg locates the pre-eminent value in modern psychology. By remaining irreducible to this trait or that predisposition, the protagonist of this frustrated *Bildungsroman* can hope to short-circuit *Bildung* itself, allowing his being to remain undetermined, rich and multifarious.

[18] August Strindberg, *Son of a Servant*, trans. Claud Field (New York: G. P. Putnam's Sons, 1913), 253. The whole tenth chapter is entitled 'Character and Destiny' and is of the greatest interest.

[19] See his *On Intelligence*, trans. T. D. Haye, Kindle edition (New York: Holt & Williams, 1872). 'The individual, animal or human, is nothing more than a system' (loc. 303) writes Taine; but this system must consistently hallucinate and misperceive its own conditions of existence in such a way as to disengage from its varied experiences 'a character common to all the successive elements of the series' (loc. 491), namely, a 'stable within' or a Self (loc. 6788), underwritten by inveterate habit and a handy pronoun.

[20] Strindberg, *Son of a Servant*, 260.

It pays to be clear on how this account agrees with, and differs from, Nietzsche, who for several years had been Strindberg's guiding light on psychology. Nietzsche, in his voluminous attention to the topic, remarks often on this sense of character as reduction and limitation to stereotype. In *Human, All Too Human*, he writes: 'If a man at first appears as something unfamiliar, never before existent, he is to be made into something familiar, often before existent. A child is said to have a good character when it is visibly narrowly determined by what is already existent.'[21] Prior to such narrowing, the self is a veritable swarm of pulsions:

> However far a man may go in self-knowledge, nothing however can be more incomplete than his image of the totality of drives which constitute his being. He can scarcely name even the cruder ones: their number and strength, their ebb and flood, their play and counterplay among one another and above all the laws of their nutriment remain wholly unknown to him.[22]

With Nietzsche, the 'individual' sits unconvincingly astride a turbulent multitude of drives. His desire is for 'nothing less than a fundamental remoulding, indeed weakening and abolition of the *individual*', in the name of this multitude.[23] The result of such a dismantling in Nietzsche is a freeing of the ethical dimension of character from any subservience to a unitary ego, and the seizure of an aesthetic possibility within 'the soul as a society constructed out of drives and affects': '*One thing is needful.*—To "give style" to one's character—a great and rare art!'[24] The subject that emerges from Nietzschean psychology is an aesthetic style imposed on constitutive multiplicity, a play of power. 'The assumption of the *single subject* is perhaps unnecessary; perhaps it is just as permissible to assume a multiplicity of subjects on whose interplay and struggle our thinking and our consciousness in general is based? A kind of *aristocracy* of "cells" in which mastery resides?'[25]

We are never far away, here, from that other source of psychological speculation dear to Strindberg, Théodule Ribot, who formulated the theory of the '*multiplicité du moi*' in his *Diseases of the Will* (1883) and *Diseases of the Personality* (1885).[26] As he wrote, 'ordinary observation shows us how little cohesion and unity the

[21] Friedrich Nietzsche, *Human, All Too Human: A Book for Free Spirits* [I.228], trans. R. J. Hollingdale (Cambridge: Cambridge University Press, 1996), 110.

[22] Friedrich Nietzsche, *Daybreak: Thoughts on the Prejudices of Morality* [II.119], ed. Maudemaire Clark and Brian Leiter, trans. R. J. Hollingdale (Cambridge: Cambridge University Press, 1997), 74.

[23] Nietzsche, *Daybreak* [II.132], 83.

[24] Friedrich Nietzsche, *The Gay Science* [IV.290], ed. Bernard Williams, trans. Josefine Nauckhoff (Cambridge: Cambridge University Press, 2001), 232.

[25] Friedrich Nietzsche, *Writings from the Late Notebooks* [40(42)], ed. Rüdiger Bittner, trans. Kate Sturge (Cambridge: Cambridge University Press, 2003), 46.

[26] It should also be noted that Paul Bourget's novel, *L'Irréparable* (1883) is full of this idea; and his *Le disciple* (1889) features a criminal protagonist, inspired by Taine and Ribot, who writes an opus entitled *Contribution à l'étude de la multiplicité du moi*. See Jean-François Braunstein, 'Antipsychologisme et Philosophie du Cerveau Chez Auguste Comte', *Revue Internationale de Philosophie* 52.203 (1) (March 1998), 14n42 [7–28].

normal ego has. Apart from fully integral characters (in the strict sense of the word, there are none), there are in each of us tendencies of all kinds, all the possible contraries; between these opposites all the intermediate shadings, and amongst these tendencies all possible combinations. The self is not only a memory, a reservoir of souvenirs linked to a present, but a set of instincts, tendencies, desires, those innate and acquired constituents which feed into action.'[27] There is in truth only a 'sum of conscious, sub-conscious, and unconscious (purely physical) states which at the [given] moment constitute the person, the ego.'[28] Consciousness itself, he suggests, 'exists only under the condition of a perpetual change; it is essentially discontinuous. An homogeneous and continuous consciousness is an impossibility' (101). The only stable element here, Ribot writes, is that of character; and

> character—that is to say, the ego, in so much as it reacts—is an extremely complex product, that heredity, prenatal and post-natal physiological conditions, education, and experience have contributed to form. It can be stated [. . .] that what constitutes it are much rather affective states, a peculiar manner of feeling, than an intellectual activity.
>
> (23)

Grounded in affect, character is understood by Ribot as 'the psychological expression of a certain organised body, drawing from it its peculiar coloring, its special tone, and its relative permanence' (113). Such a recentring of characterology around the aleatory tone poems of an 'organized body' upended centuries of idealist metaphysics. And this psychological expression from the body could best be imagined, as per Nietzsche, in a political figure. 'It is the character which gives to the co-ordination its unity,—not the abstract unity of a mathematical point, but the concrete unity of a consensus' (132).

Miss Julie

Strindberg, deeply fascinated by these physiological, pluralistic, affective accounts of character, added to them a Naturalist cynicism of impressionability, social hierarchy, and adaptive mimesis; and, in his famous account of the characterizations of *Miss Julie* (1888), offered the following anatomy:

> I do not believe in simple stage characters, and the summary judgements that authors pass on people—this one is stupid, that one brutal, this one jealous, that one mean—ought to be challenged by naturalists, who know how richly

[27] My translation. See Théodule Ribot, *Les maladies de la personnalité* (Paris: Alcan, 1885), 75.

[28] Théodule Ribot, *Diseases of the Will* (c.1883), trans. Merwin-Marie Snell (Chicago: Open Court, 1894), 21.

> complicated the soul is, and who are aware that 'vice' has a reverse side, which is very much like virtue.
>
> As modern characters, living in an age of transition more urgently hysterical than the one that preceded it, I have depicted the figures in my play as more split and vacillating, a mixture of the old and the new [...].
>
> My souls (characters) are conglomerates of past and present stages of culture, bits out of books and newspapers, scraps of humanity, torn shreds of once fine clothing now turned to rags, exactly as the human soul is patched together [...].[29]

From Nietzsche and Ribot the dramatist has condensed an extraordinary amount of advanced psychological theory, adapting their figure of the 'soul' as a complex conglomeration of forces and powers, drives and reflexes, and adding to this a social insistence on class struggle, sex war, and the newer determinations of a mechanical media ecology. If character once meant 'the dominant trait in a person's soul-complex' (58), it had quickly reified under conditions of advanced capitalism into that 'middle-class expression for an automaton' (59). As the Preface continues, 'This bourgeois concept of the immobility of the soul was transferred to the stage, which has always been dominated by the bourgeoisie. There a character became a man who was fixed and set, who invariably appeared drunk or comical or sad; and all that was needed to characterize him was to give him a physical defect, a club-foot, a wooden leg, a red nose, or some continually repeated phrase such as "That's capital", or "Barkis is willin", etc.' (59).

Here we reach a critical moment in the development of 'modern character'. Character as such is denounced as a bourgeois stereotype and demoted in preference for a conception of the ego as heterogeneous and inconsistent, or *stultus*.[30] It is precisely as *stultus* that Strindberg will pursue his formal investigations into the arcane depths of the modern psyche, where he finds only 'scraps of humanity, torn shreds of once fine clothing now turned to rags'. Against the 'superficiality of characterization in the run-of-the-mill bourgeois drama',[31] he declared the rights of a 'complex of individualities, stemming from many crossbreedings affecting blood and brains, of many stages passed through for which the author simply makes himself a medium or "automatic writer"'.[32] Deposing the hereditary fiction of 'a One', Strindberg's radical liberalism unchained 'the many', whose amanuensis he declared himself. It was a principle he fully embraced, and not only in his art. His two closest companions during the Berlin years, husband

[29] Strindberg, *Miss Julie and Other Plays*, 59–60.

[30] Michel Foucault, *Hermeneutics of the Subject: Lectures at the Collège de France, 1981–1982*, ed. Frédéric Gros, trans. Graham Burchell (New York: Palgrave Macmillan, 2005), 133.

[31] Georg Lukács, *Writer and Critic and Other Essays*, 'The Intellectual Physiognomy in Characterization' (c.1936), ed. and trans. Arthur D. Kahn (London: Merlin Press, 1970), 172 [149–88].

[32] Strindberg, letter to Meijer, 11 December 1890; qtd. in Sprinchorn, *Strindberg as Dramatist*, ix.

and wife pair Ola Hansson and Laura Marholm, remarked in parallel in 1894 that Strindberg was a 'chaos where all thoughts are jammed together, scuffling, elbowing, somersaulting—an orgy of ideas, a carnival of contemporary thought, a battlefield where armed masses of nations fight without leaders'; and 'a conglomerate character' where 'no unity has imposed itself beneath the threshold of consciousness. [. . .] In his work one finds no transitions, no coherence.'[33] Indeed, we discover a remarkable consistency in Strindberg's arguments against consistency, from letters to essays to reported behaviours to prefaces and finally works of art. Where 'unity' once went, there now goes the 'conglomerate character', hammered together out of aesthetic expediency.

Miss Julie and its Preface were calling cards for Zola; the one-act play itself is a remorseless application of cutting-edge science to a weak and defenceless art, and the Preface is its manifesto. As Zola had written of the contemporary stage, 'tragedy and romantic drama are equally old and worn out. [. . .] There is nothing left.'[34] If *Miss Julie* proposes a 'clinically analytic' approach to 'a character's behaviours and interrelations',[35] that is because this recourse to science is the most effective available weapon in an aesthetic struggle over the fate of drama itself. As a thesis-drama, then, *Miss Julie* asks to be read argumentatively and semiotically (Figure 3.1).

The temporal dimension of this stage narrative allows the dual transformations—of the haughty, aristocratic Julie into a 'fallen' woman, and of the valet Jean into a figure capable of siring the new ruling class—in under two hours, chiasmically affirming the transcendence of any vestigial notion of character as a 'dominant trait in a person's soul-complex'. Each character is inverted. There is no one reason for Julie's fall, and no single explanation for Jean's rise; each is motivated by 'an abundance of circumstances', and 'I flatter myself that this multiplicity of motives is in tune with the times' (59). Julie is a mouthpiece for this very thesis, which makes for an obvious diminution of dramatic intensity, even as it brings the drama closer to theoretical Naturalism:

> Who's to blame for all this? My father, my mother, myself? Myself? But I have no self of my own? I haven't a thought I didn't get from my father, not an emotion I didn't get from my mother, and this last idea—that everyone's equal—I got from him, my fiancé—which is why I called him a swine! How can it be my own fault, then? [. . .] Whose fault is it?
>
> (108)

[33] Both qtd. by Evert Sprinchorn, 'Introduction: Strindberg from 1892 to 1897', in Strindberg, *Inferno, Alone, and Other Writings*, 39.

[34] Émile Zola, *Le Naturalisme au théâtre*, trans. George Brandt excerpted in Brandt, ed., *Modern Theories of Drama: A Selection of Writings on Drama and Theatre, 1840–1990* (Oxford: Oxford University Press, 1998), 83.

[35] William Storm, *Dramaturgy and Dramatic Character: A Long View* (Cambridge: Cambridge University Press, 2016), 89.

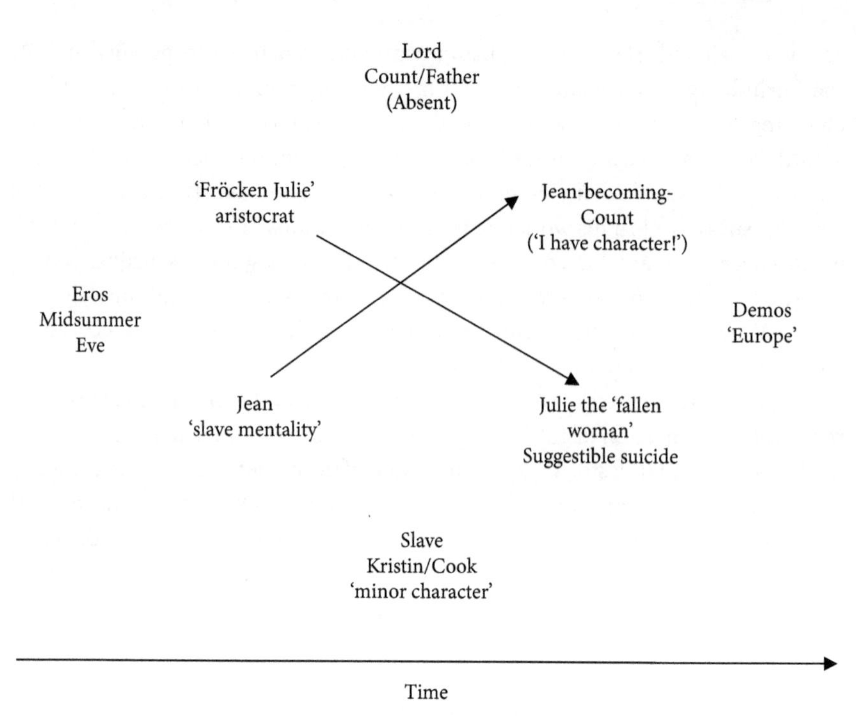

Fig. 3.1 Diachronic transformation of character semiotics in *Miss Julie*

Julie never enjoys an 'intellectual physiognomy' (as Lukács put it) of her own and is subject to various reversals within the characterological field of the play, where Jean and the minor character Kristin each rise to effective domination over the 'lady of the house' in her father's absence. Her presumed characterological superiority within the field of social distinction is undermined by sexual dynamics, on the one hand, and the stolidity of a servant's morality, on the other.

Stichomythic traducement underlines the chiasmus:

MISS JULIE. Lackey, servant, stand up when I speak to you!
JEAN. Lackey's whore, servant's tart. Shut your mouth and get out of here! (91)
MISS JULIE. You speak as though you were already above me.
JEAN. I am, too. You see, I could turn you into a countess, but you can never make me a count. (91–2)

At the bottom of our semiological table (Figure 3.1) we find the minor character as such, carrying with it some of the residual characterology of nineteenth-century character space:[36]

[36] As per the argument of Alex Woloch's *The One vs. the Many: Minor Characters and the Space of the Protagonist in the Novel* (Princeton and Oxford: Princeton University Press, 2003).

> [Kristin] is a minor character, and therefore my intention was only to sketch her in as I did the Pastor and the Doctor in *The Father*, where I just wanted to depict ordinary people as country parsons and provincial doctors usually are. And if some people have found my minor characters abstract, that is because ordinary people are to some extent abstract when working; which is to say, they lack individuality and show only one side of themselves while performing their tasks [. . .].[37]

This is quite probably a defensive response to Zola's critique of Strindberg's previous effort in this direction, *The Father*, of which he complained, 'I am not much for abstraction. I like it when characters are given a proper context, that we may elbow them and feel they are steeped in our air. And your Captain who has not even a name, your other characters who are almost [mental projections], do not give me the complete sense of life which I require.'[38] But here, the dramatist displays his lucid superiority to the novelist on matters pertaining to modern aesthetics: an anachronistic demand for 'proper context' and the 'complete sense of life' anchors Zola's characterology in the depleted paradigm of realism; whereas Strindberg's insistence on *the reality of abstraction* shows up the implicit sentimentalism of that demand.

Strindberg's aesthetic mission as the 'bridge' between Naturalism and Symbolism is perhaps best illuminated by this discovery of *real abstraction*. Rather than fleshing out and filling in the 'minor characters' who constitute the working class of nineteenth-century narrative art, this new discovery rejoins Marx's analysis of specialized and collective labour under advanced industrial capitalism.

> [A] worker who performs the same simple operation for the whole of his life converts his body into the automatic, one-sided implement of that operation. [. . .] The collective worker, who constitutes the living mechanism of manufacture, is made up solely of such one-sidedly specialized workers. [. . .] The one-sidedness and even the deficiencies of the specialized individual worker become perfections when he is part of the collective worker. The habit of doing only one thing converts him into an organ which operates with the certainty of a force of nature, while his connection with the whole mechanism compels him to work with the regularity of a machine.[39]

'The abstract', writes Enzo Paci, 'in capitalist society, *functions concretely*.'[40] If, as Alex Woloch proposed, it was the great distinction of the realist novel that it

[37] Strindberg, *Miss Julie and Other Plays*, 63.
[38] Zola, qtd. in Strindberg, *Miss Julie and Other Plays*, 292.
[39] Karl Marx, *Capital, Vol. 1*, trans. Ben Fowkes (London: Penguin, 1990), 458, 469.
[40] Enzo Paci, qtd. in Alberto Toscano, 'The Open Secret of Real Abstraction', in Gean Moreno, ed., *In the Mind but Not from There: Real Abstraction and Contemporary Art* (London: Verso, 2019), Kindle locations 3849–50.

posited a relation between 'the question of democracy and [its] distributed field of characterization',[41] and flirted with the fantasy of focalization on 'any-character-whatever', then what seriously constrained its aesthetic enterprise was an inability to recognize the real abstractions in its midst. Strindberg's observation that 'ordinary people are to some extent abstract when working; which is to say, they lack individuality and show only one side of themselves while performing their tasks', grasps the extent to which a total social organization implicitly deindividualizes, decontextualizes actual living beings, alienates them from that 'complete sense of life' that Zola demanded from his worker-characters.

Kristin the cook is indifferent to the carnivalesque happenings all around her; she labours through Midsummer Eve, participates in none of the dancing, and issues stern, moralistic judgements on the perversions of the night. She takes Jean's indiscretions as a frolic, assuming all along his strict intentions to honour his pledge to her. Moreover, while Kristin is used as a measuring stick against which to tell the extent of Julie's fall—'I'm sorry to see you sunk so low that you're beneath your cook', as Jean puts it (91)—she herself is adamant about her inflexibility on this score: 'I've never sunk below my own station. You tell me when his Lordship's cook has been with the groom or the pig man! Just you tell me!' (106). A scrupulous regard for hierarchy defines the minor character: to be minor is to have internalized the structural inequality that has so branded you in the first place; it is an inability to range, even in the imagination, beyond the prescribed bounds of action appropriate to one's station. By that same token, it is a 'moral' espousal of the hierarchy as the good itself; which is why Kristin's evaluation of Julie's declension is so harsh.

'I'm not stopping here a moment longer, not in a house where we can't respect our masters' (100). It is with this judgement that Kristin calls a halt to the 'horizontal' spread of the play's elements along an egalitarian axis identified with Europe and republicanism. 'If they're no better than we are', she responds to Jean, then 'there's no point us trying to be like them' (100). With that syllogism Kristin effectively reframes the transvaluative topsy-turvyism of the drama within a higher-order conservatism that exposes Jean's *ressentiment* as a pattern of emulation, and Julie's self-abasement as a mark of degeneracy. Dramatically, what matters is that Kristin radiates this restorationist logic through her 'minor' status and two-dimensionality. Strindberg has engineered the returning 'grey light of day' by way of the stolidity and flatness of his minor character, who uses her imperturbable figure and older values to cast a withering eye on Jean's and Julie's new ones.

This minor character functions, then, as a refutation of the major characters' interior complexity and multi-dimensionality, and a severe contraction of the character space. It is, Strindberg supposes, a quintessence of Naturalist method to

[41] Woloch, *The One vs. the Many*, 31.

insist on the inadmissibility of 'those inferior, unreliable instruments of thought called feelings' in a drama that casts its lot with 'the brutal, cynical, heartless drama that life presents' (57). Within that rigorous application of new scientific naturalism, however, the 'real abstraction' of a minor character goes much further than Zola could have imagined. Its deepest secret is to have repelled any temptations to identify with it, and it donates that same flatness (of emotion as well as intellect) to the other characters around whom it closes its narrow purview, thereby abstracting all of them. As Jon Erickson writes, 'For Strindberg [...] a "character", whether "characterless" or "non-Euclidean", is not an opportunity for personal spectator identification, but becomes an integral, even if apparently fragmentary, part of a multi-faceted "cubist" social structure, shaped by an overlapping set of perceptions and conceptions.'[42] What happens after the admission of a 'real abstraction' like Kristin into a play without conventional characters is that the field opens radically outward: even in a cast of three, what finally matters is not our feelings of identification with any of them, but the total aesthetic structure itself, now perceived as if for the first time without the alibi of sentiment.

To Damascus I

Strindberg announced his post-Inferno return to dramaturgy with *To Damascus I* (1898). In this work, the art of characterization is taken to new extremes; its conception of 'individuality' is severely exposed to the erosion of destabilizing subterranean movements. Naturalism has relaxed its strictures to admit greater degrees of abstraction and a Maeterlinckian 'stillness' via the play's recourse to a prefabricated medieval structure. That structure, the 'station drama'—marking 'the beginning of a modernist tradition of quasi-allegorical mystery plays'[43]—was to prove productive in later Expressionist drama.[44] The resurrected form permitted a new intensity of concentration on the protagonist, whose parallelism with the staged suffering and death of Christ in the station drama tended to magnify his struggles and crises. The transposition of the story of Christ's last days to the modern stage had the propensity to *psychologize* the Nazarene's ordeals; in the avatar of some merely human, ordinary, mortal, modern body, this mythic Person assumed all the qualities of modern suffering—angst, alienation, dread, terror,

[42] Jon Erickson, 'The *Mise en Scène* of the Non-Euclidean Character: Wellman, Jenkin and Strindberg', *Modern Drama* 41.3 (Fall 1998), 361 [355–70].
[43] Elinor Fuchs, *The Death of Character: Perspectives on Theater after Modernism* (Bloomington: Indiana University Press, 1996), 32.
[44] See Fuchs' discussion in *Death of Character*, Ch. 2, 36–50. See also Kela Kvam, *Max Reinhardt og Strindbergs visionaere dramatik* (Copenhagen: Akademisk Forlag, 1974), 103–39; and Göran Stockenström, '*To Damascus* (I): A Dream Play?', in Stockenström, ed., *Strindberg's Dramaturgy*, 205–22.

ennui, and nausea at the world. The conditions for Expressionist drama subsist in this modern affective chaos grafted onto a theological Absolute.

Strindberg's critical rediscovery of this archaic form entailed an inflection of its use in the direction of what would be called his subjectivism. This subjectivism goes much further than a mere attentiveness to the peculiar personality of his Christological protagonist—for the most extraordinary feature of *To Damascus* is the profoundly autobiographical nature of its narrative and conception.[45] The Stranger (an apparent echo of the figure in Ibsen's *Lady from the Sea*) is as much a figure of his author as he is of the Christ he ironically symbolizes, and it is this double valence that defines the allegorical nature of this play. In the history of aesthetics, there is perhaps no more startling break with the convention that—as Stephen Dedalus was to put it—in dramatic form the 'personality of the artist [...] finally refines itself out of existence, impersonalises itself, so to speak'.[46] In *To Damascus*, The Stranger represents the 'personality of the artist', Strindberg, with an almost embarrassing candour. Having become publicly notorious, with the sordid details of his life—his abandonment of his wife and children, alcoholic excesses, sexual promiscuity, paranoia, flirtations with occultism, alchemical experiments with carbon and gold—all a scandalous matter of record, Strindberg first burnished that notoriety with the publication of *Inferno* in 1897, an autobiographical novel that deliberately courts charges of immorality and insanity, then doubled down on his personal identification with this nefarious persona in the character of The Stranger. There is no escaping the web of explicit cross-referencing with Strindberg's life in the construction of this protagonist—constant echoes, not only of the textual specifics of *Inferno*, but of those myriad intimate personal details that tie *To Damascus* to the genre of autobiography.

This remarkable development, which takes the rudimentary autobiographical qualities of a character like Jean in *Miss Julie* and elevates them to an architectonic dominant like nothing else in the history of theatre, has the further consequence of arranging those personal details around one psychological trait in particular—paranoia. As The Stranger retorts to the Lady upon her judgement that he is 'hyper-sensitive', 'There you are again. You mean I'm paranoiac?'[47] This prevailing mood is particularly useful in the degree to which it is adapted, in advance, to the Christological form of the station drama; since the paranoiac is he who feels the full theological extent of his victimization, his martyrdom to circumstance. In the absolute sacrifice of Jesus Christ the paranoiac finds a suitably grandiose self-image: 'I was condemned to death! Of that I was convinced. By whom?', asks

[45] See William Conrad White, 'The Autobiographical Elements as Manifested in Selected Plays of John August Strindberg' (MA thesis, Department of Drama, University of California, 1950), 212–45.

[46] James Joyce, *A Portrait of the Artist as a Young Man*, ed. Jeri Johnson (Oxford: Oxford University Press, 2000), 181.

[47] August Strindberg, *To Damascus I*, in *The Plays*, Vol. 2, trans Michael Meyer (London: Secker & Warburg, 1975), 59.

the narrator of *Inferno*, begging the question that always presages the same answer: 'To struggle for the preservation of my Self against all the influences brought to bear upon me by the ambitions of any sect or party, I consider that as my duty, a duty dictated by the conscience bestowed on me by the grace of my divine protectors.'[48] Here, the overweening egotism of a true paranoiac is dignified by its referral to the stations of the cross, which are made over into explicit structuring devices in *To Damascus*: 'You have left Jerusalem and are on the road to Damascus. Go there; by the same road you came. And plant a cross at every station, but stop at the seventh. You don't have to suffer fourteen, like Him.'[49] Neither, for that matter, can the character analogues be halted at Christ, and one finds manifest in The Stranger's role the overlapping personae of Cain, Polycrates, Aeneas, Virgil, Jacob, Lucifer, and Saul, among others,[50] leading Sprinchorn to remark that the 'hero stands in the light of legend and myth in order to enjoy the giant shadows his little figure casts'.[51] Or, contrarily, the very tendency to revert to these archetypes is rendered ironic and otiose by the absurd incongruity of their reference to this pathetic 'little figure', on whom none of their sublime significance can properly be focused.

On the one hand, the psychologism of this work allows for an unprecedented degree of movement up and down the scale between the utterly trivial and delusional, and the apocalyptic and Absolute, a movement enacted by a figure in whom is invested simultaneously all the maddeningly banal confessions of an adolescent diary, and the full, divine majesty of the persecuted godhead. Here stands already operative the aesthetic principle that T. S. Eliot would canonize more than two decades later (in the name of James Joyce) as the 'mythic method', which is to say that 'continuous parallel' between a fallen contemporaneity and the august dignity of antiquity, 'giving a shape and significance to the immense panorama of futility and anarchy which is contemporary history'.[52] Maurice Valency once described *To Damascus* as 'a quasi-medieval work that was to furnish the blueprint for the most advanced drama of the twentieth century, and perhaps for the Joycean novel as well'.[53] On the other hand, however, a rather different aesthetic protocol is enshrined, according to which the prevailing mood of paranoia subjects the entire scenography and dramaturgy of the play to a principle of equivalence in line with the neurosis itself. Freud formulated the underlying rationale of paranoia a couple of years before Strindberg composed his play—'The purpose of paranoia is

[48] Strindberg, *Inferno, Alone, and Other Writings*, 198, 188.

[49] Strindberg, *To Damascus I*, 94.

[50] 'Strindberg was able to fuse personal experience and literary and mythic sources into a superbly exciting texture, at once contemporary and timeless.' Harry G. Carlson, *Strindberg and the Poetry of Myth* (Berkeley: University of California Press, 1982), 93.

[51] Sprinchorn, *Strindberg as Dramatist*, 101.

[52] T. S. Eliot, '"Ulysses", Order, and Myth', *Selected Prose of T. S. Eliot*, ed. Frank Kermode (London: Faber & Faber, 1975), 177 [175–8]. As Sprinchorn puts it, 'Joyce complicated the system of allusions and parallels without adding anything essential to the method.' *Strindberg as Dramatist*, 102.

[53] Maurice Valency, *The Flower and the Castle: An Introduction to Modern Drama* (New York: Macmillan, 1963), 304.

thus to ward off an idea that is incompatible with the ego, by projecting its substance into the external world'[54]—thereby establishing the relationship between a persecution complex and the phenomenon of projection, which indeed swallows up the world of *To Damascus* in what Fredric Jameson has described as 'an inescapable swarm of allegories [established] with all the exegetical obsession of a garden-variety paranoiac'.[55] In the words of Adorno and Horkheimer, paranoiacs

> perceive the outside world only in so far as it corresponds to their blind purposes, they can only endlessly repeat their own self, which has been alienated from them as an abstract mania. [. . .] The closed circle of perpetual sameness becomes a surrogate for omnipotence. [. . .] He creates everything in his own image. [. . .] His will permeates the whole universe; nothing may be unrelated to him. His systems know of no gaps.[56]

So it is with The Stranger in *To Damascus*. 'I feel myself swell and stretch, rarefy, become boundless; I am everywhere, in the sea which is my blood, in the mountains which are my skeleton, in the trees, in the flowers. And my head reaches to heaven. I look out over the Universe which is I, I feel the strength of the Creator within me, for I am the Creator.'[57] But this plenum of Self is internally fissured. Wherever he may turn, The Stranger is confronted with avatars of himself, and of those few others—the Lady, the Mother, and Grandfather—who are capable of forming some nidus of resistance within the hall of mirrors that is this play's field of action. Several of the major characters are simply 'projections' in the paranoiac sense of The Stranger's own inassimilable qualities and tendencies, cast abroad in all their alienated stereotypicality: the Beggar (sceptical ego), the Madman (unconscious), the Doctor (superego), and the Corpse (death drive), 'each the dream self of the other'.[58] His crisis is thus not historical or social, but *moral*, in the sense that, all his questionable acts and judgements now returning in so many scenes on the stage of himself, he is forced, as *stultus*, to confront his own 'complex of individualities' in a panorama of self-persecuting paranoia.

Morality, for Nietzsche as for Strindberg, concerns the 'self-division of man'—'In morality man treats himself not as *individuum* but as *dividuum*'.[59] In his paranoiac projections, The Stranger arraigns himself as dividuum, making tableaux of his divided psyche in order to fashion, not a plausible unity, but a dynamic

[54] Sigmund Freud, 'Draft H: Paranoia' (1895), in *The Standard Edition of the Complete Psychological Works of Sigmund Freud*, Vol. 1, *1886–1899: Pre-Psychoanalytic Publications and Unpublished Drafts*, trans. James Strachey (London: Vintage, 2001), 109.

[55] Fredric Jameson, *Allegory and Ideology* (London: Verso, 2019), 1.

[56] Theodor W. Adorno and Max Horkheimer, *Dialectic of Enlightenment: Philosophical Fragments*, ed. Gunzelin Schmid Noerr, trans. Edmund Jephcott (Stanford: Stanford University Press, 2002), 157.

[57] Strindberg, *To Damascus I*, 58.

[58] Sue Prideaux, *Strindberg: A Life* (New Haven: Yale University Press, 2012), 202.

[59] Nietzsche, *Human, All Too Human* [#57], 41–2.

passion of the soul in which all the parts are played by reified aspects of a fractured identity.[60] As Williams put it, 'in this agony the self fragments and is finally alienated'.[61] Strindberg's great innovation is to present his dramatis personae as 'figures in an internal landscape of doubt, ambivalence, insurrection, and submission; his characters [are] agents of his own self-division'.[62] The antagonisms, being internal, no longer need to be worked through via external action and reaction; they remain irresolvable due to their containment by a force-field of 'perpetual sameness' or real abstraction. In *Miss Julie*, the real abstraction concerned what Alfred Sohn-Rethel called 'the economic fetishism of manual labor ("value")', but in *To Damascus I*, it concerns 'the epistemological fetishism of intellectual labor ("logic")'[63]—moral logic vivisecting the ego portrayed as a dividuum. What this play performs, for the first time, is not a 'drama' but the monism of real abstraction, strung out along an empty and recursive continuum of 'static, futureless'[64] scenes.

Drama cedes to eternal recurrence. 'I lay there and saw my whole life unreel in a kind of panorama from my childhood, through my youth, right up to . . .', declares The Stranger. 'And when it was finished, it began to unreel again.'[65] The lack of development is written into the form (here the numbers refer to the play's seventeen scenes, the words their setting).[66]

17, 1 Streetcorner

16 Doctor's home 2 Doctor's home

15 Hotel room 3 Hotel room

14S ea 4 Sea

13 Road 5 Road

12 Ravine 6 Ravine

11 Kitchen 7 Kitchen

10 Rose room 8 Rose room

9 Asylum

[60] See Herbert Lindenberger, *The Historical Drama: The Relation of Literature and Reality* (Chicago: University of Chicago Press, 1975), 88; Ann-Charlotte Gavel Adams, 'Delacroix Murals in Eglise Saint-Sulpice and Strindberg's *Jacob Wrestles* and *To Damascus I*', *Stage and Screen: Studies in Scandinavian Drama and Film* (Seattle: DreamPlayPress Northwest, 2000), 38–53.

[61] Raymond Williams, *Modern Tragedy*, ed. Pamela McCallum (Toronto: Broadview, 2006), 140.

[62] Gilman, *Making of Modern Drama*, 101.

[63] Alfred Sohn-Rethel in Theodor Adorno and Sohn-Rethel, *Carteggio 1936/1969* (Rome: manifestolibri, 2000), 112. Translation by Alberto Toscano.

[64] Peter Szondi, *Theory of the Modern Drama*, Critical Edition, ed. and trans. Michael Hays, *Theory and History of Literature 29* (Minneapolis: University of Minnesota Press, 1987), 26.

[65] Strindberg, *To Damascus I*, 87.

[66] Adapted from Egil Törnqvist, *Strindbergian Drama: Themes and Structure* (Stockholm: Almqvist & Wiksell International, 1982), 72.

Within this perfect circle, one of the great achievements of modernist form, The Stranger meets only himself, dividuated into instantly recognizable emanations. What makes this play fully satisfying is the fact that, however rooted in pathological autobiographical symptoms and a paranoiac *grande malaise*, its dramatis personae are also *social* forms, commensurable and legible precisely in their abstract equivalence with what the audience spontaneously discovers in itself. Doctor, Lady, Madman, Mother, Beggar, Corpse: Strindberg found that a dramatic form could crystallize around such threadbare abstractions, because they were real and immanent in psychosocial space. A drama built out of real abstractions proves vastly superior to dramas patched together out of the shattered romance of yesterday's forms.

This radicalization of naturalism has transposed Ribot's '*multiplicité du moi*' into characters on the stage. In becoming aesthetic, they escape the clutches of the 'personal' altogether and turn into allegories of an undocumented social process. Figments of a now general story—of specialization, reification, self-division, and incessant recrimination—these characters configure, in their patterned disposition on the stage, an allegorical image of modernity itself; so that a distress signal sent up from the intimate depths of a morbid crisis of individuality creates a universally recognizable aesthetic constellation, a hieroglyph of modern character as such. The patchwork of real abstractions that we are obliged to carry around within us has, as it were, disclosed itself on Strindberg's stage as that which we have already become. The older 'Self' has been consumed and replaced by the parasites it once merely hosted.

A Dream Play

Strindberg is the first great literary artist to realize that, under the economic conditions of capitalism, 'the issue is not one of increasing abstraction, nor one of the failure of the abstract, but of the *becoming-real, becoming-concrete, becoming-productive of abstraction itself*.'[67] The characters in his late plays are all figures of this historic process, only serving, as such, to testify to the aesthetic's incapacity to accommodate them. None more graphically than the dramatis personae of his oneiric experiment, *A Dream Play* (1901), where the dreamwork is no longer constrained to a purely moral domain, and a cosmogonic purview is enjoined to show the limitless quantities of human suffering and futility in light of that most Hadean of real abstractions: repetition. 'I wake up in the morning with a headache; and then the repetition begins—a repetition that perverts the past, however. Everything that was beautiful, pleasant, and witty yesterday evening appears

[67] Sven Lütticken, 'Concrete Abstraction—Our Common World', in Moreno, ed., *In the Mind but Not from There*, 153 [149–76].

in recollection as ugly, vile, and stupid. Pleasure turns sour, it seems, and happiness dissolves. [. . .] That is what life amounts to, doing the same thing over and over again.'[68] But, although the structure and mood of this play are medieval (and akin to the revue), this is not the same as a reprisal of the theme of Fortuna. Repetition in this Kierkegaardian sense does not amount to a fable of variable fortune; it is the infinite regress of joyless recapitulation from one situation to the next, such that even the radiant moments are stricken and barren. 'Repetition! – – –Doing the same thing over and over again!! – – – Going back over everything!' (221). This recognition of the existential infertility of the everyday is the polar opposite of Nietzsche's eternal return. The circularity of the play's structure confirms what the cast of forty characters only appears to vitiate: that repetition is an abstraction of experience from which there is no escape. Those characters duly have their ostensible multiplicity reduced and resolved, exposing their participation in a singular ordeal. 'The characters of *A Dream Play* may be allegorical figures, but they also comprise fragmented aspects of one particular self.'[69] As Strindberg wrote in his note to the play, extending the lesson of *To Damascus*, the 'characters split, double, multiply, evaporate, condense, disperse, and converge. But one consciousness holds sway over them all, that of the dreamer; for him there are no secrets, no incongruities, no scruples, no law. He neither acquits not condemns [. . .]'.[70] The play is a psychodrama of self-division and fissiparity whose project is to refute any dramatic potentiality under the real abstraction of repetition; it ends where it begins, and the many resolve back into the one they allegorized. A 'single character dissolves into several, who merge into one again', the author wrote.[71]

In these plays, as Szalczer remarks, 'Strindberg replaced causal plot-construction, rational linguistic patterns, and realistic character motivation with a "dream-logic" of perceptual associations, in which images, sound effects, and verbal fragments are interwoven into a collage in which a leitmotif emerges from a texture of repetitions with variations.'[72] But a better way of putting this is to say that Strindberg admitted real abstractions into dramatic form in so thoroughgoing a way that they obliged the form to reinvent itself around them. Figures who look and sound like characters are not; they may move and speak like dramatis personae from the tradition, but they have been seared by the blight of abstractions so potent as to shatter their consistency and reassemble the fragments in Dantean mosaics. 'This is paradise!' proclaims Indra's Daughter in *A Dream Play*, to which the First Coal-Heaver immediately replies 'This is hell!' (223). Inferno

[68] Strindberg, *A Dream Play*, in *Miss Julie and Other Plays*, 221–2.

[69] Erikson, 'The *Mise en Scène* of the Non-Euclidean Character', 360.

[70] Strindberg, *Miss Julie and Other Plays*, 176.

[71] Strindberg, letter to Emil Schering, *Selected Letters*, Vol. 2, ed. and trans. Michael Robinson (Chicago: University of Chicago Press, 1992), 692.

[72] Eszter Szalczer, 'Strindberg & the Visual Arts', *PAJ: A Journal of Performance and Art* 25.3 (Sept. 2003), 43 [42–50].

and Paradiso are henceforth the undecidable recto and verso of a new plane of immanence, where the reigning abstractions—Value, Logic, and Repetition—lock human beings into functions, self-recriminations, and empty loops of recurrence that alienate them from all that had passed for a dramatic telos: destiny, fate, or some other inherited goal. Freed from these ends, they can face abstraction in its real dimension. It is in this sense that Adorno maintained that Strindberg's 'formal innovations, the dissolution of dramatic realism and the reconstruction of dream-like experience, are objectively critical', and that these plays are 'socially progressive, the dawning self-consciousness of that catastrophe for which the bourgeois individualistic society is preparing: In it the absolutely individual becomes a ghost as in *Ghost Sonata*',[73] or a plethora of self-dividing mirror-phantoms unable to do more than rue that things are as they are.

[73] Theodor Adorno, *Aesthetic Theory*, ed. Gretel Adorno and Rolf Tiedemann, trans. Robert Hullot-Kentor (London: Continuum, 2002), 334.

4
Chekhov

The Seagull

In the first act of Chekhov's play *The Seagull* (1895)—first performed (disastrously) at the Alexandrine Theatre in St Petersburg in mid-October 1896, and then, more happily, at the Moscow Art Theatre in December 1898—a young man with a pronounced Hamlet-syndrome presents an original play-within-the-play to woo his lover, with unhappy consequences. The proscenium that frames this play-within-the-play is plausibly worldly; Chekhov calls for an outdoor setting on Sorin's estate, with a broad avenue of trees by a lake. The design of the framed drama, on a clumsy improvised stage which blocks the view of the lake, contradicts the uncomplicated realism of the surrounding set with its otherworldly ambience and exaggerated stage devices (olfactory effects; red eyes in the darkness; will-o'-the-wisps). This discordance speaks indirectly to the young playwright Konstantin Treplyov's Maeterlinckian insistence on the need for 'new forms' in the theatre:

> I think the modern theatre is just cliché and prejudice. When the curtain goes up and there in a three-walled room with three walls, lit for the evening, these great talents, priests of the sacred art, show how people eat, drink, love, walk, wear their jackets; when out of these trite images and phrases they try to fish out a moral—a little moral, one easy to understand, useful in the home [. . .].[1]

Treplyov's critique of bourgeois Naturalism resonates ironically on Chekhov's stage, but the irony is not definitive, since there is much in this sally that *The Seagull*, too, wishes to endorse. (The play overall will deploy unmistakably 'Symbolist' tropes, such as the lake, the moon, and the seagull itself.) What Konstantin (Kostya) calls for in this context is a more adequately 'universal' and Symbolic vocation for the characters of drama, able to lift the theatre out of its entropic, mimetic attachment to the status quo.

The problem is that his play, a monodrama set in a lifeless post-apocalyptic wasteland, is not nearly equal to these ambitions for it. 'This is a bit of Decadent theatre', his mother mutters from her seat (92), and her complaint is validated by the dramatic awkwardness and jejune attitudinizing of the production—and here,

[1] Anton Chekhov, *The Seagull*, in *Plays*, trans. Peter Carson (London: Penguin, 2002), 86.

Modern Character. Julian Murphet, Oxford University Press. © Julian Murphet (2023).
DOI: 10.1093/oso/9780192863126.003.0005

'Decadence' decodes as 'Symbolism', a reduction of lived complexity to static simplifications.[2] At the heart of Kostya's distillations of Naturalism's 'messy life' into Symbolist 'pure images' stands the problem of character. The 'World Spirit' who survives the ruins of humanity in Kostya's drama does so in a brimming state of absorptive unity (not unlike the Dreamer of Strindberg's later *Dream Play*):

> The bodies of living beings have turned into dust and eternal matter has changed them into stones, into water, into clouds, and all their spirits have merged into one. I . . . I am that universal spirit . . . In me is the spirit of Alexander the Great and Caesar and Shakespeare and Napoleon, and that of the meanest leech. [. . .] Only one spirit in the universe remains constant and immutable.
>
> (92)

This condensation is theatrically disappointing. By absorbing the infinite variety of beings into a spiritualized essence, the Spirit loses any defining particularity. As Nina Zarechnaya, who plays the Spirit, complains to the author:

NINA: It's difficult to act in your play. It has no living characters.
KONSTANTIN: Living characters! Life should be shown not as it is, and not as it ought to be, but as it appears in dreams.
NINA: Your play doesn't have much action, only speeches. (89)

So, the metatheatrical contretemps of the play-within-the-play crystallizes around the problem of character, as well it might. For *The Seagull* is the first development made by Chekhov in what will turn out to be his most important dramatic innovation: the dismantlement of the very function of the protagonist, and its substitution by a decentralized, fractured site of characterological interest. To see this clearly, a backward glance at the author's previous play, *Ivanov* (1887), will be instructive.

At the core of this earlier play lies the conventional *fin-de-siècle* problem of a nobleman protagonist who lacks any remaining will. The final act, in which Ivanov's possible redemption through remarriage is finally thwarted by the malevolent honesty of Lvov, turns on the representativeness of Ivanov as a prototypical decadent, obliged to rattle off the various failures of his own personhood—thus serving as a metatheatrical mouthpiece for the contemporary irrelevance of his

[2] 'In standard turn-of-the-century parlance, "decadent" and "symbolist" were synonymous terms.' Laurence Senelick, 'Chekhov's Drama, Maeterlinck, and the Russian Symbolists', in Jean-Pierre Barricelli, ed., *Chekhov's Great Plays: A Critical Anthology* (New York and London: New York University Press, 1981), 161 [161–80].

type for the new theatre. That type is the superannuated Hamlet-figure,[3] and its function, here, is to raise the crisis of protagonicity as an avowed dilemma:

> To whine, to be sorry for myself, to bore people, to realize that my vital energy is gone forever, that I've rusted up, had my day . . . that I've lost my will and got mired up to my ears in this vile melancholy . . .
>
> If I go to a gathering, if I pay a visit or go shooting, wherever I go, everywhere I bring boredom, despair, discontent.[4]

In the absence of any credible motivation of the device for this kind of anachronistic figure, the plot dissolves around it. The dramatic process of *Ivanov* is one of mutual disintegration: the plot deliquesces around the morbid space of a protagonist incapable of anything besides the generation of 'boredom', that key Chekhovian term, which decodes as 'absence of decisive action' and which finds the dramatist resorting to the facile get-out clause of that most hackneyed of gestures, the suicidal pistol-shot.[5] The act of self-slaughter confirms, at the level of action, the character of Ivanov ('Character in a play is that which reveals the choice of the agents'[6]) as the one with nothing to choose but nothing.

'I've been playing Hamlet', Ivanov tells his betrothed Sasha, 'and you the maiden of high ideals—enough of that' (73). It is not a question of the permanent banishment of this Ivanov type from Chekhov's stage. As at least one commentator has asked, why, after all, 'did [Chekhov] continue, year after year, to fill both his stories and his plays with whole processions of Ivanovs? The ineffectual Konstantin in *The Seagull* shoots himself like Ivanov; the ineffectual Uncle Vanya, after shooting at (and of course missing) his pedant of a brother-in-law, relapses at the play's end into the same melancholy frustration with which he began', and so forth.[7] The question is, rather, with the matter of protagonicity itself, which now faces a major crisis. As *The Seagull* demonstrates, Chekhov's intuitive answer to the problem of Ivanov is to bar his type's claim to the central dramatic position, and indeed

[3] On this figure and its importance for this critical period, see Stéphane Mallarmé, 'Hamlet', in *Divagations*, trans. Barbara Johnson (Cambridge, MA: Belknap Press of Harvard University Press, 2007), 124–8; 'Opinions singuilères et curieuses touchant le seigneur Hamlet', *La Revue Blanche* 19.145 (15 June 1899): 283–94; Maurice Maeterlinck, 'Menu Propos: Le Théâtre', *La Jeune Belgique* 9 (1890): 331–6; Laurence Senelick, 'Moscow and Monodrama: The Meaning of the Craig-Stanislavsky *Hamlet*', *Theatre Research International* 6.2 (Spring, 1981): 109–24.

[4] Chekhov, *Ivanov*, in *Plays*, trans. Carson, 73–4.

[5] 'Chekhov's characters suffer from aboulia—the loss or impairment of the ability to act or to make decisions.' David Krasner, *A History of Modern Drama*, Vol. 1 (Oxford: Wiley-Blackwell, 2012), 110.

[6] Aristotle, *The Poetics*, 1450b1, 9, in *The Complete Works of Aristotle*, Vol. 2, ed. and trans. Jonathan Barnes, Bollingen Series LXXI: 2 (Princeton: Princeton University Press, 1984), 2321.

[7] F. L. Lucas, *The Drama of Chekhov, Synge, Yeats, and Pirandello* (London: Cassell, 1963), 33–4.

to dismantle the protagonist as such—to disable the advent of any single character so central, so determining of plot, theme, and style, that it exclusively defines the drama's movement and aesthetic complexion. For the remainder of Chekhov's brief career as a dramatist, there will be *no further protagonists.*

In the vacated place of the protagonist, Chekhov now—in *The Seagull*—elaborates a quartet of interrelated characters, each defined by distinct stylistic traits yet all related by the metatheatrical fact that they are professionally occupied with the depiction of character as such (actors, writers). With this multiplication of the protagonist function the drama is liberated to discover new capacities. Where before there had stood Ivanov, there now stand the four primary figures, none of whom belongs properly to the ruling class: Treplyov, the young aspiring writer; Nina, the young aspiring actress; Arkadina, the mature successful actress; and Trigorin, the mature successful writer. These four are implicated with one another in multiple, over-determining ways: Arkadina is the mother of Treplyov, who is in love with Nina, who is in love with Trigorin, who is the lover of Arkadina; Arkadina is an actress jealous of the younger actress Nina, who acts in the drama written by Treplyov, who disdains the easy commercialism of Trigorin, who sketches a story based on Nina's life, which threatens to repeat Arkadina's; Treplyov and Nina struggle, while Arkadina and Trigorin bask in their success, but the elders' jealousy of these younger talents expresses itself in an openly sexual way—Trigorin's easy conquest of Nina; Arkadina's Oedipal stranglehold on her son—that fails to contain the generational threat; Arkadina and Nina perform fictional characters who inspire Trigorin and Treplyov to write fictional characters that Arkadina and Nina might perform; and so on. These densely interwoven lines attest to a singularity of purpose expressed through the cluster of personae. Such is the tenacious shadow of protagonicity over this breakthrough drama: no 'hero' as such, but a matted characterological space knitted together by incestuous intergenerational sexual vectors.

Moreover, each of these characters is 'realized' distinctly on the stage; each has its own technical dominant and, indeed, its own privileged place in the dramatic structure. This can be schematically mapped as shown in Table 4.1.

Particularly interesting here is Chekhov's evident determination to break down the function of protagonicity into revolving foci of attention without ever losing the sense that each individual component of the quartet is inextricable from the totality of their relations.

Each of these characters is separately engaged in the representation of character, and here, too, a combinatory of variable components is allowed to do the work of what would otherwise have been a singular character 'arc'. Treplyov's conception of character, in his Symbolist drama, is one of cosmic typicality: the 'World Spirit', in its absolute generality, lacks any character as such. Yet he himself is, of course, the advance prototype of a new character in the twentieth century: the split Freudian subject divided between a melancholy ego and a voracious unconscious. Trigorin,

Table 4.1 Structured variation of character technique and type in *The Seagull*

Character	Place within dramatic structure	Technique within the quartet	Type
TREPLYOV	Act I	'Unconscious' self-revelation through dialogue	Oedipus
TRIGORIN	Act II	Conscious self-performance in monologue	Egoism
ARKADINA	Act III	Unselfconscious enactment of character via 'theatricality'	Vanity
NINA	Act IV	Realization of character through separation	Bildung

on the other hand, untroubled by any unconscious, sees character everywhere in the distinctive, embodied traits of actual persons, each one of whom might serve as the basis of some brief narrative sketch: character as an aleatory, frangible, and 'charming' constellation of features. His critique of Treplyov turns on the younger man's approach to character: 'Not one live character', as he echoes Nina's earlier complaint (134). But, in a critical reversal, Treplyov also accuses Trigorin himself of showing a 'true lack of character' [бесхарактерности] (129) in the way he treats Nina, and Trigorin admits to Nina that the *jeunes filles* in his own stories are 'seldom living characters'.[8]

The two actors, meanwhile, stage a rather different antagonism over the concept of character. If Arkadina is all 'talent', she has nevertheless exhausted any potential for her own character; she is the body that follows the name around, like the protagonist-narrator of 'A Boring Story', without anything to offer in the way of genuine dramatic identity.[9] Arkadina is less a character than the embodiment of a type of theatrical performance, a projection of the conventional stage on to life, and back again on to the stage. As Senelick puts it, she is a 'distilled' embodiment of 'the prima donnas of the [Sarah] Bernhardt school'.[10] She is both what 'character' looks like, and its blank cipher; and it is the peculiar genius of Chekhov's method to present that stark contradiction as the recto and verso of a single figure. Nina, on the other hand, pursues character asymptotically. She strives for the 'modern

[8] This (anonymous) translation of the Russian phrase 'обыкновенно фальшивы' [usually false] comes from the Project Gutenberg edition of *The Seagull*, available at: http://www.gutenberg.org/files/1754/1754-h/1754-h.htm

[9] See the discussion in the Introduction to this volume, pp. 6–9.

[10] Laurence Senelick, 'Introduction', in Senelick, ed., *Russian Dramatic Theory from Pushkin to the Symbolists: An Anthology* (Austin: University of Texas Press, 1981), xxxvi. We will see her type again in D'Annunzio's character of La Foscarina in *Il Fuoco* (1900).

character' she has never yet become on stage; her ardour and willingness to climb back from serial defeat constitute the play's most optimistic vector from within the disintegration of the functions of protagonicity.

The character of Dorn is representative of the 'minor characters' in *The Seagull*. These assume a rather different function from their former role and place, memorably mapped by Alex Woloch in relation to the nineteenth-century novel. There, of course, it is correct to say that the 'strange significance of minor characters [...] resides largely in the way that the character disappears [...] for *every* minor character does—by strict definition—disappear'.[11] But in Chekhov's play the minor characters do not disappear. Indeed, they are the more durable figures, fetched from the former background in order to stabilize the ground of the focal quartet's dynamic relations, in such a way that it has ceased to be a background at all. Harvey Pitcher observed that 'What is distinctive about Chekhov's treatment of his minor characters is that he gives them independent status, so that they do not strike the audience as being subordinate to those characters who are more in the limelight.'[12] Masha, Medvedenko, Sorin, Dorn: these are mirrors of the dominant quartet in more ways than one,[13] but principally in the way they insist on their existence as persons interlocked with the locale and the dramatis personae who occupy centre stage. They do exactly what Nina says all true characters must—they *endure*. This peculiar quality of *The Seagull* will be taken up and developed extensively in the works for the stage that followed, and it is worth saying that it was only in his dramatic works that Chekhov was able to make this decisive alteration to the characterological economy of his writing—his short stories never offering the right character space for it.

Chekhov had already complained of the inadequacy and undramatic qualities of Ibsen's work—'complicated, involved, and cerebral'[14]—and endorsed the startling new qualities of Maeterlinck's drama; whose 'odd wonderful plays [he wrote Suvorin] make an enormous impression, and if I had a theatre, I would definitely put on "les Aveugles"'.[15] Yet the difficulty of forcing new 'Symbolist' dramatic forms through the bottleneck of Naturalist theatrical praxis proved stubborn without a company willing to take the aesthetic leap of faith beyond the fourth wall. As he cautioned Björnstjerne Björnson on the touchy subject of the latter's 'metaphysical' play *Over Ævne* [*Beyond Human Power*] (1895), in words

[11] Alex Woloch, *The One vs. the Many: Minor Characters and the Space of the Protagonist in the Novel* (Princeton and Oxford: Princeton University Press, 2003), 38.

[12] Harvey Pitcher, *The Chekhov Play: A New Interpretation* (Berkeley: University of California Press, 1985), 42.

[13] 'Each of these artistically oriented couples has a less intense analogous couple.' See Michael Heim, 'Chekhov and the Moscow Art Theatre', in Barricelli, ed., *Chekhov's Great Plays*, 135 [133–43].

[14] Letter to Suvorin (2 November 1895), translated by and quoted in Senelick, ed., *Russian Dramatic Theory*, xxxvi.

[15] Letter to Suvorin (20 June 1896), in Senelick, 'Chekhov's Drama, Maeterlinck, and the Russian Symbolists', 162.

that again echo Nina's critique of Treplyov's drama, 'it won't do for the stage, because it can't be played, there's no action, no living characters, no dramatic interest'.[16] The mounting of Treplyov's play-within-the-play must, then, be read ambivalently. Its commitment to Symbolist principles is tacitly satirized by its ineffective stagecraft, and the larger Naturalist sympathies of the surrounding drama cannot, finally, be dismantled.[17] Chekhov was relatively constrained by his understanding of the theatre as a conventional harness thrown over the living body of drama, and had routinely made compromises (melodramatic plot points, sudden surcharges of 'action') to vitiate his authorial participation in what Meyerhold was to call the literary 'foreshadowing' of the New Theatre in literature: 'Literature has always taken the initiative in the breaking down of dramatic forms. Chekhov wrote *The Seagull* before the Art Theatre appeared and staged it. It was the same with Van Lerberghe and Maeterlinck. [. . .] The theatre is prompted by literature.'[18]

A New Form

Something in *The Seagull* convinced Meyerhold and the other performers at the Moscow Art Theatre that a 'new form' was already latent in it. Meyerhold (who played Treplyov in 1898) wrote of this elusive quality as a kind of 'music' made manifest in 'the power of *atmosphere* on [Chekhov's] stage'.[19] He attributed it, first, to 'the rhythm of his language', by which he doubtless meant the intermittent flashes of verbal intensity from amidst the ebb and flow of meaningless triviality that washes over the characters; the oscillations typical of Chekhov's dialogue between inanity, vanity, and profundity. It was a rhythm—latent, subsonic, and fugitive—that, without the intuitive (and venerating) responses of a 'definite group of actors' (37) to the script and collaborative contributions of the author, would forever have gone unheard. Meyerhold's point here is of the utmost dialectical importance, since the relationship between Chekhov and this 'definite group of actors' at the Moscow Art Theatre (1898–1904) was to have been one of those happy world-historical conjunctures, the like of which is so rare and fruitful as to have altered the course of aesthetic history.

[16] Letter to Suvorin (20 June 1896), in Senelick, ed. *Russian Dramatic Theory*, xxxvi.

[17] 'Chekhov apparently based Treplev's experiment in new forms on Maeterlinck's spooky one-acts, but at the same time denuded it of Maeterlinck's intellectual commitment and knack for effective stage situations.... The allegory is much cruder than anything in Maeterlinck's writing, and Treplev's fustian and his lurid use of Sulphur and red flares . . . are more reminiscent of Chekhov's parodies of the sensational melodramas staged by Mikhail Lentovskiy in Moscow in the 1880s.' Senelick, 'Chekhov's Drama, Maeterlinck, and the Russian Symbolists', 163.

[18] Vsevolod Meyerhold, *Meyerhold on Theatre*, ed. and trans. Edward Braun, 4th ed. (London: Bloomsbury, 2016), 39.

[19] Meyerhold, *Meyerhold on Theatre*, 36.

The form of its fruition was, according to Meyerhold, a synthesis of the mature Naturalist drama and an embryonic 'theatre of mood' whose consequence was a liberated Symbolist dramaturgy.[20] Here is his description:

> The new aspect of the theatre was created by a definite group of actors who became known as 'Chekhov's actors'. The key to the performance of Chekhov's plays was held by this group which almost invariably acted in them, and which may be regarded as having created Chekhov's rhythm on the stage. Every time I recall the active part which the actors of the Art Theatre played in creating the characters and the mood of *The Seagull* I understand why I believe firmly in the actor as the principal element in the theatre. The atmosphere was created, not by the *mise en scène*, not by the crickets, not by the thunder of horses' hooves on the bridge, but by the sheer musicality of the actors who grasped the rhythm of Chekhov's poetry and succeeded in casting a sheen of moonlight over their creations.[21]

The drama's emancipation from the protagonist function precipitates this epochal shift from narrative to musicality, from plot to rhythm, from realism to moonlight. It was as though the actors' immersion in the material and rapport with the *auteur* had transcended the merely representational roles of what was given them to play in the form of characters and attained instead to a level of abstraction where those residual forms were dissolved into a collective pulse of rhythm, tone, and pitch.

Although written two years before its performance at the Moscow Art Theatre, Chekhov's *The Seagull* broadly anticipated the theatrical mission-statement of that group: 'its emphasis on ensemble playing or, in negative terms, the abolition of the star system'.[22] As described by Pitcher, and in line with other 'small theatre' operations after Saxe-Meiningen:

> Members of the company were told that 'there are no small parts, there are only small actors', and they might find themselves playing an important role one day, and a walk-on part the next. But the walk-on part was to be treated with the same seriousness as the big role, and here Chekhov's small parts, which are not really small at all, offered ample scope for creative interpretation. [. . .] The absence of leading roles in the Chekhov play, his interest in the group rather than the individual, his reliance on what is implied or hinted at rather than what is actually said—all this was perfectly suited to the 'ensemble' approach and introspective style of the Moscow Art Theatre.[23]

[20] See here, too, Andrei Bely: 'Nowadays the realists who depict reality are symbolists; at the very point where everything once ended, everything has now become transparent, pellucid. Such is Chekhov.' 'The Cherry Orchard', in Senelick, ed. *Russian Dramatic Theory*, 91 [89–92].

[21] Meyerhold, *Meyerhold on Theatre*, 37.

[22] Heim, 'Chekhov and the Moscow Art Theatre', 135.

[23] Pitcher, *The Chekhov Play*, 20.

Yet this is an insufficient account of what was at stake in the new ensemble theatrical style of the Moscow Art Theatre; since for Meyerhold it was precisely Stanislavski's ensemble approach that had subsequently captured and domesticated the music of Chekhov's dramaturgy.[24] Democratization was usurped by the dictatorial will of the conductor-director. The truly radical effect of Chekhov's plays lies elsewhere, in the distributed tonal colorations that the actors as a group assumed and discharged under cover of their assigned characters.

About this democratic 'music' of the Chekhovian play, Andrei Bely wrote:

> The spirit of music is extremely diverse in its manifestations. It can penetrate all the characters of a given play equally. Each character is then a string in the general chord. Chekhov's plays of mood are musical. Their symbolism is a guarantee of this, for a symbol is always musical in an abstract sense.[25]

Attending to the conventional realistic surface, we are likely to miss this latent music, whose orchestral combinations and movements depend upon something other than mimetic fidelity to the status quo. Chekhov's characters assume the crucial position within his aesthetic force field. It is only in and through them, as performative bearers of subliminal ground- and grace-notes, that the 'musical symbols' of the play can sound, 'reverberating on a background of minutiae'.[26] On one level these are characters drawn more or less realistically and from life (as Chekhov always insisted they should be[27]); but, on another, something in them exceeds their representability. This latter, obscure quality is intermittent and impersonal, and cannot be reduced to any particular *characteristic* of the represented persons. It resides in them like timbre in a musical instrument; a latent aesthetic *Schein* that resounds only when the prattle of some trivial melody is played, and especially when, over the course of a scene, various overlapping melodies of dialogic discourse lock into new modal complexes.

It has often been observed how the 'rhythm' of Chekhov's dialogue works according to a principle of dissociation and inconsequence:

> He gave his dialogue a much more unpredictable, 'broken-up' quality. A significant part of a Chekhov play consists of small talk, where the conversation is likely

[24] Meyerhold, *Meyerhold on Theatre*, 37.
[25] Bely, 'The Cherry Orchard', 91.
[26] Bely, 'The Cherry Orchard', 89, 91.
[27] Chekhov: 'After all, in real life people don't spend every minute shooting each other, hanging themselves and making declarations of love. They don't spend all their time saying clever things.... Life must be exactly as it is, and people as they are—not on stilts. Let everything on the stage be just as complicated, and at the same time just as simple, as in life. People eat their dinners, just eat their dinners, and all the time their happiness is being established, or their lives destroyed.' Qtd. in David Allen, *Performing Chekhov* (London: Routledge, 2000), 4.

> to switch rapidly from person to person, or from subject to subject. The thoughts of the person speaking may veer off in an unexpected direction; and the reply that is given often bears an unexpected relation, sometimes no relation at all, to what has gone before.[28]

Nils Åke Nilsson remarks how the playwright typically preferred to imbricate 'a lyrical or elated with a banal, everyday atmosphere, a melancholy and serious with a comic atmosphere, a lively and active with a calm and pensive atmosphere', in such a way that these contrasting affective moods 'not only succeed each other [across the course of a play], but are also to be found in balance in the same scene'.[29] Here a key is provided for understanding what is at stake in Chekhov's characters serving two discontinuous ends simultaneously; they are subjected, in the midst of expressing their characters, to a process that has nothing to do with characterization at all, but seems to emanate from an altogether different seat of dramatic power. The inconsequential dramatic diction, the plethora of overlapping indifferent and colloquial lines, bypasses the represented person altogether, and accesses a realm of impersonal affects and intensities, whose arrangement in the dialogue appears—at one level—abstract and detached from the immediate situation. There thus emerges a pattern of modal overtones and dialectic diatonics where the characters are simultaneously speaking their self-interested, banal lines, and participating in a polyphonic choral arrangement—expressing and projecting far beyond their characters as such.

This remarkable capacity of Chekhovian dialogue was taken up and elaborated extensively by the actors and writers of the Moscow Art Theatre, who saw in it the password to a new theatre. As one character is made to proclaim in a work by the Moscow Art Theatre's co-director, Nemirovich-Danchenko: 'To be quite honest the words don't exist for me. I disown them completely. They never show me what the human soul in reality wants. But the sounds—they affect me. Do you follow me? The sounds of the voice.'[30] Construing characters as bearers of such impersonal sounds, this new dramaturgy operated according to a dialectical principle that permitted the character to be split into two simultaneous aspects, one aimed squarely at the mimetic characterization of lifelike persons, the other projected upward, away from representational selves altogether, towards an atmosphere woven of sonic symbolism and rhythmic abstraction, where individuals are dissolved into the impersonal affects they bear.[31]

[28] Pitcher, *The Chekhov Play*, 21.

[29] Nils Åke Nilsson, 'Intonation and Rhythm in Chekhov's Plays', in Robert Louis Jackson, ed., *Chekhov: A Collection of Critical Essays* (Englewood Cliffs, NJ: Prentice-Hall, 1967), 167 [161–74].

[30] Nemirovich-Danchenko qtd. in Nilsson, 'Intonation and Rhythm', 163.

[31] The discussion of the double-faced quality of the human voice in Mladen Dolar, *A Voice and Nothing More* (Cambridge, MA: MIT Press, 2006) is of the highest interest here. See esp. 133–7.

Uncle Vanya

We can now track this extraordinary effect across the three great plays that followed *The Seagull*, once the relationship with the Moscow Art Theatre had stabilized. In *Uncle Vanya* (1898), we are concerned with the theme of provincial backwardness and tedium and asked to participate in a metatheatrical disquisition about character in such inhospitable climes: 'life here', as Astrov tells Marina at the outset of the play, 'gets you down. You're surrounded by the oddest people . . . Spend a couple of years among them, and you gradually turn into a freak yourself and don't even notice it.'[32] Progressively, any potential of a protagonistic sort is worn down to mere oddity and eccentricity; in other words, into minorness as such, which now dominates the terrain. Sure enough, Astrov's moustache has drooped to the proportions of a provincial stereotype, and his character has retreated into itself: 'Somehow I don't feel things keenly any more. I don't want anything, I don't seem to need anything and there's no one I'm fond of' (120). Such ruminations are justified by the theme of generational ageing, but they also shed allegorical light on the inability of anybody here, even—and especially—the visiting 'professor' Serebryakov, to amount to anything more than a protagonist manqué (at best) and a self-conscious nonentity (at worst). 'I've worked myself to a standstill and become thoroughly second-rate' (140): Astrov's self-summation applies to everybody in the drama. 'This filthy atmosphere has poisoned our blood and we've become as second-rate as the rest of them' (161).

The plot of *Uncle Vanya* concerns the division of labour shouldered by the members of Serebryakov's 'second-rate' family that he might amount to something in the big city: the work that promotes characterological (intellectual) eminence from out of the provincial morass, undertaken by figures who, thanks to that work, sink deeper into the 'minorness' that is its element. Only, it turns out that the professor's supposed eminence, his character as such, is a sham; the glorious promotion from the ranks of the minor to the major never took place, and his retirement finds him sunk in indistinction and teetering into dotage. The willing sacrifice of the 'minor' figures who remained on the estate and earned the capital necessary to effect Serebryakov's transfiguration was wasted; their obscurity never afforded the central character the salience required to cut a figure on the world stage. The political ethics of the drama thus turn on a pragmatic reorientation of the sacrificial element internal to the characterological division of labour (the task of 'becoming-minor' in order to promote a major character), away from any synchronic hierarchy of the sociological sort, and towards a non-hierarchical diachrony—that is, the task of 'becoming-minor' here and now, in order that 'future generations' will flourish

[32] Anton Chekhov, *Uncle Vanya*, in *Five Plays*, trans. Ronald Hingley (Oxford: Oxford University Press, 1998), 119.

in freedom at some indeterminate date when all the play's characters are nameless dust.

Serebryakov is a vestigial figure, the quondam protagonist of some unwritten earlier play. His persistence here, beyond the limit marked by *The Seagull*, attests to a newly ironic purpose that stands as Chekhov's final investment in the anachronistic hero function. 'Those who dress themselves up as professors and learned pundits, so people can't see how cheap, stupid and utterly callous they are' (160), as Vanya puts it, are implicated in a deceitful characterization. Meanwhile, the ageing scholar's second childhood—'Old folks are like children', Marina quips (133)—allows for the expression of copious amounts of ridicule and exasperation at the role. 'Please stop behaving like a child' is not a line that traditional dramatic form can generally tolerate being directed at the protagonist; here Vanya utters it to Serebryakov in the first act, as if to underscore the lengths to which this play will now go to displace the 'central character' from his pedestal. Neither is the belittlement merely verbal. It extends to the sphere of action reserved for this figure, who attempts only one significant act in the play—the selling of the estate—which is criticized and countermanded by the rest of the dramatis personae. At the level of 'character', and of 'action', then, the verdict is clear: 'He's totally obscure' (123); 'obscure, a nonentity. A soap-bubble!' (135).

On the other hand, eponymous Vanya is placed in a position where protagonicity is barred from the outset, both by his menial relationship to Serebryakov and the estate itself, and by the emphatic insistence that he and the other characters place on that most Chekhovian of qualities, his 'boredom'. Bored and boring, Vanya can never raise himself to the seriousness and purpose of a worthy action; and his rallying point turns out to be around the work ethic as such, to which he is prepared to return after the forced interlude of the professor's visit (and of the play itself), in the final act. The burden of his monologue, and of his participation in dialogue, is the smallness and insignificance of his allotted role in this provincial wasteland: 'I've grown lazy and don't do anything apart from grousing away like an old fogy' (122); 'the stupid way I've wasted time when I might have had everything I can't have now because I'm too old' (125). Missed opportunities and the collapse of potential dictate the terms of this character's regretful plaints. Helen recognizes in him the living image of her own mortal tedium: 'Do you know why you and I are such good friends, Vanya? It must be because we're both such abysmal bores. Yes, bores!' (129). Formally, the function of Vanya's repetitive complaints is to focus on the dimension of the past. Vanya's soliloquy conjures 'the spectre of a life hopelessly wasted. I've never lived. My past life has been thrown away on stupid trivialities and the present is so futile, it appals me' (134). The purpose of the titular character is, then, to illuminate the hold of the past on the present as a death-grip, whose power is to abolish all signs of character. Vanya is a man without a character; least of all, of course, in the dimension of the Act. His assumption of the conventional burden of melodramatic revenge against Serebryakov is indulged only to be farcically negated: his two shots at the enemy with a loaded pistol miss their target, and nothing changes except the extra burden of humiliation Vanya must then shoulder.

Helen's character is related to Vanya's, not by exhaustion but by proclivity and that other distinctive quality of the Chekhovian character-system: 'laziness'. 'As for me, I'm just a tiresome character and not a very important one. In my music, in my husband's house, in all my romantic affairs—in everything, that is—I've always played a minor role' (142). Within the character space cleared by the collapse of the protagonist figure, such deliberate and innate (rather than circumstantial) minority has a peculiar effect, one that the other characters begin to perceive as infectious and chronic. 'You're bored', Sonya tells her, 'you don't know what to do with yourself and boredom and idleness are infectious' (144). 'You have nothing in the world to do, you may as well admit it', opines Astrov, 'no object in life, nothing to occupy your mind' (162), and the net result of that kind of vacancy of purpose in one of the main characters of the play is a contagious inaction:

> No sooner do you and your husband turn up in this place than people here who were getting on with their work, all busy creating something, have to drop everything and do nothing all summer but attend to you and your husband's gout. You two have infected us all with your idleness. I've been under your spell and I've done nothing for a whole month . . .
>
> (163)

The plot of the drama is as much about the suspension of dramatic activity—the spread of distracted idleness across the characterological landscape, to the extent that nothing happens of any consequence throughout the length of the play—as it is about the characterological division of labour itself. Helen's character concentrates this suspended nature of all dramatic purpose in *Uncle Vanya* in a single person. The play's three attempted Acts (Vanya's seduction of Helen; the selling of the estate; the shooting of Serebryakov) all fail miserably; and the end of the play returns us to the situation immediately before the beginning, with the sole difference that the work newly resumed will no longer be dedicated to bankrolling Serebryakov's exceptionalism.

Astrov is what the drama requires to soak up and reshape the shattered protagonicity lying around the figure of Serebryakov; despite his self-confessed minority, Astrov intermittently occupies the vacated pace of the protagonist, only *as a minor character*. As Helen puts it in her soliloquy, 'In the middle of all this ghastly boredom, where there are no real people, but just dim, grey shapes drifting round, where you hear nothing but vulgar trivialities, where no one does anything but eat, drink and sleep—*he* appears from time to time, so different from the others . . .' (147). The periodicity of his appearance is the index of his minority; while the allure and resonance of his presence—the one true person in a wilderness of shades and nonentities—is decidedly 'major'. 'I'm bored when he's not about' (147); yet he is often not about. Indeed, Astrov seems to occupy a dramatic space adjacent to the one in this play. His figure is somewhat anamorphic in that sense, stretched out between two dramatic realities that keep him coming back to the Serebryakov estate: the decadent allure of Helen, and the sustaining pleasures of his historical-geographical mapping of the area's forests. It is this last intensity which truly animates him, his language and gestural economy vibrating from within thanks to his passion for agronomy. It is what breathes majority into his minority. His great monologue in Act III is the only sustained moment of concentrated enthusiasm in the play; its vistas dwarfing the stage of the play's desultory action, both geographically and historically.

The formal punchline to this great speech is that its addressee, Helen, hears none of it. Establishing what will become, for Chekhov, a major innovation taken to further lengths in his subsequent plays, this kind of misalignment of address and audience forces a monologue into the status of soliloquy, despite the presence of an auditor drawn from the principal dramatis personae. 'To be perfectly honest, I was thinking about something else' (149), she responds to his crushed realization: 'I can see this bores you' (148). That 'something else' concerns Sonya's closeted desire for the doctor, and predictably bores him as much as Helen is bored by his monologue. Dramatically, the point is underscored that the moments of maximal affective transference in the dialogue lead to missed opportunities and failed encounters; the best chances available for centripetal concentration of the play's emotional energy are squandered, making for a centrifugal entropy that afflicts the web of characterological interconnection. Helen's failure to attend to Astrov's speech, which is on one level an attempt to seduce her with his enthusiasm, is the play's clearest evidence that the characters are not the bearers of reconciliation here.

This is the point to revive a critical term pioneered by Harvey Pitcher to account for Chekhov's centrifugal dramatic energy: the 'emotional network' of his dramas, figured as an 'electric field' strung out amongst the dramatis personae. Chekhov's distributive affective patterns do not concentrate themselves into any one character's 'goal-oriented' desires, actions, or narrative arcs. Rather, they are patterned *across* the gulfs and schisms that irrevocably divide the characterological domain into monads. That is why the dialogue so often falls apart or fails to achieve cathexis between the agents who speak it: because the network of affective intensities moves in electrical undercurrents beneath the frustrated surface semantics. Pitcher's case, against Prince Mirsky and others, was that the result is not testament to some prevailing pessimism about the 'failure of communication', but a higher-order communication (of aesthetic moods, atmospheres, and disembodied affective networks). It is a position borrowed from one of the earliest critics of *The Cherry Orchard*, Aykhenval'd: 'Each one hears the other's silence. Each one wordlessly, subtly understands the other. Voicelessly soul converses with soul. Amidst it all there is a certain wireless contact, and during the pauses unheard words are enunciated distinctly on light wings across the stage.'[33] Musical metaphors best characterize the resultant polyphony, in which the narrative agents are effectively disaggregated as 'individuals' and transformed into communicating vessels for a multitude of tones and modal complexes. Chekhov's most acerbic critic, Zinaida Gippius, loved to lambaste him for this 'atomic' and molecular quality: 'He discovered the microscope, he founds atoms and shows them to us. [. . .] It is unfortunate that the grey and the white, the most miniscule atoms of dust and diamonds are so mixed in him, life and death so horribly, trivially and fleshily intermingled.'[34]

At this disaggregated level, we begin to sense the purpose of the desultory plot and the retreat of regular signs of character: to amplify the autonomy of moods. Take, for example, the instance of Astrov's enthusiasm for the forests. 'When I plant a young birch and later see it covered with green and swaying in the breeze, my heart fills with pride' (128). There is little else in the drama to compare with this fresh note of pleasure and pride; but the remarkable thing is that, once sounded, it is susceptible to propagation and echo. Each of the major characters has occasion to take up this affect in turn, assimilate and give voice to its contagious intensity, even despite its incompatibility with their prevailing 'bass notes': 'it's extremely interesting' (127), cries Sonya, while Vanya declares that it 'is all very charming' (127). Astrov's existential joy in the planting of forests is communicable and able to take root in the most unlikely of soils. Later in the play, Vanya is found voicing a most improbable mood, fetched from the well dug by Astrov's hobbyhorse: 'be a mermaid', he says to Helen; 'fall madly in love with a river god, dive head-first into deep water' (145). That this mood coexists with his more frequent ugly feelings is testament to its impersonal propagation throughout the characterological matrix. Vanya's shame—'This feeling of shame, it hurts so much. It's worse than any pain. [*With anguish.*] I can't stand it' (160)—and his mortal boredom are not, then, essential to him, any more than they are to Helen or Astrov; rather, these qualities radiate through them in unpredictable atmospheric patterns, now tending towards an utter gloom, now shimmering with ecstatic enthusiasm.

The 'electrical field' of affects in Chekhov's mature plays is contraindicated by the exorbitant dialogical emphasis on the past as what ruthlessly dictates the form of the present; since in that sense, the present is immutable and irreconcilable with the unpredictable chromatic modal complexes here glimpsed. Rather, these abrupt shifts in the modal complexion of the drama seem oriented towards that contradictory temporal dimension, the future, whose note is sounded in the opening of the play and then again repeatedly thereafter, as if to offset the gravitational force of the past: 'And I thought of the men and women who will live a hundred or

[33] Yuly Aykhenval'd, 'Sovremennoye iskusstvo', *Russkaya mysl'* (1904), qtd. in Senelick, 'Chekhov's Drama, Maeterlinck, and the Russian Symbolists', 170.

[34] Anton Krayniy (pseud. of Zinaida Gippius), 'Chto i kak', in *Literaturnyy dnevnik: 1899–1907*, qtd. in Senelick, 'Chekhov's Drama, Maeterlinck, and the Russian Symbolists', 166.

a couple of hundred years after we've gone, those we're preparing the way for. Will they have a good word to say for us? You know, Nanny, they won't even remember us' (120). Astrov's pathos is ironic because it is immediately self-cancelling in the grammatical figure of a utopian 'future anterior', whose denizens will have led such charmed and perfect lives that there could be no imaginable purpose to recollecting this cast of self-consciously 'second-rate' personages. 'If man is happy a thousand years from now', Astrov continues later, 'I'll have done a bit towards it myself' (128)—but this is the opposite of egotism, since that 'something' is simply the planting of the new forests, his anonymous gratuity to the future that will always already have forgotten him. Helen grasps the logic of this: 'When he plants a tree he's already working out what the result will be in a thousand years' time, already glimpsing man's future happiness' (142). There is hope, no end of hope, Astrov's project seems to accept; but not for us.[35] 'Those who live a century or two after us and despise us for leading lives so stupid and tasteless, perhaps they'll find a way to be happy, but as for us—. There's only one hope for you and me, that when we're resting in our graves we may have visions. Even pleasant ones perhaps' (161).

This insistence on the future as a jubilee of species redemption in a fulfilled and meaningful characterology is the corrective to the play's otherwise moribund emphasis on the past's stranglehold on the present. The characters inhabit a temporal situation defined by their inability to effect Nietzsche's 'strong forgetfulness of the past', whilst being able only distantly to envisage a new future that they themselves, as biological individuals and historical social subjects, can do little to realize. Mortgaged to the crushing ontological supremacy of the past and sundered from the chance to effect the changes necessary to surmount it, these characters drift in a state of suspended animation, redoubled by the visit of Helen and her husband, that only leads to despair. Vanya's terrible cry is emblematic: 'I'm 47. Suppose I live to be 60, that means I still have 13 years to go. It's too long. How am I to get through those 13 years? What am I to do? How do I fill the time? [...] Can you think what it would be like to live the rest of one's life in a new way? Oh, to wake up some fine clear morning as if you'd started living all over again, as if the past was all forgotten, gone like a puff of smoke. [*Weeps.*] To begin a new life—' (160).

These characters, stranded in time, are no longer defined by their emotional weathervanes. Something has taken the place of the named emotions; complex compounds made of distinct, anonymous intensities traversing the dramatis personae with an impersonal logic. Melancholic upsurges are no longer native or peculiar to any one character; and ecstatic shimmerings burst out unexpectedly across the stage. The distributive nature of these affective sequences is such that

[35] The proximity of the thought here to Kafka's quip—*Oh Hoffnung genug, unendlich viel Hoffnung,—nur nicht für uns*—can hardly be overlooked. See Max Brod, *Franz Kafka: Eine Biographie* (Berlin: S. Fischer Verlag, 1954), 94–5.

they move like interpenetrating waves of sound through the available media of human bodies. The characters of *Uncle Vanya* have become aspects of a larger dynamic whose ultimate consequence is the liquidation of personification itself. Vanya may seem to 'personify' melancholy, Sonya unreciprocated love, and Serebryakov disappointment; but none of these two-point associations will hold. There is too much lateral interference from the affective network itself, and gradually it becomes apparent that what we are dealing with is a situation in which the expected equations are undone by the subliminal music of these transpositions and overtones. It is not unlike Arnold Schönberg's idea of *Klanfarbenmelodie*: 'a melody made up of a sequence of timbres and the material qualities of specific instruments rather than by the series of notes generally understood to constitute a theme or a musical "subject"'.[36] *Uncle Vanya* earned a very precise description from the champion of contemporary Naturalism, Sergei Glagol: the play 'has a symbolic character', a two-level oscillation between the surface depiction of characters and situations, and a higher-level abstraction, where this other melody is heard.[37]

Three Sisters

Three Sisters (1900) continues the critical innovations of *Uncle Vanya*: the emphasis on provincial distance from true life, and consequent absence of any real character; the failed scholar (lapsed protagonist) who hasn't lived up to the familial sacrifice that made his work possible; the distant future horizon of human flourishing; and so on. All these repeated motifs serve to underline the sense of radical achievement, the breakthrough, of the previous work, and to provide a context in which to perceive the new developments on show here for the first time. Of these, more soon. But first we can allow Andrei's monologue from Act IV to stand as perhaps the definitive statement of Chekhov's general understanding of the 'becoming-minor' or 'second-rate' that his characters are obliged to grasp as the essence of their situation in the far-flung reaches of the Russian tsarist state:

> Where is my past life, oh what has become of it—when I was young, happy and intelligent, when I had such glorious thoughts and visions, and my present and future seemed so bright and promising? Why is it we've hardly started living before we all become dull, drab, boring, lazy, complacent, useless and miserable? This town's two hundred years old and we've a hundred thousand people living here, but the trouble is, every man jack of them's exactly like every other one, and no one here does anything really worth while. Or ever has. We've never produced a single scholar or artist or anyone else with a touch of originality to make

[36] Fredric Jameson, *Allegory and Ideology* (London: Verso, 2019), 44. See Arnold Schönberg, *Theory of Harmony*, trans. Roy E. Carter (Berkeley: University of California Press, 1978), 421–2.
[37] Qtd. in Senelick, 'Chekhov's Drama, Maeterlinck, and the Russian Symbolists', 167.

> us envy him, or decide we were damn well going to get one better ourselves. All these people do is eat, drink and sleep till they drop down dead. Then new ones are born to carry on the eating, drinking and sleeping. And to save themselves getting bored to tears and put a bit of spice in their lives, they go in for all this sickening gossip, vodka, gambling, litigation. Wives deceive their husbands and husbands tell lies and pretend they're deaf and blind to what's going on, and all the time the children are crushed by vulgarity, lose any spark of inspiration they might ever have had, and—like their fathers and mothers before them—turn into a lot of miserable living corpses, each one exactly like his neighbour.[38]

A subtle new note is sounded here, from inside the familiar tune of provincial 'secondrate-ness', which is to say, the note of *seriality* as such, which will become such a dominant motif of twentieth-century art and fiction—the idea that *we are all the same*. This infernal vision of serial repetition is one of Chekhov's signature moments, and its essence concerns the destiny of character itself in such a wilderness of pseudo-forms and Strindbergian 'real abstractions'.

Andrei's sisters agree on this definitive 'minorness' of their sibling, in whom so much hope and faith had been invested: 'I must say poor old Andrew has gone to seed. Living with that wretched woman has put years on his life and knocked all the stuffing out of him. At one time he was aiming to be a professor, and there he was yesterday boasting he'd got on the county council at long last' (216), as Irina puts it (not before adding the salt of the council chairman's affair with Andrei's wife), while Masha pursues the same theme from the vantage point of the division of labour necessary to sustain protagonicity in the first place: 'All our hopes have come to nothing. Imagine thousands of people hoisting up a huge bell. Then after all the effort and money spent on it, it suddenly falls and is smashed to pieces. Suddenly, for no reason at all. That's how it's been with Andrew' (226). This is the summative statement of the fate of the protagonist in Chekhov's mature drama: a shattered bell amid whose wreckage the former hoisters now find themselves wondering what they had been at, and why. The restating of the founding presupposition of *Uncle Vanya* in this new context effectively amounts to a forgetting of the problem altogether, which will no longer trouble the dramatist.

For all this is now tertiary stuff in the dramatic field of *Three Sisters*, whose title shifts the focus away from the vestigial protagonist figure and allows it to decline to farce. 'The whole town's talking about it, everyone's laughing at him and he's the only one who doesn't know or see what's going on' (216); the marriage to Natasha attracts to Andrei only the most scornful attention, terminating in a theatrical tableau like none other in Chekhov's work, with the family party congregated in the garden below while Natasha brazenly carries out her tryst with

[38] Chekhov, *Three Sisters*, in *Five Plays*, trans. Hingley, 231.

Protopopov behind the upstairs window. It is with Natasha herself that the principal dramatic tension is achieved, so that the three sisters are obliged to realize their fate as dictated by their presumptive sister-in-law, who proceeds to muscle them out of the family home altogether. This demotion of the masculine element to the far background is critical to the effects of this play, whose feminine dominant makes for some major adjustments to the character space—not least the final supersession in Chekhov's stagecraft of that disreputably melodramatic prop, the pistol; or at least, its demotion to the far fringes of the offstage, where we understand that Captain Solyony has deployed its firepower against the hapless Baron Tuzenbakh during the final Act, without our even hearing its report.

With violence displaced from the domestic interior for the first time, theatrical space assumes a more decisive function. Over it all hangs the distant telos of Moscow itself, of course; but this presiding structural magnetism towards the capital is then allegorized in any number of ways in the scenography itself, where the deep gulfs between foreground and background, upstairs and downstairs, inside and outside, and either side of a closed door, are rendered meaningfully internal to almost every scene. Maeterlinck's theatrical pressure on Chekhov is perhaps best felt here, in the growing importance of obstacles and partitions on the stage. This charges the bodies on stage with an active significance, not on the basis of any presumed hierarchy of persons, but purely physically according to where they stand. The play's major events—the fire, the carnival celebrations, the affair between Natasha and Protopopov, and the climactic duel on the streets—where opportunities for action and heroism may arise, none are presented on stage; while the luncheon of Act I happens in the distant background, inaudible and obscure. We, like the characters, hear of them via gossip. Chekhov's concern is clearly to project the provincial distance of the country town onto the dramaturgy itself, where obstacles divide the dramatic space against itself, and often find the principal characters on the side of redundancy and ineffectuality.

More significant still, characters appear most often in ensembles, rather than individually or in pairs. It is their disposition across the entire stage, rather than some privileged part of it, that is the very point of the marvellous opening scene, where we find the three Prozorov sisters clustered in the foreground of their house's drawing room, while behind them, beyond the columns that stand monumentally as a border between this intimate space and the space of the ballroom, three military men are similarly grouped. This elaborate mirroring in depth, and across the gender divide, is the most obstreperous sign yet that Chekhov has attained to a dramatic form that can no longer be constrained to the trials of the individual but must now be apprehended as the space of interactions between groups and clusters. The spatial dynamics that set Irina, Masha, and Olga apart from their military counterparts Tuzenbach, Chebutykin, and Solyony, are not meant to be symbolic or embedded in one-to-one correspondences; rather, it is the principle of organized multiplicity itself that rises to the surface of the play here, in a display of counterpoint and polyphony. It is a matter of complete indifference who is speaking when Olga's line 'I felt I just had to go back home to Moscow' is immediately answered by Tuzenbach's line 'Absolute nonsense of course' (171), and then again Olga's 'I'd love my husband' by Tuzenbach's 'You talk such nonsense' (172), since either individual is at this stage a mere emissary of a group whose component parts have yet to emerge as definite subjects, and there is no question of the sequent lines being a conscious response to the prior ones (as the space is too large for either party to hear the other). And yet the truth of the rejoinders is the more certain for that disjunction. The theatrical space delivers 'character' over to another, quite different principle, for which the individual is an unwitting instrument of larger constructive forces, and groups define the context in which impersonal messages are exchanged.

In *Three Sisters* Chekhov arranges for a decentring of the drama's traditional relationship with the hero or heroine via these large group dynamics and counterpoints. Many of his critics have positioned these distributed patterns over and against the dictates of characterization. Ronald Gaskell was particularly sensitive to the notion that Chekhov's 'characters do not just drift', but 'group themselves in a pattern that holds for a moment and then collapses. The pattern has no significance, yet we feel it should have'[39]—an admission that says more about the imperturbable humanism of his critics than it does about the plays, which do precisely allow for these metastable patterns to form and dissolve before our eyes and ears in a matter of moments, without the characters being aware of them. J. L. Styan, similarly, notes that 'his most deceptive technique may be that of arranging for his characters to fall into patterns that indicate order in what otherwise seems to be at random—a kind of dramatic *Gestalten* awaiting the perception of an audience watching a performance'.[40] These patterns are not finally to be distinguished from Pitcher's 'emotional networks', which likewise show through the dissolution of protagonicity: nodes and overtones dependent upon the compresence of represented persons not listening to one another, not attending to the impersonal flows of discursive and affective energy through the space. With *Three Sisters*, this principle displaces any residual interest in the space of the hero.

As in *Uncle Vanya* the remarkable Dr Astrov gives rise to expressions of potential protagonicity, so too in *Three Sisters* Vershinin holds out the tantalizing prospect of 'heroic' distinction from the 'lot of miserable living corpses, each one exactly like his neighbour'. Vershinin reprises something of Astrov's character here and repeats too its infectious animation by the future jubilee: 'Before very long—in two or three hundred years, say—people will look back on our way of life with the same horror and contempt, they'll regard our times as rough, hard, strange

[39] Ronald Gaskell, *Drama and Reality: The European Theatre since Ibsen* (London: Routledge & Kegan Paul, 1972), 98.

[40] J. L. Styan, 'Chekhov's Dramatic Technique', in Toby W. Clyman, ed., *A Chekhov Companion* (Westport, CT: Greenwood Press, 1985), 120.

and most uncomfortable. Why, life is going to be absolutely wonderful, it really is' (214). And yet this future anterior—the present glimpsed from the standpoint of redemption—is repeated so often by this character, without any accompanying call to action, that its effect is weakened as the play progresses—to the point that, by Act IV, Vershinin has become scarcely distinguishable from the rest of the artillery company. It is conspicuous that, unlike Astrov who is universally known and loved, Vershinin's name is immediately forgotten by the 'minor character' Anfisa, the nurse to Natasha's daughter (199). His anonymity goes with the territory on an estate where 'I'm already beginning to forget [Mother's] face . . . Not that anyone will remember us either. We'll be forgotten too' (179); and 'I've forgotten, forgotten everything [. . .] I'm always forgetting things, I forget something every day. And life is slipping away, it will never, never come back again, and we shall never go to Moscow either . . .' (217). Vershinin is obliged to accept this law: 'Yes, we'll be forgotten. Such is our fate, and we can't do anything about it. And the things that strike us as so serious and important, they'll all be forgotten one day or won't seem to matter' (179).

On the other hand, Natasha's conspicuous villainy here—she remains one of the very few outright antagonists in Chekhov's oeuvre—attests to a countervailing force of memorable acts, gestures, and functions within the drama; memorable in the sense that they dictate the terms of the collapse of the Prozorov familial nest, and the erection of a new domestic order founded on Natasha's ruthless will and desire. Her individuation is all the more disconcerting for being situated within such a diffracted, multitudinous character space, where characteristics are felt more as component parts of larger group formations than riveted to any specific persona. In Natasha the principle of individuation, distinction, separation, is associated explicitly with villainy and the grasping egotism of a new order. This is further confirmation that, under the coming bourgeois order, what 'character' means is a ruthless drive and ambition; by comparison with which the older characterology of settled provincial types and threadbare nobility has come to seem positively exhausted. There can be no plot in such a situation, merely the concatenation of representative incidents in a protracted provincial life, all of them occurring offstage, so that the prevailing mood is of time emptily passing, not only between the acts, but very much within them, too; where the most important question is when the artillery regiment will be reposted elsewhere and the balanced groups finally dissolve under the arbitrary hand of history. For groups do not a tale unfold; that is a task for individuals. Instead, groups achieve patterned integrities, conduct a range of moods and intensities, diffract them, create myths and caricatures, stabilize a lore, and ultimately establish an ethos.

The minor characters in such a situation enjoy a degree of comfort and nativity, since where permanent anonymity hovers and plotlessness presides, the already relatively anonymous and narratively extrinsic will thrive. Kulygin, provincial schoolmaster and walking illustration of the dismal level of culture in the region;

Rode and Fedotik, the indistinguishable second lieutenants; Chebutykin, the superannuated army doctor; Solyony, the splenetic staff captain with a penchant for *non sequitur* couplets; Ferapont, the ancient council watchman—it is a comic menagerie of the inconsequent, the dull, and the redundant. Yet it is through these witless 'second-raters' that much of the truth of the drama is conducted. Nary a commentator on this great play who does not pause to consider the *non sequitur* dropped into a higher-order conversation about the meaning of life by Chebutykin in Act II: 'Balzac got married in Berdichev' (198). Ostensibly disrupting the flow of the dialogue between 'major characters' Masha, Vershinin, and Tuzenbakh, the phrase, summoned from a newspaper, intrudes into that pretentious discussion with the discordant note of the contingent, the trivial, and the extrinsic (not to mention the automatic and partial: see below). Taken up by Masha as something of a formula, the phrase pulverizes the dominant movement of the Act. Such is the force of the minor character in this space, who, with sufficient verbal power, is permitted to derail the dramatic action and reset the field of play with a word.

Chebutykin himself has the more significant function of anticipating and instantiating the coming reign of inconsequence and anonymity within the present, as when he opines on the duel between Solyony and Tuzenbakh that, 'one baron more or less in the world—what does that matter? Let them get on with it. Who cares?' (227). Indeed, it is Chebutykin's role to inflict this indifference on all the contending parties, the entire dramatis personae of the drama. He enters the play with a significant virtual company of other doctors in Chekhov's work—Astrov, Dorn, and Lvov, to speak only of the preceding plays—at his back but disappoints the expectation of being 'interesting' because of it: 'I know absolutely nothing. What I did know I've forgotten. I don't remember a thing, my mind's a blank.... Perhaps I'm not even a human being, perhaps I only pretend to have arms and legs and a head, perhaps I don't even exist at all, and only imagine I walk about and eat and sleep. [*Weeps.*] Oh, how nice not to exist' (211). Not yet 'existential', such a complaint functions metatheatrically to cast a formal doubt over his own status as a character and raises the larger question of the ontology of character per se: its inevitable quotient of 'pretence' and 'inexistence' *d'hors texte*. By the end of the play, this note has expanded to absorb them all, the theatre and all its players: 'We're not real, neither is anything else in the world. We aren't here at all actually, we only think we are. And who cares anyway?' (227). The privileged relationship between the theatre-goer and the minor character in the Moscow Art Theatre—for which this play was the first explicitly to be written by Chekhov—is avowed.

If 'we aren't here at all', then what is? One answer to that concerns the semi-autonomous play of language that passes through characters like unconscious impulses: the voice as a carrier of viral linguistic supplements, 'speaking' the subject with catchphrases and meaningless sounds and stutters, like Chebutykin's ejaculation about Balzac. Solyony's 'Chuck, chuck, chuck' (in a high-pitched voice) (180, 185 [twice], 215) and nonsense recitations, '"I may be old but who is not?"

Aleko, be not angry . . . Aleko, be not angry. Forget, forget your dreams' (201–2), or 'I could develop my idea, / But might annoy the geese, I fear' (215), or 'Before he'd time to turn a hair / He'd been knocked over by a bear' (228, 229)—'he frightens me', says Irina, 'he says such stupid things' (186)—; Kulygin's Latin declensions and pompous Latin mottos (e.g. '*In vino veritas*, as the ancients used to say', 212; '*Omnia mea mecum porto*, as the saying goes', 216); Chebutykin's couplet-aphorism, 'That love alone might rule this earth / Kind Nature gave us mortals birth' (181, 187), his tuneless 'Tararaboomdeay' (223, 226, 236, 237) and echoing of one of Kulygin's declensions '*Bunki, bunko, bunko*' (226); Masha's haunting refrain, 'A green oak by a curving shore; / And on that oak a chain of gold—/ And on that oak a chain of gold' (188, 234 [twice])—'[*Tearfully*] But why do I keep saying that? Those words have been going through my head all day' (188) and her angry conjugation of the Latin verb *amore* (216); Rodé's 'Halloo-oo!' (222, 223, 224, 227, 229, 230); the stichomythic singing of Tuzenbakh, Andrei, and Chebutykin (202); and the flirtatious automatisms of Masha and Vershinin in Act III:

VERSHININ: [*sings*] 'As everyone has always found,
It's love that makes the world go round.' [*Laughs*]
MASHA: Ti tum ti tum ti——
VERSHININ: Tum tum tum——
MASHA: Tara tarara
VERSHININ: Tum ti tum. [*Laughs*] (214)

All of it 'doesn't add up to much, does it? It's just a lot of hot air, there's precious little sense in it' (225), as Kulygin summarizes this dimension of the drama—its extension into nonsense, verbal automatisms, and formulaic refrains. As Masha worries about the persistence of her own leitmotif, 'What does it mean . . .? Why can't I get those words out of my head?' (234). Once out of the bag—and it is Solyony's 'chuck, chuck, chuck' that applies the first, fatal dose—this tendency affiliates itself with what Deleuze calls 'a trait of expression that contaminates everything, escaping linguistic form', the verbal *formula* whose 'contagious character is immediately evident'.[41] And in part, this is an effect of this play's uniquely multilingual character, whose Russian dialogue is riven by French, Latin, and German.

These flotsam and jetsam of the linguistic unconscious are like so many pieces of evidence of what lies beneath the dull surface of provincial conformity and its corresponding representation in the play's characterology—a deeper and elusive material substratum, of language in its purely physiological dimension, of voice as such, and of the insensible 'music' that plays through the agents of a drama

[41] Gilles Deleuze, *Essays Critical and Clinical*, trans. Daniel W. Smith and Michael A. Greco (Minneapolis: University of Minnesota Press, 1997), 77, 70.

that is scarcely worth the title. Jameson has referred this kind of material to minimalism in the modern period, which bears a strong resemblance to Rancière's and Deleuze's 'molecular' domain: 'It is not here a question of the smallest component of the work, such as the sentence or the narrative event; but rather the components of those components, the notes and overtones of a musical phrase, the parts of speech and even their phonemics, the particles and their mysteries and dynamics, which take place below the level of human perception.'[42] The dramatis personae are subject to a multiplicity of impersonal 'tones' that play through them, in excess of their lacklustre attempts at communication, and combine into gestural motifs and patterns that do anything but express this or that 'character'. Such verbal traits evince not a depth model of the represented subject, but the animation of all these inert dramatic selves by prefabricated and nonsensical syllables, lively and dispersed, fetched from the surrounding buzz of media noise that makes communication possible in the first place.[43] Chekhov's play demonstrates the unique dialectic between signal and noise in the nascent media ecology of 1900, according to which characters *speak* lines that drift inexorably into the status of verbal waste material (they fail to communicate at an explicit level) but are energetically *spoken by* meaningless lexical clusters and syllabic sequences, testifying to a livelier, larger, and more distributed agency: the real abstraction of commodified speech. Minor and major characters both are susceptible to taking up these depersonalized, automatic speech-acts, whose function is levelling in an entirely new fashion, since their effect is to depose the rational seat of subjective authority from within and establish a mechanical babble in its stead.

Doubtless Peter Szondi is right to claim of *Three Sisters* that it 'is exclusively a presentation of lonely individuals intoxicated by memories and dreaming of the future. Their present, overwhelmed by past and future, is merely an interim, a period of suspended animation during which the only goal is to return to the lost homeland'; and that this state of 'suspended animation' is the key to what is most modern about the drama.[44] Yet we have also seen that this present, if evacuated of characterological intention or action, is nevertheless occupied by other forces equally capable of detaining us within it. If the 'dialogue carries no weight' here (20), still, potent verbal automatisms and a latent tonal structure become the more conspicuous in that weightless environment. If 'empty dialogue turns into substance-filled monologue' (20) thanks to the distinctive lack of developmental

[42] Jameson, *Allegory and Ideology*, 313.

[43] Lacan's discussion of 'la langue' in the later Joyce is also apropos here. See Jacques Lacan, *The Sinthome: The Seminar of Jacques Lacan Book XXIII*, ed. Jacques-Alain Miller, trans. A. R. Price (Cambridge: Polity, 2016), esp. 141–8.

[44] Peter Szondi, *Theory of the Modern Drama*, Critical Edition, ed. and trans. Michael Hays, Theory and History of Literature 29 (Minneapolis: University of Minnesota Press, 1987), 18.

dialogical to-and-fro in *Three Sisters*, a 'lyric of loneliness' (20) is not the inevitable result. Rather, a higher-order aesthetic structure becomes intermittently audible, whose order is not of solitude and alienation, and not of emotional identification, but of elusive harmonics and overtones, polyphonic interpenetrations that lead us towards a more affirmative appreciation of what we might call the post-characterological uses of onstage characters: their subsumption by a communal energy.

The Cherry Orchard

All of which comes to its ultimate fruition, formally and otherwise, in the final masterpiece of this artist's creative life, *The Cherry Orchard* (1903), written solely with the Moscow Art Theatre in mind. In this work the inner principle of Chekhovian drama can finally be revealed. At a stroke, the author visits a very specific affliction upon the fallen gentry siblings Lyuba Andreyevna and Leonid Andreivich Gayev, which is simultaneously their freeing up for concerns other than the dynastic: namely, the absence of a male heir, the death by drowning of little Grisha five years before the action of the play. This leaves the dramatic energy usually reserved for the protagonist figure free to circulate around its vacated place at the heart of an aborted succession plan. The residual Hamlet-figure is meanwhile occupied by Trofimov, the eternal student, but now scavenging on the periphery of the estate (he is little Grisha's former tutor). This class distance from the family plot is somewhat compromised by his alliance with Anya, the distaff heir of the clan; but the effect is more to loosen her from the dynastic succession than to implicate him in it. Trofimov's Tolstoyan ethics of renunciation and the simple life gather Anya up into that principle of the negation of class altogether.

The action of the play consists in the radical undoing of the Gayevs' claim to any status or property whatsoever, as their inability to pay the interest on their debts results in the forfeiture of their title in the estate to whose heavily mortgaged remnants they cling. Their nobility is merely residual in that sense, and in scene after scene, Chekhov will make the point that there is only a vanishing gap between them and their class inferiors, into whose amorphous anonymity they are seen to be sinking without redress. Indeed, what sets Lyubov and Leonid apart from their *déclassé* contemporaries on the stage is the vestigial superiority that neither of them believes in enough to make any strong effort to maintain its 'effect in the Real'—they have neither the money nor the authority to conjure from those around them much more than an embarrassed awareness that, in their persons, 'essence' and 'appearance' will never be made to agree again. Lyubov has brought the patronymic into disrepute by marrying a commoner, and then taking up with a swindler who has robbed her of her fortune: 'a loose woman and you can't get away from it', as her brother accuses.[45] While Gayev, absurdly effeminate and passionately attached to his memory of the 1880s, gives himself preposterous airs in a kind of self-sustaining delusion that will not stand the light of public scrutiny.

It is Gayev who, in his aloof manner and the tonality of his diction, carries into *The Cherry Orchard* a living memory of the Romantic stage, where protagonists declaimed in high style and attained an eloquence in keeping with their essence as subjects of striving and accomplishment. Only here, in the context of his straitened circumstances and history shifting inexorably under his feet, this high style is traduced, its strain grating excruciatingly on the ears of the younger, more pragmatic generation of realists. On three separate occasions, Gayev is found delivering an epideictic prosopopoeic address to inanimate or abstract entities: a bookcase, the house, and Nature. He is the bearer of a style that is the verbal hangover of a superannuated class of stage character:

> Dear and most-honoured book-case. In you I salute an existence devoted for over a hundred years to the glorious ideals of virtue and justice. In the course of the century your silent summons to creative work has never faltered, upholding [*through tears*] in several generations of our line confidence and faith in a better future and fostering in us the ideals of virtue and social consciousness. [*Pause.*]
>
> (251)

And again later, his apostrophe during Act II's 'idyll':

> Nature, glorious Nature, glowing with everlasting radiance, so beautiful, so cold—you, whom men call mother, in whom the living and the dead are joined together, you who give life and take it away
>
> (267)

Before the flurry of rhetorical questions in Act IV:

> My friends, my dear good friends! As I leave this house for the last time, how can I be silent? How can I refrain from expressing as I leave the feelings that overwhelm my entire being?
>
> (292)

Gayev's instrumentation by the rhetoric of high dramatic, Romantic style, his possession by its customs and periods, is consistently met on Chekhov's stage by mute embarrassment or outright complaint: 'Uncle dear!' 'Uncle, you're off again' (267); '[*beseechingly*] Uncle'. 'Uncle dear, please don't' (292). Anya's and Varya's

[45] Chekhov, *The Cherry Orchard*, in *Five Plays*, trans. Hingley, 255.

case against 'poetic diction' is pursued with conviction: 'Uncle dear, you should keep quiet, just keep quiet.' 'It's true, Uncle dear, you oughtn't to talk. Just don't talk, that's all' (256). This metatheatrical contretemps is rooted in Gayev's anachronism, his archaic comportment and dress, his manner and style—an anachronism that is simultaneously diegetic (it recalls a sequence in the life of the character) and metatheatrical (it recalls an episode in the history of dramatic form).

GAYEV. I'm a man of the eighties. No one has a good word to say for those days, but still I've suffered quite a bit for those convictions, I can tell you. Do you wonder the peasants like me so much? You have to know your peasant of course. You have to know how to—
ANYA. Uncle, you're off again.
VARYA. Uncle dear, do be quiet. (257)

In this commitment to theatrical anachronism, Leonid is evidently the partner of old man Firs, his manservant, with whom he forms a kind of pseudo-couple, each tacitly trying to outdo the other in the extent of his reactionary recoil from the present, and from the revolutionized stage on which they are compelled to perform their ludicrously antiquated parts.

The brilliance of *The Cherry Orchard*, surely the greatest work of modern theatre, consists above all in this extraordinary formal consonance that Chekhov established between its 'content' (the decay and obsolescence of an anachronistic class faction) and the theatrical dynamics of its character system. For what Leonid's penchant for Romantic characterization means within the character system around him, where all such rhetoric is felt as hackneyed and shameful dross, is the immanent collapse of an entire ethical system of noble honour and pride, and its subsumption by a nascent bourgeois moral order, beyond good and evil. This intrinsic crisis of the old order of honour is allowed to ripple through his speech of reassurance to the two nieces who, in this one case, want to hear him speak:

> We shall pay that interest, I'm sure of it. [*Puts a sweet in his mouth.*] I give you my word of honour, I swear by anything you like, this estate isn't going to be sold. [*Elatedly.*] As I hope to be happy, I swear it. Here's my hand and you can call me a good-for-nothing scoundrel if I let it come to an auction. I won't, on that I'll stake my life.
>
> (256)

It is not just that the compulsive consumption of the sweet ('People say I've wasted my substance on boiled sweets', 262) undermines the heroic stance of the oration; it is that the very speech genre of the oath, the pledge of a life, the self-staking act of avowal, is invalidated by the verbal atmosphere where this rhetoric sounds like so many dead tokens. In speaking these lines, Gayev both affirms his anachronism and articulates the wish-fulfilment of the family that knows full well the worthlessness of the promises here made—yet cannot silence them, this once, since to do so would be to sacrifice the dramatic substance of the play itself. Just as Falstaff represents a depleted medieval dramatic structure embedded within the more Machiavellian matrix of Prince Hal's story in *Henry IV*, Leonid figures more than his own superannuation in *The Cherry Orchard*'s modern setting; like Falstaff, he is attractive and affecting on its basis. The nostalgic wish that both incarnate is felt as formally 'eccentric' but is not rejected. Rather, the character whose obsolete qualities decide in advance the ultimate fate of his 'tendency' in the drama is redeemed from satirical deflation by the underlying yearning, for simpler times and clearer social relations, that he movingly embodies.

Chekhov's strategy for registering the character's internalization of this problem is a kind of continuation by other means of the previous play's interest in the 'automatic' domain of involuntary verbal tics and clichés. For alongside his compulsive ingestion of boiled candies, Gayev is subject to his own verbal automatism, concerning his love of billiards. 'Off two cushions into the middle. Pot the white' (257); 'Pot the red in the middle' (260, 288); 'Double the red into the middle' (292); 'In off into the middle, double the white into the corner' (293). These and many other like interjections serve as a mask or a shield behind which the anachronistic character can dissemble his ordinariness. Gayev's recourse to such verbal nuggets contradicts the flowery rhetoric of his more exposed moments. He is even encouraged by other characters to change track from one to the other: after his apostrophe to Nature, Trofimov follows the nieces' stern counsel of silence with the direct advice, 'You'd far better pot the red in the middle' (267). The character space of *The Cherry Orchard* is one in which the loyalist to the dying order is rendered indistinguishable from a mere eccentric. The pounding imperatives to be silent, and the ready availability of this repertoire of meaningless verbal tics, mean that Gayev is shunted away from his Romantic-heroic predilections and into a harmless empty mannerism of speech, thereby sinking into a 'degree zero' of prattle and eccentric jargon. The effect is once again metatheatrical, in that we cannot finally distinguish between this as a plausible subjective syndrome, and an effective dramatic solution to the problem of the formal anachronism at issue. Visibly 'switching tracks' between the two orders of reality his character straddles, Leonid loses any footing he may have had in either and is rendered ineffectual.

It is not the younger generation as such, however, that delineates the fault-line between Gayev and the rest of the play's character space, but his nemesis and antitype, the 'businessman' and former muzhik, Yermolay Lopakhin. This delineation is best perceived in the antagonistic relationship either character has towards the object world. For if Leonid clings to the world from which he is in the process of being evicted—its furniture, its grounds, its very demesne—then it is surely the case that, for Lopakhin, there is no stately object that cannot be converted into liquidity, no precious node of the vanishing substance of the nobility that cannot be treated as an 'aliquot part' of the total pool of value available on the marketplace. Gayev's fetishism of the material, as historical matter, is in the process of being displaced by a new fetishism, of commodities—which is to say, of *value* as it manifests in material things, and from which it can be wrested in turn, in the infinite fungibility and amnesia of things that is capitalism.[46] For Lopakhin, nothing is sacred because everything is value:

> If you divide the cherry orchard and the land along the river into building plots and lease them out for summer cottages you'll have a yearly income of at least twenty-five thousand roubles. [. . .] You'll get at least ten roubles an acre from your tenants every year. And if you advertise right away I bet you anything you won't have a scrap of land left by autumn, it'll all be snapped up.
>
> (249)

This is not the speech of deference and decorous respect that one might expect from one whom Leonid calls 'a lout of a peasant out for what [he] can get' (248); it is uttered, so to speak, on the plane of immanence, where all hierarchies have ceded to the implacable melting pot of equivalence that is the market.[47] Bearing the rhythm and inflections of the auction block (where it will ultimately succeed in uprooting the Gayev family from 'their soil'), such speech is already sufficient to commit Leonid's flowery apostrophes to the dustbin of history. And its speaker is fully aware both of the implications of its utterance, and of their historical inevitability. Berating the servant woman Dunyasha for appearing above her station, Lopakhin seems still to belong to the world his money is disintegrating: 'You dress like a lady and do your hair like one too. We can't have that. Remember your place' (242). He is fully prepared to accept Gayev's characterization of himself as 'a lout of a peasant', and indeed seems to relish the part. But he relishes it for a reason: it does not belong on the stage that privileges the minor aristocracy.

It is in the context of a discussion about the contemporary stage that Lopakhin particularly distinguishes himself as a comic figure incompatible with the tragedy of disintegrating noble fortunes. Telling Mrs Ranevsky about his visit to the theatre the night before, to see something 'really funny', he is checked by her aesthetic strictures:

MRS RANEVSKY. I don't suppose it was a bit funny. You people shouldn't go and see plays, you should try watching your own performance instead. What drab lives you all lead and what a lot of rubbish you talk!

[46] Not only should every reader of *The Cherry Orchard* be intimately familiar with Karl Marx's *Capital, Vol. 1*, but every reader of *Capital* ought to be reading *The Cherry Orchard*.

[47] On the philosophical implications of what they call the 'plane of immanence', see Gilles Deleuze and Félix Guattari, *What is Philosophy?*, trans Hugh Tomlinson and Graham Burchell (London: Verso, 1994), 35–60.

LOPAKHIN. Quite right. To be honest, the life we lead is preposterous. [Pause.] My father was a peasant, an idiot who understood nothing, taught me nothing and just beat me when he was drunk, with a stick too. As a matter of fact I'm just a big numbskull and idiot myself. (263)

Implicit in Lyubov's rebuke is the claim that peasants do not belong on stage; for they do not belong to the theatre of representations. The peasantry, and its petit-bourgeois upstarts, would do better to 'watch their own performance instead', which is to say, learn how to conform to the time-honoured rules about what is, and what is not, a fitting part of the distribution of the sensible.[48] Lopakhin is perfectly prepared to accept these inherited strictures of the aesthetic, and to own his allotted role: 'a big numbskull and idiot'. But he is only happy to do so because he is actively involved in 'bumping out' the very stage on which such rules have always applied, here and now, in the play called *The Cherry Orchard.*

Lopakhin feels the historical wind in his sails, in a purely formal sense, even as Gayev feels the discursive ground shifting under his feet; and the aesthetic fault-line where these mutual realizations are clearest felt is the site of the hyphen in the phrase 'tragi-comedy', the most privileged generic descriptor of *The Cherry Orchard* since it was first performed.[49] Lopakhin, the figure of comedy, has intruded so far upon tragedy here that, in a transubstantiation of form with little precedent, he fatally undoes it from within. He does so with a style of speech and self-presentation that augurs 'a new way of linking the sayable and the visible, words and things',[50] specifically, one in which the tragic stage, as a 'stage of visibility for an orderly world governed by a hierarchy of subject matter and the adaptation of situations and manners of speaking to this hierarchy',[51] is finally left behind. Neither can the resultant ruins of the tragic be straightforwardly identified with the comic, since that traditional genre 'for the people of meagre means' (32) is not exactly what we are left with after the irresistible rise of Lopakhin. Rather, when Chekhov entitles his play *The Cherry Orchard: A Comedy in Four Acts*, he is gesturing at a new generic space made possible by the historical conversion of 'people of meagre means' into people who own the means of production, the transformation of a fraction of the former muzhik class into capitalists. And this is comic precisely because it is progressive in relation to the captivation of the stage by an undead tragic-noble paradigm, whose inability to comprehend its destiny in either class or aesthetic terms is exemplified by the following exchange:

[48] See Jacques Rancière, *The Politics of Aesthetics: The Distribution of the Sensible*, trans. Gabriel Rockhill (London: Continuum, 2004).

[49] 'In the theatre of Chekhov such thought and feeling, such laughter and tears, alternate perpetually. Hence the constant wrangles whether his plays are meant to be tragic or comic. In reality they are both, ceaselessly passing from the poignant to the ridiculous and back again.' Lucas, *The Drama of Chekhov, Synge, Yeats, and Pirandello*, 85. See also Martin Esslin, 'Chekhov and the Modern Drama', in Clyman, ed., *A Chekhov Companion*, 138.

[50] Jacques Rancière, *The Politics of Literature*, trans. Julie Rose (Cambridge: Polity, 2011), 9.

[51] Rancière, *The Politics of Aesthetics*, 18.

LOPAKHIN. You must act at once, without delay, the auction's almost on top of us. Do get that into your heads. Once you definitely decide on those cottages you can raise any amount of money and you'll be all right.
MRS RANEVSKY. Cottages, summer visitors. Forgive me, but all that's so frightfully vulgar.
GAYEV. I entirely agree.
LOPAKHIN. I'm going to burst into tears or scream or faint. This is too much. I've had about all I can stand! [*To* GAYEV.] You're an old woman.
GAYEV. What's that?
LOPAKHIN. I say you're an old woman. [*Makes to leave.*]
MRS RANEVSKY [*terrified*]. No, don't go away, my dear man. Stay with us, I implore you. (262)

Leonid's late realization that, in life as on the stage, 'We've suddenly become unnecessary' (339), is counterbalanced by his sister's intuitive understanding that the family's connection to Lopakhin is necessary and indispensable. Her sudden terror at his threatened departure is the signal of an underlying crisis of representation. Its lesson is that her own class's irrelevance is a progressive and 'democratizing' effect that will revolutionize the theatre and bring it within the grasp of millions. This is what the 'comedy' of the play's title intends: that a new situation is possible, where no one figure is any more valid or important than any other, where nobody will amount to the stature of a 'giant' (since, as Lyubova tells Lopakhin, 'They're all very well in fairy tales, but elsewhere they might be rather alarming,' 267), and where everybody is equally 'a big numbskull and an idiot', or at best a holy fool.

It is Trofimov who is charged with representing this last, Dostoevskian type here; his deadbeat Hamlet-ism allowing for a generic conversion of any residual tragic overtones into affirmatively comic ones. His wisdom is never hierarchical but conveniently all-purpose, flattened into a humanistic common-sense. While Lopakhin 'objectively' assails the obsolete idiom of honour and pride, Trofimov does so 'subjectively' at the level of ideology and perception:

> But if we look at the thing quite simply and don't try to be too clever, then what room is there for pride and what's the sense of it anyway, if in fact man is a pretty poor physiological specimen and if the great majority of the human race is crude, stupid, and profoundly miserable? It's time we stopped admiring ourselves. The only thing to do is work.
>
> (265)

The aesthetic narcissism of pride and vanity consists in a misrecognition of the 'crude, stupid' human animal as though it were a worthwhile specimen, a compelling imago—a *character*—when in fact, in this individual shape or that, it is an unprepossessing prototype of a species beneath contempt insofar as it is blindly engaged in *the reproduction of the relations of production*. And the misrecognition is nowhere sharper or more injurious, ethically, than in the case of the so-called 'intellectuals', the educated elite, who in failing to recognize their own mediocrity, serve to perpetuate conditions that, ultimately, proscribe the emergence of anything like character to begin with.

> The kind of Russian intellectuals I know . . . aren't looking for anything. They don't do anything. They still don't know the meaning of hard work. They call themselves an intelligentsia, but they speak to their servants as inferiors and treat the peasants like animals. [. . .] They talk of nothing but weighty issues and they discuss abstract problems, while all the time everyone knows the workers are abominably fed and sleep without proper bedding.
>
> (266)

Playing from a script that history is now in the process of invalidating, the 'intelligentsia' from which Trofimov here distinguishes himself *à la* Tolstoy speaks its empty lines to an empty house: 'they speak to their servants as inferiors and treat the peasants like animals'. The aesthetic milieu of the tsarist 'distribution of the sensible' runs on these very lines, these gestures of address and act that serve to maintain social distinctions by shoring up a characterology of 'us and them'. But nobody is listening, because everybody with any sense is at the Moscow Art Theatre, listening to an actor speak these lines to other actors, in what feels like the announcement of a new dramaturgy, a new 'work' that will cut across all these established lines and transform the horizon of possibility.

The play makes it clear just what opportunity has been missed, what event it has not yet occurred to the Russian intelligentsia to swear their fidelity to, since Chekhov has gone to great lengths to announce the date that must serve as a permanent marker between 'now' and 'then', but which so few of the leading personae in this play seem able to comprehend in its immensity.[52] That date is, of course 1861—a date not dissimilar from the date of 1863 in the USA—when the serfs were liberated and the feudal mode of production altered at a stroke. The only two characters who respond to this singular event with due reverence and grasp the monumental tasks ahead as inherently transfigurative of the space and ground of character itself, are Lopakhin and Trofimov. Generally, the rest of the cast, including old Firs, tend to carry on as if the liberation of the serfs has not taken place, or as if it were possible to continue in their current course without taking the full, radical measure of what that event portends to the character space itself. Firs can stand as emblematic of the stubborn cultural persistence of the *ancien régime*, his dress and carriage a walking testament to unconscious atavisms and 'returns of the

[52] The idea of a subjective fidelity to an event as the sine qua non of a radical ethics is developed the work of Alain Badiou, especially *Being and Event*, trans. Oliver Feltham (London: Continuum, 2005), esp. 173–254.

repressed' that underscore the perseverance of a certain distribution of the sensible. Costumed in traditional livery, jacket and white waistcoat, and even in tails during the ball of Act III, the deaf old man voices unapologetic homilies on behalf of the old dispensation.

FIRS. Well, I've been alive a long time. They were arranging my wedding before your Dad was so much as thought of. [*Laughs.*] And when the serfs were freed I was already head valet. But I wouldn't have any of their freedom, I stayed on with the master and mistress. [*Pause.*] As I recall, everyone was very pleased, but what they were so pleased about they'd no idea themselves.

LOPAKHIN. Oh, it was a good life all right. At least there were plenty of floggings.

FIRS [*not hearing him* .] Yes, those were the days. The serfs had their masters and the masters had their serfs, but now everything's at sixes and sevens and you can't make head or tail of it. (264)

But Lopakhin's memories of being beaten by his own father, a muzhik on the estate, leads him to more ambivalent conclusions. Being protected by the young Lyobov Andreyevna from his father's violence, and her affectionate epithet for him 'little muzhik', prompts the reflection: 'Little peasant. It's true my father was a peasant, but here I am in my white waistcoat and brown boots, barging in like a bull in a china shop. The only thing is, I'm rich. I have plenty of money, but when you really get down to it I'm just another country bumpkin' (241). On the one hand, then, Lopakhin can give voice to a conception of 'class essence' that should trigger in the actor a suite of conventional performance traits to evince this 'lout of a peasant': whatever the costume, the underlying character-type is programmed to be boorish, rude, and comical. And yet, of course, nothing could be further from the truth; he is the play's most decent and attractive character, sincerely trying to help save the Gayevs from themselves, but perfectly prepared to step in and administer the advised dose himself, for his own benefit, when they inevitably succumb to the prejudice that dismisses it as 'vulgar' and unbefitting of their action.

Here we see how far Chekhov has come, even from *Three Sisters*, where he had been quite prepared to associate the 'bourgeois' aspirational figure of Natasha with structural villainy. In *The Cherry Orchard*, Lopakhin's function as the nouveau-riche upstart who buys the precious cherry orchard from under the sleeping noses of the sunken gentry, and in the final act even has workmen actively axing it into kindling, could so easily have been dealt the same ethical hand in the distribution of dramatic values. But instead Lopakhin's objective villainy as the liquidator of the estate is offset and trumped by his subjective attribute as the agent of a powerful affective redemption. His long monologue at the end of Act III, the play's single most powerful scene, seizes hold of the fact of 1861 as a whip with which to punish the present, and for the first time in a Chekhov play, to irradiate the present with the vector of a true act. It is entirely to the point that the true act can only be felt as a fantasy, a dream, an impossibility within the frame offered by the tragic distribution of the sensible; and Lopakhin's *Tempest*-like wonder is, if you like, the affect that spills over from the wrenching out of one generic frame and into another:

> Mine! [*Gives a loud laugh.*] Great God in heaven, the cherry orchard's mine. Tell me I'm drunk or crazy, say it's all a dream. [*Stamps his feet.*] Don't laugh at me. If my father or grandfather could only rise from their graves and see what happened, see how their Yermolay—Yermolay who was always being beaten, who could hardly write his name and ran around barefoot in winter—how this same Yermolay bought this estate, the most beautiful place in the world. I've bought the estate where my father and grandfather were slaves, where they weren't even allowed inside the kitchen. I must be dreaming, I must be imagining it all. It can't be true. This is all a figment of your imagination wrapped in the mists of obscurity. (282)

Here is a character caught in the extreme situation of seeing himself, his actions and speech, from the outside, as a player in a vast historical sequence whose logic exists to prevent what has just happened from happening. Putting himself in the third person—'their Yermolay'—Lopakhin brings home to himself, and to his audience, the radical lack of consistency in his person, the extreme rupture in his character, which has transformed him from the son of a serf to the master of the estate, while yet being 'the same' person. The full lesson of all this can only come out in dialogue with Trofimov, the other 'supporter' of the truth of 1861, who answers Lopakhin's obsessive rehearsal of his class background with the following, stunning, response: 'Your father was a peasant and mine worked in a chemist's shop, all of which proves precisely nothing' (286). On the plane of immanence where a new characterology now works out its various parts, everything that had mattered so profoundly to the former distribution of the sensible has ceased to be meaningful, other than in one remaining sense: the dimension of redemption.

Trofimov answers Lopakhin's astonishment at 1861's lesson of characterological discontinuity with a deeper and more complex lesson descending from the same event. It is a lesson aimed not at the former peasantry, but at the falling nobility, which now has one task before it: to unbecome everything it has been, to learn how to live on the plane of immanence, not in a state of radical forgetfulness, but with a deeper humility and the internalization of the dead. For Trofimov, to be a character after 1861 (and on the revolutionary threshold of 1905) means to assume and assimilate the innumerable dead into one's own person, to open oneself to the multiple that one, as a member of the ruling class, has been all along:

> Just think, Anya. Your grandfather, your great-grandfather and all your ancestors owned serfs, they owned human souls. Don't you see that from every cherry tree in the orchard, from every leaf and every trunk, men and women are gazing at

> you? Don't you hear their voices? Owning living souls, that's what has changed you all so completely, those who went before and those alive today, so that your mother, you yourself, your uncle—you don't realize that you're actually living on credit. You're living on other people, the very people you won't even let inside your own front door. We're at least a couple of hundred years behind the times. So far we haven't got anywhere at all and we've no real sense of the past. We just talk in airy generalizations, complain of boredom or drink vodka. But if we're to start living in the present isn't it abundantly clear that we've first got to redeem our past and make a clean break with it? And we can only redeem it by suffering and getting down to some real work for a change.
>
> (269)

Here the inner truth of Chekhov's lifelong accent on 'hard work' and 'suffering' achieves its ultimate expression, as the ethical imperative to break from the past by internalizing it, admitting its anonymous multiple—'the very people you won't even let inside your own front door'—into the inner sanctum of the self. It is incumbent upon the children of the former ruling class to repay the vast credit, the centuries of unpaid labour, that had made their distinction possible in the first place, by repaying it in the present to the collective essence of the people. Becoming anonymous, humble, 'low', and toiling on the land, is of course synonymous with losing all characterological distinction, sinking into the great masses and off the stage of history; but that, and only that, will be sufficient to the time now arriving, the revolutionary upsurge of 1905, to which this play is both propaedeutic and user's manual.

If it is the case that, in *The Cherry Orchard*, the 'ensemble had taken over entirely'[53] from the vestiges of melodramatic protagonicity, then the exact terms of that assumption can be determined with some precision. As Bely had pointed out, apropos of this play in particular, 'His heroes are outlined by external strokes, but we apprehend them from within. They walk, drink, talk rubbish while we behold the spiritual poverty transpicuous within them. They talk like men confined in prison, but we have learned something about them that they themselves have not noticed in themselves. In the minutiae by which they live, a certain secret cipher is revealed to us—and the minutiae cease to be minutiae.'[54] It is of the essence of *The Cherry Orchard* that, in its presentation, something is witnessed in the characters *more than themselves*, a principle of transvaluation whereby the very parts they are playing are caught in the act of slipping out of coincidence with themselves. The *characters*, then, are not the *character* of the play, which is situated outside their immediate concerns and travails, and which registers itself as a 'secret cipher' written upon the very banality and venality of their interactions. Martin Esslin once remarked that in his drama 'Chekhov created a new focus of attention: the

[53] Heim, 'Chekhov and the Moscow Art Theatre', 141.
[54] Bely, 'The Cherry Orchard', 91.

situation itself, the conjunction of characters, the subtle use of seemingly incongruous details [. . .] put the emphasis on the complex audiovisual image of the stage and made the stage itself into a poetic metaphor. Chekhov was one of the pioneers in moving theatre away from putting its main emphasis on action in the simple, literal sense. A great deal is still happening in the seemingly static images of Chekhov, behind the apparently trivial dialogue. But it is complex and covert rather than on the surface and direct.'[55] It is here again that we can distinguish a critical distinction between the *characters* of the play and the *character* it gives rise to, which I am now going to insist has to be read as the cipher of a characterology to come, an absent configuration of roles and agents glimpsed amid the wreckage of this one.

Traditionally, the critical record has tended to read this covert message in the code of music. 'After the first performance of *The Cherry Orchard*', notes Nils Åke Nilsson, '[Meyerhold] wrote a letter to Chekhov in which he criticizes Stanislavski. It is interesting to note that here, too, he was looking for the key to the play in precisely its rhythmical-acoustic character. He compared it to a symphony by Tchaikovsky—a comparison many were to make after him. But he had in mind not so much its melancholy mood as its abstract, musical structure; he especially pointed out the rhythmical contrasts in Act III.'[56] Or, as Jean-Pierre Barricelli puts it, 'The meaning of *The Cherry Orchard* is rooted in a kind of recondite music, or unmusic, contrasting intensely with the clumsiness of the characters or their inability to harmonize (*neskladnyy*).'[57] And we have seen the usefulness of this metaphor for thinking of Chekhov's innovations in characterology. But no statement comes so near to formulating the full radicalism of this play's achievement as that made by Meyerhold himself, just after its initial performance, in which he took part:

> In *The Cherry Orchard*, as in the plays of Maeterlinck, there is a hero, unseen on the stage, but whose presence is felt every time the curtain falls. [. . .]. For Chekhov, the characters of *The Cherry Orchard* are the means and not the end.
>
> (33)

Maeterlinck's 'third person' is transfigured into Chekhov's composite prefiguration of a character-to-come, unseen hero of another dramaturgy, emerging at the complex intersections of genre (tragedy, comedy), style (mock-heroic, vulgar, 'idiotic'), class, and historical event (1861, 1905). Chekhov's dramatis personae are allegorical figures of their own historical and aesthetic sublation into another character we intuit only through their collective redundancy.

[55] Esslin, 'Chekhov and the Modern Drama', 142–3.
[56] Nilsson, 'Intonation and Rhythm in Chekhov's Plays', 173–4.
[57] Jean-Pierre Barricelli, 'Counterpoint of the Snapping String: Chekhov's *The Cherry Orchard*', in Barricelli, ed., *Chekhov's Great Plays*, 121.

PART TWO

5
Wilde and Huysmans

It was a novel without a plot and with only one character.[1]

Strindberg's misogyny radiated its animus over the cultural landscape of the *fin-de-siècle*, in ways that were socially and politically deleterious while yet promoting appreciable benefits in the arena of aesthetic innovation. If the 'negation of woman' at the heart of the Decadent enterprise[2] was not meant entirely seriously as a social and political doctrine, then it was arguably offered instead as a rebarbative corrective to the conventionality of the marriage plot and 'emotional equations' which held literature back from its more serious vocation.[3] So much can already be construed from Huysmans' remarkable claims for what he was trying to achieve in *À rebours* (1884):

> to shake off prejudices, to break the boundaries of the novel, to introduce into it art, and science, and history; in a word to no longer to use this form except as a frame in which one could incorporate work of a more serious nature. As for me, what seemed to me especially important at that period was to get rid of the traditional plot, to get rid even of love, of woman, to concentrate the beam of light on one single character, to do something new regardless of the cost.[4]

The movement away from Woman is a movement against the traditional plot and against the novel itself.[5] It is also a move away from questions of procreation, dynasty, and lineage, in line with 'the biological teleology of a life that aims at extinction', on the track of fatal repetition.[6] If this shudder at the female proceeds from a 'philosophical pessimism that is itself but the intellectual exposition of some more concrete lived experience', it is also a frisson of 'radical innovation' in the

[1] Oscar Wilde, *The Picture of Dorian Gray* (London: Penguin, 2012), 127.

[2] See Monique Marie LaRocque, 'Decadent Desire: The Dream of Disembodiment in *À rebours*, *The Picture of Dorian Gray*, and *L'Eve future*' (PhD dissertation, Dept. of Comparative Literature, Indiana University, 2001), 2–3.

[3] See Joseph Carroll, 'Aestheticism, Homoeroticism, and Guilt', *Philosophy and Literature* 29.2 (October 2005), 295 [285–304]. For 'emotional equations', see Ezra Pound, *The Spirit of Romance* (New York: New Directions, 1968), 14.

[4] Joris-Karl Huysmans, 'Preface, Written Twenty Years After the Novel', *Against Nature*, trans. Margaret Mauldon (Oxford: Oxford World's Classics, 1998), 194.

[5] The discussion in Katherine Snyder's *Bachelors, Manhood, and the Novel, 1850–1925* (Cambridge: Cambridge University Press, 1999) is significant here; see the Introduction, 1–17.

[6] Robert Ziegler, 'The Pervert, the Aesthete, and the Novelist in Huysmans's *À rebours*', *Romance Studies* 25.3 (2007), 207 [199–209].

Modern Character. Julian Murphet, Oxford University Press. © Julian Murphet (2023).
DOI: 10.1093/oso/9780192863126.003.0006

precincts of art[7]—whose most ironic side-effect is the feminization of the single character in question.[8]

A further benefit of this campaign against Woman—'Woman is the *radix malorum*'[9]—is the opportunity to move along from the 'homosocial desire [of the] mid-eighteenth- to mid-nineteenth-century novel',[10] to a more overtly homosexual desire, which, channelled through what I will follow Duchamp in calling 'bachelor-machines', radically unsettles the established conventions of literary characterology.[11] The rejection of all things naturally fruitful (organic, reproductive, embodied, female) in favour of high artifice, degeneration, and death—of the sort practised by des Esseintes, Dr Jekyll, and Dorian Gray—licenses the writers' defection from the novel form in favour of the spindly and generically promiscuous novella. Form is radically simplified to enable the flourishing of a style. If, as Huysmans implies, the suspension of Woman is verily a suspension of plot itself, then what emerges to take its place is the prototypical 'Anatomy' of aestheticism: encyclopaedic lists that catalogue souvenirs of a stupendously various experience.[12] 'I have known everything', says Lord Henry wearily, 'but I am always ready for a new emotion'.[13] The bachelor-machine 'knows everything', is held back from no perilous extreme of the 'passion for sensations' (48)—but to no other end than their meticulous itemization: 'as though satisfied at having exhausted every possibility, as though worn out with the strain, his senses were overpowered by inertia, and impotence was close at hand'.[14] Going nowhere, the bachelor-machine's sterile ethos is nevertheless a veritable gold mine for that most precious of contemporary artistic jewels: *affect*.

The project of the bachelor-machine, as articulated by Lord Henry Wotton, is 'to become the spectator of one's own life' (112), to convert otherwise inchoate sensations and affective stimuli into the prime object of aesthetic attention—to cultivate novel affects, moods, sensitivities the way one might cultivate pigments

[7] Fredric Jameson, *The Ideologies of Theory* (London: Verso, 2008), 311; Georg Lukács, *Writer and Critic and Other Essays*, trans. Arthur D. Kahn (London: Merlin Press, 1970), 13.

[8] See Rita Felski, 'The Counterdiscourse of the Feminine in Three Texts by Wilde, Huysmans, and Sacher-Masoch', *PMLA* 106.5 (October 1991): 1094–105.

[9] George C. Schoolfield, *A Baedeker of Decadence: Charting a Literary Fashion, 1884–1927* (New Haven: Yale University Press, 2003), 9.

[10] Eve Kosofsky Sedgwick, *Between Men: English Literature and Male Homosocial Desire*, 30th anniversary ed. (New York: Columbia University Press, 2016), 1.

[11] Duchamp's bachelor-machines are servo-mechanical thralls to the Bride, to be sure, but here I imagine them liberated from the great top panel of *The Large Glass*, in pursuit of other fare.

[12] 'The impression of formlessness results from the enumerative, descriptive, cataloguing tendencies of the literary genre of the anatomy, to which *À rebours* belongs.' Laurence M. Porter, 'Huysmans' *À rebours*: The Psychodynamics of Regression', *American Imago* 44.1 (Spring, 1987), 52 [51–65]. Regenia Gagnier hails Wilde's 'astonishing lists in *The Picture of Dorian Gray*' and calls *À rebours* Huysmans' 'anatomy of Taste from the perspective of one interior life'. Regenia Gagnier, *Individualism, Decadence and Globalization: On the Relation of Part to Whole, 1859–1920* (Basingstoke: Palgrave Macmillan, 2010), 91, 165.

[13] Wilde, *Picture of Dorian Gray*, 80.

[14] Huysmans, *Against Nature*, 8.

or scents. '[S]tirred by some new emotion for which we cannot find expression' (23), the bachelors strive to prevent it from settling into anything resembling a conventional experience, or a 'named emotion', which would be merely vulgar; to sequester and persevere with a bodily intensity until it is effectively depersonalized, autonomized, and spiritualized into an 'essential oil' or 'succulent extract'.[15] That is the work of style on those otherwise inert, non-dynamic materials arranged into lists and networks; and in the world of the story, the work of style masquerades as science. Jekyll is a scientist, as is Lord Henry in his amateur way, and des Esseintes in his. In Strindberg's *I havsbandet* [*On the Seaboard*] (1890), too, the decadent protagonist is a scientist. Villiers de l'Isle Adam's *L'Ève future* (1886) applies its tonic of scientific misogyny via the dream figure of Thomas Edison. The bachelor-scientist sits apart from experience to study and classify it, modify it, intensify it—beyond empathy for his specimens as he is beyond good and evil in his method, committed only to the accumulation of knowledge as a will to power. In these experiments, 'the body is analytically broken down into its smallest components and then scientifically reconstructed as an abstraction, all the while releasing a flow of affect hitherto stored and bound by its traditional unities and their named feelings'.[16] As Jameson goes on to insist, however, this atemporal anatomization does not 'exclude narrative' in the textual artefact but 'in reality harbors new kinds of narrative movement' in the stylistic working up of the material (41). It is these 'new kinds of movement', molecular and chromatic, that are the secret goal of the aesthetic of decadence, and they are incompatible with the reigning protocols of the novel.

So, what is unfairly called the 'unproductive aestheticism' of these bachelor-machines is better understood as prodigiously productive—not of action but of style.[17] This kind of productivity is anti-social, as befits the bachelor-scientist. A protagonist retracted from the market in wives, as from any form of professional or productive enterprise, is a protagonist separated from the well-strung web of characterological relations in the realist novel. With obvious precursors in the blighted scions of Poe's tales and the social misfits of Dostoevsky, the Decadent protagonist overcomes his morose alienation to proclaim, 'I am not a champion of marriage. The real drawback to marriage is that it makes one unselfish. And unselfish people are colourless. They lack individuality.'[18] The individuality of the bachelor-machine consists in the extreme plurality of his mode of existence. The bachelor-machine contains, *is*, as many 'selves' as are convoked by the affects he assiduously pursues, indulges, and then sheds like a worn skin. He is properly multifarious. Multiplicity begins with doubleness that rapidly metastasizes. Dorian Gray 'felt keenly the terrible pleasure of a double life' (180), but the matter scarcely

[15] Huysmans, *Against Nature*, 162.
[16] Fredric Jameson, *The Antinomies of Realism* (London: Verso, 2013), 41.
[17] Ziegler, 'The Pervert, the Aesthete, and the Novelist', 199.
[18] Wilde, *Picture of Dorian Gray*, 74.

ends there. Dr Jekyll may be 'committed to a profound duplicity of life', and convinced of 'man's dual nature'; he is aware of 'the two natures that contended in the field of my consciousness', and that he is 'radically both'—but as a true scientist of affect he knows that this convenient dualism is a mere prejudice.[19] His acute 'consciousness of the perennial war among his members' (55) points in a much more troubling direction than the easy distinction between Good and Evil. His great discovery is limited only by the state of the art, the science, the *style* in which it can be written:

> man is not truly one, but truly two. I say two, because the state of my own knowledge does not pass beyond that point. Others will follow, others will outstrip me on the same lines; and I hazard the guess that man will be ultimately known for a mere polity of multifarious, incongruous and independent denizens.
>
> (55–6)

It will remain for others, Huysmans and Wilde among them, to outstrip Stevenson's scientist and map this new *stultitia*.[20] With Strindberg's John they will ask, 'where is to be found the central "ego",—the core of character?' and find that 'individuality was a fairly rich but chaotic complex'.[21] With Nietzsche they will hail 'a multiplicity of subjects on whose interplay and struggle our thinking and our consciousness in general is based'.[22] And with Théodule Ribot they will proclaim that 'what constitutes [character] are much rather affective states' than moral and intellectual consistencies.[23] Wilde puts the matter on a moral footing in Henry Wotton's defence of insincerity: 'It is merely a method by which we can multiply our personalities.'[24] And des Esseintes spreads his person across so many diverse sensory and intellectual domains, each with its own dedicated chapter—colour, scent, flavour, tone, tincture, flora, gemstones, and so on—that his tactical retreat from society and the 'loathsome age of shameful duplicity' (44) becomes in fact a performance of its vast polity of beings, 'multifarious, incongruous and independent'.

While Huysmans' non-narrative model was the anatomy, Wilde's was the modern Platonic dialogue as mastered by Dryden, Peacock, de Quincy, and Wilde himself in his 'Intentions' (1891), particularly 'The Art of Lying' and 'The Critic

[19] Robert Louis Stevenson, *The Strange Case of Dr Jekyll and Mr Hyde and Other Tales of Terror*, ed. Robert Mighall (London: Penguin, 2002), 55.

[20] On *stultitia*, see Michel Foucault, *Discourse and Truth and Parrhesia*, ed. Daniele Lorenzini, Henri-Paul Fruchaud, and Nancy Luxton, trans. Nancy Luxton (Chicago: University of Chicago Press, 2019), 29; and Michel Foucault, *Hermeneutics of the Subject: Lectures at the Collège de France, 1981–1982*, ed. Frédéric Gros, trans. Graham Burchell (New York: Palgrave Macmillan, 2005), 133.

[21] August Strindberg, *Son of a Servant*, trans. Claud Field (New York: G. P. Putnam's Sons, 1913), 260.

[22] Friedrich Nietzsche, *Writings from the Late Notebooks* [40(42)], ed. Rüdiger Bittner, trans. Kate Sturge (Cambridge: Cambridge University Press, 2003), 46; 40/42.

[23] Théodule Ribot, *Diseases of the Will* (c.1883), trans. Merwin-Marie Snell (Chicago: Open Court, 1894), 23.

[24] Wilde, *Picture of Dorian Gray*, 144–5.

as Artist'. Wilde thrilled to the form's dialectical toleration of contradiction and paradox, its lifeblood of inconsistency. 'I can invent an imaginary antagonist', he exulted of the dialogue's advantages over the essay, 'and convert him when I choose by some absurdly sophistical argument'.[25] Or not. The dialogue required no final taking of sides, for it existed in the *agon* and *aporiae* of the exchange itself; if one side proved more charismatic, the other seemed more responsible, and the laurels went to the engineer of the encounter. As a result, the figures in the dialogues—Cyril and Vivian, Gilbert and Ernest—could scarcely be called characters. Their artful thinness is an effect of not having to bother with interiority, existing as they do entirely on the surface, at the interface of wit and erudition. They do nothing but spar. It is this quality that is transposed, with only minor alterations, to the world of *Dorian Gray*, with effects that compromise standard novelistic form. 'I am afraid [the book] is rather like my own life', quipped Wilde, '—all conversation and no action. I can't describe action: my people sit in chairs and chatter.'[26] Basil Hallward and Lord Henry Wotton assume the lounging positions of Cyril (defender of truth) and Vivian (defender of lying) respectively. Only now, besides intellectual intercourse, they have more serious coupling to do.

If Sheldon Liebman is right to argue that the 'flat' characters of Basil Hallward and Lord Henry serve principally to provide the impressionable Dorian Gray with countervailing 'moral positions', it seems fair to push the matter further.[27] They are his progenitors. Dorian's true parents can hardly be the heiress Margaret Devereux and some 'penniless young fellow, a mere nobody' (33) (a melodramatic pairing plucked straight from the Victorian stage), when the pseudo-couple of Hallward and Wotton is explicitly responsible for his figure, face, and form. Basil (as *mater*) conjures Dorian's physical appearance, his stupid beauty and charm, from the blank canvas;[28] while Lord Henry (as *pater*) lures Dorian out of choric innocence into the worldly-wise experience of the Symbolic Order: language, literature, and original sin. Basil donates the physical, spatial, and visual, Lord Henry the verbal, temporal, and intellectual components of Dorian's character. It is not only that these two parental figures then compete jealously for possession over Dorian's soul, but that Dorian, their creature, embodies their *agon*—a fracture running through his character so deep that it permits subsequent internal doubling and redoubling, a feverish multiplication of selves. Among them, Dorian must find his way, which he does in a most peculiar manner. Holding fast to the gift of *mater* (to Beauty) whilst going pell-mell into *pater*'s doctrine of Experience,

[25] Qtd. in Richard Ellmann, *Oscar Wilde* (New York: Vintage Books/Random House, 1988), 306.

[26] Qtd. in Ellmann, *Oscar Wilde*, 314.

[27] Sheldon W. Liebman, 'Character Design in *The Picture of Dorian Gray*', *Studies in the Novel* 31.3 (Fall 1999), 311 [296–316].

[28] Christopher Craft concurs that 'Basil has endured a tough gestation.' Christopher Craft, 'Come See About Me: Enchantment of the Double in *The Picture of Dorian Gray*', *Representations* 91.1 (Summer 2005), 121 [109–36].

Dorian straddles their differences until finally he cracks and does the Oedipally unthinkable: slaying his Mother, having enjoyed his Father's body, he does himself in.[29]

The advantage of this schema, particularly over the earlier model of *À rebours*, is that it charges Dorian Gray, as a protagonist, with heightened allegorical significance in relation to the function of art. As the bastard son of a visual artist and a wordsmith—of the dialogue between Painting and Literature—Dorian is the living allegorical emblem of 'character' in the space of this text. '[N]ow and then a complex personality took the place and assumed the office of art, was indeed, in its way, a real work of art, life having its elaborate masterpieces, just as poetry has, or sculpture, or painting' (57). Basil's and Henry's irreconcilable aesthetic debate made flesh, Dorian incarnates their theoretical tensions, to which he comes as the characterological solution—not by resolving the *agon*, but by living it to the letter. No wonder he is drawn first to the theatre, where the red herring of Sibyl Vane lays traps for all unsuspecting moralists.[30] As the novella's ostensible concession to the female, Sibyl emanates some alarming signals undermining the sufficient homosociality of the scene, much to Basil's chagrin. But Henry understands Dorian's attraction as one of like to like, a narcissistic self-rapturing. Sybil is the *character of character*. She is 'all the great heroines of the world in one'. Like Dorian, 'She is more than an individual' (54). 'Lips that Shakespeare taught to speak have whispered their secret in my ear. I have had the arms of Rosalind around me, and kissed Juliet on the mouth' (77). Any reader of that other portrait story of the day, 'The Portrait of Mr W. H.' knows full well that 'Viola and Imogen, Juliet and Rosalind, Portia and Desdemona, and Cleopatra herself', all of them, 'Beatrice to Ophelia', are but erotic ciphers for that 'wonderful boy-actor of great beauty, to whom [Shakespeare] entrusted the presentation of his noble heroines', and who goes by the convenient name of Willie Hughes, dedicatee of the Sonnets.[31] What Dorian recognizes in Sibyl is, first, his own homoerotic desire looking back at him; and, second, his very status as a fictional being, situated in a fiction about fictionality. But then she makes the fateful error of forgetting what she is, defecting from an exquisite aesthesis and boyish charm that holds her aloft, and stumbles into female sexuality and melodrama. At once, 'Sibyl Vane seemed to him to be absurdly melodramatic. Her tears and sobs annoyed him' (88–9). Becoming all-too realistic, she ceases to be true. 'Without your art you are nothing', the lad accurately puts it (87). Lord Henry is literally right to go still further:

[29] Dorian and Henry share residences together during their orgies abroad (143); moreover, Henry enjoys 'projecting' himself into Dorian's 'gracious form', 'conveying [his] temperament into [him] as though it were a subtle fluid' (36).

[30] Even the great Richard Ellmann cannot prevent himself from looking askance at Dorian's indifference to her fate. 'Only her brother, and the reader, are left to mourn, and to judge.' Ellmann, *Oscar Wilde*, 316.

[31] Oscar Wilde, 'The Portrait of Mr W. H.', in *The Soul of Man Under Socialism and Selected Critical Prose*, ed. Linda Dowling (London: Penguin, 2001), 41, 50, 42.

'The girl never really lived, and so she has never really died' (104). It is the final lesson Dorian needs before assuming his full allegorical function.

That lesson is already implicit in the inaugural scene of the text itself: the finishing of the portrait. It is worth remembering what Barthes says of the portrait in 'Sarrasine'. 'Meanings abound in the portrait', writes Barthes, 'proliferating through a form which nonetheless disciplines them: this form is both a rhetorical order (declaration and detail) and an anatomical cataloguing (body and face); these two protocols are also codes; these codes are superimposed on the anarchy of signifiers, they appear as the operators of nature'.[32] Barthes' point is that a portrait in a literary text is never a copy of a body, but always a pattern or 'diacritical paradigm' (61) of prior meanings which a fictional body then comes along to exemplify. As François Delaporte has written of Lavater, 'with the description of [his] portraits, he was giving in advance the qualities that he was claiming to deduce from representation'.[33] In Wilde's text this is so true as to be virtually the premise of the fable; the rhetoric of the image here exceeds its denotative or anatomical function by an order of magnitude matched only in fairy tales.[34] 'The portrait [. . .] is not a realistic representation, a related copy, an idea such as we might get from figurative painting; it is a scene made up by blocks of meaning [. . .]; out of the arrangement of these blocks comes a diagram of the body, not its copy.'[35] This diagram of the body is all Basil Hallward's, its rhetoric pluripotent as he confesses repeatedly: 'I have put too much of myself into it' (2). '[E]very portrait that is painted with feeling', he admits, 'is a portrait of the artist, not of the sitter' (5). What he has 'put into it' is a feeling different in kind but not in intent from what Lord Henry 'projects' into Dorian, namely his unspeakable desire, of which he is ashamed (and which the book version, too, shamefacedly excises from the *Lippincott* original: 'It is quite true that I have worshipped you with far more romance of feeling than a man usually gives to a friend. Somehow, I had never loved a woman.'[36]) The portrait is an objectification of that queer 'romance of feeling', transposed into form. 'It is the real Dorian Gray', says Lord Henry of the portrait, a phrase that is duly echoed by Basil (27, 29). Latecomer Dorian can only concur, as he has not existed textually prior to the portrait. He is 'seduced into specular identification with an erotically charged image of himself; the portrait supplies the very prototype of the being Dorian will work to become'.[37] 'It is, after all, the

[32] Roland Barthes, *S/Z*, trans. Richard Miller (Oxford: Blackwell, 1990), 60.

[33] François Delaporte, *Anatomy of the Passions* (Stanford: Stanford University Press, 2008), 40.

[34] Julian Hawthorne could not decide if *Dorian Gray* was 'a novel or romance (it partakes of both)'. He went with 'parable' and found Wilde's novel 'a salutary departure from the ordinary English novel'. Hawthorne, 'The Romance of the Impossible' (c.1908), at https://www.gutenberg.org/files/33689/33689-h/33689-h.htm

[35] Barthes, *S/Z*, 61.

[36] Wilde, 'The Picture of Dorian Gray' as published in *Lippincott's Monthly Magazine* in July 1890; reproduced at: https://en.m.wikisource.org/wiki/Lippincott%27s_Monthly_Magazine/Volume_46/July_1890/The_Picture_of_Dorian_Gray/Chapter_7

[37] Craft, 'Come See About Me', 121.

picture and not the character that gives the story its title, just as it is the copy that confers upon "the original of the portrait" his first sense of being Dorian.'[38] This is one of those many cases in Wilde's work where life's imitation of art is happily affirmed; his animadversions against the chronic misuse of Hamlet's line about art 'holding the mirror up to Nature' in 'The Decay of Lying' turn on the contradictory conviction that 'Life is in fact the mirror, and Art the reality.'[39]

If this is a rhetoric, its privileged figure is *hysteron proteron* and its ground is *ekphrasis*. The effect precedes the cause; the described work of art antecedes the body it supposedly represents. The 'blocks of meaning' implicit in the portrait are clear from its oblique literary description: the 'young man of extraordinary personal beauty' (1) with 'gracious and comely form' (2) who is a 'young Adonis, who looks as if he was made out of ivory and rose leaves' (3). As with most *ekphrasis*, description rapidly veers off into connotation, allusion, and vague metaphors. The name Dorian itself is a noun denoting a Doric-speaking Hellene from the Peloponnese; like the 'Adonis' portrait that bears this name, its denotative references blur backward in the mists of time—to ancient Greece, where the rhetoric of this image would have been entirely familiar. Ephebophilia personified and deified, what 'the face of Antinous was to late Greek sculpture' (9), is what gleams out of the canvas; it is 'the visible incarnation of that unseen ideal' (116) which justifies a world without women.[40] Dorian steps into the world not as a person, then, and not even as a type, but as the shadow of an *icon*.

Thus the aesthetic revolution betokened by the portrait—'an entirely new manner in art, an entirely new mode of style', 'a fresh school' (10)—part romantic, part ancient Greek, has little to do with representation in the realist sense, and (just as Epstein, Hulme, Worringer, and Gaudier-Brezska would recommend a generation later) thrives on abstraction, transcendence, and perfection. If it 'is Dorian Gray', then the character who later enters to claim that name assumes the heady responsibility of reincarnating the incarnate ideal already gazing from the picture. And the point at which, the medium through which, this transference can take place is none other than the 'wonderfully beautiful face' itself (22), which youth and portrait share. According to one venerable theory of the subject, crucial to this tale, the human face is character reified: the permanent trace record of all the emotional agitation suffered by the individual. 'In the face alone', writes Georg Simmel, 'emotion first expressed in movement is deposited as the expression of permanent character'.[41] As Basil Hallward puts it, 'Sin is a thing that writes itself across a man's

[38] Craft, 'Come See About Me', 113.

[39] Wilde, 'The Decay of Lying', in *Soul of Man*, 178.

[40] The prevalence of references to Antinous in Decadent fiction is charted in Schoolfield, *A Baedeker of Decadence*, xiv–xv.

[41] Georg Simmel, 'The Aesthetic Significance of the Face', trans. Lore Ferguson, in Kurt H. Wolff, ed., *Georg Simmel, 1858–1918: A Collection of Essays* (Columbus: Ohio State University Press, 1959), 279.

face' (152); and Lord Henry, 'Sin is the only real colour-element left in modern life' (29). Such indelible coloration then creates, on Wilde's own account, a living fossil of everything that individuates and rescues the human being from type: 'By its curiosity Sin increases the experience of the race. Through its intensified assertion of individualism it saves us from monotony of type.'[42] 'One can fancy an intense personality being created out of sin';[43] and the face is the badge of that 'liberation of the personality' through sinful 'self-expression'.[44] The problem is, of course, that such exposure of the face to its accumulated inner wealth of sin tends to produce ugliness. The wicked man appears wicked because of it; and with that formula, we are back in the world of melodrama and realism, which it was precisely the motive of Dorian's picture to abolish—to found a 'new school of art'.

Physiognomy, the expressive theory of facial character, develops a belief in the indexicality of facial signs as regards the moral history of the 'soul'—a belief apparently hard-wired into the cerebral cortex. As one contemporary psychological study puts it, 'Face-to-trait inference appears to be intuitive and automatic among human adults',[45] and this inveterate reflex has left deep traces in the literary and cultural record. Physiognomy begins with Aristotle's claim in the *Prior Analytics* that it is 'possible to infer character from features', is restated in Sir Thomas Browne's assertion that 'there are mystically in our faces certaine characters which carry in them the motto of our Soules', attains an apotheosis in the work of Johann Caspar Lavater, and has run like a river through the entire history of literary characterization.[46] What a godsend it was to novelists that 'whenever we behold a new face, we involuntarily form some conclusion respecting the one who wears it; that it is the index of a mind either honest, or dishonest; cultivated, or barren; generous and friendly, or inimical and covetous'—their labour consisting only in crafting descriptions that catered to this enormous repertoire of assumed understanding.[47]

As John Frow points out, ancient wax death masks (the Roman *imagines*) 'were a direct impression of the deceased person's face, metonymically linked to it and thus not distinct from the face they represent and whose person they preserve; their function is like that of the English word *stamp* or the Greek *kharakter*: at once the instrument and the mark it leaves. After the funeral the *imago* was locked in a chest in the family atrium [. . .]. It was normally never seen.'[48] The *imago*'s

[42] Wilde, 'The Critic as Artist', in *Soul of Man*, 231.
[43] Wilde, 'Pen, Pencil, and Poison', in *Soul of Man*, 211.
[44] Ellmann, *Oscar Wilde*, 329.
[45] Emily J. Cogsdill, Alexander T. Todorov, Elizabeth S. Spelke, and Mahzarin R. Banaji, 'Inferring Character from Faces: A Developmental Study', *Psychological Science* 24.5 (2014), 1132 [1132–9].
[46] Aristotle, *Prior Analytics*, 2.27, trans. A. J. Jenkinson, http://classics.mit.edu/Aristotle/prior.mb.txt; Sir Thomas Browne, *Religio Medici*, 2.2, in *The Major Works*, ed. C. A. Patrides (London: Penguin, 1977), 135.
[47] Editorial in the *Lancaster Hive*, 1805; qtd. in Christopher J. Lukasik, *Discerning Characters: The Culture of Appearance in Early America* (Philadelphia: University of Pennsylvania Press, 2010), 33.
[48] John Frow, *Character and Person* (Oxford: Oxford University Press, 2014), 248.

'incorruptible and yet mortal form' was then directly the 'incarnation of [the ancestors'] numinous force' (249), out of sight but never out of mind. It seems logical to think of *The Picture of Dorian Gray* as an overturning and rewiring of this Roman custom. In Wilde's text, the 'incarnation of numinous force' is already impressed on the canvas as Basil paints it, by the intensity of his desire: the portrait is a 'character'—an *ikon*, a *mask*—of the Ephebe à la Antinous and Adonis. But once it is caught up in the mirror-relation of portrait to subject, once a person appears to claim the image as his own, the ambivalent function of *kharaktēr* is starkly revealed. It is impossible to decide whose face it is that these two figures share: did the living Dorian's face leave its impression on the canvas, or did the canvas imprint its image on the waxy flesh of the unformed youth? The answer lies in the nature of the image being discussed: a mask. As Michael Taussig writes, 'the face itself is a contingency, at the magical crossroads of mask and window to the soul', and the extraordinary value of Dorian's situation is that he can operate the magic of that crossroads.[49] A new rhetorical structure suggests itself. The *hysteron proteron* figure is converted, imperceptibly, into a figure of chiasmus: 'the portrait reverses the usual relation between surface and depth, core and facia. It turns Dorian inside out so his eyes may witness what, by definition, they cannot see at all—the legible condition of his inner being.'[50] Dorian's fairy-tale wish is chiasmic, seizing on the unrealistic, iconic, abstract mask-like quality of the face Basil has painted. It is this that he decides to wear, while he confers upon the portrait all the inherited physiognomic wisdom of literary realism and melodrama. One aesthetic is swapped for another. The literary character will assume the mask of the painterly *imago*; the painting will acquire the sinful face of a novelistic character. It is the latter that ends up in 'the family atrium' while the former walks the streets.

And here a secondary characterological theory can be discerned, the Strindbergian theory of will and influence. The problematic of the face is not narratively satisfying; it is only a clever conceit. But the story of influence is properly Shakespearean, and our textual Iago here, Lord Henry, is its chief proponent.

> There was something terribly enthralling in the exercise of influence. No other activity was like it. To project one's soul into some gracious form, and let it tarry there for a moment; to hear one's own intellectual views echoed back to one with all the added music of passion and youth; to convey one's temperament into another as though it were a subtle fluid or a strange perfume: there was a real joy in that—perhaps the most satisfying joy left to us [. . .]. He was a marvellous type, too, this lad [. . .], or could be fashioned into a marvellous type, at any rate. Grace was his, and the white purity of boyhood, and beauty such as old Greek

[49] Michael Taussig, *Defacement: Public Secrecy and the Labor of the Negative* (Stanford: Stanford University Press, 1999), 3.

[50] Craft, 'Come See About Me', 114–15.

> marbles kept for us. There was nothing that one could not do with him. He could be made a Titan or a toy.
>
> (35)

Wearing the abstract mask of the Doric Ephebe, Dorian's 'gracious form' is but unmoulded clay, uncarved marble, requiring a Satanic whisper in the ear to lift out of the 'white purity of boyhood' into the salience of character. Henry's point is explicit here: a mask is not a character. Character formation is literary not visual, and its undertaking is a joyous release of affect and sensation. The dominator or influencer takes the raw material of a visual icon, a mere prototype, and shapes it via literature (the 'Yellow Book' or pseudo-*À rebours*) into a complex dynamic living text, 'Dorian Gray', whose vivisection supplies the necessary rush of sensation. 'To note the curious hard logic of passion, and the emotional coloured life of the intellect—to observe where they met, and where they separated, at what point they were in unison, and at what point they were at discord—there was a delight in that! What matter what the cost was? One could never pay too high a price for any sensation' (56–7).

The idea is to release our concept of character from any idea of the primacy of experience, from the lingering protocols of the *Bildungsroman. The Picture of Dorian Gray* is a programmatic anti-*Bildung* novella, and its 'scientific analysis of the passions' (58) rests upon a thoroughgoing anti-moralism. 'Experience was of no ethical value. It was merely the name men gave to their mistakes. Moralists had, as a rule, regarded it as a mode of warning, had claimed for it a certain ethical efficacy in the formation of character, had praised it as something that taught us what to follow and showed us what to avoid. But there was no motive power in experience' (58). In the Satanic text of influence and domination, however, character is a result of hard-won victories over material inertia and the social pressures of conformity; it must be fashioned out of 'those irresistible impulses to which the will is subject without recognizing them'.[51] The clay is moulded, the marble carved, by each application of a precise verbal instrument—not to produce a moral subject, but rather to yield delirious affective intensities in the bachelor-scientist. 'I am always ready for a new emotion', sighs Henry Wotton, and Dorian is his vicarious supplier. 'In this way', remarks Sheldon Liebman, 'Dorian becomes one of Henry's multiple selves.'[52]

Dorian's tragedy is not unlike that of the Creature in Mary Shelley's great Gothic novel. Manufactured in the aesthetic laboratory, his inner life animated by literary murmurings, he must confront his derivative status as a character, daily, in the mirror of the portrait, whence stares back at him the evolving physiognomy of his creators' pitiless quests for affect. Basil, having projected his own passionate

[51] Huysmans, *Against Nature*, 155.
[52] Liebman, 'Character Design in *Dorian Gray*', 302.

domination by the Ephebe onto the portrait, and so exorcized it, releases a potential seized upon by Henry in the person of Dorian. When Dorian wonders after Basil's confession 'if he himself would ever be so dominated by the personality of a friend' (117), it is already too late. The 'hideous corruption of his soul' (124) is a collateral effect of Henry's ruthless pursuit of pleasures for which he will not have to pay himself.[53] The experience is all Wotton's and not Dorian's, as Dorian has no accessible character with which to filter and adjust its intensities. He must make do with their visual hypostases on the canvas, those 'characters which carry in them the motto of our Soules' according to Browne. Henry's experiment has been to fashion a character and then separate it from its body, in which gap his own lurid sensations can expand and multiply.

'Dorian', Liebman remarks, 'is a major figure in the development of the modern novel'.[54] He is a 'wonderful creation' whose purpose it is to blast through 'the same wearisome round of stereotyped habits' that atrophies affective spontaneity, and win the precious bourn of a 'perpetual present with a diminishing sense of temporal or indeed phenomenological continuities':[55] 'a world in which things would have fresh shapes and colours, and be changed, or have other secrets, a world in which the past would have little or no place, or survive, at any rate, in no conscious form of obligation or regret'.[56] In a word, Dorian is a palette brush or chisel designed particularly to bring modernism, that 'entirely new manner in art' (10), into our world. The cost to his character is any sense of consistency; the gain to aesthetics is a plethora of new worlds shimmering with affect.

> It was the creation of such worlds as these that seemed to Dorian Gray to be the true object [. . .] of life; and in his search for sensations that would be at once new and delightful, and possess that element of strangeness that is so essential to romance, he would often adopt certain modes of thought that he knew to be really alien to his nature, abandon himself to their subtle influences, and then, having, as it were, caught their colour and satisfied his intellectual curiosity, leave them with that curious indifference that is not incompatible with a real ardour of temperament, and that, indeed, according to certain modern psychologists, is often a condition of it.
>
> (134)

Having discovered this 'method by which we can multiply our personalities' (145), Dorian transcends the ground of the classical novel. His ardour is a function of his

[53] Lord Henry is a sentimentalist. 'For a sentimentalist is simply one who desires to have the luxury of an emotion without paying for it.' Oscar Wilde, *De Profundis and Other Prison Writings*, ed. Colm Tóibín (London: Penguin, 2013), 146.

[54] Liebman, 'Character Design in *Dorian Gray*', 297.

[55] Jameson, *Antinomies of Realism*, 28.

[56] Wilde, *Picture of Dorian Gray*, 21, 134.

insincerity; his romance an avid pursuit of chromaticism and strings of intense singularities. Affect, 'feeding on itself, and perpetuating its own existence' finally trumps experience, becoming the sufficient motive power for a transvaluation of all the inherited values. 'Affects are singularities and intensities, existences rather than essences, which usefully unsettle established psychological and physiological categories.'[57] And with those categories fall the associated characterological ones as a matter of course.

Modern character is simultaneously a shattering of the ego as an organizing centre of moral responsibility—a prising apart of the expressive relationship between soul and face, interior essence and exterior sign—and an admission of that innumerable succession of 'others' whom history has kept in store for the bachelor-machine.

> There were times when it appeared to Dorian Gray that the whole of history was merely the record of his own life, not as he had lived it in act and circumstance, but as his imagination had created it for him, as it had been in his brain and in his passions. He felt that he had known them all, those strange terrible figures that had passed across the stage of the world and made sin so marvellous and evil so full of subtlety. It seemed to him that in some mysterious way their lives had been his own.
>
> (146–7)

'I am all that exists', proclaimed Nietzsche, that inveterate bachelor-machine, while Wilde was planning his novel: 'every name in history is I!'[58] Deleuze and Guattari clarify that 'It is not a matter of identifying with various historical personages, but rather identifying the names of history with zones of intensity on the body without organs; and each time Nietzsche-as-subject exclaims: "They're *me*! So it's *me*!" [. . .] He consumes all of history in one fell swoop.'[59] Dorian's egregious 'ancestors in literature' are superimposed on the plastic substance of his 'rose-white boyhood' (226) where they balloon into three dimensions—the only depth of character he will attain. The one thing they have in common, these Filippos and Viscontis, Malatestas and Baglionis, rays of sheer affective brilliance dancing prismatically over the surface of Dorian's soul, is their resolute distance from and opposition to the pedestrian middle class. After all, *il faut être absolument moderne*, and as Lord Henry puts it emphatically, 'the middle classes are not modern' (77). Having tarried for two centuries with these insufferable puritans and pedants, in an effort to pattern its formal modernity on their material achievements, the novel had at last

[57] Jameson, *Antinomies of Realism*, 36.

[58] Friedrich Nietzsche, letter to Jakob Burckhardt, 6 January 1889, in *Selected Letters of Friedrich Nietzsche*, trans. Christopher Middleton (Chicago: University of Chicago Press, 1969), 347.

[59] Gilles Deleuze and Félix Guattari, *Anti-Oedipus: Capitalism and Schizophrenia*, trans. Robert Hurley, Mark Seem, and Helen R. Lane (Minneapolis: University of Minnesota Press, 1983), 21.

to abandon its post. Modern character lay elsewhere. If Huysmans' obloquy upon the bourgeoisie shared 'numerous similarities to anarchist ideology',[60] Wilde had openly committed himself by 1894: 'We are all of us more or less Socialists now-a-days.... I think I am rather more than a Socialist. I am something of an Anarchist, I believe, but, of course, the dynamite policy is very absurd indeed.'[61] *The Picture of Dorian Gray* applies its own formal dynamite to the teetering edifice of bourgeois characterology to release energies and possibilities that will ripple across the next several decades.

[60] Richard Shryock, '*Ce Cri rompit le cauchemar qui l'opprimait*: Huysmans and the Politics of *A rebours*', *The French Review* 66.2 (December 1992), 252 [243–54].

[61] Wilde speaking to Almy, 'New Views of Mr O.W.', in *Theatre* (1894), 124; qtd. in Ellmann, *Oscar Wilde*, 290n.

6
D'Annunzio

The 'decadence' of a Huysmans or a Wilde, with its basis in the rapid commercial break-up of a lingering organic sense of feudal order in France and the United Kingdom, acquired in Italy a more acute political spin. After centuries of foreign occupation and rule, Italian culture was by and large the mythic property of a perilously thin urban stratum of literate men and women, antennae turned to the West and North, insisting on the grandeur of Ancient Rome and the spirit of the Renaissance, as the heroic days of 1861 were frittered away by decades of political disorder. As Marja Härmänmaa puts it, at the turn of the century 'Italy's unification was largely considered "incomplete", because it failed to create a truly national spirit',[1] and that incompleteness was fatally imprinted on the psyche of a generation. A symptom of this lapse of national character is the absence of any national press as late as 1890, when Gabriele D'Annunzio first emigrated from the barbarous Abruzzo to take up his role as a columnist for the Roman daily *La Tribuna*. Here the provincial prodigy used the new capital's developed means of literary production as 'a near-national stage on which to begin to forge his own persona'.[2] He did so not as one but as many. 'In his articles published in Roman newspapers [. . .] D'Annunzio wrote, hidden behind a multitude of pseudonyms (Happemouche, Vere de Vere, Il Duca Minimo, Lila Biscuit, etc.), about Roman high society.'[3] His literary persona was, from the start, a flamboyant voice 'diffracté [en plusieurs personnages], usant de contrepersonnages, de doubles, d'opposants'.[4] His work as a social chronicler and gossip columnist gave him a unique vantage on the incomplete project of unification, as the ostentatious new bourgeoisie failed to find any common ground with the older nobility immured behind impenetrable palace walls, and the city merchants and nascent proletariat bore little sensible relation to the vast surrounding peasantry.

But it also forced him back upon himself as a medium in which the *membra disjecta* of an incomplete national experiment might find some temporary

[1] Marja Härmänmaa, 'Anatomy of the Superman: Gabriele D'Annunzio's Response to Nietzsche', *The European Legacy: Toward New Paradigms* 24.1 (2019), 63 [59–75].

[2] Giuliana Pieri, 'Gabriele D'Annunzio and the Self-Fashioning of a National Icon', *Modern Italy* 21.4 (2016), 330 [329–43].

[3] Monica Jansen, Srećko Jurišić, and Carmen Van den Bergh, 'Life as Art, Art as Life, and Life's Art: The "Living Poetics" of Italian Modernism', *Arcadia* 51.1 (2016), 27 [24–45].

[4] '. . . diffracted [into several characters], using counter-characters, doubles, antagonists'. Jérôme Meizoz, *Postures littéraires. Mises en scène modernes de l'auteur. Essai* (Genève: Slatkine érudition, 2007), 28.

Modern Character. Julian Murphet, Oxford University Press. © Julian Murphet (2023).
DOI: 10.1093/oso/9780192863126.003.0007

accommodation—'d'Annunzio as Italy's foremost aesthete and dandy; a modern *arbiter elegantiarum*, whose impeccable and exquisite taste became the hallmark of the poet throughout his life'.[5] No less a judge than Henry James was inspired to declare in 1902 that, 'ostensibly, transcendently, Signor D'Annunzio's *is* the most developed taste in the world'.[6] Taste, then, proved a useful substitute for character, which he lacked radically; a way of promoting a plausible persona without any *ethos*. The young poet's '*sacro egoismo*' was deployed as a self-conscious strategy for managing (and masking), both ideologically and rhetorically, an insufficient quantity of objective unity, in the nation and in himself—forcing it through the impress of a singular sense of style.[7] Here we must pause to remark some correspondences between Italy's epic poet of the Ego and Sweden's. Strindberg was, like D'Annunzio, an early convert to Naturalism, and as passionate a defector from the cause under the impetus of Symbolism. Like D'Annunzio he moved indiscriminately between essays, poems, novels, memoirs, and works for theatre; all heavily marked by the obsessive and recurrent concerns of the author. He, too, wrestled extensively with the raw material of personal lived experience, fashioning it into a string of luminous artworks in which the figure of the artist is invariably perceived, thinly veiled in characterological guise and excruciated: 'the Egotist as a divine figure on the Cross', as D. H. Lawrence would put it, associating the image directly with 'D'Annunzio and the Strindberg set'.[8] Each of them discovered Nietzsche at a crucial moment in his trajectory as a writer, drawing on the philologist's baroque psychology to frame an image of the modern *stultus*. But the question of taste arises as a significant disjunction between these two otherwise aligned artists: D'Annunzio's excess of it proved unnecessary to the Swedish artist who discovered better reasons to eschew it altogether, in the unholy war he waged against his nation's self-satisfied middle class.

D'Annunzio's highly refined sensibility was an instrument for governing and reconciling the heteroclite particulars of a dissociated national culture. Taste was here the sovereign faculty of experience, disciplining the proliferating sensory qualities that besieged a detached and disinterested observer. 'Life is not an abstraction of aspects and events, but a sort of diffused sensuousness, a knowledge offered to all the senses, a substance good to touch, smell, taste, feel. In fact, I feel all the things near to my senses', he wrote in 1915, in a manner that encapsulates

[5] Pieri, 'Gabriele D'Annunzio', 331.

[6] Henry James, 'Gabriele D'Annunzio', in *Literary Criticism: French Writers, Other European Writers, The Prefaces to the New York Edition*, ed. Leon Edel (New York: Library of America, 1984), 925 [907–43].

[7] Theodor W. Adorno, 'Richard Strauss', *Perspectives of New Music* 4.1 (Fall/Winter 1965), 15 [14–32].

[8] D. H. Lawrence, letter to Gordon Campbell, 19 December 1914, *Collected Letters of D. H. Lawrence, Vol. 1*, ed. Harry T. Moore (London: Heinemann, 1962), 301.

his aesthetic feeling for atomized sensation.[9] What James called D'Annunzio's 'rare notation of states of excited sensibility', his virtuosic way with 'the play of sensibility from end to end of the scale'[10] thus turns on this exceptional category. Without taste, such exquisite sensitivity to sensory phenomena might well dissolve the subject, rendering him (like *La trionfo della morte*'s Giorgio Aurispa) 'un mero flusso di sensazioni, di emozioni, di idee, privo d'ogni fondamento sostanziale'.[11] Taste intervenes with the whip-hand capable of ordering this diffuse and threatening maelstrom of qualia; while in its absence, 'I nervi lo dominavano, gli imponevano il disordine e l'eccesso delle loro sensazioni.'[12]

The sign of taste in the text itself is, of course, its sumptuous commitment to *style*. 'I have such a sensitive ear', he complained, 'that the repetition of a word irritates me three pages away. [. . .] I am and I wish to be above all a stylist. Compare any page of mine with that of any contemporary Italian writer and you will see the difference.'[13] The 'whole thing', wrote James of *Le vergini delle rocce* (1895), 'is in the largest sense but a theme for style, style of substance as well as of form'.[14] D'Annunzio had wanted, in this novel above all others, to indite 'a work of style presenting the character of a great symphony through which the four themes of Hair, Hands, Waters and Rocks move like ever-recurring melodies'.[15] But the effort is general, and its effect is uniquely sonorous and rhythmic. Transposing the criteria of taste—value, sensibility, aesthetics, discrimination—onto the singular voice that runs through the various texts, becomes a well-nigh musical exercise. The Italian language's 'musical elements, various and powerful enough to compare with the great Wagnerian orchestras', would permit the most exorbitant chromaticisms of writerly style, not strictly tethered to the material but floating serenely above it.[16] Sense is subordinated to sound; 'l'opera e' il prodotto dell'intelligenza tecnica. Il significato conta poco. Il valore semantico tende a sparire e la creazione artistica diventa esercizio barocco.'[17] As Michael Syrimis explains, 'aestheticism and

[9] D'Annunzio, from an article published in English in *The Daily Telegraph*, 29 December 1915, entitled 'A Poet's Adventures: Laying Mines on an enemy's Coast'. Qtd. in Stefano Bragato, 'Of Attention: D'Annunzio's Sixth Sense', *Forum italicum* 51.2 (2017), 397 [396–412].

[10] James, 'Gabriele D'Annunzio', 914, 915.

[11] '[A] mere flux of sensations, of emotions, of ideas, without any substantial ground'. Gabriele D'Annunzio, *Trionfo della morte* (Milan: Fratelli Treves, 1894), 381.

[12] 'His nerves dominated him, imposed on him the disorder and excess of their sensations.' D'Annunzio, *Trionfo della morte*, 167.

[13] D'Annunzio, qtd. in Anthony Rhodes, *The Poet as Superman: A Life of Gabriele D'Annunzio* (London: Weidenfeld & Nicolson, 1959), 46.

[14] James, 'Gabriele D'Annunzio', 934.

[15] D'Annunzio, qtd. in Philippe Jullian, *D'Annunzio*, trans. Stephen Hardman (New York: Viking Press, 1973), 98.

[16] D'Annunzio, qtd. in Rhodes, *Poet as Superman*, 30.

[17] '[T]he work is the product of technical intelligence. Meaning matters little. The semantic value tends to disappear and artistic creation becomes a baroque exercise.' Giovanni Gullace, 'D'Annunzio teorico dell'arte e della critica', *Annali d'Italianistica* 5 (1987), 22 [21–41].

musicality are essential in D'Annunzio's style'.[18] '[T]he virtue of style', D'Annunzio claimed in 'Il romanzo futuro', 'will be a virtue of pure creation. Style will no longer look like a literary exercise, but almost a direct continuation of life',[19] provided 'life' is understood as an incessant detonation of quivering intensities. The artist's 'exalted Symbolist style'[20] is, then, a reckoning with multiplicity and sensory variety, not at the level of concept or narrative design, but sheerly as musicality (rhythm and timbre, tonality and pitch) and lexical innovation (unique verbal clusters, odd words, striking images), stamped with a recognizable temperament holding the performance together.

What we will want to map in what follows is the trajectory of the D'Annunzian protagonist-figure, 'a transcendent young man—always pretty much the same young man',[21] as he morphs from a high decadent into a Nietzschean prophet of the Overman. Later critics have tended to concur with James: 'condemned to a monotonous and oppressive repetition, his is an illusory fecundity. D'Annunzio's heroes, male and female, all have the same flesh [. . .]. In their verbose falsity, their maniacal hyperboles and obsessive repetitions, their boundless nullity of useless and sick beings, his heroes are a portrait of D'Annunzio himself, the "superlative histrion". This is why D'Annunzian characters of whatever sex, age, and condition all have the same voice, the voice of their author refractory to every idea and every ideal.'[22] The Strindbergian deployment of the novel form (*The Red Room*, *Son of a Servant*, *Defence of a Fool*, *Inferno*) as a quasi-fictionalized self-anatomy transplanted itself to Italian soil and established a break in the history of fictional characterization. Never before had a series of protagonists so obviously been offered as avatars of the single, evolving persona of their author; and this had consequences for the form and its character system. The multi-volume progress of this protagonist is charted against an unhappy novelistic backdrop, or what James calls 'the almost complete absence of other contacts to which D'Annunzio systematically condemns his creatures'.[23] That radical deficiency of broader social relations or any meaningful collective project is manifest in a tightly constricted cast of dramatis personae. The abiding paradox is consistent and symptomatic: the larger and more imposing the represented Ego, the more threadbare and abstract the character space onto which it is projected. Time and again, D'Annunzio's protagonists are absorbed into 'the cult of personality that he himself crafted', avatars of a distributed consciousness that touches down in the novels only where some major

[18] Michael Syrimis, *The Great Black Spider on Its Knock-kneed Tripod: Reflections of Cinema in Early Twentieth Century Italy* (Toronto: University of Toronto Press, 2012), 14.

[19] D'Annunzio, qtd. in Bragato, 'Of Attention', 400.

[20] Fernando Esposito, *Fascism, Aviation and Mythical Modernity* (Basingstoke: Palgrave Macmillan, 2015), 80.

[21] James, 'Gabriele D'Annunzio', 932.

[22] P. Giuseppe Venturini, 'Spiritualita e religiosita di D'Annunzio', *Quaderni de Vittoriale* 4, Special Issue: D'Annunzio e Jung (July–August 1980), 43 [39–74].

[23] James, 'Gabriele D'Annunzio', 921.

stylistic effort is at stake.[24] This has the very curious effect, in a textual environment entirely mediated by that ambient taste and style, of vitiating the substance of the hero, along the lines first adumbrated by James' early review: 'It would be difficult perhaps to find elsewhere in the same compass so much expression of the personal life resting so little on any picture of the personal character and the personal will.'[25] The absence of anything like a mature novelistic plot—of sophisticated narrative teleology, reversals of fortune, an evolved actant-system, subsidiary and countervailing story arcs, and so on—deprives the text of its nuanced 'picture of personal character' and 'personal will', despite the many rhetorical assertions of these elements. In place of character, we find an abundance of attitude, pose, style; in place of concerted action, we discover heady annunciations of 'the will' that crash upon the wider social world like so much weightless sea-foam. And over the arc of D'Annunzio's brief novel-writing career, this deficiency transforms from the satiric thrust of a decadent critique of high society into an out-and-out affirmation of the need for a new type of 'hero' to undertake 'the gesture of resistance and self-distancing from social demands' appropriate to the Nietzschean artist-god.[26] The central character of these texts is one who has reneged on the world because it has reneged on him; it is a new sort of protagonist, one who, like his author, is full of the sound and fury of a noble will, but remains 'almost ideologically inclined to dispersion. The artist's self-dissolution is in itself the last stage of an evaporation of sense extended to all levels in his novels.'[27] If he resists this centrifugal dissipation, he will do so purely as a matter of style.

Il Piacere

In *Il piacere* (1889), his first completed novel, D'Annunzio attempts a trenchant critique of a social stratum, the idle rich, that had served as the *objet du désir* of his early journalism.[28] But he also seeks to reimagine the form of the novel itself, setting himself the task of starting anew after the 'total abolition of literary tradition.'[29] '[T]his is what D'Annunzio intended when he wrote *Il piacere*, a completely new

[24] Lara Gochin Raffaelli and Michael Subialka, 'Introduction: D'Annunzio's Beauty, Reawakened', *Forum italicum* 51.2 (2017), 313 [311–34].

[25] James, 'Gabriele D'Annunzio', 912.

[26] Jeffrey Schnapp, Translator's Introduction to D'Annunzio, 'The Beast Who Wills', first published in *Il Mattino (di Napoli)*, 25–26 September 1892; reprinted in Thomas Harrison, ed., *Nietzsche in Italy* (Saratoga: Anma Libri, 1988), 267.

[27] Giulia Ricca, 'Like an Alchemist: The Artist between D'Annunzio and Joyce', *MLN* 132.1 (2017), 126 [121–34].

[28] 'I study, with sadness, so much corruption and so much depravity and so much deviousness and falsity and futile cruelty.' D'Annunzio, qtd. in Lucy Hughes-Hallett, *The Pike, Gabriele D'Annunzio: Poet, Seducer and Preacher of War* (London: Fourth Estate, 2013), 178. The novel was literally worked up, in the first instance, from his notes as a society columnist. See Rhodes, *Poet as Superman*, 31.

[29] D'Annunzio, qtd. in Hughes-Hallett, *The Pike*, 177.

form of novel, with diction—decadent prose—never used before—that projected the *lettore futuro* into the new era.'[30] Impatient with the epistemological rigours of satire, *Il piacere* vaults easily into a fantasy of an upper class its author scarcely knew apart from its graceful social manners and auctioned bibelots. Moving determinedly away from the '*verismo*' of his early short stories, D'Annunzio was less concerned with accurate social portraiture than he was with atmosphere, mood, and tone. For the first time, as Croce wrote, 'risuonô nella letteratura italiana una nota fino ad allora estranea, sensualistica, ferina, decadente'.[31] If the book 'reveal[s] the inanity of a self-indulgent upper-middle class and a bourgeois logic of reification', it does so with a superficial eye for class analysis.[32]

Its animus is directed principally at the urban lower middle class; but this is an ambivalent disdain. At the culminating scene in the auction room, we are besieged by 'traders, secondhand furniture sellers, junk dealers: common people. As there were no connoisseurs around in summer, the dealers were rushing there, sure of acquiring precious objects at low prices. A bad odor spread through the warm air, emanating from those impure men' (324).[33] That 'bad air', the palpable stench of the petit bourgeoisie, is a kind of miasma through which the eyes of the text strain to see what remains of the noble world, a mercantile fog liquidating the cultivated habitus of the gentry. But it is that liquidation which brings close to the senses the very objects—'pieces of furniture made of carved wood and some large triptychs and diptychs of the Tuscan school of the fourteenth century; four Flemish tapestries representing the Story of Narcissus', etcetera (59)—out of which the supremely tasteful world of the text is woven. The narrative's disgust for the 'common people' who trade these objects for money is a structural disavowal of the fetishism it shares with them. If for the merchants these treasures of the nobility are convertible to aliquot parts of the substance—money—that will save Italia from its backwardness, for the narrator they are the materials on which his discriminating faculty, taste, can go to work and so make an international literary career out of the 'prolific eclecticism [and] long catalogues of descriptions' that define literary decadence.[34] If 'D'Annunzio's descriptions are often mere inventories, painfully minute, like a mosaic with millions of little word cubes—a multiplicity of words', then that is a studied and artful declaration of aesthetic principles that builds on

[30] Moira Di Mauro-Jackson, 'D'Annunzio's *Il piacere*: A Generational Gaze on New Values', *Forum italicum* 51.2 (2017), 526 [525–48].

[31] '[A] hitherto foreign, sensualistic, feral, decadent note resounded in Italian literature.' Benedetto Croce, qtd. in Renato Barilli, *D'Annunzio in prosa* (Milan: Mursia Editore, 1993), 42.

[32] Michaela Barisonzi, 'Mother Italy: The Female Role in the Rebirth of Italian Nationalism in Gabriele D'Annunzio's *Le Vergini delle Rocce*', *Studi d'Italianistica nell'Africa Australe* 28.1 (2015), 32 [22–48].

[33] In Italian: Gabriele D'Annunzio, *Il piacere*, a cura di Giansiro Ferrata (Rome: Arnoldo Mondadori, 1974), 422.

[34] Raffaelli and Subialka, 'Introduction', 326.

the 'molecular' Flaubertian instance to forge a pathway into the twentieth century.[35] The name of that pathway is *commodification*, and Adorno liked to insist that 'the sensations of Wilde, d'Annunzio, and Maeterlinck [...] served as preludes to the culture industry. Progressive subjective differentiation, the heightening and expansion of the sphere of aesthetic stimuli, made these stimuli manipulable; they were able to be produced for the cultural marketplace.'[36] D'Annunzio's style is the manipulation of an object-world thrown onto the auction block, where it is 'bought back' at interest, as style, for a spiritual nobility to come.

Like the narrator, the Roman protagonist, Count Andrea Sperelli, 'mirrors himself in the "*Roma delle ville, delle fontane, delle chiese*", [and] creatively fashions his own identity in reference to it'—but only fitfully.[37] This 'literary descendant from the duke Des Esseintes'[38] is animated, too, by a 'disgust for the commonplace, the popular, the uncouth, the democratic',[39] and in the force of that recoil he has lapsed from any consistent identity: 'it [. . .] seemed to him that he had been reduced to nothing; and he shivered in the face of the great empty abyss of his being: [...] his entire past, his entire present dissolved; they detached themselves from his consciousness and fell, like a fragile slough, an empty garment'.[40] This is the open fault line where we detect a 'clear and distinct separation between narrator and main character', and whence 'modern character' as such draws its nutrients.[41] D'Annunzio himself, a lambent presence throughout, is expert at depicting such dissolution without falling victim to it; his characterization of his protagonist turns, as so often in his oeuvre, on a stylized negation or liquidation of qualities. The mellifluous Italian—*si dissolvevano; si distaccavano*—chimes with the general subsidence of salience here, as the metaphors take wing and the personality decomposes before our eyes. Sperelli may be theoretically true to his father's Nietzschean dictum, which dovetails with the official programme of decadence: 'One must *fashion* one's life, as one fashions a work of art. A man's life must be of his own making. This is where true superiority lies' (35). But there is very little self-fashioning at work here, as the Roman *stultus* drifts desultorily from assignation to auction, steeplechase to duel, lover to lover.[42] Rather than forcibly making

[35] Rhodes, *Poet as Superman*, 45. Jacques Rancière makes the case for Flaubert's style as a 'molecular'. See Jacques Rancière, *The Politics of Literature*, trans. Julie Rose (Cambridge: Polity, 2011), 26.

[36] Theodor W. Adorno, *Aesthetic Theory*, ed. Gretel Adorno and Rolf Tiedemann, trans. Robert Hullot-Kentor (London: Continuum, 2002), 239.

[37] Luca Cottini, 'D'Annunzio, Bernini, and the Baroque Prelude of *Il piacere*', *Forum italicum* 51.2 (2017), 343 [335–55].

[38] Jansen, Jurišić, and Van den Bergh, 'Life as Art, Art as Life', 29.

[39] Raffaelli and Subialka, 'Introduction', 323.

[40] Gabriele D'Annunzio, *Pleasure*, trans. Lara Gochin Raffaelli (London: Penguin Classics, 2013), 26; *Il piacere*, 98.

[41] Mauro-Jackson, 'D'Annunzio's *Il piacere*', 536.

[42] On the *stultus*, see Michel Foucault, *Discourse and Truth and Parrhesia*, ed. Daniele Lorenzini, Henri-Paul Fruchaud, and Nancy Luxton, trans. Nancy Luxton (Chicago: University of Chicago Press, 2019), 29; and Michel Foucault, *Hermeneutics of the Subject: Lectures at the Collège de France, 1981–1982*, ed. Frédéric Gros, trans. Graham Burchell (New York: Palgrave Macmillan, 2005), 133.

himself, he is passively susceptible to every stray datum of sense perception: 'The sensitivity of his nerves was so acute that every minimal sensation that came to him from external things felt like a deep wound [. . .]. The clusters of sensations would suddenly pass through his spirit, [. . .]; and they disturbed and alarmed him' (75). His one true dedication, to pleasure itself, contributes to his inner disorganization, Adorno's 'subjective differentiation', since it encourages stunted powers of reflection. The result is perhaps the high-water mark of decadent stultification, the modern subject framed as Plato's 'excitable and multicolored character' without sufficient rationality to bind it into unity.[43]

The following passage is a prototypical D'Annunzian characterization:

> No longer able to conform itself, adapt itself, assimilate itself to a superior dominating form, his soul, chameleon-like, mutable, fluid, virtual, transformed itself, deformed itself, took on every form. [. . .] The habit of falsity blunted his conscience. Due to the continuous absence of reflection, he gradually became impenetrable to himself, remained outside his mystery. Little by little he almost reached the stage of no longer seeing his inner life, in the way that the external hemisphere of the earth does not see the sun, despite being tied indissolubly to it. One instinct was always alive, ruthlessly alive in him: the instinct of detachment from everything that attracted him without binding him. And his will, as useless as a badly tempered sword, dangled as at the side of a Jew or a paralyzed man. (95–6)[44]

That striking final simile, which caught the admiring eye of Henry James,[45] clinches the truth that, for Sperelli, such 'superiority' as crowns the application of will to one's inner life must remain a distant fantasy. In its suspension, 'his forces returned to their original disorder [*al primitivo disordine*]' (95).

The disorder of *stultitia* is *primitivo* indeed ('d'Annunzio's primitivism is striking and obvious').[46] It is rooted not in the person but in the disorganized flux of phenomena for which the named persona is merely a screen. This great novel of Rome which takes an extended vacation in the villa of Shifanoja (a glorified version of D'Annunzio's natal home in the Abruzzi), places the subject on an existential sliding scale from the '*grandi abissi vacui*' to the oceanic Whitmanisms of the Upanishads: *Hae omnes creaturae in totum ego sum, et praeter me aliud ens non est* [I am all this creation collectively and besides me there exists no other being] (124)—between the dandy's instinct of detachment and the mystic's instinct

[43] Plato, *Republic* X, 605a, trans. G. M. A. Grube and C. D. C. Reeve, in John M. Cooper, ed., *Plato: Complete Works* (Indianapolis: Hackett, 1997), 1209.

[44] Italian: D'Annunzio, *Il piacere*, 174–5.

[45] James, 'Gabriele D'Annunzio', 914.

[46] Jessica Susan Wood, 'Portraits of the Artist: Dionysian Creativity in Selected Works by Gabriele D'Annunzio and Thomas Mann' (PhD dissertation, Department of Modern Languages, University of Birmingham, 2015), 145.

of total immersion, between the city and the countryside. In the urban, a riot of becomings and a general nullity; in the rural seat, a pantheist egotism: 'Instead of transmuting into other forms of existence, or placing himself in different states of consciousness or losing his particular being in general life, he [... wrapped] himself up in a nature that was a completely subjective conception of his intellect' (126). Between these two poles there is no space for social relations. Even erotic relations are subsumed within the overarching dualism, for this is also the choice between his two privileged love-objects, the voluptuous and sensual Elena Muti and the sacred and intellectual Donna Maria Ferres y Capdevila: a carnal dissolution of self, or a spiritual exaltation? As so often in D'Annunzio's narratives, the barely existent plot boils down to 'the supreme moment of salvation or of perdition, the decisive moment' of Choice (229), which is the only action of which the protagonist is capable—as it is the expression of the solitary active quality he possesses, namely taste. Invariably, however, he chooses badly, because he cannot avoid the feeling that the Choice has already been made for him. There looms beneath the anticipated application of will a far deeper determinism, of passion and instinct, that the aesthete cannot finally resist. What James saw as the underlying 'problem' of D'Annunzio's work, its invariable lapses of taste, is in fact the whole of its narrative substance. Where the Ego is, the Id shall go.

Pleasure itself, specifically sexual pleasure, subverts a rounded psychology, which the text cannot inscribe because it is soundly shaken by the pleasure principle.[47] The carnal body is the refuge and alibi of a fugitive characterization, effective precisely to the extent that it has been left out of most serious fiction since Rabelais; a lightning rod driven into the text, it can pass as a sign of selfhood. As Adorno put it, 'In Jugendstil, sex fills the place of inwardness. It has recourse to sex because only there does the private individual encounter himself or herself not as inward but as corporeal. This applies to all Jugendstil art, from Ibsen to Maeterlinck and D'Annunzio.'[48] The 'progressive' element of this substitution consists in its universality; 'D'Annunzio demonstrates his modernity in *Il piacere*, not only in recognising an equal sexual drive in men and women as a basis for desire, but also [...] he rejects the idea of sickness, commonly attributed in the nineteenth century to those women considered sexually proactive.'[49] James himself remarked, breathlessly, the degree to which Giuliana in *L'Innocente* (1892) is 'a creature of organs,

[47] Samuel Beckett remarked of D'Annunzio that 'He has a dirty juicy squelchy mind, bleeding and bursting, like his celebrated pomegranates.' Letter of 7 July 1930, in *The Letters of Samuel Beckett, Vol. 1: 1929–1940*, ed. Martha Dow Fehsenfeld and Lois Lore Overbeck (Cambridge: Cambridge University Press, 2009), 41.

[48] Theodor W. Adorno, letter to Walter Benjamin, 2–4 August 1935, in Howard Eiland and Michael W. Jennings, eds., *Walter Benjamin: Selected Writings, Vol. 3: 1935–1938* (Cambridge, MA: Belknap Press of Harvard University Press, 2002), 60.

[49] Michela Barisonzi, 'The Death of the Angel: Games of Seduction and Moral Destruction in Gabriele D'Annunzio's *Il piacere*', *MLN* 130.1, Italian Issue (January 2015), 130 [124–44].

functions and processes, palpable, audible, pitiful physical conditions';[50] her scandalous corporeality here registering for the Anglo-American author as a peak in Darien. But then of course, 'fear for the integrity of the male body is an aspect of all of D'Annunzio's writings'[51]—a misogynist horror stimulated by the very object it most desires, 'so weak, so sickly, so imperfect, irremediably equal to the females of the beasts by the laws of nature which impose on them the duties of the Species'.[52]

L'Innocente

Tullio Hermil, 'the ideologist, the analyst, the sophist of an epoch of decadence', and the lead character of *L'Innocente*, marks a progression from his predecessor's *stultitia*, for he has become an 'alchemist' of the soul, 'combining the several products of my mind' the way an expert might mix chemicals or scents, in the interest of 'increasing the intensity of the sensations that I wished to experience'.[53] This '*dilettante di sensazioni*' (as Croce said of D'Annunzio[54]) pursues a scientific refinement of affective states that is incompatible with morality, at the expense of his devoted wife Giuliana's emotional health. Again, the application of a superior taste lapses irrevocably into narrative tastelessness, as these exquisite voluptuary pleasures and delicious stings of conscience are sought for in the most vulgar quarters. Yet there is no question of somehow reverting to the moral law and becoming merely conventional, as the 'several products of his mind' are too numerous to be straitjacketed by any norm. In one of the author's great diagnoses of modern character, we read of:

> an illogical, fragmentary, incoherent life. There were in him all kinds of tendencies, the possibility of every opposite, and, between these opposites, an infinity of intermediary degrees, and, between these tendencies, an infinity of combinations. According to the weather and according to the place, according to the accidental shock of circumstances, of an insignificant fact, of a word, according to the inner influences, even still more obscure, the permanent basis of his being assumed the most changing, the most fugitive, the strangest aspects. In him a special organic condition corresponded to every special tendency while strengthening it, and this tendency became a centre of attraction toward which converged all the conditions and tendencies directly associated, and the association spread further and further. Then his centre of gravity was displaced; his personality was changed

[50] James, 'Gabriele D'Annunzio', 922.

[51] Derek Duncan, 'Choice Objects: The Bodies of Gabriele D'Annunzio', *Italian Studies* 52.1 (1997), 135 [131–50].

[52] Gabriele D'Annunzio, *The Intruder* [*L'Innocente*], trans. Arthur Hornblow (Boston: L. C. Page, 1897), 15–16.

[53] D'Annunzio, *The Intruder*, 153, 26.

[54] Benedetto Croce, qtd. in Jansen, Jurišić, and Van den Bergh, 'Life as Art, Art as Life', 26.

> to another personality. Silent floods of blood and ideas caused to blossom on the permanent basis of his being, either gradually or all at once, new souls. He became multanime.
>
> (27)

There is nothing the text, or the protagonist, can do to overcome this condition, apart from flood it with affective intensities that have the momentary effect of stilling the fissiparous and protean swarm of beings that constitute the 'I'. The sensibility under the microscope here is one that is infinitely suggestible, sensitive, determined, in ways clearly recognizable from the Naturalist tradition ('according to the weather and the place', 'floods of blood'), but now dropped into a stylistic kaleidoscope where the soul or character is revealed anew as a cascading multitude of curious shapes. Thus anatomized, Tullio discovers that by alternating his sexual current between the devout wife and the absent lover he can create something like an electrical field dynamically surcharging the *uomo multanime*: 'This parallelism gave to my inner life an incredible intensity and acceleration' (36). More and more intensity; greater and greater acceleration—the production of affect knows no limit here.

> A multitude of sensations, involuntary, spontaneous, unconscious, and instinctive, made up my real existence. Between the exterior and the interior there was established a play of minute actions and instantaneous minute reactions, that vibrated in endless repercussions, and each one of these incalculable repercussions became converted into an astonishing psychic phenomenon. My entire being was modified by the slightest odor of the circumambient atmosphere, by a breath, by a shadow, by a flash of light.
>
> (56–7)

What need for any plausible social space when the phenomenal realm is so stuffed and various, and when the narrative voice has enough to do to record it? To be sure, a melodramatic novelistic machinery is put in place to organize this extraordinary material into a form that at least provides it with a semblance of closure: Giuliana pursues her own desire, falls pregnant to another man's progeny, which threatens to usurp the Hermil family name (the couple has only two daughters); and so the familial hearth is restored and defended jealously by Tullio who dooms the human cuckoo to an infant death. But the plot limps along as an afterthought to the rhapsodically realized condition of a character so attuned to his inner multitude that he verily anticipates Septimus Warren Smith:

> And all these flowers shed by the elms, that rained, rained ceaselessly, all these dead flowers, almost unreal, almost bereft of being, induced in me an inexpressible sensation, as if that psychic vision were transformed in me into strange

> internal phenomena, as if I had been present at the continuous passage of these thousands of impalpable shadows in an inner sky, at the bottom of my soul. (77)

Affective chromaticism has rarely been so exhilaratingly pursued for its own sake as in this threadbare excuse for a novel, which prefers to chase the intensities as they rain ceaselessly from phenomena, creating in the music of its prose rare scintillations of tone and shimmers of overtone, than to force these 'strange internal phenomena' into something as pedestrian as a self. Modern character is the 'inexpressible sensation' created by 'thousands of impalpable shadows' cast on an 'inner sky', a radiant void opened by the vacation of the self.

Trionfo della morte

If *Trionfo della morte* (1894) remains D'Annunzio's masterpiece it is because the autobiographical elements remain nearest to the surface, and least subject to this author's clumsy attempts at satire or narrative judgement.[55] This is autobiography as phenomenology. As he promises in his manifesto-like Preface, the protagonist here, Giorgio Aurispa, is presented in more comprehensive phenomenal detail than any literary character hitherto:

> The play of actions and reactions between his sensibility and the external world is established through a precise web of direct observations. His feelings, his ideas, his tastes, his habits do not vary according to the incidents of a page-turning adventure, aided by an exact logic; but present the true character of an organic life, consisting of a definite balance between what changes and what is stable, between fixed forms and fleeting, illogical forms. A sensation, a sentiment, appearing on the first pages, is then developed—according to the laws that govern phenomena—through a forest of innumerable signs that all correspond to one and the same understanding and insightful soul.[56]

As it appears to him in the midst of his own story, 'The innumerable phenomena that, instant by instant, succeeded one another in his inner world made the comprehensive power of his soul appear to be illimitable.'[57] The narrative that is

[55] 'It is a novel in which the author's own love letters are quoted verbatim, and one which describes in exact detail the place in which it was first written. D'Annunzio told Romain Rolland that it was "not imaginary at all".' Hughes-Hallett, *The Pike*, 167.

[56] Gabriele D'Annunzio, *Il trionfo della morte*, 2nd ed. (Milan: Fratelli Treves, 1896), vi–vii. My translation.

[57] Gabriele D'Annunzio, *The Triumph of Death*, trans. Arthur Hornblow (New York: Richmond & Co., 1897), 282. ['I fenomeni innumerevoli che si succedevano nel suo mondo interiore, d'attimo in attimo, gli facevano apparire illimitata la potenza comprensiva della sua anima.']. D'Annunzio, *Trionfo*, 329.

strung together to allow this exceptionally developed sensibility to unfurl its ornate physiognomy is episodic, in a manner that will come to characterize literary modernism: the individual parts are discrete, folded in on themselves, and each features a 'sensational' focal point.[58] This is a feature remarked by James in one of the earliest adumbrations of this tendency—'Each of his volumes offers thus its little gallery of episodes that stand out like the larger pearls occurring at intervals on a string of beads'[59]—but it reaches its apotheosis here in *Trionfo*. The episodes include a lurid visit to the family home in the Chietian town of Guardiagrele (another version of D'Annunzio's Pescara in the Abruzzo); a lovers' weekend in Albano-Laziale; a suicide off the Pincian cliff; the drowning of a peasant boy in the Adriatic; the parade of frenzied supplicants at the House of the Virgin outside Casalbordino; the ecstatic immersion in *Tristan und Isolde*; and the final murder-suicide. Each of them, set pieces all, presents a risk and a temptation to the protagonist, who experiences them as specific moments in a general dissolution of identity and agency, and the creeping, wishful 'triumph of death' that Freud will theorize only after the First World War.[60]

For instance, the trip to Guardiagrele—one of the great contributions to modern prose made by this extraordinary writer—toys with all the appeals of nostalgia and the national fetish for *la Mama*; but stonily refuses all the expected sentiment with a prevailing mood of disgust. Giorgio's outward character is shown in its provincial, genetic aspect, but his exposure to other, Roman, currents of modernity have corroded the familial ties to such an extent that what is presented to us, through his alienated eyes, is only a congeries of grotesques. The toothless crone of an aunt with her insatiable appetite for confectionery; the surly stupid younger brother; and *Mama* herself, sadly altered beyond recognition. As it is with his mother, so it is with the hero: 'he did not succeed in filling the interval between the *I* of long ago and the *I* of to-day' (53). The voyage to the past is non-conciliatory to the extent that it only reveals the rifts and inconsistencies within the personal substance.

> 'But what is the substance of my life? To what forces is it subjected? What laws govern it? I do not belong to myself—I escape from myself.' [. . .]
>
> 'What do I lack? What is the lacuna of my moral being? What is the cause of my impotency? I have the most ardent desire to live, to give all my faculties a rhythmic development, to feel myself complete and harmonious. And, on the contrary, I secretly destroy myself every day; each day my life goes out by invisible

[58] The argument about literary modernism's privileging of episodes, chapters, self-sufficient entities within the whole, is made repeatedly by Fredric Jameson. See Fredric Jameson, *The Cultural Turn: Selected Writings on the Postmodern, 1983–1998* (London: Verso, 1998), 148–50; and *The Modernist Papers* (London: Verso, 2007), 181–95.

[59] James, 'Gabriele D'Annunzio', 917.

[60] In his *Beyond the Pleasure Principle* (1920).

> and innumerable fissures [in vece io perisco segretamente; ogni giorno la vita mi fugge da varchi invisibili e innumerabili].'
>
> (81–2)

Neither can the 'deep, yet puzzling, existential crisis' that defines Aurispa (who 'in many ways personifies the pessimism and sense of crisis that lie at the very heart of *fin-de-siècle* culture'[61]) be resolved through any Oedipal confrontation. The *retour au pays natal* revolves around an inevitable scene with the father—it is the anticipated Act of this episode—but Giorgio's moral cowardice and revulsion from his familial essence mean that all he can do is recognize in himself the same character that defines his crude, meretricious, voluptuary sire. 'And I—I am that man's son!' (86). Finally, the hope on which this episode is pinned comes to nothing. 'In burying again the roots of my being in the natal soil, shall I not suck up a pure and revivifying sap, which will have the power to expel all that is false and heterogeneous in me, all that I have consciously and unconsciously received by a thousand contagions [*ricevuto consapevole ed inconsapevole per mille contagi*]?' (231). No; the modern *stultus* is incorrigible, and tapping back into the racial essence does nothing to hinder the progressive loosening and autonomization of the psychic part-objects.

It is once again the erotic knot, the dyad defined by Giorgio Aurispa and his lover Ippolyta Sanzio, that drives the novel's unique characterology. Put starkly, D'Annunzio's solution is to break apart the singularity of the Beloved, to show her constitution by the same multitudinous forces that define his avatar's own *stultitia*. Aurispa's inveterate 'analytical zeal' shatters the sacred unity of Ippolyta's person. She is irradiated by a multiple—of class origin, organic constituency, and imaginary projection—from which she cannot recover.[62] Henceforth the Enemy, in an openly Strindbergian register that even the Italian cult of Eros cannot vanquish, Ippolyta is incapable of being One. 'All in her dissolved, melted, dilated [*Tutto si dissolveva in lei, si fondeva, si distendeva*], returned to the original fluidity, to the immense elementary ocean in which the forms were born, in which the forms disappeared to become renewed and to be reborn' (377). It is all an emanation, this chthonic multiplicity, of the feminine itself, a spontaneous affinity with the primitive and 'natural.'

> The facility she exhibited in entering into communication with every form of natural life and of finding a world of analogies between human expressions and the appearances of the most diverse things; this rapid and diffuse sympathy,

[61] Marja Härmänmaa, 'The Seduction of Thanatos: Gabriele D'Annunzio and the Decadent Death,' in Marja Härmänmaa and Christopher Nissen, eds., *Decadence, Degeneration, and the End: Studies in the European Fin de Siècle* (Basingstoke: Palgrave Macmillan, 2014), 227.

[62] Paul Barnaby, 'Superuomini e no: Dannunzian Hypotexts in Capuana's *Rassegnazione*,' *Forum italicum* 51.2 (2017), 438 [432–51].

> which attached her not only to objects with which she was in daily contact, but also to foreign objects; that sort of imitative virtue which often permitted her to express by a single sign the distinctive character of an animate or inanimate being, of talking to the domestic animals and understanding their language—all these mimic faculties properly concurred in rendering more visible, in George's eyes, the predominance in her of the inferior life.
>
> (201)

The living metaphor of all metaphors, Ippolyta presents Being in its infinite multiplicity.[63] It is her proximity to the inanimate and animal, to the inhuman, that infects Giorgio's desire for her with that other, more diffuse and disorienting passion for dissolution itself. Touched by her power, 'he languished, dissolved [. . .]. It was as if all the effeminations of his soul had blossomed at the same time' (358). Masculine countours erode. While throbbing together to Wagner, she grants him 'a glimpse of the possibility of freeing himself from space and time, of detaching himself from the individual will that confined him in the prison of a personality enclosed in a restricted place' (331). Thomas Mann's description of D'Annunzio as 'Wagner's monkey' hangs on his subscription to the morbid ecstasies of *Tristan's Liebestod*, its 'nocturnal empire of marvels' (331).[64] Wagnerian chromaticism grants the context in which Giorgio 'believed that death would be a means for prolonging his existence in the infinite, that he would become dissolved in the continuous harmony of the Great All [*dissolversi nell'armonia continua del Gran Tutto*] and would participate in the endless voluptuousness of the Eternal' (331).

But it is on the social plane that this problematic assumes its most potent and problematic form. When D'Annunzio ran for Parliament for the district of Ortona in 1897, three years after *Trionfo* was published, he wrote in a letter: 'I have just come back from an electoral trip and my nostrils are still full of an acrid smell of humanity.'[65] The antithesis of a democrat, he had written in his political credo, 'The Beast Who Wills' (1892), that 'the State founded on universal suffrage and on equality, held together mostly by fear, is not only an ignoble edifice, but also a precarious one.'[66] The demotic 'multitudes' evoked in that screed are classified as

[63] Ontology, the 'science of being-qua-being', is '[r]ealized as thought of the pure multiple', 'without recourse to the One'. Alain Badiou, *Being and Event*, trans. Oliver Feltham (London: Continuum, 2005), 517.

[64] Thomas Mann, *Reflections of a Nonpolitical Man*, trans. W. D. Morris (New York: Viking Press, 1983), 420–35. See here also Jameson's descriptions of Wagner's innovations in musical form: 'the reorganization of sonata-form temporality into the repetitions of the *Leitmotiven*, the transformation of heightened dissonance (the diminished seventh and ninth) into vehicles for affect rather than simple preparations for resolution; chromaticism itself and the very conversion of the key system into [the] sliding scale [suggestive of] quarter-tones and their eventual disaggregation of the Western tonal system'. Fredric Jameson, *The Antinomies of Realism* (London: Verso, 2013), 39.

[65] D'Annunzio, qtd. in John Woodhouse, *Gabriele D'Annunzio: Defiant Archangel* (Oxford: Oxford University Press, 1998), 165.

[66] D'Annunzio, 'The Beast Who Wills', 274.

'the inferior race', to be permitted 'little or close to nothing' in the coming social order, so that true human nobility will once again rule in the form of a 'superior race, lifted up by the sheer energy of its will'; 'a privileged few whose personal nobility is such that it will make them worthy of every privilege' (277). Drawing his inspiration explicitly from Nietzsche,[67] of whom he was the first sworn disciple in Italy, D'Annunzio clarifies an important distinction between this coming nobility and 'the decrepit heirs of the ancient patrician families' with whom his fictions have not been able to identify: 'the essence of the noble is an inner sovereignty' (277). The Overman is the one able to manage his inner multitude, and to use that discipline of the self as the means with which to govern effectively.

Nietzsche had been adamant on this score. 'However far a man may go in self-knowledge, nothing [. . .] can be more incomplete than his image of the totality of drives which constitute his being. He can scarcely name even the cruder ones: their number and strength, their ebb and flood, their play and counterplay among one another, and above all the laws of their nutriment remain wholly unknown to him.'[68] It is a paraphrase of D'Annunzio's fictions to date: a man especially gifted in introspection comes to recognize that his own 'totality of drives' exceeds his capacities for nomination, let alone management; disaster ensues. 'But the path lies open', cried Nietzsche, 'for new versions and sophistications of the soul hypothesis—and concepts like the "mortal soul" and the "soul as subject-multiplicity" and the "soul as a society constructed out of drives and affects" want henceforth to have civil rights in the realm of science'.[69] The 'enchanting and crazy *half-barbarism* into which Europe has been plunged through the democratic mixing of classes and races' (114) is a result of the failure of strong personalities to regulate their own drives. But Nietzsche adumbrates a nascent force, cultivated by philosopher-artists, that can resist this entropy: it is the 'desire to give form to oneself as a piece of difficult, resisting, suffering matter, to brand it with a will, a critique, a contradiction, a contempt, a "no", [the] uncanny, terrible but joyous labour of a soul voluntarily split within itself' that will overcome the ignoble European *stultus* and its *Weltschmerz*.[70]

> One thing is needful.—To 'give style' to one's character—a great and rare art! It is practised by those who survey all the strengths and weaknesses that their nature

[67] The only existing English translation of *Trionfo*, a worthy 1896 effort by Arthur Hornblow, omits in its entirety the ecstatic hymn to Zarathustra, the anti-Christ, which culminates the third chapter of the fifth book, 'Tempus Destruendi'.

[68] Friedrich Nietzsche, *Daybreak: Thoughts on the Prejudices of Morality*, I: 119, ed. Maudemarie Clark and Brian Leiter, trans. R. J. Holingdale (Cambridge: Cambridge University Press, 1997), 74.

[69] Friedrich Nietzsche, *Beyond Good and Evil*, I: 12, ed. Rolf-Peter Horstmann and Judith Norman, trans. Judith Norman (Cambridge: Cambridge University Press, 2002), 14.

[70] Friedrich Nietzsche, *On the Genealogy of Morality*, II: 18; III: 15, ed. Keith Ansell-Pearson, trans. Carol Diethe (Cambridge: Cambridge University Press, 2006), 59–60; 96.

> has to offer and then fit them into an artistic plan until each appears as art and reason and even weaknesses delight the eye.[71]

It is the very ethic of D'Annunzio's novels, reduced to an aphorism. That his characters so often fail is the thrust of his satire; that they do occasionally prevail is the lesson of his creed. And in *Trionfo*, what gets in the way is the destructive presence of the masses driven by religious zealotry.

The transcendent stylistic effort expended by D'Annunzio on the pilgrimage episode—a dizzying synthesis of Zola, late Flaubert, and Huysmans—is aimed at something properly Dantean and constitutes the author's vision of hell on earth: the multitudinous poor.

> Nothing—not the whirlwind of madness that drove the fanatic bands around the temple, nor the hopeless cries that seemed to issue from a place on fire, from a shipwreck or a massacre, nor the inanimate and bloody old men who lay in heaps along the court of the votive hall, nor the convulsed women who crawled towards the altar tearing their tongues against the stone, nor the supreme clamor that issued from the entrails of the multitude confounded in an unique anguish and in an unique hope—nothing, nothing, was as terrible as the spectacle of that great dusty hillside blinding in the glare of the sun, where all these monsters of human misery, all this débris of a ruined race, these bodies vilified to the level of the unclean beast and excremental matter, opened their rags to expose their impurities and proclaim them. The innumerable horde occupied the slope and the ditches; they had with them their family, their progeniture, their relatives, their household goods. One saw women half-naked and as lean as bitches who have just littered, children green as lizards, emaciated, with rapacious eyes, their mouths already withered, taciturn, breeding in the blood the hereditary disease. Each tribe possessed its monster: one-armed, bandy-legged, subject to goitre, blindness, leprosy, epilepsy.
>
> (293)

These are not 'characters' in any meaningful sense; neither are they personae. Rather, they designate the very limit of what is human as it subsides into a nether-region of monstrosity and the *bios* itself. For twenty pages the nauseating catalogue of Otherness, of everything that is not subsumable within an ethic of mastery, grace, taste, and poise, rolls and roils—the beast itself, *la moltitudine, una tribù innumerevole*—to engulf the slender reed that would withstand its trials. If it is true that 'Giorgio's failure to become the *superuomo* is predicated upon his inability to

[71] Friedrich Nietzsche, *The Gay Science*, IV: 290, ed. Bernard Williams, trans. Josefine Nauckhoff (Cambridge: Cambridge University Press, 2001), 163.

aestheticize life in the way he understands Nietzsche to advocate',[72] that failure is allegorized here most dramatically as the collapse of the sovereign, aestheticizing Ego before the grotesque Demos. The Wagnerian *Liebestod* is an infinitely more manageable and attractive prospect.

Il fuoco

Of D'Annunzio's final novel, *Il fuoco* (1900)—of which Joyce once marvelled that it 'was the most important achievement in the novel since Flaubert, and an advance upon Flaubert'[73]—it only remains to say that, in it, the person inhabited by the *multanime* is no longer the protagonist, who has attained his Style (he is a celebrated author, resembling D'Annunzio to an exceptional degree), but the object of his desire, La Foscarina (a fabled actress, modelled on Eleanora Duse, D'Annunzio's lover). For once, the protagonist, Stelio Effrena, has achieved a rapport and a communion with the multitude, and with his own multiple, which we might not unfairly characterize as *the aestheticization of politics*: 'In that communion between his soul and the soul of the people an almost divine mystery had existed; something greater and more exalted was added to the habitual feeling he had for his own person; he had felt then an unknown power converged within him, abolishing the limits of his earthly being and conferring on his solitary voice the full harmony of a chorus.'[74] The idiom of Italian heroism is transposed out of the realm of conventional politics and into the Wagnerian cult of the Artist-God, in whose 'sliding scale' all discord, all tumult, is reconciled via the sacred mystery of the Dionysian dithyramb. D'Annunzio goes so far as to feature the dying Richard Wagner as one of the tiny cast of characters in this remarkable novel, carried on his bier to his final resting place by the protagonist, in an appeal for the succession, and migration, of Wagnerian art from a Northern to a Southern sphere of influence, to a great Latin theatre of state from the Teutonic exaltations of Bayreuth.[75]

But it is his Perdita, La Foscarina, in whom the lively and unresolved multiplicity of modern subjectivity now resides, and this because—like Wilde's Sibyl Vane—she is an actress. 'She is the empty vessel through which his desire for other men is channelled and concealed', writes Derek Duncan. 'This ventriloquism allows him to withdraw his body, the material site from which he speaks, from the public gaze.'[76] But her exposure leaves her thrumming with all the residual roles and voices her vessel has channelled from artist to crowd. Her body vibrates to the

[72] Jessica Susan Wood, 'The Art of Dying in *Trionfo della Morte*', *Forum italicum* 51.2 (2017), 469–70 [469–87].
[73] Richard Ellmann, *James Joyce*, new and revised ed. (Oxford: Oxford University Press, 1982), 59.
[74] Gabriele D'Annunzio, *The Flame* [*Il fuoco*] (London: The National Alumni, 1906), 115.
[75] See on this Raffaelli and Subialka, 'Introduction', 328.
[76] Duncan, 'Choice Objects', 137.

tremors of 'all the barbarous crowds she had visited as the messenger of Latin genius; all the ignorant masses [...] all the human herds' (98). She is mortal and ageing; but she is freighted with 'an illimitable mass of reality and poetry' (98) which lifts her into the sublime.

> All her thirst had burned in the delirium of Phædre, and in the submissiveness of Imogen had trembled all her tenderness. Thus Life and Art, the irrevocable Past and the eternal Present, had made her profound, many-souled [*multanime*], and mysterious, had magnified her ambiguous destiny beyond human limits, and rendered her equal to great temples and natural forests. Nevertheless, she stood there, a living, breathing woman, under the gaze of the poets, each of whom saw her, and yet in her many others.
>
> (99)

D'Annunzio's list of the *multanime* she incarnates is similar to Sibyl Vane's: Phædre, Imogen, Antigone, Cassandra, Medea, Cleopatra, Mirra, Giulietta, et cetera. She 'appears as one who really does have "*mille anime* [a thousand souls]" and "*mille maschere* [a thousand masks]"'.[77] La Foscarina maintains as a feminine virtue the unsynthesizable modern multiplicity that Stelio's Wagnerian aestheticization of politics would sublate; she keeps open the wound of modernity. As such, she is D'Annunzio's greatest character, and the one for which he was most openly dependent on the living example of an artist every bit his equal; the one, too, on whom he broke the lance of the novel form and so took up a more direct and deplorable means for regulating the multitude, as a Fascist.

[77] Lucia Re, 'Author and Actress between Decadence and Modernity', in Mario Moroni and Luca Somigli, eds., *Italian Modernism: Italian Culture Between Decadentism and Avant-Garde* (Toronto: University of Toronto Press, 2004), 105.

7
Henry James

Really, universally, relations stop nowhere, and the exquisite problem of the artist is eternally but to draw, by a geometry of his own, the circle within which they shall happily appear to do so.[1]

'What is character but the determination of incident? What is incident but the illustration of character?' Henry James' ruminations in 'The Art of Fiction' turn on this traditional association and depart from it in the same breath. 'It is an incident', he continues, 'for a woman to stand up with her hand resting on a table and look out at you in a certain way'.[2] This recalibration of the status of 'incident' will preoccupy the last phase of James' career and propel the novelistic art of characterology into uncharted terrain. If a 'look' be an incident, then a character can be anything a look might engender in its percipient. Further, if it is not a singular 'you' being looked at, but a plural you, already caught in webs of relations that 'stop nowhere', then the gaze of the woman, like the gaze of the artist, is *incidental* above all in the circle it draws—by a geometry of its own—around the characters it binds together within the specific quality of her own affect.

Geometry simplifies to ascertain first principles. 'James is on occasion guilty of sacrificing human plausibility to economy and symmetry', writes Barbara Hardy; for the later James, such sacrifice has become an art.[3] There is a progressive deracination of the variegated character space that had surrounded and buttressed the heroes and heroines of Dickens, Trollope, and Thackeray.[4] That richly peopled background of the 'minor' undergoes a thorough campaign of weeding and routing, to the point that, in *The Golden Bowl*, we have attained something like a logical minimum of supporting players. The author's apology there for the 'fundamental fewness' of his 'elements' turns on the rich compensations on offer: 'We see very few persons in "The Golden Bowl", but the scheme of the book, to make up for that, is that we shall really see about as much of them as a coherent literary form

[1] Henry James, 'Preface' to *Roderick Hudson*, in *Literary Criticism: French Writers, Other European Writers, The Prefaces to the New York Edition*, ed. Leon Edel (New York: Library of America, 1984), 1041.

[2] Henry James, 'The Art of Fiction', in *Literary Criticism: Essays on Literature, American Writers, English Writers*, ed. Leon Edel (New York: Library of America, 1984), 55.

[3] Barbara Hardy, *The Appropriate Form: An Essay on the Novel* (London: Athlone, 1964), 6.

[4] Alex Woloch, *The One vs. the Many: Minor Characters and the Space of the Protagonist in the Novel* (Princeton: Princeton University Press, 2003), esp. 12–42.

Modern Character. Julian Murphet, Oxford University Press. © Julian Murphet (2023).
DOI: 10.1093/oso/9780192863126.003.0008

permits.'[5] And what we see, in these late fictions, is not exactly 'internal' either; the prose is 'remarkably resistant to an interest in psychological depth', but attends richly to the fine, dynamic interplay of the surfaces displayed, linguistic and otherwise.[6] Character, here, is a web strung between four principal anchors, on which vibrations pass from one region to another without the need for psychology.

What Maisie Knew

It all begins in *What Maisie Knew* (1897), which proceeds from an 'extraordinarily "ironic centre"' to embrace an unexpected form of characterology.[7] Maisie, the child protagonist, is a passive point of view with little capacity to affect the course of events; she is a bound witness, and she bears witness to a set of adult relationships whose shifting configurations will (and this is the irony) decide her fate outside them altogether. Looked at in Maisie's 'certain way', the principal relationships lock into a pointedly rectangular formation. Maisie is 'the subject of the manoeuvres of a quartette',[8] and this nominates James' new formula for modern character, the verso of which is that remote inner sense, 'privatised and peripheral', of the heroine's spectatorial suspension before those quadrilateral intrigues.[9] Again and again, from this point forward, the author will experiment with variations on this fundamental schema. What 'character' comes to mean in this organization of the materials is less and less anything resembling a depth-model of the interior and increasingly something like a cybernetic feedback loop between a geometrical form and its 'being-looked-at'. The geometrical figure permits a radical abstraction from social models, from all concessions to the *vraisemblable*; while its 'being-looked-at' determines a detour of that abstraction through the equally abstracted mode of its perception.

Paul Theroux is not wrong to remark that *Maisie* is a 'novel of threes', but these threes are resolved into that larger configuration of which Maisie is herself the

[5] Henry James, *The Golden Bowl*, in *Novels 1903–1911*, ed. Ross Posnock (New York: Library of America, 2010), 436.

[6] Leo Bersani, *A Future for Astyanax: Character and Desire in Literature* (Boston: Little, Brown & Co., 1976), 130.

[7] Henry James, 'Preface' to *What Maisie Knew*, in *Literary Criticism: French Writers, Other European Writers, The Prefaces to the New York Edition*, 1162.

[8] Henry James, *What Maisie Knew*, in *Novels 1896–1899*, ed. Myra Jehlen (New York: Library of America, 2003), 536.

[9] Terry Eagleton, *Criticism and Ideology: A Study in Marxist Literary Theory* (London: Verso, 1978), 141. I remark in passing the strange coincidence of the similarity between this plot, the plot of *The Golden Bowl*, and that of Freud's 'Dora' (1901/05), in which what Lacan calls a 'quadrille' is set in motion between a heterosexual couple and a father–daughter pair. 'Fragment of an Analysis of a Case of Hysteria' (1905 [1901]), in *The Standard Edition of the Complete Psychological Works of Sigmund Freud, Volume VII (1901–1905): A Case of Hysteria, Three Essays on Sexuality and Other Works*, trans. James Strachey (London: Hogarth Press, 1953), 3–124.

proximate cause.[10] Her parents, Beale and Ida, appear to have been united solely for the purposes of procreating her, after which they swiftly part. Each attracts a new lover—Beale wins the pretty governess Miss Overmore, while Ida secures the dashing Sir Claude—and Maisie then sits at the intersection of these two overlapping triangles, where she acquires the power of a catalyst.[11] As she had first brought together and then separated her parents, so she now brings together her step-parents (the original couple having spun off into an escalating series of other bonded compounds), only to have these nearly separate in turn, before separating instead from Maisie herself. As John Frow writes of Goethe's *Elective Affinities*, this, too, is a novel that 'would exemplify the chemical workings of character and dispense with psychological motivation and differentiation in favour of a narrative of underlying and impersonal forces'.[12] But here the 'underlying' is all on the surface. What Maisie *knows* is what she *sees*: 'a change in the nature of the struggle she appeared to have come into the world to produce' (430). In bearing witness to this battle of affective permutations whose reagent she is, Maisie undergoes the only 'growth' allotted her; and that growth is in her aesthetic, and not her moral sense—as her stalwart companion Mrs. Wix is never shy of complaining. It is a matter of symmetries minutely observed, suggestive parallelisms and limpid echo-effects, all conducted within what James himself called 'this intensely structural, intensely hinged and jointed preliminary frame'.[13] Here, where everything is 'a question of sides', where 'the distribution of parties [leads] to a rushing to and fro and a changing of places' (464), moral accountancy cedes to ideas of balance, proportion, and harmony. 'Her little world was phantasmagoric', writes her narrator; '—strange shadows dancing on a sheet. It was as if the whole performance had been given for her—a mite of a half-scared infant in a great dim theatre' (401). It is out of this geometrical shadow-play that Maisie, with her 'sharpened sense of spectatorship' (472), is obliged to eke out her little 'idea of an inner self or, in other words, of concealment' (406). The two-dimensional figures she sees projected on her 'pane of glass' (472) are characters, not as unplumbable depths of inner motivation, but as configurations of the pictorial mosaic: 'character here becomes a compositional device, part of the patterning of the text'.[14]

The oft-used term 'squared' supplies a geometrical key to this overarching pattern. Maisie is herself 'squared' by her step-parents into a convenient fig-leaf for their outrages against Mrs. Wix's moral sense; but in that very squaring, Maisie is caught up, cathected by the libidinal currents that embower her delicious aesthetic

[10] Paul Theroux, Introduction to *What Maisie Knew* (London: Penguin, 1985), 13.

[11] Maisie is 'the embodied catalyst for compounding complications' in the text. Michelle H. Phillips, 'The "*Partagé* Child" and the Emergence of the Modernist Novel in *What Maisie Knew*', *The Henry James Review* 31.2 (Spring 2010), 96 [95–110].

[12] John Frow, *Character and Person* (Oxford: Oxford University Press, 2014), 5.

[13] Henry James, *The Complete Notebooks of Henry James*, ed. Leon Edel and Lyall H. Powers (Oxford: Oxford University Press, 1987), 161–2.

[14] Frow, *Character and Person*, 6.

sense of concealed spectatorship.[15] As a term, 'squared', remarks Glenn Clifton, 'is not an empty hieroglyph but rather a placeholder with which Maisie navigates what she is able to observe without words. Such terms are pointers toward the perceptions that language cannot accommodate directly.'[16] To 'be squared' is simultaneously to be internally quartered, as an inaugural crack in Maisie's being—her quality as the '*partagé* child' divided by her parents' divorce[17]—is doubled and redoubled, and each of her impressions plays out along various seams and angles in the perceptual and affective quadrature. 'Nothing was less new to Maisie than the art of not thinking singly' (553). She is become a kaleidoscope, and the ornate shadow-play of an adult quartet on the sheet of her senses, 'attended and amplified' by the narrator into a proper 'register of impressions',[18] is the shifting ground on which her 'inner self, or in other words [her] concealment' is built. The result is what Michelle Phillips calls 'a modernist figure', her squared consciousness an exemplification of 'the inexplicable, the restrained, and the strictly and uniquely formed', those new values in the repertoire of literary forms.[19] If Maisie ultimately 'forges her own dynamic subjectivity', shedding 'rigid, typological models of identity' in order to embrace 'an identity of flux', what that spells for the art of the novel is a relative demotion of the laws of realist form—of narrative structure, complex character systems, and thematic organization—in the name of those ambient affects and percepts clinging to Maisie like beads of dew strung on the 'geometrical precision' of her squared point of view.[20]

The Sacred Fount

That James had 'no very great narrative sense' is nowhere better proven than in *The Sacred Fount* (1901).[21] 'Plot, setting, and characterization are suppressed',[22] so that nothing happens in this novel other than conversations which confabulate a hypothetical incident taking place while the central narrating instance (himself a player, another bachelor-machine) ruminates tirelessly on the plausibility and

[15] 'James's novel invites an attention precisely to the relations between affect and sexuality.' Adam Frank, 'Maisie's Spasms: Transferential Poetics in Henry James and Wilfred Bion', *Studies in Gender and Sexuality* 17.3 (2016), 171 [165–80].

[16] Glenn Clifton, 'More Perceptions than Terms to Translate Them: The Enigmatic Signifier and the Jamesian Unconscious in *What Maisie Knew*', *The Henry James Review* 36.2 (Spring 2015), 169 [163–76].

[17] Henry James, *The Notebooks of Henry James*, ed. F. O. Matthiessen and Kenneth B. Murdock (New York: Oxford University Press, 1947), 126, 134.

[18] James, 'Preface' to *What Maisie Knew*, 1157.

[19] Phillips, 'The "*Partagé* Child"', 108, 104.

[20] Mary Grace Albanese, 'Experimental *Maisie*: Zolien Naturalism and the Compulsion to Convert', *The Henry James Review* 38.1 (Winter 2017), 55, 61 [53–70].

[21] Ezra Pound, *Literary Essays of Ezra Pound*, ed. T. S. Eliot (London: Faber & Faber, 1960), 299.

[22] Marcus Klein, 'Henry James's *Sacred Fount*: The Theory, the Theorist, and the Lady', *Arizona Quarterly* 62.3 (Autumn 2006), 88 [83–104].

elegance of his cherished 'theory'. It is a novel seemingly extrapolated from the sketch of a play, and a Symbolist play at that: observing *à la* Maeterlinck the classical unities of time (thirty-six hours) and place (Newmarch), while eschewing any expectation of action, *The Sacred Fount* displays the abstract scenic logic of a sequence of dialogues disposed around the premises of a country house, interspersed with a good deal of first-person commentary, in which, at last, 'nothing takes place but the place'.[23] The novel is, according to R. P. Blackmur, 'not a novel at all but a vast shadowy disintegrating parable, disturbing distressing distrait, indeed distraught'.[24] At its core is a refinement of James' bold new characterology, which is, finally, all the plot the book can boast: a perceiving consciousness, a perceived quartet, and the resonant affective transference that obtains between them.

James' unusual decision to surrender narrative responsibilities to a first-person voice which seems increasingly to be a parody of his own—intellectually presumptuous, minutely discriminating, voluble to a fault, subjunctive and conditional by preference, and devoid of the faintest shadow of an idea that is not an aesthetic one—has formal consequences. Where 'there is no place "outside" the mind', all variety must come from the play of percepts and affects that the mind organizes for itself.[25] First, to the extent that the narrator subjects his fellow house-guests to his theory of character, he becomes their 'author', and they his characters, in a 'social text' that sits alongside them and becomes an active irritant to their otherwise vacuous rituals of social elevation. Second, in the absence of any objective action or rotating point of view, we have a characterology defined by spatial configurations, patterns, and tableaux; *L'Année dernière à Marienbad*, but in words. Third, given this eclipse of individuated motivation and purpose by group figures and effects, there is a gravitation of the signs of character to the surface of things—a punctilious behaviourism trumping any hint of expressionism. Fourth, there is thus no question of anything like consistency or unity of the person in this textual space, where 'everyone changes' and characters as 'stable and unified centers of meaning' do not exist, since character is roundly understood to be an effect of contingent propinquities and associations that change within the general drift of forms.[26]

The entire situation emerges from a brace of discoveries made by the narrator as he shares a railway car with Mrs. Grace Brissenden and Mr. Gilbert Long from Paddington to the country house of Newmarch where they are to share a weekend away with forty or so other guests: that, since last they met, Mrs. Brissenden

[23] On James' relationship with Maeterlinck's work around this time, see Heath Moon, 'Is *The Sacred Fount* a Symbolist Novel?', *Comparative Literature* 39.4 (Autumn 1978): 307–9. See also Adeline Tintner, 'Henry James and the Symbolist Movement in Art', *Journal of Modern Literature* 7.3 (Sept. 1979): 397–415.

[24] R. P. Blackmur, 'In the Country of the Blue', *Kenyon Review* 5.4 (Autumn 1943), 597 [595–617].

[25] Sharon Cameron, *Thinking in Henry James* (Chicago: University of Chicago Press, 1989), 161.

[26] Ann-Marie Priest, '"In the Mystic Circle": The Space of the Unspeakable in Henry James's *The Sacred Fount*', *Style* 34.3 (Fall 2000), 437 [421–43].

is 'changed so extraordinarily for the better. How could a woman who had been plain so long become pretty so late?'; and that Long is changed from a 'stupid' if 'fine piece of human furniture' into a man whose 'perfectly graced' intellectual eminence puts him, inexplicably, 'in possession of the scene'.[27] That they appear so animatedly together, of course, alerts the reader to a more prosaic explanation of their altered personae, but our narrator looks elsewhere for an adequate account of these conjoint 'miracles' (19) of character transformation. The matter at issue is the perfectly confounding sense that neither of these individuals is at all the same as they were the year before; a sense that belongs to the narrator first and foremost, but which will be corroborated by a few choice conspirators. If Grace Brissenden has shed twenty years and transmogrified from 'plain' to 'pretty' (she will culminate as 'beautiful', 153), then Gilbert Long has made the even more unaccountable passage from asininity to wit (8). Here is a conundrum for any theory of character, especially one steeped in the modes of realism: if there is no personality trait that cannot be reversed, no quality that cannot be suspected of radical impermanence, then in what does character consist? That such miracles occur is out of the bounds of any storytelling mode but fairy tale—the narrator will compare himself to 'the messengers and herald in the tale of Cinderella' (157)—and, as if to clinch the hanging thread of Romance, it appears that a party close to Mrs. Brissenden, namely Mr. Guy Brissenden himself, shows all the signs of a complementary condition. If she has grown young and lovely, he has declined into premature senility and hunched age: 'It was he who was old—it was he who was older—it was he who was oldest' (15), appearing 'quite sixty' despite being not 'yet thirty' (5).

Thus is hatched the theory of character on which the narrator's plot depends: that intimate union (sex, as all the commentators agree, but also simply constant availability) permits a dominant partner to draw vitality, privately, from the 'sacred fount' of the submissive other's storehouse of the *élan vital*. The Brissendens have the signal virtue, for the narrator, of rather giving this game away—in the logical complementarity of their states and the public legitimacy of their intimacy. The real question is, then, what could possibly account for the even more miraculous condition of Gilbert Long? It is thus as a characterological algebraic equation that the 'plot' of *The Sacred Fount* announces itself. The missing 'x' (Long's sacred fount) compels the narrator to build an immense and 'perfect palace of thought' (188), in whose symmetrically proportioned grounds, like a better mousetrap, the victim should stand revealed, having disclosed the requisite amount of psychic damage: 'whoever she was, she must logically have been idiotised' (84), 'having *de*formed and idiotised herself' (185) to create the reborn Long.

This algebraic coordination dovetails nicely with a parallel investigation, concerning the transmutation of another member of the party, Mrs. May Server, who

[27] Henry James, *The Sacred Fount*, in *Novels 1901–1902*, ed. Leo Bersani (New York: Library of America, 2006), 5, 3, 11.

(although known to the narrator only remotely) appears sufficiently altered to a cognate intelligence—that of the fellow bachelor-artist, Ford Obert—to arouse a deep anxiety. She's 'different now' (13) he warns, 'too beastly unhappy' to be anything other than 'uncanny' (14); which shudder communicates itself to the narrator, who shares with Obert his pet theory, and between them they wield the 'torch of [his] analogy' (40, 130) in a hunt for the mysterious party benefiting from the drainage of May Server's 'sacred fount'. Analogy is thus played in two directions simultaneously from the same shining instance, to either end of a speculative union: to the strange case of Gilbert Long's impossible, miraculous conversion; and to the sad case of Mrs. Server's uncanny self-estrangement, her '*difference from herself*', as Obert phrases it (38). With Mrs. Brissenden the narrator pursues the former line of inquiry; with Ford Obert, the latter.

Grace Brissenden hits upon the correlation that the situation has logically called for: that May Server must serve as Long's sacred fount. It is this deeply satisfactory squaring of the circle, the solution of the algebraic equation, that comes so wholly to persuade the narrator that, by the end of the text, he will hold to it despite being objectively 'smashed' 'utterly to pieces' (180) by contrary evidence. We will have noted, in all the preceding summary, that none of it offers a single ray of light into anything psychologically 'interior', apart from this very passionate attachment to a foursquare formal arrangement on the part of the narrator. His 'externalist, objectifying way with characters' here is truly remarkable.[28] The theory has not required the merest suggestion of an intention, a motive, or a purpose in any of the concerned parties; their 'agency' has consisted, rather, entirely in their involuntary submission to a formal analogy—as A is to B, so X is to Y. The challenge was to have observed intensely enough to perceive the latent diagram, the perfect quadrilateral figure, created by the persons implicated in this analogy, despite their intentions or designs of subterfuge. This theory of character, then, has nothing of the psychologic about it; it hangs upon an *architectonic* that conceives of character purely as a reflex of pattern and implication.

Here we need to say a word on the form of which this novel is a weirdly mutated instance: the comedy of manners. Just as the outline of *Maisie*'s plot can be seen in Goethe's *Elective Affinities*, so *The Sacred Fount* shares a good deal of its overtly satiric concerns with the plays of Congreve, Wycherley, and Sheridan. A suspected scandal lurks beneath the decorous play of appearances and courtly manners held fast to by a sophisticated faction of the dominant social class, whose wit and ingenuity is called upon to preserve the brittle superficialities of their *demi-monde* against the impending revelation of shocking indiscretions. That all this should take place in the elegant, formal, above all *proportioned* environs of a stately country house—a 'great asylum of the finer wit' (60)—is then the final guarantee that we are housed within a generic space that has more than a merely symbolic relation

[28] Myra Jehlen, *Five Fictions in Search of Truth* (Princeton: Princeton University Press, 2008), 59.

to the algebraic method, the quadrilateral throb, that so animates the narrator's perfectly geometrical plot. It is of the essence of the comedy of manners that its society is so refined as to have had abstracted from it all vulgar trace of the natural man; nature itself can make no impression on this artificial realm. 'We were all so fine and formal, and the ladies in particular at once so little and so much clothed, so beflounced yet so denuded, that the summer stars called to us in vain. We had ignored them in our crystal cage' (121). Character in this space is, virtually by definition, less an innate property of the figures who populate the landscape, than a shifting function of the fine formality itself: the inevitable stock caricatures of the Restoration model, and here (in this turn-of-the-century pastiche) deprived of even those reliable signs of stereotypy and agreed rules of engagement.

There is a gap between the polite surface of 'fine formality' and the barbs and thrusts of a deeper, unarticulated, layer of signification. The comedy of manners thrives on this duplicitous deployment of the decorous codes of civility to discharge otherwise inexpressible, unmentionable energies in plain view in the form of *wit*. James' abiding interest in this aspect of the genre has been much remarked, as by Laurence Holland: a characterology privileging 'a significant community in which elemental human activities are at once constrained and given release, veiled and given room to play, by forms'.[29] *The Sacred Fount*'s narrator enjoys this frisson particularly in his interlocutions with Mrs. Brissenden.

> It could *not* but be exciting to talk, as we talked, on the basis of those suppressed processes and unavowed references which made the meaning of our meeting so different from its form. We knew ourselves—what moved me, that is, was that she knew me—to mean, at every point, immensely more than I said or than she answered; just as she saw me, at the same points, measure the space by which her answers fell short.
>
> (165)

It is on this basis—that what is said is merely a cipher for 'suppressed processes and unavowed references'—that our narrator constructs his edifice of speculation, fully authorized by the laws of the genre to do so. The question remains whether the other characters are indeed participating in a generic operation as archaic as this one; or whether the narrator has taken it upon himself to project an ageing generic protocol on social materials that have, circa 1900, evolved beyond them entirely. This question defines the irony of the text from beginning to end, and remains irresolvable precisely to the extent that, even given his final 'shattering into pieces', we are allowed no other point of view to balance his own. Moreover, what the novel of manners is called upon to grapple with here is nothing less than the decline of an entire class faction: the steady erosion of the English leisure class as such,

[29] Laurence Bedwell Holland, *The Expense of Vision: Essays on the Craft of Henry James* (Princeton: Princeton University Press, 1964), 190.

that component of the minor aristocracy which, having ridden high in the 1870s and 1880s, is now in an objective crisis thanks to 'inexorably mounting debts', the decline of agricultural rents, and slumping land values.[30] If 'something was happening to ranked and ordered English society once so full of enviable typicalities', then that makes the generic procedure itself anachronistic enough to create dissonance.[31] It is this that undergirds the 'physiological degeneration, the vampirism, and the reduced scope of the novel's point of view', and deflects attention away from the shady personae to the grounds themselves.[32]

The Wings of the Dove

From the weirdly abstract character space of *The Sacred Fount* (where James arguably attains 'form, perfect form, his form'[33]) to the ostensibly more reputable characterology of *The Wings of the Dove*, James' next novel, seems a retreat from daring formalism into the weathered textures of a more agreeable (and commercial) fictional mode. Yet hovering over this text, with its aggressive war of position against Trollope, Thackeray, Dickens, and De Maupassant, is the twice-invoked spirit of Maeterlinck; and through it runs another variation on the geometrical model we have been examining, a model which now tends to transform the apparently conventional *Portrait*-like interiorities on show into *Gestalt*-figures constituted out of 'morsels of coloured glass' or the tiles of Ravenna mosaics.[34] At the same time, there is a 'mutation of personality into allegorical function' so extreme as to force the various 'principal centres' of narrative perspective to 'merge'.[35] In *The Wings of the Dove*, woven as it is from 'triangular relationships', the quartet strains for the first time to become a 'meta-character' in its own right.[36] The emphasis is no longer on what it looks like to an external observer (a function it internalizes), but how it feels to be part of it, refracted and morselized by the infinite play of looks and suppositions strung out between its revolving 'centres'.

Characterologically, the novel is a critical disquisition on fictional 'type' at the end of the nineteenth century. Here are types of a particularly novelistic sort, delivered with purring irony: Aunt Maud's prodigious 'personality' of 'Britannia

[30] Francis M. L. Thompson, 'English Landed Society in the Twentieth Century', in Didier Lancien and Monique de Saint Martin, eds., *Anciennes et nouvelles aristocraties: De 1880 à nos jours* (Paris: Éditions de la Maison des sciences de l'homme, 2007), 11–27.

[31] Millicent Bell, '"Type" in *The Wings of the Dove* and the Invention of Kate Croy', *Cambridge Quarterly* 37.1 (March 2008), 94 [90–7].

[32] Moon, 'Is *The Sacred Fount* a Symbolist Novel?', 326.

[33] Pound, *Literary Essays*, 327.

[34] Henry James, *The Wings of the Dove*, in *Novels 1901–1902*, ed. Bersani, 375, 384.

[35] Bersani, *Future for Astyanax*, 142.

[36] John Goode, 'The Pervasive Mystery of Style: *The Wings of the Dove*', in Goode, ed., *The Air of Reality: New Essays on Henry James* (London: Methuen, 1972), 247.

of the Market Place', some 'parts doubtless magnified and parts certainly vague' (236–7); Sir Luke Strett, 'the highest type of scientific mind' (373), who wears his professional 'character scientifically, ponderably, proveably—not just loosely and sociably' (366); Lord Mark, the prowling hypocrite and opportunist, 'a type with which the preaching of passion somehow so ill consorted' (524); the depraved Lionel Croy, 'his type reflecting so invidiously on the woman who had found him distasteful' (223); and Mrs. Condrip, the sullen drudge, hovering between the stereotypes of other novelists, 'a mixed, wandering echo of Trollope, of Thackeray, perhaps mostly of Dickens' (324). In each case there is a certain ambiguity as to whether such typicality is properly social or purely literary, and that hesitancy between 'the logic of folk taxonomy' and 'typologies relevant to the modal world of genre' is, as John Frow argues, essential to the meaning of realist literary character, with its constant movement between cultural generality and textual particularity.[37] 'In this way', notes Alex Woloch, 'a character is simultaneously projected *outside* the discourse and embedded *within* a narrative structure'.[38] This is exactly the double-valence that Henry James struggles to transcend in his later fiction, whose purpose it is to prohibit as much of the *projection outside* as possible. 'Character "types", a foundation of the realist art [James] had greatly admired in Balzac, constrict personality, after all, to a bundle of predictable features', and the only personality worth developing now was the consistently surprising one of intra-referential resonance between multiple nodes.[39]

The most interesting work being done with 'type' in *The Wings of the Dove* concerns the four major centres of consciousness in the book, who belong to two kinds: Kate Croy and Milly Theale, and Merton Densher and Susan Stringham. Of this latter pair of writer-figures, on whom we will speak more later, what matters most is that their 'type' is under erasure. Densher, the handsome journalist, is 'not unamenable, on certain sides, to classification', but remains above all 'vague', his elements 'so in fusion and fermentation that the question of the final stamp, the pressure that fixes the value, must wait for comparative coolness' (248). Indeed, it could be said that his character awaits the stamp of his last scenes to have its value fixed. He is a disorganized prototype, rather than a type.[40] Susan Shepherd, the widow Stringham, meanwhile, is a very definite type—the independent Boston lady writer, making her way in the magazines—who by the stroke of a higher power is undone. Thanks to the unmentionableness of her 'rare passion' (446), her 'proto-lesbian identity' as Milly's helpmeet and companion,[41] 'Susan Shepherd [. . .] was

[37] Frow, *Character and Person*, 122, 125.
[38] Woloch, *The One vs. the Many*, 260.
[39] Bell, '"Type" in *The Wings of the Dove*', 90.
[40] On the *stultus*, see Michel Foucault, *Discourse and Truth and Parrhesia*, ed. Daniele Lorenzini, Henri-Paul Fruchaud, and Nancy Luxton, trans. Nancy Luxton (Chicago: University of Chicago Press, 2019), 29; and Michel Foucault, *Hermeneutics of the Subject: Lectures at the Collège de France, 1981–1982*, ed. Frédéric Gros, trans. Graham Burchell (New York: Palgrave Macmillan, 2005), 133.
[41] Eve Sedgwick, *Tendencies* (Durham, NC: Duke University Press, 1993), 79.

not anybody else. She had renounced that character; she had now no life to lead; and she honestly believed that she was thus supremely equipped for leading Milly's own' (291). Each of these singularly untypified personae—one irresolute, the other cancelled—serves in the court of a true Type, the struggle between whose spheres of influence defines the plot.

The novel begins on a telling grammatical micro-drama at the level of the pronoun: 'She waited, Kate Croy, for her father . . .' (217); and this cataphoric precedence of the pronoun over the proper name, an increasingly common narrative fact in the modern novel,[42] opens a zone of indecision about the 'true' centre of consciousness (Kate or Milly) in this long novel which perhaps has none. It is perfectly right, within the parameters set by the fiction, to continue to wonder up to the very end if it isn't Kate Croy after all who has sufficient weight to claim the prize. 'She virtually takes the novel over from Milly', it has been remarked;[43] Kate is 'the dominant centre of consciousness'.[44] But here—as the Preface insists—the novelist's own 'inveterate displacement of his general centre' should chasten any headlong rush to decide this question.[45] The text's poly-centredness (it has four focalizers) rather encourages us to think through the structural relationship between *the perception of type* as a habit of consciousness and *type itself* as an ineluctable habit of genre, and of the novel especially. That is to say, if this novel has no proper centre, what comes to matter more is the very tendency *to fix a centre upon a type*; and this means that, over and against the claims of Kate and Milly as the types par excellence of this fiction, it is rather the collateral pressures of Densher and Susan, courtiers-in-chief of the rival factions, that may be the higher subject matter of *The Wings of the Dove*. The quartet of this novel is the form through which this subject is developed.

Milly, who tends towards an 'apotheosis', is ever 'the American girl as [Densher] had originally found her' in New York (563).[46] Buoyant, plucky, spontaneous, yet somehow unequal to the hypocrisies and subterfuges of Europe, Milly is the *femme fragile* incarnate.[47] 'The type was so elastic that it could be stretched to almost anything; and yet, not stretched, it kept down, remained normal, remained properly within bounds' (588). It is this plastic quality that attracts Susan Shepherd to

[42] See Jameson's discussion in *The Antinomies of Realism* (London: Verso, 2013), 163–70.

[43] Bell, '"Type" in *The Wings of the Dove*', 97.

[44] Anna Despotopoulou, 'The Price of "Mere Spectatorship": Henry James's *The Wings of the Dove*', *The Review of English Studies* 53.210 (May 2002), 232 [228–44].

[45] James, 'Preface' to *The Wings of the Dove*, in *Literary Criticism: French Writers, Other European Writers, The Prefaces to the New York Edition*, 1299.

[46] Brian Lee, 'Henry James's "Divine Consensus"', *Renaissance and Modern Studies* 4 (Spring 1966), 17 [5–24].

[47] 'The ambiguous appeal of the *femme fragile* is partly what makes Henry James's portraits of the American girl at the end of the nineteenth century memorable, especially because they often seem to imply something about America itself.' Sofia Ahlberg, 'Scenes of Instruction: Representations of the American Girl in European Twentieth-Century Literature', *Journal of Modern Literature* 33.3 (Spring 2010), 65 [64–77].

her and fixes her at her side, Milly's typicality resolving itself into the outline of 'one of her own New England heroines' in the stories Susie writes for the magazines (348). It is also what suggests to Kate her own shadier novelistic uses for Milly. Kate Croy, of whom 'no sum in addition would have made up the total' (218) is then 'the wondrous London girl in person', a type familiar to her American observers 'from the tales of travellers and the anecdotes of New York, from old porings over *Punch* and a liberal acquaintance with the fiction of the day' (228). Susie's 'feeling that she, Kate, had "type"' (447), is made up of 'English, of eccentric, of Thackerayan character' (329), renders Kate susceptible to further authorial modification by the American scribbler who 'felt that with such stuff as the strange English girl was made of [. . .] there was none other to be employed' than that of 'Chop[ping] me up fine or serv[ing] me whole', as Kate later shudders (447). This is what types do: they offer themselves as models for further work, conscripted to the cause of an ongoing fictional anatomization and elaboration. Milly 'placed this striking young person from the first in a story, saw her, by a necessity of the imagination, for a heroine, felt it the only character in which she wouldn't be wasted' (228); and the same could be said for Kate's vision of Milly.

Yet this typology is only the beginning, and each of these grand types absorbs many others besides. The 'London girl' is also the 'penniless girl' (219), while the 'American girl' is the avowed 'princess'—a mildly chiastic (though familiar Jamesian) resetting of the terms that offers a welcome economic footing to the *agon*. Milly Theale's allegorical embodiment of Money itself (so much it cannot be spent)[48] chafes against Kate's awful penury and dependency, her frightful status as a 'middle-class nobody [from] Bayswater' (330). Yet it is very much Kate who stands here for sexual 'Experience' against Milly's unblemished purity and 'Innocence', the 'Dark Lady' to her 'Pale Maiden', a further ironic twist in this typological extravaganza.[49] Most startling, perhaps, is Kate's livid personification of 'Life', as against Milly's grim embodiment of 'Death', about which more in a moment.[50] There is an especially rich interfusion of types here, all of which should properly be referred to a presiding distinction between the world of prose and that 'embodiment of poetry' as which Milly ends up in Venice (564), if not between Naturalism and Symbolism as such—the squalid calculations of Kate's 'quasi-utilitarian' exchange set against Milly's 'sublime' (646) sacrifice of all calculation

[48] See, on Milly Theale's representativeness of American money, Michael R. Martin's 'Branding Milly Theale: The Capital Case of *The Wings of the Dove*', *The Henry James Review* 24.2 (Spring 2003): 103–32.

[49] Leslie A. Fiedler, *Love and Death in the American Novel* (Funks Grove, IL: Dalkey Archive Press, 1997), 304–5.

[50] The 'negation of Kate's drive and vigor is embodied in Milly Theale, who by her own reckoning has no talent for life at all'. See Constance Wilmarth, 'Framing the Subject: Jameson's James and *The Wings of the Dove*', *The Henry James Review* 36.3 (Fall 2015), 243 [241–8].

to the Infinite.[51] It is notable that Kate begins and concludes the novel in the company of her *déclassé* progenitor; able to perceive 'the persistence of class in ways that Milly cannot', she is an emissary from the precincts of a seedy Naturalism the novel will do everything in its power to obscure.[52] While Milly, with her hunger for 'abysses' (338), emerges from and recedes into a fabular realm of Romance set apart from the mundane. Naturalism vs. Symbolism is not, after all, an outrageous way of putting the terms of this allegorical encounter between rival protagonists. The narrator is forced to a theatrical analogy:

> Certain aspects of the connexion of these young women show for us, such is the twilight that gathers about them, in the likeness of some dim scene in a Maeterlinck play; we have positively the image, in the delicate dusk, of the figures so associated and yet so opposed, so mutually watchful: that of the angular pale princess, ostrich-plumed, black-robed, hung about with amulets, reminders, relics, mainly seated, mainly still, and that of the upright restless slow-circling lady of her court who exchanges with her, across the black water streaked with evening gleams, fitful questions and answers.
>
> (512)

The reflexive typology of *The Wings of the Dove* commits its method to an abstract plane of crepuscular Maeterlinckian vibrations, thus subtly shunting the vestiges of Naturalism that Kate brings to the encounter to a further periphery.[53]

What matters, as I have suggested, is how this typological profusion is 'fixed' by the spectators drawn to the two major figures. There is an instability in the very ground of such fixing, between Kate's sphere of influence (a novelistic libidinal economy of cause-and-effect, quid pro quo transactions), and Milly's (a 'poetic', thoroughly modern shimmer of intensities in the key of melancholy). Densher is the stage on which this indecision between the terms of engagement is played out. As against Kate's sexual down-payment on their pledge, he must weigh 'that something had happened to him too beautiful and too sacred to describe' (647) in Milly's 'glorious great *salone*' (636); and he cannot, in the end, consciously decide the issue. The locution 'something had happened' joins an open thread of other such nameless Events: the disgrace engulfing Lionel Croy—'Something had happened to him that could never be undone' (278)—the fateful meeting of Kate and Densher themselves—'something for each of them had happened' (251)—the final collapse of Milly after Lord Mark's visit—'Something had happened—he didn't

[51] Phyllis van Slyck, 'Charting an Ethics of Desire in *The Wings of the Dove*', *Criticism* 47.3 (Summer 2005), 306 [301–23].

[52] Martin, 'Branding Milly Theale', 113.

[53] That 'Kate's world view is as limited as that of a naturalist writer' is something the novel progressively brings out. Goode, 'The Pervasive Mystery of Style', 252.

know what' (591)—and, sure enough, Densher's again meeting Kate in London—'Something *had* in this case happened to him' (653). This recurrent passive phrase belongs also to the narrator of *The Sacred Fount*, and we find it (or its equivalent) popping up in Conrad and Faulkner, running through literary modernism like a seam of possibility. By enshrouding a character's agency in the heat of a decisive narrative moment, and marking him out as suspended before his fate, withheld from the vulgarity of any Act that might tip the scales, the phrase leaves him to confront it only in the retrospect of the perfect past tense—Lord Jim's 'I had jumped', which yields a very distinct kind of tragic dénouement from the melodramatic machinery of even the richest Dickens or Eliot novel.[54]

What 'had happened' to Densher at the Palazzo Leporelli shall not be named, an aspect of the narrative tact that underwrites the novel's organization of characterological interest.[55] This tact is a theme in the novel itself, where Lionel Croy's crime must remain, with Milly's illness and Susan's desire, unspoken by any character. Such namelessness is the very condition, we might say, of the typological excess of the two major figures: Kate is all the types she is on the basis of her unmentionable paternity; Milly on the basis of her unutterable condition. And this is precisely why they need to be 'fixed'. If Densher fixes Kate as the idol of his fancy, and so threatens all the intrigues and machinations of Aunt Maud with his incalculable quantity of desire, so too Susan Shepherd fixes Milly as the sublime, the imponderable Absolute, and proposes her as a 'trophy' to the worlds of Lancaster Gate and Matcham. It is the degree and quality of 'interest' supplied by these satellite figures that springs the character system into action. Kate hatches her plot of 'squaring' the 'American ladies' to their unsuspecting function as a screen for her lovemaking with Densher (426), and then seeks to devour the substance of the Maeterlinckian 'pale princess', to feed the sordid novel of adultery she is sketching in the margins of her frustrated love-plot; while Milly seeks to capture Densher from that love-plot for an entirely different, 'Symbolist' economy of desire—pining, spiritualized, infinite—of the sort that Susan already enjoys with her.

James' late characterology, begun in *What Maisie Knew*, undergoes a decisive modification. The spectator figure has been fully absorbed into the quartet it regards. That extrinsic relation, which had given rise to such morbid abstractions as the 'joke' of *The Sacred Fount*, is henceforth rendered immanent, albeit in a complex way.[56] The role of ineffective spectator belongs most conspicuously to Milly herself, who, 'heir of all the ages', is by virtue of her illness (the equivalent

[54] See the final chapter in this volume.

[55] See Samuel Cross, 'The Ethics of Tact in *The Wings of the Dove*', *Novel: A Forum on Fiction* 43.3 (Fall 2010): 401–23.

[56] Henry James, *The Letters of Henry James, Vol. 4: 1895–1916*, ed. Leon Edel (Cambridge, MA: Harvard University Press, 1984), 186.

of Maisie's childhood) 'balked' of her 'inheritance'.[57] Milly's enormous 'liberty' as a heroine withers in the bud and turns to agential ash. Her heroism must, then, turn to the business of watching and waiting as, yet again, a quadrilateral forms itself in reference to her—only, now, with her as one of its cardinal points. Then, too, Densher and Susan are watchers and waiters, prototypical subjects of a quartet. This leaves to Kate the abundant sum of action (plotting, planning, scheming) necessary to sustain the quadrilateral in its given form, a fund from which the various kinds of observation at play can draw their nourishment and so set the diameter of the circle where their relations are squared.

It is only the dullest reader who fails to appreciate the pleasing ratio that obtains within the square: Densher is to Kate Croy as Susan is to Milly Theale. Both couples meet under the sign of 'opposed curiosities' (288) or 'the famous law of contraries' (249); and in both cases the one (the 'weaker' who is actually stronger) is attracted to the other for their representative portion of 'culture' (288) and the life of 'the mind' (249), of which s/he feels the lack. Diagonals are thus implied: Kate and Milly being arch antagonists, it remains to the other two to realize a more surreptitious relation. Densher's 'broad brotherhood with Mrs. Stringham' (441), their 'mute communion' (443) as spectators, is one of the more satisfying formal homonyms of the novel. Colleagues of ink and pen, and with similar international childhoods, there is ever for Merton and Susie 'a hint of possibilities between them, of a relation, beneficent and elastic for him' (559) that is critical to the dénouement of the novel itself, as this prolepsis makes clear:

> They were not, as a pair, as a 'team,' really united; there were too many persons, at least three, and too many things, between them; but meanwhile something was preparing that would draw them closer. He scarce knew what: probably nothing but his finding, at some hour when it would be a service to do so, that she had all the while understood him. He even had a presentiment of a juncture at which the understanding of every one else would fail and this deep little person's alone survive.
>
> (547–8)

This intimation of the novel's final vindication of everything Susan has all along quietly understood anticipates Densher's defection from his own pact with 'the London girl', and his higher fealty to the doomed 'American girl'—when 'the joys of Kate's body are forsaken for the consecrated splendours of Brompton Oratory',[58] and for that brand of melancholia associated with 'the excision of homosexual possibility'.[59]

While the Densher-Croy pair hails from the storied kingdom of Naturalist protagonicity, Susan and Milly have their deeper roots in the minor. Susan, who, in

[57] James, 'Preface' to *The Wings of the Dove*, 1290–1.
[58] Goode, 'The Pervasive Mystery of Style', 244.
[59] Sedgwick, *Tendencies*, 89.

'our Maeterlinck picture, might well have hovered in the gloaming by the moat' (512), is minor in her structural repeat of that cognate figure in *The Portrait of a Lady*, Henrietta Stackpole, and to the extent already noted that she 'had renounced her character' (291) to become Milly's companion. Milly, meanwhile, is uniquely qualified by the leading question that James raises in the Preface: the perverse 'idea of making one's protagonist "sick"'.

> Why should a figure be disqualified for a central position by the particular circumstance that might most quicken, that might crown with a fine intensity, its liability to many accidents, its consciousness of all relations? This circumstance, true enough, might disqualify it for many activities—even though we should have imputed to it the unsurpassable activity of passionate, of inspired resistance.
>
> (1288)

Here we have the outline of a very new idea of protagonicity which it will be the purpose of 'modern character' to canonize and elaborate infinitely: the association of the central position not with the 'many activities' of busy realism, but with a 'fine intensity' of 'consciousness' and 'passionate' resistance to circumstance, which is to say, exclusively with affect, mood, and perception. More telling still is the genetic origin that James traces of this strange turn in the precincts of heroism: its source in the minor or secondary. 'One had had moreover, as a various chronicler, one's secondary physical weaklings and failures, one's accessory invalids' (198), James writes, clinching the link between his heroine and Ralph Touchett and so her wellspring in novelistic minority.

It is in Venice that the fracture in our quadrangle becomes apparent to all parties, broken into two triangles along a shared hypotenuse extending between Densher and Milly (Fig. 7.1). The mutual repulsion of Susie and Kate closes each triangle upon itself, where completely different affective intensities are on offer for Densher, who must straddle both. From Kate, Densher takes the plentiful cues of Eros, and is obliged to use Milly as the only sure path to Kate's bed. From Susan Shepherd, meanwhile, in a much longer and more arduous pedagogy, he must learn the trials of hopeless and melancholic passion for the Unattainable—Susie's inadmissible sapphic desires for Milly setting the tone for an altogether more poetic, anti-teleological spectrum of moods.

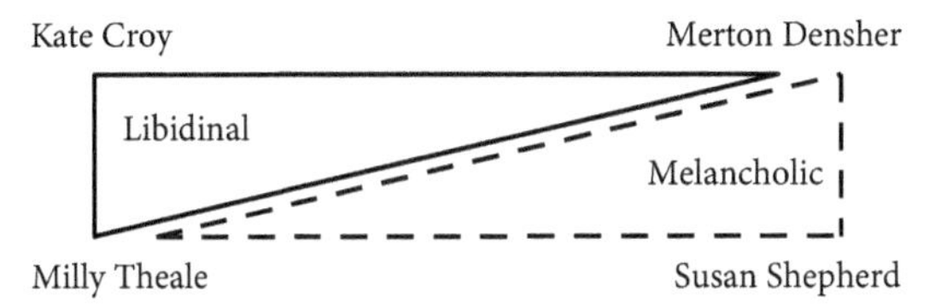

Fig. 7.1 The fractured semiotic rectangle of *The Wings of the Dove*'s character relations

In this way, the novel's characterology is, yet again, its plot, as the fracture internal to the presiding quadrilateral figure is the very crisis of the narrative itself. The 'ultimate concern of the novel is the way in which one person's geometry squares with everybody else's'[60]—until it doesn't, and the breaking of the rectangle spins the geometry out beyond the bounds of novelistic attention, towards a 'poetry—it was also history—Mrs Stringham thought, to a finer tune even than Maeterlinck and Pater, than Marbot and Gregorovius' (289). Naturalism cedes to Symbolism.[61]

The Golden Bowl

In *The Golden Bowl* (1903), finally, these lessons are taken to their outer limit. By the time that, as the Princess Margaret reflects, 'it seemed as easy for them to make a quartette as it had formerly so long appeared for them to make a pair of couples' (778), the form has shed its auxiliary function in this novel and established a provenance in James' art. The 'quartette' has become an organism of its own, a character at a higher level, whose form permits an ingenious exchange and delegation of characterological attributes between the individuals and couples concerned. The spectatorial function inherited from *Maisie* and the *Sacred Fount* narrator is still here, but in residual form, in the person of Fanny Assingham, who indeed—with her 'small still passion for order and symmetry' (836)—is the perspective in reference to which the quartet best 'shows' itself. But the 'point of view' most at issue is the hypothetical one distributed among the four corners of the square itself, the higher-order networked consciousness of a group sensitive above all to its internal 'precious equilibrium' (742, 781). It is, once the geometry is in place, 'quite as if a sense for the equilibrium was what, between them all, had most power of insistence' (758); suggesting an immanent metabolic self-awareness of intra-relatedness, as though a work of art had become cognizant of its own serene 'happy balance' (743).

The plot, such as it is, rests entirely, 'almost miraculously' (846), 'extraordinarily' (861), on that 'most wonderful of chances' (843, 865) betokened by Maggie's rediscovery four years later of a talisman already stroked, already rejected by the desiring gaze of the Prince her husband and Charlotte Stant, his lover and Maggie's childhood friend. This unsubtle declaration of formal dependency upon the fairy-tale fantastic of Balzac's *Peau de chagrin* and Dickens' *Old Curiosity Shop*, on a melodramatic 'coincidence [so] extraordinary' as to evince 'the sort of thing

[60] Goode, 'The Pervasive Mystery of Style', 247.

[61] '*The Wings of the Dove* even more than *The Sacred Fount* (which, Beardsleyan in tone, involves simply one aspect of the Symbolist visual spectrum) should be considered James's Symbolist novel, because of the inclusion of practically all the icons of that movement in painting.' Tintner, 'Henry James and the Symbolist Movement in Art', 408.

that happens mainly in novels and plays' (865), places James in a kind of formal jeopardy for which only the fine geometrical play of the quartet's internal balancing acts can compensate. What begins as two separate couples (Amerigo and Charlotte; Maggie and Adam) undergoes a chiasmic amalgamation into a perverse family unit (father and stepmother; daughter and mother-in-law), which then quickly separates back into the older couples thanks to a law of representativeness (the 'darker' pair doing the social and sexual work of the 'innocent' dyad). The moment a crack appears in the crystal, however, Maggie works assiduously towards a 'fresh distribution of the different weights' in their 'equilibrium' (781), re-establishing the quartet on a higher plane. It is this that, now ringing out its 'beautiful harmony' (782) at frequencies beguiling and transformative, sets up a resonance in each of the participant members, most of all in Maggie herself, whose final heroic effort will be to re-divide the quartet into two couples, only this time the 'right' ones (the Prince and Princess; Mr. and Mrs. Verver) on either side of the Atlantic.

The Ververs, as they enter the picture, are quite without character—amiable, meek, modest, and (as the others repeatedly put it) 'simple'. They lack even the most minimal perquisites of 'personality' or 'agency'; figures of a vulgar new wealth buying off its *gaucherie* in a great campaign of European cultural asset-stripping. Whereas the Prince and Charlotte are somewhat in excess of character, a property lavished in inverse proportion to their paltry quantities of ready cash. When the rectangle snaps into place, when the two couples are chiasmically and 'perversely' (the word appears twenty-four times, and chimes with 'Ververs') arranged, something miraculous happens. The poorer pair provides a great charm and worldliness, a 'frivolous' (669) public face of 'character' for the retiring Ververs' fortune; while the Ververs' fortune provides the poorer pair with the elegant frame and shelter necessary to pursue their rich erotic entanglement. Sex particularly matters here; the Ververs are sexless ciphers, 'abjectly innocent' (721), while 'the clever son-in-law and the charming stepmother' (679) abound in sexual attributes. The pervading puritanical moral atmosphere of the Ververs, those 'primitive parents before the Fall' (681), absolves the active couple's sexual immorality, like 'a vicarious good conscience cultivated on [their] behalf' (680). These internal delegations of function and form are always 'proportionate', obeying a strict law of 'working harmony' (678) and a conservation of energy. The internal metabolism allows for a stable balancing of complementarities, which creates in turn, as the novel progresses, a remarkable feedback effect: the sudden salience of Maggie.

Maggie, to be sure, has 'in perfection her own little character', but this seems always 'to simplify itself' (672) into indistinction. It is the littleness, exposed to the brilliance and scale of the characters of the Prince and Charlotte, that allows these two to take 'advantage of her character', her utter absence of 'selfishness', her 'modesty' (524–5). But what the quartet does for this undeveloped quality, having provided it with larger organic frame, is to force its growth. Within the space of the quartet, what Fanny Assingham calls Maggie's 'no small amount of character' (808) is allowed to bloom, entirely as a result of the redistribution—the blowback—of qualities from the 'lions' to the 'lambs' (820). It is not, then, 'the precious little innermost [. . .] golden personal nature' of Maggie (808) that blossoms, but its germination by foreign spores released within the 'happy spell' of the quartet. In the end, it is as a 'princess' that Maggie will find her full scope. 'That was what she was learning to do, to fill out as a matter of course her appointed, her expected, her imposed character' (780).

'In the later James, "character" is [. . .] in an extreme crisis: it can only exist at all through possession, and so it becomes in itself a monistic concept.'[62] John Goode's observation holds good, and comes into focus around the figure of Adam Verver, who has all the elements of a larger-than-life 'character'; it is what stares out at Maggie as she plans their separation: the '"successful" beneficent person, the beautiful bountiful original dauntlessly wilful great citizen, the consummate collector and infallible high authority' (916). Yet this is not at all how he figures in the text, where he is impossibly mild, modest, quiet, and unassuming. He abounds in metaphorical exemplifications of radical innocence, frequently referred to as a child, 'always marvellously young' (917), and once even as 'some precious spotless exceptionally intelligent lamb' (788). He just 'was simple, he was a revelation of simplicity', but in such a way, the Prince comes to realize, as to be anything but straightforwardly what he is. Adam's 'simplicity' is in fact an abstraction. It is a precipitate, not a medium. What the Prince recognizes as Adam's 'resources, possessions, facilities and amiabilities amplified by the social legend' depend, as he puts it, 'on no personal "equation", no mere measurable medium' (673).

> He was meagre and modest and clear-browed, and his eyes, if they wandered without fear, yet stayed without defiance; his shoulders were not broad, his chest was not high, his complexion was not fresh and the crown of his head was not covered; in spite of all of which he looked, at the top of his table, so nearly like a little boy shyly entertaining in virtue of some imposed rank, that he *could* only be one of the powers, the representative of a force—quite as an infant king is the representative of a dynasty.
>
> (673)

The man without qualities is none other than the 'person' (the *representative of a force*) of Money itself. The imposed rank of wealth he so 'modestly' incarnates means that, like Dostoevsky's idiot, he needs no further 'personal equation'. His body is not a medium on which any character can settle. Money is not a *property of a character*; rather, it makes *a person of a nobody.*

[62] John Goode, '"Character" and Henry James', *New Left Review* I/40 (December 1966), 73 [55–75].

'Money is representative', as Emerson wrote.[63] But of what, and for whom? We need to take stock of what it has meant, particularly in these last two novels, to have predicated a geometrical characterology on this very element. We can put it that, in late James, the great protagonistic potentiality of money celebrated by Balzac is broken cleanly in two: into *potentiality* and *protagonicity*. Money marks the *potential* of those made into 'persons' by its social power; *protagonicity* belongs to those without money who seek it fervently. The 'quartette' brings these moments together, as one couple latches on to another for mutual advantage. Money is the meeting house of the characterless rich and the fortune hunters with character to spare. It is the medium in which 'characters act as surrogates and substitutes for each other', and nicely squares the circles of their transactional relations.[64] 'Money in the later James becomes an attribute of innocence', as John Goode puts it, 'blatantly offered as a magic wand in the capitalist fairy-tale'.[65] Money elevates, abstracts those who have it out of the class antagonisms and exploitation from which it was extracted; it propels them ever upward, away from sordid everydayness, into that 'remoteness from the real' that best characterizes their situation.[66] This distance is also that of the artwork: 'Remote from reality, the purposiveness of artworks has something chimerical about it', writes Adorno; but inevitably '[c]ontent makes its mark in those works that distance themselves from it'.[67] So it is with the infallible 'aesthetic principle' of the plutocrats (589). Adam's radical innocence is the end result of a decades-long process of deracination from the social substrate. He finds himself 'quite at the top of his hill of difficulty, the tall sharp spiral round which he had begun to wind his ascent at the age of twenty, and the apex of which was a platform looking down, if one would, on the kingdoms of the earth and with standing-room for but half-a-dozen others' (543). In just the same way, Milly Theale 'was looking down on the kingdoms of the earth. [. . .] Was she choosing among them or did she want them all?'[68] It is the scant remaining standing-room left for social 'content' on the fairy-tale eyrie that really tells on novelistic composition. The putative 'half-a-dozen' simplifies itself to four, and the perfect crystal formed by their union is held intact by the immense social power of money to keep society at bay; only, in the end, the pressure is too much, a crack runs through the crystal, and the form breaks. The quartet is the precipitate of an immense amount of social carbon; the four-cornered diamond is the figure in

[63] Ralph Waldo Emerson, 'Wealth', in *Essays and Lectures*, ed. Joel Porte (New York: Library of America, 1983), 997 [987–1011].

[64] John Vernon, *Money and Fiction: Literary Realism in the Nineteenth and Early Twentieth Centuries* (Ithaca: Cornell University Press, 1984), 192.

[65] Goode, '"Character" and Henry James', 66.

[66] Eagleton, *Criticism and Ideology*, 141.

[67] Theodor W. Adorno, *Aesthetic Theory*, ed. Gretel Adorno and Rolf Tiedemann, trans. Robert Hullot-Kentor (London: Continuum, 2002), 184–5.

[68] James, *Wings of the Dove*, 298.

which social relations inscribe themselves in the mathematical language of abstraction. Into its crystalline precincts the underlying dynamics and antagonisms, long deferred and immensely diffracted, carry their lethal charge.

In the 'happy spell' of the quadrilateral's equilibrium, as the Ververs are ultimately to make out, there lurks the suspended question of the aesthetic's moral and social indifference. Being absorbed into what Adam calls 'a selfish mass' of four guarantees that, even 'living [. . .] in the biggest crowd in the world', they 'get nothing but the fun', with not 'enough of the sense of difficulty' 'not to be selfish'. There is a looming sense of unpayable debts.

> . . . we're selfish together—we move as a selfish mass. You see we want always the same thing [. . .] and that holds us, that binds us together. We want each other [. . .]; only wanting it, each time, for each other. That's what I call the happy spell; but it's also, a little—possibly—the immorality.
>
> (794)

So it is, too, that the work of art holds itself together through a purposiveness without a purpose, the immanent relatedness and harmony of its parts, its elements unified within 'the nonviolent synthesis of the diffuse',[69] and yet is haunted by the guilt of its innumerable broken pledges, the back it has turned on the world. There is, Adam surmises, 'something haunting—as if it were a bit uncanny—in such a consciousness of our general comfort and privilege' (794). This is nothing more, finally, than a sense of the immense and irresistible pressure of 'other people' breaking asunder the immoral 'happy spell' of persons, or a corporate person, held aloft in the woven golden bower of Capital.

'Mathematization as a method for the immanent objectivation of form is chimerical. Its insufficiency can perhaps be clarified by the fact that artists resort to it during historical periods when the traditional self-evidence of forms dissolves and no objective canon is available.'[70] Henry James, working at just such a moment (as the English leisure class decayed and the American plutocrat was launched) on the frontier between Naturalism and Symbolism, found himself resorting to characterological mathematization—his recurrent triangles and quartets—as a way of persevering with the novelistic work of art, allegorizing the 'insufficiency' of all its available models while performing the insufficiency of its own. The 'formal perfection of symmetrical, compact, and carefully composed character systems' in the late work profoundly defamiliarizes fictional character itself.[71] 'Character' is here a distributed function, not an embodied one. While James' late novels show heavy traces of the decadent French and Italian reaction away from realism in Huysmans and D'Annunzio, whom he read avidly, they attempt a markedly different

[69] Adorno, *Aesthetic Theory*, 189.
[70] Adorno, *Aesthetic Theory*, 188.
[71] Albanese, 'Experimental *Maisie*', 61.

path towards abstraction and affective chromaticism.[72] The fading European aristocracy could no longer supply the over-refined sensibilities, aestheticism, and narcissism that provide the frame for those artists' prose works; protagonicity is thus displaced onto bland American figures of colossal, fairy-tale wealth—which, like blood dripped onto a vampire's lips, stimulates the impoverished older gentry and the residual naturalist personae into action. Narrow subjectivism is sublated through James' geometrical rearrangement of the terms: decadence is offset and raised to a higher level by the symbiosis that holds the 'selfish mass' in place. While they last, miraculously, these geometrical figures of four 'shut out the rest of life' (as sex did in D'Annunzio according to James[73]), allowing unprecedented access to the inner workings of intersubjectivity as ambiguous signals are sent, relayed, refracted, and read across multiple nodes of the circuit-board. Qualities are separated from hosts and reappropriated by other carriers; and a higher-order consciousness is developed with no precedent in world fiction. Yet, under the pressure of everything these units are purpose-built to keep out, they inevitably collapse or shear in two, the elements spinning out of novelistic orbit, in directions that will have to be tracked by other novelists, in other forms.

[72] D'Annunzio exemplified James' call for a 'luxuriant independence from rules and restrictions'. See Moon, 'Is *The Sacred Fount* a Symbolist Novel?', 314.

[73] Henry James, 'Sex: An Immense Omission', in *Theory of Fiction: Henry James*, ed. James E. Miller Jr. (Lincoln: University of Nebraska Press, 1972), 150.

8
Knut Hamsun

Of the many new writers of the 1890s who proclaimed a new era for literature—D'Annunzio, Maeterlinck, and Jarry amongst them—none made a more pronounced push into uncharted characterological terrain than Knut Hamsun (born Knud Pedersen). While others used the available aesthetic language of Symbolism to steer away from rounded realist styles of characterization, back to simpler, more abstract modes, Hamsun deranged the coordinates for prose narrative to such an extent that the very concept of character was itself largely undone. In the stark absence of anything resembling a plot or a generic ground tone, his early protagonists—whether displayed in the first person or third, and often modulating between a simple past and present tense—like Strindberg's and D'Annunzio's drew on a rich autobiographical seam to fashion a style of literary persona defined by presentism, a fecund interiority, and a rhetoric of the 'stranger' or the 'exception.' As the ground of this prose shifts under our feet, shattering long-held assumptions about the functions of action, desire, will, and integrity in the various attributes of character, we find that the category unravels, only to knit itself back together around a new set of functions: passivity, eccentricity, affectivity, and self-referentiality. No longer obliged to bear the stresses of a plausible world of social interactions, of aims and consequences, but allowed to drift and skip across the aleatory surfaces of text, Hamsun's early characters adumbrate a rupture within the very codes of fiction.

To make sense of the enormity of Hamsun's achievement,[1] we need first to affirm the vituperation he shared with Strindberg, D'Annunzio, Huysmans, Egerton, Maeterlinck, and others and that he put into the mouth of his mysterious character Johan Nilsen Nagel: 'I loathe your bourgeois life—phony, orderly, meaningless. I loathe it with a vengeance, and I feel the wrath rising within me, like the wrath of the Holy Spirit, when I think of you.'[2] This familiar *fin-de-siècle* execration is in lockstep with a generational disdain for the culture of the market. A 'coarse and

[1] His early novels have been described as 'an influential contribution—mainly by way of their German and Russian translations—to the process of re-orientation to which the European novel was at that that time being subjected.' J. W. McFarlane, 'The Whisper of the Blood: A Study of Knut Hamsun's Early Novels,' *PMLA* 71.4 (September 1956), 563 [563–94]. Isaac Bashevis Singer went further: 'he is the father of the modern school of literature in his every aspect—his subjectiveness, his fragmentariness, his use of flashbacks, his lyricism. The whole school of modern fiction in the twentieth century stems from Hamsun, just as Russian literature in the nineteenth century "came out of Gogol's greatcoat."' Singer, 'Afterword,' in Knut Hamsun, *Mysteries*, trans. Gerry Bothner (New York: Farrar, Straus & Giroux, 1999), 344.

[2] Hamsun, *Mysteries*, 220.

Modern Character. Julian Murphet, Oxford University Press. © Julian Murphet (2023).
DOI: 10.1093/oso/9780192863126.003.0009

simple marketplace mentality' has sapped the world of its richer meanings and blinded us to our variegated inner complexion;[3] the capitalist order of things is anathematized for its vulgarity, standardization, and anomie. Within this detestation for the modern bourgeois a more focused contempt was hatched for the cultural and literary forms that kept it in place. Literature was to be condemned for its capitulation to the banal and conventional, to social reproduction: 'Ordinary fiction about dances and engagements and excursions and marriages is nothing but reading for sea-captains and coachmen looking for an hour's entertainment. Cheap writing!'[4] For Hamsun, *épater les bourgeois* meant liquidating the accumulated literary means for stabilizing their worldview, and that meant an entire characterology which traded in *types* rather than individuals:

> Now what if literature on the whole began to deal a little more with mental states than with engagements and balls and hikes and accidents as such? Then one would, to be sure, have to relinquish creating 'types,'—as all have been created before,—'characters'—whom one meets every day at the fishmarket. And to that extent one would perhaps lose a part of the public which reads in order to see if the hero and heroine get each other. But in return there would be more individual cases in the books, and these in a way more appropriate to the intellectual life which mature people now live.[5]

In these remarkable formulations, drawn up in 1890 as he was launching *Hunger*, Hamsun identified the proliferation of 'character types' with the stereotypical plot-points of the bourgeois comic novel: balls, engagements, dances, marriages. Plots entail characters, and characters incur plots, in a vicious circle of determination that trapped bourgeois fiction in a 'phony, orderly, meaningless' repetition of its commercial forms. In his own estimation, this charge could equally be levelled at Zola and his Naturalist school of literature, a barb that shares its venom with Huysmans and Strindberg in their pivots away from Zola in the 1890s.

> The so-called 'Naturalists', Zola and his period, wrote about people with dominant traits. They had no use for the more subtle psychology, and people all had this 'dominant characteristic' which ordained their actions. [. . .] From the time I began I do not think that in my entire output you will find a character with a single dominant characteristic. They are all without your so-called 'character'. They are split and fragmented, not good or bad, but both at once, ever subtle and changeable in their attitudes and deeds.[6]

[3] Knut Hamsun, 'From the Unconscious Life of the Mind' (c.1890), trans. Marie Skramstad de Forest, in *Two Essays*, Heaven Chapbook Series #48 (Louisville, KY: White Fields Press, 1994), 6.
[4] Hamsun, qtd. in McFarlane, 'The Whisper of the Blood', 565.
[5] Hamsun, 'From the Unconscious Life of the Mind', 7.
[6] Hamsun, aged 80 in 1946, giving written evidence in his trial for having been a member of the Nasjonal Samling during the Second World War; quoted and translated by Joseph A. Slavin, 'The

Here the elderly Hamsun lucidly recalls the presiding animus of his earliest work against Taine's idea of the *faculté maîtresse*, an inert psychological category that, in Zola's work particularly, had stymied the growth of a 'subtle psychology' and those 'more individual cases' that might flourish out of its shadow.[7] But in Hamsun's push against 'your so-called "character"', Strindberg was the key correspondent.[8] Having declared Dickens' characters 'puppets', and the characters on the bourgeois stage 'automata'—'A well-drawn character is synonymous with a caricature'[9]—the great Swede prefaced the 1888 published version of his *Miss Julie* with the assertion that his drama's 'souls (characters) are conglomerates of past and present stages of culture, bits out of books and newspapers, scraps of humanity, torn shreds of once fine clothing now turned to rags, exactly as the human soul is patched together'.[10] This became an article of faith for Hamsun's 'post-characterological' prose narratives. 'Strindberg is in my opinion the only writer in Scandinavia who has made a serious attempt to produce modern psychology [. . .]. Strindberg realizes, realizes and recognizes, the inadequacies of the character psychology prevailing at present for describing the split and disharmonic mind of modern man.'[11]

Hamsun's campaign was thus overtly *against character*, against the lazy automatisms and repetitions of bourgeois fiction's trait-defined types; and for that same reason, *against plot*, against the forced organization of his material into spurious formal statements, developments, and reversals, inherited from the Ancients, having nothing to do with the 'ever subtle and changeable' phenomena of daily life under the capital-relation. As he wrote in 1890 about the narrator-protagonist of *Hunger*, 'This "I" is no ordinary person, no type; he is a [. . .] finely tuned, strange, sensitive, impressionable nature.'[12] Hamsun undertakes his double campaign via a compensatory development of hitherto underdeveloped technical means, their transformation into ends. Specifically, his prose, stepping away from analyses of action and mores, shifts its emphasis towards point of view—voice, tone, mood, temperament—as an end in itself, radically complicating narrative perspective. 'Hamsun's intention was not so show *Entwicklung* but rather a soul's dialogue with

Wound, the World, and the Word: Narrating Consciousness and Continuity of Hamsun's Authorship', in *Two Essays*, 7.

[7] For an excellent early discussion of Taine's *faculté maîtresse*, see André Chevrillon, 'Les Principes Critiques de Taine: II: La Faculté Maîtresse', *La Revue des Deux Mondes, Septième Période* 46.1 (July 1928): 116–44. Taine himself pursues the idea in the prefaces to his *Essais de critique et d'histoire*, vol. 1 (1858), and the Introduction to his *Histoire de la littérature anglaise*, 4 vols. (1863–4).

[8] 'August Strindberg's autobiography, *Son of a Servant* [. . .] fell into his hands in Minneapolis. There he also discovered that Strindberg had recommended the autobiographical documentary as the only acceptable novel of the future.' Harald Næss, *Knut Hamsun* (Boston: Twayne, 1984), 32.

[9] August Strindberg, *Son of a Servant*, trans. Claud Field (New York: G. P. Putnam's Sons, 1913), 253.

[10] August Strindberg, 'Preface' to *Miss Julie* in *Miss Julie and Other Plays*, ed. and trans. Michael Robinson (Oxford: Oxford University Press, 1998), 59–60.

[11] Knut Hamsun, *Artikler*, ed. Francis Bull (Oslo, 1939), 44; translated in McFarlane, 'The Whisper of the Blood', 567.

[12] Knut Hamsun, letter to Gustav af Geijerstam, 1890, *Briefe* (Munich: Langen-Müller, 1957), 87; qtd. in Daniel Rees, *Hunger and Modern Writing: Melville, Kafka, Hamsun, and Wright* (Köln: Modern Academic Publishing, 2016), 88.

its alter or superior ego.'[13] 'I could hear myself uttering this drivel', *Hunger*'s narrator informs us, 'but took in each word I spoke as though it were coming from another person.'[14] So far did Hamsun pursue this agenda that 'in *Hunger* he produced perhaps the first novel to make consciousness itself a hero.'[15] In place of character, consciousness; and in place of plot, episodes. Indeed, Hamsun takes enormous strides, particularly in *Mysteries* (1892), in the direction of 'stream of consciousness' narration. 'His was a technique distinguished by fracturing the first-person narrator into several voices placed in peculiar dialogue with each other, alternately observing, reflecting and commenting on each other.'[16] As André Gide wrote of *Hunger*, the book had '[a]ucune histoire, aucune intrigue' [no story, no intrigue], and focused entirely on the dialogical, multifaceted egoism of its protagonist.[17] It is, exemplarily, 'a novel without plot, without any orthodox development or culmination in the action, without moral lesson or social significance.'[18] 'With its dissolution of plot, self-indulgent lyricism, and blunt irrationality, the novel marked a turning-point in Scandinavian literary modernity.'[19] Character here is not what imprints itself on social space according to some expressive personality trait, but what feels, reacts, and ruminates freely among a range of internal personae and moods that are rarely externalized. Inverting centuries of association around this concept, character is not, for Hamsun, a writing of the self in legible phrases on the commonplace book of Life; rather, it is the secret space in which a writing must now take shape, a new writing without any language, sprung from morbid introspection and the spontaneous productivity of desire.

The formal carapace within which these remarkable developments are pursued, if not defined by the mechanics of novelistic plot, must then be governed by a different principle, which we can identify as that of the *episode*. Doubtless, the episode is as central to novelistic form as the chapter and the scene; but episodic fiction proper is distinct from the novel, including the serialized novel, by virtue of its thoroughgoing disregard for the molar unities of traditional aesthetics. Like medieval *chansons* and the Elizabethan picaresque, truly episodic fiction eschews those harmonious thematic statements and gestures of closure that bourgeois art imposes on its forms; its molecular energies remain committed to local effects and fade rapidly from the mind once the next episode heaves into view. That this curious form should resurface at the end of the nineteenth century is not accidental; it is of the logic of commodity production in the sphere of culture that, not wholes,

[13] Næss, *Knut Hamsun*, 32–3.

[14] Knut Hamsun, *Hunger*, trans. Sverre Lyngstad (Melbourne: Text, 2006), 102–3.

[15] Robert Ferguson, *Enigma: The Life of Knut Hamsun* (London: Faber, 2011), 112.

[16] Ingar Sletten Kolloen, *Knut Hamsun: Dreamer and Dissenter*, trans. Deborah Dawkin and Erik Skuggevik (New Haven: Yale University Press, 2009), 28.

[17] André Gide, Preface to *La Faim*, trans. Georges Sautreau (Paris: PUF, 1961), 5–6 [1–10].

[18] McFarlane, 'The Whisper of the Blood', 576.

[19] Stefano Evangelista, *Literary Cosmopolitanism in the English Fin de Siècle: Citizens of Nowhere* (Oxford: Oxford University Press, 2021), 125.

but parts should predominate. Decadence itself will be crystallized in Havelock Ellis' well-known formulation:

> A style of decadence is one in which the unity of the book is decomposed to give place to the independence of the page, in which the page is decomposed to give place to the independence of the phrase, and the phrase to give place to the independence of the word. A decadent style, in short, is an anarchistic style in which everything is sacrificed to the development of the individual parts.[20]

The plotless novel is one in which this sacrifice has been made a priori vis-à-vis its own form. In the absence of any larger plot design, the individual episodes now attach themselves narratively to the protagonist as expositions of whose mysterious complexes they are articulated. In his discussion of epic form in Brecht (who admired Hamsun's objectivity[21]) Fredric Jameson makes these points:

> [T]he effect of narrative is rather different when it is the subject or the character, the protagonist, who is its object. Now the result is [. . .] to bring an uncanny strangeness to the subjective moment of decision and action itself, the 'proairesis' of the protagonist, with its wavering motives and intentions, its psychological impulses as well, and even its unconscious drives.[22]

This was Hamsun's gamble with his rejection of the well-made novel form—that the results would reorient prose narrative towards the inchoate psychological materials and the unconscious drives of a modern *stultus*, which he explicitly heralded in 1890, promising to map 'the whole unconscious life of the mind.'[23]

Freeing the narrative voice to treat the 'whole unconscious life of the mind' as though it were a submerged plot, an occult text, in relation to which the individual could be exposed as a series of dispositions, appetites, stirrings, meanderings of the psyche, and chaotic perceptions, Hamsun brought an 'uncanny strangeness' to his depiction of the wellsprings of deliberative agency. And he was adamant that the result should not be confused with that despised form, the novel.

[20] Havelock Ellis, *Views and Reviews: A Selection of Uncollected Articles 1884–1932* (Boston: Houghton Mifflin, 1932), 52.

[21] 'Our literature is astonishingly free of opinions. When you read Kipling and Hamsun the subject matter is completely different, just like the point of view, but behind the subject matter you can clearly see a standpoint and the man to whom it belongs, and it is the man that counts. He states his opinion, whether right or wrong—that is, whether it suits our taste or not—and the man allows us to place ourselves above him and observe him writing.' Bertolt Brecht, in Tom Kuhn and Steve Giles, eds., *Brecht on Art and Politics*, trans. Laura Bradley, Steve Giles, and Tom Kuhn (London: Bloomsbury, 2003), 27.

[22] Fredric Jameson, *Brecht and Method* (London: Verso, 1998), 52.

[23] Hamsun, *Artikler*, 60–1; quoted and translated in Harald Næss, 'Strindberg and Hamsun,' in Marilyn Johns Blackwell, ed., *Structures of Influence: A Comparative Approach to August Strindberg* (Chapel Hill: University of North Carolina Press, 1981), 129 [121–32].

> My book must not be regarded as a novel. There are enough people who write novels when they want to write about hunger—from Zola to Kielland. They all do it. And if it is the lack of this kind of novel, which perhaps makes my book monotonous, then that is quite simply a commendation, in that I had determined quite deliberately not to write a novel.[24]

As he wrote to his German translator in 1890, 'I am completely incapable of writing for the masses; novels with betrothals and dances and childbirth, overlaid with an external apparatus, are a bit too cheap for me and have no interest for me.'[25] The war against character, against plot, and against the novel form, are interdependent moments of an aesthetic-philosophic mission to arraign bourgeois narrative art, to hijack its faltering formal energies and expropriate them for very different artistic and ethical purposes: what Rancière calls the *aesthetic regime*'s interest in a molecular, atomistic egalitarianism of perception and affection, where no preexisting hierarchy or 'distribution of the sensible' intervenes to decide in advance the value of any hard-won crystal of aesthetic energy.[26]

One of the most pertinent consequences of this multi-front war for literary characterology is the foreshortening of the rich social topographies of the Victorian novel in Hamsun's text. *Hunger* and *Mysteries* are set in a city and village respectively;[27] but even these early concessions to the metropole and the provincial 'knowable community' are scarcely recognizable for any genetic relation to Balzac and Zola, Dickens and Hardy, Trollope and Tolstoy. The sudden evacuation of social space here—the stark absence of boudoirs, assembly rooms, churches, private parlours, inner chambers, offices, and so on—deracinates the foundation of the extended prose narrative form in spatial heterogeneity and prohibits any appearance of the broad mix of social 'types' who naturally inhabit these *topoi*. In place of that familiar, teeming novelistic topography, we are given a radically myopic (and 'de-realized') view of Kristiania in *Hunger*, and the typical small coastal town in *Mysteries*. It is as if, to take only the first novel, Poe's eponymous Man of the Crowd had been elevated from the position of a curious eccentric the narrator must track, to the status of protagonist himself. 'This noisy traffic everywhere put me in a brighter mood immediately', he remarks at the outset, 'and I

[24] Hamsun, Letter to Georg Brandes, 1890, in Knut Hamsun, *Selected Letters, Vol. 1: 1879–1898*, ed. Harald Næss and James McFarlane (Norwich: Norvik Press, 1990), 114.

[25] Hamsun, quoted and translated in McFarlane, 'The Whisper of the Blood', 578.

[26] Jacques Rancière, *The Politics of Aesthetics: The Distribution of the Sensible*, trans. Gabriel Rockhill (London: Continuum, 2004), 7–46.

[27] We will not follow Hamsun to the homestead or farm where he would relocate and re-engineer his aesthetic mission, from *Pan* through *The Growth of the Soil* and the long chain of Volkish romances that would draw him resistlessly towards Fascism. A popular joke about Hamsun during the Second World War ran as follows: 'The Germans have decided to divide Hamsun's works between themselves and the Norwegians. The Germans will get *The Growth of the Soil* and *Victoria*, while Norwegians will keep *Hunger*.' Qtd. in Kathleen Stokker, *Folklore Fights the Nazis: Humour in Occupied Norway* (Madison: University of Wisconsin Press, 1995), 147.

started feeling more and more contented'. 'I went with the flow, borne from place to place this happy morning, rocking serenely to and fro among other happy people.'[28] For this article of urban flotsam, there is simply no 'deep space' at all,[29] and we are pulled erratically from park bench to police cell to alleyway to a cheap rented room with the landlady in the doorway, without any sanctuary or stable recess within which (like Dostoevsky's Raskolnikov or the narrator of *Notes from the Underground*[30]) to recharge. The novel is entirely situated on the shallow surfaces of urban space; even its interiors, like the nightmarish family parlour in Part Four, seem indistinguishable from the punishing round of the street.

The protagonist who drifts across the city surface is almost entirely invisible to the propertied citizens who surround him while ignoring him: 'I sat on the same spot for a quarter of an hour or more. People came and went and nobody bothered me' (79). Neither do they make any impression on his own cognitive map of the city, which is peopled instead by pawnbrokers, streetwalkers, shopkeepers, beggars, editors' assistants, cab drivers, and, above all, the ubiquitous police. Indeed, the corollary of the narrator's invisibility to the typical bourgeois citizen is his hyper-visibility to the constabulary—this is a novel about the conspicuousness of the homeless vis-à-vis the eye of the state in its role as the executive will of the governing class.

> A police officer forces his way up to me and wants to know what's up.
>
> 'Nothing', I answer, 'nothing at all. I just wanted to give my waistcoat to that little girl over there . . . for her father. . . . It's nothing to laugh at. I will simply go home and put on another one.'
>
> 'No rumpus in the street!' says the officer. 'So, move along now!' And he nudges me on my way.
>
> (76)

This raffish familiarity between protagonist and police, so different from the horror of Dickens or Dostoevsky, extends to an evening spent in prison, which far from being a nadir in this character's odyssey represents a victory over the authorities, inasmuch as it affords welcome shelter on a freezing night. It is a victory purchased via the narrator's ability to invent and proliferate names, to evade objective identification and classification through fictive ruses and a spontaneous

[28] Hamsun, *Hunger*, 19, 20.

[29] David Trotter, *Literature in the First Media Age: Britain Between the Wars* (Cambridge, MA: Harvard University Press, 2013), 184–95.

[30] It is worth pointing out that, ever since, in 1888, Edvard Brandes told Axel Lundegård that 'there was about it [the *Hunger* fragment] something of a Dostoievsky', there has been a great deal of commentary on Hamsun's debts to the great Russian. The problem is that he had only read snatches of the author while in America, and it wasn't until after the publication of his short story 'Hazard' in 1889 that he began any systematic approach to Dostoevsky. See Hanna Astrup Larsen, *Knut Hamsun* (London: Gyldendal, 1922), 33; Kolloen, *Knut Hamsun*, 48, 59.

characterology. Our protagonist, like many in the subsequent annals of modern character, has no written name; but he can produce dozens of them on demand. In what follows, note the degree to which he seizes more than just the first-person pronoun in his drive to become the author of his own text:

> 'Name?' the officer on duty asked.
>
> 'Tangen—Andreas Tangen.'
>
> I don't know why I lied. My thoughts fluttered about in disarray and gave me more fanciful notions than I could handle. I hit upon this far-fetched name on the spur of the moment and tossed it out without any ulterior motive. I lied unnecessarily.
>
> 'Occupation?'
>
> Now he was forcing me to the wall. Hmm! I thought first of turning myself into a tinsmith but didn't dare; I had given myself a name not borne by each and every tinsmith, and besides I was wearing glasses. Then it came into my head to be foolhardy—I took a step forward and said, firmly and solemnly, 'Journalist.'
>
> (64)

Such are the advantages of being exiled from bourgeois character space: with no hearth, no office, no club, no inner sanctum to certify his identity, the narrator may extemporize names and occupations fitted to circumstance. If, in the standard novel form, space and character, name and location, are always mutually implicating, then when the relationship breaks down, new and 'far-fetched' configurations become possible. Playing novelist in his own anti-novel, the protagonist abides by certain rules of typification: if he is 'Andreas Tangen', he cannot be a tinsmith, and his spectacles designate a white-collar profession. Extrapolation fills in the blanks. He is no longer a homeless writer starving to death on the streets of Kristiania; rather he 'Sat at the Prime Minister's dressed to the nines till two o'clock, forgot my gate key and a wallet with several thousand at home!' (65). And he sleeps in the jailhouse bunk 'Like a cabinet minister!' (69). Even his tattered clothes cannot shatter the illusion created by a name used judiciously in context; in bourgeois social space, the world is already a novel, a palimpsest of types and clichés.

Nor does it stop here, this authorial will to inscribe names, characters, on the city which, because it has no depths for him, is virtually all surface, all text. The narrator of *Hunger* is the first properly metafictional character self-consciously to project a world with words rather than lapse into objectivity, realism, sentiment, and morality; just as Hamsun himself writes *Hunger* as a weapon against the novel and Naturalist psychologism. Aware that he requires a love-interest to sustain a focus on sexual desire, he produces a near-palindrome of one—'a name with a nervous, gliding sound: Ylajali' (24)—who may or may not correspond with a woman walking the streets of Kristiania. 'Ylajali' is one of the few constants of the book, a recurring presence that is really an absence, token of the desire from which she springs as an obvious wish-fulfilment. That she, too, abandons the narrator by the end of the book without any consummation is testimony to the love-plot as deliberately missed opportunity, evidence of a generic '"road not taken", the direction *Hunger* might have gone' had it been a bourgeois novel.[31] Ylajali is also deployed in another characterological manoeuvre, in relation to a different name, 'Happolati', used to distract and befuddle a little old man who sits down beside our narrator on a park bench. 'Happolati' is, variously, the narrator's landlord at 2 St Olaf Place, the brother of a sailor, an agent 'for all sorts of things, lingonberries to China, feathers and down from Russia, hides, wood pulp, writing ink—' (32), inventor of the electric hymn book, a former Persian cabinet minister, and father to Ylajali, 'a fairy princess who owned three hundred women slaves and slept on a bed of yellow roses' (34). Once the name is out, there is nothing that cannot attach itself to it as a literary predicate, on a swelling, global frame of reference. 'The situation was running away with me, and one lie after another sprang up in my head' (33). His auditor contributes further characteristics—an able man, owner of vast properties—and 'Happolati' has ceased to be 'the foreign name I had invented' (34), to become a palpable figure in the civic and commercial life of the capital. So it is, too, with that other projected person, Joachim Kierulf, whom our narrator seeks in a sudden urge to hail a coach and commit himself ardently to the 'realist floor-plan' of actual Kristiania streets, addresses, and residents.[32] '"37 Ullevaal Road!" I cried. And we rolled off' (114) to find this Kierulf, a 'trader in wool', but he isn't in; 'Drive to 11 Tomte Street', he barks at the cabbie, who agrees that 'there was no mistaking that man [Kierulf]. Didn't he usually wear a light-coloured coat?' (115). No, the narrator won't accept that; the 'light coat was extremely unwelcome and spoiled the image of the man I had made for myself', although the driver's next suggestion, that Kierulf is a redhead, is much more satisfactory.

> I was instantly convinced he was right. I felt grateful to the poor driver and told him he had caught the spitting image of the man; what he had said was perfectly correct. It would be something quite exceptional, I said, to see such a man without red hair.
>
> 'It must be the same person I've driven a couple of times', the coachman said. 'He even had an ashplant'.
>
> This made the man come vividly alive to me, and I said, 'Ha-ha, to be sure, no one has ever yet seen that man without his ashplant in his hand. You may rest assured as far as that goes, quite assured'.
>
> Yes, it was obviously the same man he had driven. He had recognised him . . . .
>
> (115)

[31] Arnold Weinstein, *Northern Arts: The Breakthrough of Scandinavian Literature and Art, from Ibsen to Bergman* (Princeton: Princeton University Press, 2008), 253.

[32] Fredric Jameson, 'The Realist Floor-Plan', in Marshall Blonsky, ed., *On Signs* (Baltimore: Johns Hopkins University Press, 1985), 373–83.

In this dazzling comic passage, Weinstein has observed, the 'entire construct/consort of character is being jerked around, taken for a ride, hauled out for inspection and then blown sky-high'.[33] Hamsun's narrator is so *au fait* with the assortment of types that comprise a novelized city that he can confidently draw the merest sketch of one and sit back as his interlocutors supply physiognomy and dress. Character types are, in that sense *real*: they persist as social imagos patched together out of various overlapping codes and make it possible to recognize a purely fictive fabrication as a plausible citizen who has ridden your coach several times. But by that same token, they are patently *abstract*: if all it takes is a proper name traversed by a couple of 'semes' (an address, a trade, a hair colour, a prop) to establish a viable persona, then character is being governed by formulae and patterns that precede the individual who assumes it.[34] *Real abstractions* walk the streets.

Out of his radical solitude, the narrator can fashion any number of personae to flesh out a social and sexual existence for himself, and irradiate the flat, numbing world of economic necessity with the light of his desire. His is an exemplary case of the extent to which the One of modern character is always and already a multitude of others whom he either suffers as an internal schism or projects onto the world with comic aplomb. As a metafictional illustration of the situation out of which he grew, the narrator of *Hunger* could scarcely be improved upon; the book's 'peculiar authority is that it was in many ways Hamsun's own story'.[35] As Hamsun wrote much later, at the end of his career, he had 'created several hundred different characters, every one of them spun from myself'.[36] 'The multitude of characters spun out of the hunger artist's perceptions—characters suffering from a kind of holy anorexia—have this in common: they are the narrators of their own stories and themselves, concerned with the sovereign word in the realm of fiction.'[37] It is only that, in the space of the text itself, these characters, like their author, have nothing to do and nowhere to go. They are thumbnail sketches and half-drawn portraits, pockets of narrative possibility drawn on the run without even the epiphanic mode of the short story to fulfil their potentials. The narrator, a struggling writer, knows all too well the experience of beginning a fiction, peopling it with figures and activating its narrative engines without having the wherewithal to finish, and so moving desperately on to the next job—an essay, a treatise, or a witty commentary. In the one-act allegory he begins in Part Four, 'The Sign of the Cross', the 'gorgeous fanatical whore' who sins 'simply from a

[33] Weinstein, *Northern Arts*, 268.
[34] The formula is Roland Barthes', in his *S/Z*, trans. Richard Miller (Oxford: Blackwell, 1990), 67.
[35] Ferguson, *Enigma*, 110. 'From America Victor Nilsson wrote asking him whether the events described in Hunger had really happened to him: "Yes, all of it, and much more, right here at home", replied Hamsun' (110–11).
[36] Hamsun in 1946, qtd. in Slavin, 'The Wound, the World, and the Word', 7.
[37] Slavin, 'The Wound, the World, and the Word', 9.

voluptuous contempt of heaven' (148) obsesses our protagonist with the enormity of her personality:

> Her body was to be misshapen and repulsive: tall, very skinny and rather dark, with long legs that showed through her skirts at every step she took. She would also have big, protruding ears. In short, she would not be easy on the eye, barely tolerable to look at. What interested me about her was her wonderful shamelessness, the desperate excess of premeditated sin that she had committed. (149)

But the lights go out, he hasn't a candle, and the landlady is about to evict him; the drama is never completed, despite the potential of its protagonist—who exists in despite of the failure of any narrative to congeal around her. So it is with all his people, his motley tribe of half-finished personae who have no story, no plot in which to inscribe their destinies.

The links between our protagonist's vocation, his economic situation, his physical and emotional debility, and the status of his characters, are material and determining. To write in the Kristiania of the end of the nineteenth century, 'following two decades of the hardest economic times modern Norway had seen, where increased integration into the global capital market made many traditional professions obsolete', is to imagine oneself as a professional, but to be treated, willy-nilly, as an unemployed manual labourer or artisan.[38] 'Didn't I have the same right to life as anyone else, like Pascha the second-hand book-dealer, or Hennechen the steamship agent?', the narrator asks, before immediately acknowledging that 'I have the shoulders of a giant and two stout arms for work, and [...] I even applied for a job as a woodcutter on Møller Street to earn my daily bread' (62). He wants the bourgeois status of a name and a station but his proletarian anonymity is stamped upon him like the brawn of his physique. Trapped in the time-honoured holding pattern of job-seeking, scrounging, and bill-dodging, while his body wastes away, the narrator's narrative has no project beyond the immediate one of surviving. 'Throughout *Hunger*, the human residue of a rapidly changing economic system hovers at the margins of the narrator's starved consciousness. Yet no figure in *Hunger* better embodies the economic context of the novel than the nameless narrator himself.'[39] So too his metafictional characters who, even if they are fabulously wealthy like Happolati, or holy like the 'gorgeous fanatical whore' of his play, cannot be imagined in a plot because their creator hasn't the wherewithal to give them one.

[38] Eveliina Pulkki, 'Failing Authorship in Knut Hamsun's *Sult* (1890)', *Forum for Modern Language Studies* 54.3 (2018), 294 [293–306].

[39] Timothy Wientzen, 'The Aesthetics of Hunger: Knut Hamsun, Modernism, and Starvation's Global Frame', *NOVEL: A Forum on Fiction* 48.2 (August 2015), 211 [208–23].

Character, like the labour that produces it, is interrupted, itinerant, contingent, unfinished. The 'fragmented and discontinuous' nature of the mental presentation of the protagonist, a reflection of his working conditions, is amplified in his own quasi-autonomous, amputated personae.[40] If it is true, as Kittang writes, that '[i]nstead of presenting us with a fully-fledged character, the text shows how a human subjectivity is beginning to take shape', it is also the case that, for reasons already elaborated, there is only ever beginning and beginning again; nothing can be completed or reconciled in a labour market where supply outstrips demand.[41] The one material that serves to unify and mediate what is otherwise a chaotically miscellaneous, episodic narrative is the inevitable one of *paper*, the medium of contingency and exchange at the end of the nineteenth century, and of subjectivity and character itself. It is worth wondering whether *Hunger* is not, after all, a critical early instalment in the twentieth-century reflection on 'what will have been meant', as Derrida puts it in his ruminations on the 'paper machine', 'by the *trait* or mark, of course, and retreat (*retrait*), but first of all by *being-beneath*, the submission or subjectedness of subjectivity in general' to paper as such.[42] From the opening scene in his cheap room, wallpapered with pages from the *Morgenbladet* festooned with advertisements, to the trusty papers he keeps in his pockets at all times (which attract flies), the shaving coupons that fall out of his pocket, the sightless old man in the park who holds his old grease-stained newspaper in such a way as to make the narrator think of 'documents, dangerous records stolen from some archive!' (31), to the page on which he 'wrote mechanically the date 1848 in every corner of the page' (36), or those happier leaves whereon 'one word follows another, they connect with one another and turn into situations; scenes pile on top of other scenes, actions and dialogue well up in my brain, and a wonderful sense of pleasure takes hold of me' (38), to the wrapping paper out of which he fashions a pillow, the scrawled note of departure he leaves for his first landlady, the newspapers for which he drafts his articles, the 'few sheets of paper, coated with dust' (72) that are also 'the cleanest thing I had left' (81) and are his sole possession, the papers the editor tosses into the wastebasket, the paper cornucopia full of imaginary coins which fools the police constable, the small boy tying together strips of paper in a chain as a man with a red beard spits on him from a second-floor window, the torn scraps of his play floating around the streets, and of course the paper money, the five- and ten-krone notes, that periodically save the narrator from immediate demise, above all the one he crumples up and throws into the face of the landlady who has evicted him—it is a novel, printed on paper, in which

[40] Rees, *Hunger and Modern Writing*, 95.

[41] Atle Kittang, 'Knut Hamsun's *Sult*: Psychological Deep Structures and Metapoetic Plot', in Janet Garton, ed., *Facets of European Modernism*, essays in honour of James McFarlane presented to him on his 65th birthday, 12 December 1985 (Norwich: University of East Anglia, 1985), 297 [295–308].

[42] Jacques Derrida, *Paper Machine*, trans. Rachel Bowlby (Stanford: Stanford University Press, 2005), 43.

paper is the only true constant, and becomes the great spiritual test of its central character, himself a set of marks [*traits*] on paper:

> When I just couldn't get any further, I began staring with wide-open eyes at those last words, that unfinished sheet of paper, peering at the strange, trembling letters which stared up at me from the paper like small unkempt figures, and at the end I understood nothing at all and didn't have a thought in my head.
>
> (100)

Sitting and writing, or walking, or sleeping: this character is a maker of marks, *kharaktēr*, on the singular support of everything he can claim to be, paper, which finally cannot subdue the inner, autonomous life of each letter, each *kharaktēr*, 'small unkempt figures' like their author, in a trembling of affect no sentence can constrain. Social inequalities, remarks Derrida, 'separate the rich and the poor, and one of the indicators of this is "our" relationship to the production, consumption, and "waste" of paper.'[43] In no other novel has this relationship been subjected to such a searching and moving analysis as in *Hunger*. As the narrator tells us, 'The intelligent poor individual was a much finer observer than the intelligent rich one' (136), and the choice object of his observations is the waste paper that blows along the streets.

Paper is the privileged medium of the aesthetic regime of the arts: the silencing of speech's dominance over representation, the space in which a pure style is cultivated, the anonymity of a faceless, genre-less, disseminated discourse; but also the de-differentiation of all kinds of writing, the collapse of the division between what is 'fiction' and what is not.[44] So it is, emblematically, in *Hunger*, where the name of the protagonist is never broached, and the line between autobiography and novelism is permanently blurred. On paper, in the aesthetic regime, all boundaries are dissolving: between the significant and the insignificant, the narrative and the descriptive, the aesthetic and the anti-aesthetic, the proper and the improper, the named and the anonymous. There is nothing our narrator will not describe, from flies on his writing paper to chunks of meat gnawed off a dog's bone, from spit to vomit to the blood drying in a gnawed navel; the sordid world drawn by the *nature morte* of his prose belongs to no representative regime, but to a zone of pure indistinction. In this zone names are meaningless. As John Frow writes, 'Names . . . inscribe us in the social order, tying bodies to language to make us recognizable as persons or non-persons. [. . .] Naming places us, designating such things as gender, birth-order, clan, geographical provenance, ethnicity, and religion.'[45] But in the paper economy of the aesthetic regime, none of this tying down or inscription

[43] Derrida, *Paper Machine*, 63.

[44] See, for instance, the discussion of Flaubert's task in Madame Bovary in Jacques Rancière, *The Politics of Literature*, trans. Julie Rose (Cambridge: Polity, 2011), 55–71.

[45] John Frow, *Character and Person* (Oxford: Oxford University Press, 2014), 181.

can stand; names have only a bureaucratic function. In the absence of a name, the 'social order' has nowhere to land, language remains unmoored, and bodies radiate outward into the object world of which they are a constituent element, which is exactly what writing wants.[46] Persons and things are confused, interfused, the way our narrator is with his papers. And although he is an outsider, a stranger in Kristiania, it is odd that he is never asked for his 'papers', which would fail to corroborate the false names he gives; it is as if he has sunk under the radar of naming.

As a result, no semes can stick to him, and he can be recognized and hailed only on the basis of other signs: principally, the signs of progressive degeneration and decay that mark his starving body, which are ever-changing. Our Hero, writes Maud Ellmann, 'is a starving writer, and it seems to be the writing that is emptying his body, feasting words with fasting flesh. [. . .] Here the creation of the work of art entails the decreation of the artist, since his writings bleed his body dry.'[47] But prior to that, it has already consumed his name without a trace. Although there are other nameless protagonists in modern literature—in James' *Aspern Papers*, Perkins Gilman's 'The Yellow Wallpaper', Du Maurier's *Rebecca*, and Ellison's *Invisible Man*, to name a few—none comes so close to specifying the dark relation between 'pure literature' and impersonality, between writing as such and disappearing from view, lapsing from the gridwork of modernity, being 'freed from the chains of individuality':

> In this world of the impersonal, the mind loses its identity, it splits into a multiplicity of atoms of thought that collect in these things that have themselves exploded in a dance of corpuscles.[48]

'However estranged I was from myself at this moment', he tells us, 'so completely at the mercy of invisible influences, nothing that was taking place around me escaped my perception' (25). To have become impersonal has this prodigious compensation that it surcharges the perceptive apparatus with sensitivity. He is become a registering apparatus for the atomic flux of things. 'Nothing escaped my attention, I was lucid and self-possessed, and everything rushed in upon me with a brilliant distinctness, as if an intense light had suddenly sprung up around me' (25). Not being One, he is suddenly everything, and this subsidence into the waves and particles of terrestrial phenomena is a terrifying, exhilarating prospect. As Eveliina Pulkki writes, 'the narrator is stripped of conscious authorial control: instead, his

[46] 'The reader never learns where the I of the novel comes from or where he goes; in fact, one never learns who he actually is. In some respects, the novel manifests a phenomenological conception of man.' Riikka Rossi, 'The Everyday in Nordic Modernism: Knut Hamsun's *Sult* and Maria Jotuni's *Arkielämää*', *Scandinavian Studies* 82.4 (2010), 428 [417–38].

[47] Maud Ellmann, *The Hunger Artists: Starving, Writing & Imprisonment* (London: Virago, 1993), 26–7.

[48] Rancière, *Politics of Literature*, 60.

anxious thinking patterns, his body and the city together generate the text. This atomization of authorship [in] *Sult* is never treated as celebratory, but as a great source of anxiety and suffering.'[49] And also of *jouissance*—for with no overarching project to dictate his actions, what the narrator is left with are reactions, distinct impressions, which flood consciousness with currents of energy that can go either way. 'I couldn't pull myself together to make any definite effort. I was acted on and distracted by everything around me, all that I saw gave me new impressions' (30). No longer a coherent substance, he has become a surface on which the minutest vibrations of matter leave their stochastic traces, of which his 'I' is the quivering reed. 'In all that I observed in this way, there was nothing, not even a tiny incidental circumstance, that escaped me' (145).

Beneath the surface is void. In the most remarkable passage Hansun ever wrote, we find a parable of what it is to have had one's ethical substance, one's character, surgically removed:

> God had stuck his finger down into the network of my nerves and gently, quite casually, brought a little confusion among the threads. And God had withdrawn his finger and behold!—there were fibres and delicate filaments on his finger from the threads of my nerves. And there was a gaping hole after his finger, which was God's finger, and wounds in my brain from the track of his finger [Og der var et åbent Hul efter hans Finger, som var Guds Finger, og Sår i min Hjærne efter hans Fingers Veje]. But where God had touched me with the finger of his hand he let me be and touched me no more, and allowed no evil to befall me. He let me go in peace, and he let me go with that gaping hole.
>
> (29)

Far from branding him the 'holy fool', however, this becoming-void renders the protagonist an even finer observer of himself than he is of the play of molecules in matter. What he discovers within is a blooming world of anonymous affects and intensities, none yet classified within the sanctioned precincts of literature, but which must now be hauled into view. In Copenhagen during the fevered months while he was writing *Hunger*, after his second abortive trip to the USA, Hamsun met and befriended the young Danish literary critic and historian Valdemar Vedel. Vedel was completing his doctoral thesis and had published its manifesto in the journal, *Ny Jord* ['New Earth'], in August 1888, where Hamsun would publish his first fragment of *Hunger* later that year. In his manifesto, Vedel proclaimed with striking assurance that the 'modern, complex psyche had ceased to move in great waves of simple emotions like love, hate, sorrow, anger and joy. The voices that surfaced in us now were profoundly richer, stranger and infinitely more varied.'[50]

[49] Pulkki, 'Failing Authorship in Knut Hamsun's *Sult*', 305.
[50] Kolloen, *Knut Hamsun*, 36.

In another related article in *Ny Jord*, by Gustav Hetsch in 1888, entitled 'Lidt om Kunst' ['Art in Brief'], the author heralded the all-important term *stemning* ['mood'; like the German *Stimmung*] in Nordic literature:

> By 'mood' we understand precisely the background from which reciprocally related feelings emerge, and it is only a difference of degree which separates the conceptually determined feeling from the more general chaotic-dark mood, a difference of degree in the clarity and demarcation of perception . . . .[51]

The 'conceptually determined' emotions of the great heroic phases of aristocratic and bourgeois literature were played out, and in their place writhed innumerable new, 'chaotic-dark moods', 'waves of generalized sensations', as Jameson calls them, behind which language and its 'demarcations of perception' lagged helplessly; and which therefore elicited the most astounding aesthetic innovations:

> I am also insisting [writes Jameson] on the resistance of affect to language, and thereby on the new representational tasks it poses poets and novelists in the effort somehow to seize its fleeting essence and to force its recognition. For in its insatiable colonization of the as yet unexplored and inexpressed [sic, . . .], the system of the old named emotions becomes not only too general but also too familiar: to approach the emotions more closely is microscopically to see within them a Brownian movement which, although properly unnameable in its own right, calls out imperiously for all the stimulation of linguistic innovation.[52]

This is veritably Hamsun's stated mission. As he wrote after the release of *Hunger*, 'The emotions in Norwegian literature lack variety and are too rigid.'[53] Whereas, 'I felt I had described moods in *Hunger* whose total strangeness would not be likely to tire the reader by its monotony. Also, there is from the first to the last page not one single feeling which is repeated, none that resembles either the previous or the following.'[54] In line with the radical aesthetic theory of *Ny Jord* (which would also begin publishing Nietzsche in 1889), Hamsun worked to disaggregate the unwieldy abstractions of 'named emotions' and put in their place a rich molecular world of nameless 'moods'. He aimed to examine, as through a linguistic microscope, the very 'mimosas of thoughts—the delicate fractions of feelings—I want to burrow down into the finest weave of our souls—delicate observations of the fractional workings of the soul',[55] to find there 'completely

[51] Gustav Hetsch, 'Lidt om Kunst' (c.1888), quoted and translated in Daniel M. Grimley, *Carl Nielsen and the Idea of Modernism* (Woodbridge: Boydell, 2010), 27.
[52] Fredric Jameson, *The Antinomies of Realism* (London: Verso, 2013), 31.
[53] Hamsun, qtd. in Kolloen, *Knut Hamsun*, 59.
[54] Hamsun, qtd. in Næss, *Knut Hamsun*, 33.
[55] Hamsun, qtd. in Kolloen, *Knut Hamsun*, 36.

inexplicable states of perception . . . the sighing of suspected atoms . . . too transitory to be grasped and held securely, they last a second, a minute, they come and go like flashes [. . .] the secret movements which are made unnoticed in the remote places of the soul, the capricious disorder of perception . . . motionless trackless journeys with the brain and the heart, strange activities of the nerves, the whispering of the blood, the pleading of the bone, the entire unconscious intellectual life'.[56] Cut adrift from the molar compulsions of those older novelistic emotions, 'love, hate, sorrow, anger and joy', Hamsun's characters must repeatedly make these trackless journeys within, to conquer the means of recording what is discovered there: inchoate complexes of embodied affects and passions, which are never stable long enough to assume any fixed 'character', but shift constantly, reversing their polarities without warning, as 'rapture-revulsion-contempt' becomes 'pride-lust-nausea' in under a page, and then on to other far more complicated constellations of affect. 'I want', said Hamsun, 'to let [readers] listen to the breath of the mimosa—each word like dazzling white wings—a spoken mirror of movement'.[57]

The decisive step forward from Zola consists in the remarkable self-consciousness the narrator of *Hunger* displays towards his affective states, and his capacity for recording them. As Zola explained in his 1868 preface to *Thérèse Raquin* (1867), he wanted 'protagonists who were supremely dominated by their nerves and their blood, deprived of free will and drawn into every action of their lives by the predetermined lot of their flesh'.[58] Naturalist protagonicity is defined by the weakness of will in relation to biological and hereditary impulses, a predetermination of character by organic and psychological laws. In Hamsun's hands, however, while the nerves and blood remain of critical importance, it is not for their deterministic role, but the phenomenological chromaticism of complex modal transitions from state to state in which they play the decisive part. No longer a puppet of his nervous states, the narrator of *Hunger* is rather their 'lucid and self-possessed' transcriber and improvisatory artist. What happens, for instance, when you look deeply at your own feet?

> I sit up halfway and look down at my feet, and at this moment I experience a fantastic, alien state I'd never felt before; a delicate, mysterious thrill spreads through my nerves, as though they were flooded by surges of light. When I looked at my shoes, it was as though I had met a good friend or got back a torn-off part of me: a feeling of recognition trembles through all my senses, tears spring to my eyes, and I perceive my shoes as a softly murmuring tune coming toward me.
>
> (30)

[56] Hamsun, 'From the Unconscious Life of the Mind', 6–7.
[57] Hamsun, qtd. in Kolloen, *Knut Hamsun*, 37.
[58] Émile Zola, *Thérèse Raquin*, trans. Robin Buss (London: Penguin, 2004), xxii.

The existential tradition will call this 'alienation', but it is just as much *anagnorisis*, this moving recognition of one's own missing character displaced into one's footwear: 'I discover that their wrinkles and their white seams give them an expression, lend them a physiognomy. Something of my own nature had entered into these shoes—they affected me like a breath upon my being, a living, breathing part of me . . .' (31). But such writing is always also an emptying, a labour of evacuation that leaves the organism depleted:

> During this fruitless effort my thoughts began to get confused again—I felt my brain literally snap, my head was emptying and emptying, and in the end it sat light and void on my shoulders. I perceived this gaping emptiness in my head with my whole body, I felt hollowed out from top to toe.
>
> (37)

Involuntary decadence, this has been called; and it is true that the emptiness in question breeds unhealthy tumours. 'Rotten patches were beginning to appear in my inner being, black spongy growths that were spreading more and more' (51). But out of the noble rot comes literary ichor:

> A succession of fleeting associations of ideas flashed through my head at this moment—from the green grass to a Bible passage that says all flesh is as grass that is torched, and from there to Judgment Day when everything would be burned up, then a small detour to the Lisbon earthquake, whereupon I had a dim memory of a Spanish brass spittoon and an ebony penholder I had seen at Ylajali's. Alas, all was perishable! Just like grass that was torched. It all came to four boards and a shroud—at Madam Andersen's, main entrance to the right. . . . All this was tossed around in my head in this desperate moment when my landlady was about to throw me out of the house.
>
> (156)

This is what it is like not to be a character, but instead a sentient node in the nervous network of things. Not the hatcher of plots and intrigues, but the mere support of 'fleeting associations' that have no reason to exist other than that, at the moment of your final ejection from social space, they occur to you, sustaining you in being for one 'desperate moment' before perishing forever. This has been, after all, the purpose of the narrator from the start: to unbecome, to relinquish his questionable hold on things, to disappear inside the hole God has made of him. 'Few things are better suited to break down and render anonymous a human personality than prolonged want of the most primitive kind', writes Robert Ferguson,[59] and *Hunger* is one long experiment in projecting the anonymization of a human

[59] Ferguson, *Enigma*, 111.

personality through the thematic prism of his starvation. 'Hamsun's pioneering emphasis on the affective experience of the body'[60] turns the incontrovertible and Naturalist topic of hunger inside out, to expose the 'gaping hole' of capitalist social relations as a characterological vanishing point. With no name to suture him in social space, no deep space within which to take shelter from the trials of the capital-relation, the narrator has nothing to do but decompose before our eyes. 'I must be just incredibly thin. My eyes were sinking deep into my skull', he notes. 'What, exactly, did I look like?' (84). So much for the face. What about the voice, that other crucial ground of character? 'My voice sounded so strangely hollow that I almost failed to recognise it' (88); 'My voice sounded so poor, downright feeble, I was moved to tears by it' (158). The body, meanwhile, is rather less than it should be. 'Want had dried me up' (98). With no sap in his veins, he is little but husk: 'I am disgusted with myself, even my hands appear loathsome to me. This flabby, shameless expression on the backs of my hands pains me, makes me uneasy. I feel rudely affected by the sight of my bony fingers, and I hate my whole slack body and shudder at having to carry it, to feel it around me' (117). All of Beckett inheres in a sentence like this one: 'It would have been a different matter if I had met her while I still looked like a human being, in my heyday' (131); but there is still room for pathos in this modernist vanishing act. 'I was sinking, sinking everywhere I turned, sinking to my knees, to my middle, going down in infamy never to come up again, never!' (164).

Modern character in literary prose begins with Hamsun's astonishing demolition of all the cardinal points of character, which brings a millennia-old convention literally to its knees: its face become a mocking death's head, its body a slack bag of skin sloughing off brittle bones, its voice a rasping mockery of human expressiveness, its figure bent or prone, its name never breathed or recorded, its person never viable, and utterly irreducible to a type. All that remains of Frow's eight-ply definition of 'character and person' is the solitary category of 'interest', of which there is an inordinate amount at stake, largely due to the radical impoverishment of all the other categories and functions.[61] And, at base, this unflagging interest derives from the 'minimal demand' that this vanishing, implausible creature makes at the moment of his erasure, a demand that inflates him suddenly to the status of a hero, a godhead, immediately recognizable and magnificent in his status as defiant Prometheus:

> My insane anger was only heightened by this fit of exhaustion, and I lifted my foot and stamped it on the pavement. I also did various other things to recover my strength: I clenched my teeth, knitted my brows and rolled my eyes in despair,

[60] Wientzen, 'The Aesthetics of Hunger', 208.

[61] Frow's breakdown runs: figure; interest; person; type; voice; name; face; body. Frow, *Character and Person*, xv.

and it began to help. My mind cleared up, I understood I was about to go under. I stretched out my hands and pushed myself back from the wall; the street was still whirling around with me. Bursting into sobs of rage, I fought my distress with my innermost soul, bravely holding my own so as not to fall down: I had no intention of collapsing, I would die on my feet.

(163)

9
Egerton

As Terence de Vere White observed posthumously of his aunt, Mary Chavelita Dunne, her period in Norway (1887–9) coincided with a watershed in Scandinavian intellectual history, the so-called 'modern breakthrough', much of which she bravely took on. She 'was alive to the significance of what she found: Ibsen, Strindberg and Björnsen were flourishing, [Knut] Hamsun and Olaf [sic] Hansson breaking new ground. She absorbed their ideas.'[1] As those ideas were flush with the recent impact of Nietzsche's thought in Sweden and Norway, he too became part of the heritage she would mediate to the English-speaking literary world under the name 'George Egerton'. Moreover, Dunne was the first translator of Hamsun's work into English, and her translations demonstrate a remarkable sensitivity to his characterological commitments to rootlessness, *Wanderlust*, and eccentricity. The poet figure from 'The Regeneration of the Two', the culminating tale of her second story collection *Discords* (1894), is clearly an amalgamation of the biographical Hamsun (with whom Dunne entered into a sublimated erotic relationship[2]) and the protagonist of his novel *Hunger* (1890), which she translated in 1899[3]—thin, hungry, restless, trapped in Kristiania, reader of Nietzsche, perhaps on the verge of great success. A similar figure, obviously a fictionalization of Hamsun, appears in 'Now Spring Has Come', a story from *Keynotes* (1893). The attention to Scandinavia in these two story collections amounts to 'one of the most extensive treatments of modern Norway in the English *fin de siècle*'.[4] William Sharp's contemporary review of *Keynotes* acutely compared it to the work of Bjørnstjerne Bjørnson and noted its pervasive 'northern' sentiment.[5] Books are everywhere in these stories, and the name-dropping of key Northern European authors is

[1] George Egerton, *A Leaf from the Yellow Book: The Correspondence of George Egerton*, ed. Terence de Vere White (London: Richards, 1958), 18.

[2] See Ingar Sletten Kolloen, *Knut Hamsun: Dreamer and Dissenter*, trans. Deborah Dawkin and Erik Skuggevik (New Haven: Yale University Press, 2009), 54–69.

[3] Despite the censoring of her work in the reduced 1921 sixth edition of *Hunger*, Egerton's translation remains today 'arguably more radical than [Sverre] Lyngstad's translation' of 1996, having 'withstood the passage of time very well' due to its unique rapport with Hamsun's life and aesthetic ideology. See Tore Rem, 'The Englishing of Hunger: Knut Hamsun, George Egerton and Leonard Smithers', in Bjørn Tysdahl, Mats Jansson, Jakob Lothe, and Steen Klitgård Povlsen, eds., *English and Nordic Modernisms* (Norwich: Norvik Press, 2002), 61–73; and Stefano Evangelista, *Literary Cosmopolitanisms in the English Fin de Siècle: Citizens of Nowhere* (Oxford: Oxford University Press, 2021), 163n79.

[4] Evangelista, *Literary Cosmopolitanisms in the English Fin de Siècle*, 122.

[5] William Sharp, 'Review of *Keynotes*, by George Egerton', *Academy* (17 Feb. 1894): 143.

Modern Character. Julian Murphet, Oxford University Press. © Julian Murphet (2023).
DOI: 10.1093/oso/9780192863126.003.0010

striking. Fate announces itself to the protagonist of 'Now Spring Has Come' in the form of

> a paper-backed novel with a taking name. I was waiting in a shop for some papers I had ordered, when it struck me. I took it up. The author was unknown to me. I opened it at haphazard, and a line caught me. I read on. I was roused by the bookseller's suave voice,—
>
> 'That is a very bad book. Madam. One of the modern realistic school, a tendenz roman, I would not advise Madam to read it'.
>
> '"A-ah, indeed!"'[6]

Reading such books triggers a Nietzschean 'Unwerthung aller Werthe' in 'The Regeneration of the Two' (165). '[W]hen a Strindberg or a Nietzsche arises and peers into the recesses of [woman's] nature and dissects her ruthlessly', the central figure in 'A Cross Line' thinks, 'the men shriek out louder than the women' (10). The discussion of Northern literature has sweeping moral and aesthetic repercussions. 'Did we not talk about anything? Of course we did. Tolstoi and his doctrine of celibacy. Ibsen's Hedda. Strindberg's view of the female animal. And we agreed that Friedrich Nietzsche appealed to us immensely' (22). It is the specific relation to Hamsun, however, that most clearly marks Dunne's (henceforth Egerton's) work in the *fin-de-siècle.* As Evangelista writes, it was Egerton 'who was to pick up Hamsun's challenge to invent a new literary form capable of capturing the unconscious, albeit, in her case, from an explicitly gendered point of view'.[7] It was specifically her work on characterization and the unmapped spaces around the Ego—the affects, the unconscious, the other—that enabled Egerton to persevere with Hamsun's trailblazing effort, and develop it in unanticipated ways.

The nascent culture industry's implicit support of a patriarchal typology at the end of the nineteenth century was amplified in every medium—in novels, stories, operas, ballads, paintings, and so forth.[8] The determination on the part of women writers 'to expand the permissible topics in fiction' at this time turned above all on the push to dismantle that edifice of inherited representations.[9] One aspect of this work was to propose a partial deconstruction of the hierarchy on which they rested at the level of characterization. Of the so-called 'New Woman' narratives it has been said that their 'characters exhibit both masculine and feminine impulses and, in consequence, are imagined as double-sexed'.[10] Egerton's women characters

[6] George Egerton, *Keynotes and Discords*, ed. Sally Ledger (London: Continuum, 2006), 15–16.
[7] Evangelista, *Literary Cosmopolitanisms in the English Fin de Siècle*, 125.
[8] Nigel Bell, 'The "Woman Question," the "New Woman," and Some Late Victorian Fiction', *English Academy Review* 30.2 (2013), 80 [79–97].
[9] Martha Vicinus, 'Introduction', in George Egerton, *Keynotes and Discords* (London: Virago, 1983), viii.
[10] Casey A. Cothran, 'Fanged Desire: The New Woman and the Monster', *Nineteenth-Century Gender Studies* 2.3 (Winter 2006), 2 [1–15].

are feminine in certain respects (they enjoy high levels of emotional articulacy, understand the semiotics of dress,[11] move gracefully with thin wrists and waists, are nurturing and long-suffering in equal measure, and have an affinity for children) and are charged with an abundance of female sexuality, but their strong complement of supposedly masculine characteristics (they hunt and fish, ride bicycles, often make their living with a pen, are highly intellectual, and become powerfully assertive when necessary) renders them intriguing hermaphroditic complexes: 'Hermaphrodite by force of circumstances'.[12] 'Her more idealistic stories thus seem to aim for a future "beyond man and woman"', as Elke D'hoker writes of Egerton's insistent 'redistribution of gender roles'.[13] Another option was to use the potential solidarity of gender enforcement as a social bracket within which to negate or at least counteract other forms of social hierarchy, particularly social class. Egerton 'situates women's relationships with other women, particularly of different classes and ethnicities, as being of primary importance in women's lives'.[14]

Ideological support for women's emancipation is not itself a sufficient precipitant of formal change within the literary precincts of character: the work of George Meredith, for instance, empathetic as it is with the painful political and spiritual strides being taken, shows no particular wrestling with the category or its terms; the same is true of Hardy, Gissing, and Moore, in their less active identifications with the cause. The late Victorian characterization of young women in objective and subjective tension, not to say rebellion, with their social constraints under bourgeois patriarchy was to draw on a rich realist tradition of depictions of young men losing their illusions to the trials of social accommodation. Indeed, it was one of the advantages of the novel as an instrument in the struggle that it offered a readymade template. As one contemporary American critic, William Cary Brownell, put it apropos Meredith's novelistic 'treatment of women', 'it is as a sex that, currently, women particularly appreciate being treated as individuals. The more marked such treatment is, the more justice they feel is done to the sex. [. . . Mr Meredith] makes it unmistakably clear that women are psychologically worthwhile, complex, intricate, and multifarious in mind as well as complicated in nature.'[15] Regenia Gagnier's more recent case is that the 'New Women' 'took the individual, rather than the group or class, as the primary social unit'.[16] It was as individuals that, for some 150 years, generations of novelists had

[11] On the full spectrum of these rich semiotics, see the excellent discussion in Madeleine Seys, *Fashion and Narrative in Victorian Popular Literature: Double Threads* (London: Routledge, 2017).

[12] Egerton, *Keynotes and Discords*, 16.

[13] Elke D'hoker, '"Half-Man" or "Half-Doll": George Egerton's Response to Friedrich Nietzsche', *Women's Writing* 18.4 (October 2011), 533, 534 [524–46].

[14] Lisa Hager, 'A Community of Women: Women's Agency and Sexuality in George Egerton's *Keynotes* and *Discords*', *Nineteenth-Century Gender Studies* 2.2 (Summer 2006), 1 [1–11].

[15] William Cary Brownell, in John Alexander Hammerton, *George Meredith: His Life and Art in Anecdote and Criticism* (c.1911), rev. ed. (New York: Haskell House, 1971), 234–5.

[16] Regenia Gagnier, *Individualism, Decadence and Globalization: On the Relation of Part to Whole, 1859–1920* (Basingstoke: Palgrave Macmillan, 2010), 63.

presented ostensibly 'unremarkable' middle-class young men, to vindicate their claims to normative subjectivity; but for Nancy Armstrong it was women who had, by the mid-nineteenth century, become central to the now traditional idea of self-regulating individuality.[17] Given its limitation to the domestic front, what Jusová calls the 'popular narrative of the evolution of a woman's character' with its full complement of *Bildungsroman* formal features, gravitated to matrimony as the ultimate test of a female character's narrative fate.[18] But at the end of the nineteenth century, a major modification was made to the forms of prose fiction to accommodate an explicit anti-matrimonial theme: 'man demands from a wife as a right, what he must sue from a mistress as a favour; until marriage becomes for many women a legal prostitution, a nightly degradation, a hateful yoke under which they age, mere bearers of children conceived in a sense of duty, not love', as George Egerton's character Florence puts it in 'Virgin Soil'.[19] 'The preoccupation with the institution of marriage [. . .] constituted a major part of the dominant discourse of the New Woman at the *fin de siècle*', as Ledger remarks.[20]

The work of George Egerton shows both a continuity with the prevailing patterns of literary characterization and some significant breaks along the lines first laid down by Hamsun, which now need to be investigated. To a certain extent, we can recognize a sibling enterprise to that of the 'bachelor fictions' we have been analysing thus far. Thomas Hardy sharply identified the key character-type of Egerton's work in his 1912 'Postscript' to *Jude the Obscure*: 'the slight, pale "bachelor" girl—the intellectualized, emancipated bundle of nerves [. . .] who does not recognize the necessity for most of her sex to follow marriage as a profession'.[21] Egerton shares with Huysmans, Wilde, Hamsun, and D'Annunzio a cognate interest in figures sundered from the typical marriage plot—in her case, adulteresses, free-lovers, abandoned women, single mothers, widows, and spinsters. These social imagoes are adopted with a highly charged ambivalence towards their currency as personae within the patriarchal *déja-lû*.[22] There is, on the one hand, a superfine sensitivity to the extent to which such women are always-already perceived by middle-class morality as 'fallen' or 'falling', and so an association of them with pity and social forgiveness. On the other hand, new and progressive formal features are drawn into these presentations, admixed with generous portions

[17] See Nancy Armstrong, *Desire and Domestic Fiction* (New York: Oxford University Press, 1987) and *How Novels Think: The Limits of Individualism from 1719–1900* (New York: Columbia University Press, 2005).

[18] Iveta Jusová, *The New Woman and the Empire* (Columbus: Ohio State University Press, 2005), 66.

[19] Egerton, *Keynotes and Discords*, 131.

[20] Sally Ledger, *The New Woman: Fiction and Feminism at the Fin de Siècle* (Manchester: Manchester University Press, 1997), 20.

[21] Thomas Hardy, 'Postscript' to *Jude the Obscure*, ed. Patricia Ingham, rev. ed. (Oxford: Oxford University Press, 2002), xlvi.

[22] Lyn Pykett writes that the 'New Woman' was 'a construct [. . .] who was actively produced and reproduced' in the period, as well as parodied and ridiculed. Lyn Pykett, *The 'Improper' Feminine: The Women's Sensation Novel and the New Woman Writing* (New York: Routledge, 1992), 137.

of Scandinavian and German psychology, and fused with a topsy-turvy imperial romanticism that finds value outside the civilized metropole (presented as infernal for women, apart from the odd oasis like the British Museum's Reading Room). With these scandalous energies, Egerton's 'fallen women' are conscripted to a larger cultural and aesthetic struggle against the limits of representation itself—a battle over the presentability of what falls afoul of bourgeois conventionality in the precincts of art. In other words, Egerton finds ways—not always, but often enough—to combine the relatively stereotypical 'New Woman' character[23] with a zone of perceptual and affective freedom that subscribes to the high aesthetic purposes set out for literary art by Flaubert, Huysmans, and Hamsun. Her characters are often perforated by the multiple, tumbled into otherness, and so hypersensitive to sensory data as to require a relatively new concept, 'psychometrical influence', which seems to have some genetic relation to the work of Francis Galton and his German contemporaries, Wilhelm Wundt and Gustav Flechner, but is most likely rooted in an engagement with the writings of William and Elizabeth Denton.[24] This is that other aspect of characterization, identified by Hardy, which she shares with Huysmans and Wilde—her interest in the person as a highly developed 'bundle of nerves'.

Egerton's most important works—the story collections *Keynotes* and *Discords*—are often critically referred to the question of her supposed *essentialism* as regards the 'woman question', to a foundational conception of 'the essentialized passionate woman'.[25] There are numerous references across the two volumes to the 'underlying wholesome woman' (140), the 'whole woman [. . .] the woman of whom every woman was but a fragment' (169). This primordial wholeness, a psycho-spiritual grounding in the organic, the natural, and the divine, is the abiding source from which, we are led to suppose, the war against patriarchy takes its primary nourishment. 'In one word', a character says in 'Now Spring Has Come', 'the untrue feminine is of man's making; while the strong, the natural, the true womanly is of God's making' (16). This prescient distinction between sex and gender need not be obscured by the conventional invocation of the divine. As Penny Boumelha has argued, the 'true womanly' force is 'something disruptive of the very terms of [man-made] society: the "natural"—woman, instinctive, intuitive, enigmatic,

[23] Laura Marcus and Peter Nicholls once estimated that over a hundred 'New Women' novels were published over the decade of the 1890s. See Ann Ardis, *New Women, New Novels: Feminism and Early Modernism* (New Brunswick: Rutgers University Press, 1990), 70. The situation is further complicated by the fact that, from the moment that Sarah Grand first christened the character-type (1894), it began circulating as a social imago and entered the general lexicon as a mostly disparaged social type. 'Largely a media construction, it was always contested, not least by the women themselves, but it has come to indicate a public representation in literature, art, and the media of self-conscious female modernity.' Gagnier, *Individualism, Decadence and Globalization*, 61.

[24] See below, pp. 197–198.

[25] Kate McCullough, 'Mapping the "Terra Incognita" of Woman: George Egerton's *Keynotes* (1893) and New Woman Fiction', in Barbara Leah Harman and Susan Meyer, eds., *The New Nineteenth-Century: Feminist Readings of Underread Victorian Fiction* (New York: Garland, 1996), 207 [205–23].

wild.'[26] However, in case we were unsure about where the divine and the natural intersect here, 'the *only divine* fibre in a woman is her maternal instinct. Every good quality she has is consequent or coexistent with that. Suppress it, and it turns to a fibroid sapping all that is healthful and good in her nature.'[27] And this rubs against the grain of much feminist thinking today, not to mention the trans campaign against assigned sexual identities; though it is perfectly consistent and viable as an anti-patriarchal ideological position, with no small quotient of political potentiality. Our question is simply what difference it may have made to Egerton's art of characterization; that is, while it may have filtered into the text as theoretical statement, placed always in the mouths of certain women characters, did this conception in fact determine the author's literary portraiture of contemporary women? And the short answer must be negative, since, taking place as they do in a realistically proportioned world of 'man's making' (whose misogyny was 'indiscriminate, incessant, and injurious'[28]), these stories are prohibited from projecting in any rounded way the utopian 'whole woman' periodically invoked. As Bliss Perry put it in 1902, the short story 'deals not with wholes but with fragments.'[29] Cut up into part-objects, the putative 'whole woman' devolves into what patriarchy has made of her. The 'maternal instinct' is subverted by the characters' pursuits of non-procreative sexual liaisons (especially in 'A Cross Line') or by the option of fostering (in 'Spell of the White Elf' and 'Regeneration of Two'); the children are too often subject to infanticide or avoidable deaths; the damage done by the 'feminine' to the 'womanly' is presented as traumatic and sometimes catastrophic. The sole exception to this rule, which proves it, comes in the fairy-tale of 'The Regeneration of the Two': 'Now you are a whole woman' (169)—but this is the rousing utopian note on which to end two collections that remain, overall, committed to the horizon of the actual. To answer the question more methodically, it will be important to establish the author's distinctive characterology.

On this score, several interrelated matters need to be considered. First, while it is true that there is almost always some conspicuous avatar of the 'New Woman' in these stories—she smokes, she rides a bicycle, she studies and writes in genteel poverty, she fishes, she engages in extra-marital affairs, she is almost always going somewhere by ship or by train—she is not invariably the central figure. We will look carefully at the exceptions shortly, as these are the most propitious for Egerton's development of the art of character, but in many cases there arises in the narrative a significant division of labour, which dictates that the 'New Woman' shall become a relatively passive witness to a melodramatic incident involving a

[26] Penny Boumelha, *Thomas Hardy and Women: Sexual Ideology and Narrative Form* (Brighton: Harvest, 1982), 89.

[27] Egerton, *Keynotes and Discords*, 108.

[28] Elaine Showalter, *A Literature of Their Own: From Charlotte Brontë to Doris Lessing*, rev. ed. (London: Virago, 1999), 189.

[29] Bliss Perry, 'The Short Story', *Atlantic Monthly* 90 (1902): 249–50.

'fallen woman', who is then the proper centre of narrative interest, and whose social class tends to be a few rungs lower than the shabby-genteel *petit-bourgeois* daughters of vicars and officers who are our routine focalizers. Thus these stories tend by and large to split the 'woman question' into two related but separate instances: the *sufferer* and the *sympathizer*. By the same token, this division aligns with another moral one: the object of sympathy has followed 'her sexual needs and desires' and faced 'the huge social cost of attempting to realize them', while the writer/observer parses the meaning of this object-lesson for her own self-knowledge and social relations more generally.[30] On the one hand, then, a *déclassé* third-person character positioned in a testing narrative situation; and on the other, a 'busy brain, with all its capabilities choked by a thousand vagrant fancies, [. . .] always producing pictures and finding associations between the most unlikely objects' (3). Such a textual division of labour is explicitly written into the narrative fabric of the tales, as when in 'Wedlock' we read: 'The other woman observes her closely as she does most things—as material. It is not that her sympathies are less keen since she took to writing, but that the habit of analysis is always uppermost' (120). There is no question of the 'fallen women'—the childless mothers, the child murderers, the sex workers, and the drunks—being the agents of this kind of 'analysis' since they lack the requisite education and sensibility; rather, they lapse into 'material', the grim anecdotal stuff out of which the New Woman forges her critical weapons, tempered by her tears. It is important that, in this characterology, there is still room for pity—since that is an index of the marketability of the writing such encounters must generate.[31] Egerton's broadly socialist 'sympathy with human suffering' (112) is a strong residue of Victorian sentimentality, inflected in a political direction. The relation between writer and material, however, is increasingly one of observation and analysis. The sympathy remains keen but has ceased to be the real point at issue—which is henceforth a kind of *Neue Sachlichkeit*, beyond good and evil ('she takes both sides of the question impartially', 7). This is a characterology that, having separated its functions into observer and observed, writer and object, bears within it the potential for a pitiless Naturalism and brutal social topography, along with the microbial spores of a Flaubertian 'molecularity' of vision.[32] It is only that, within the prevailing economy of *fin-de-siècle* textual production, the automatisms of commercial fiction continue to waylay that latter tendency, for as long as this structural division is in place.

[30] Rosie Miles, 'George Egerton, Bitextuality, and Cultural (Re)Production in the 1890s', *Women's Writing* 3.3 (1996) 251 [243–59].

[31] '*Keynotes* sold over 6000 copies in its first year alone, was translated into seven languages and had run through eight printings by 1898. The second edition, issued in 1894, was used by [John] Lane to launch his "Keynotes Series" of novels and volumes of short stories by contemporary writers.' Miles, 'George Egerton, Bitextuality, and Cultural (Re)Production in the 1890s', 243.

[32] On this see Jacques Rancière, *The Politics of Literature*, trans. Julie Rose (Cambridge: Polity, 2011), 55–71.

The men, meanwhile, in this distinctive characterology, are frequently cast as villains, narrow and mean; but perhaps their most striking characteristic is that peculiar 'denseness of man, his chivalrous conservative devotion to the female idea he has created [which] blinds him, perhaps happily, to the problems of her complex nature' (9). That relatively unconscious service to patriarchy is motivated by a singular lack of penetration: an inveterate reduction of women's complexity to simplicity due to a self-serving inability to detect the complexity in the first place. Alcohol comes in aid of that blindness, to be sure, as does a helpless tendency to womanize and multiply the bourgeois male's erotic entanglements. The exceptions are either working-class or poetic-artisanal, or both. The sympathetic bricklayer in 'Wedlock', surely Egerton's most lurid and melodramatic tale, is himself virtually converted to the status of 'New Woman' by virtue of his own domestic situation and signal empathy for the central figure's looming tragedy. The poet in 'The Regeneration of Two' is ultimately subject to the same kind of gender deconstruction that the New Woman figure in this story goes through (it is what foments their union): 'She marvels at the strange tangles of his poet nature, the child, and man, ay, the woman in it' (166). But perhaps the finest treatment of this kind of figure comes in 'Her Share'—a 'foreign workman' from the Baltic countries, Catholic, sensitive, a reader of Heine, Stirner, and Marx (98–9). This is what an illegitimate love-object looks like to a Victorian Englishwoman, and what she needs to be remade.

A significant aspect of Egerton's character system is its genuine commitment to rootlessness and itineracy, the degree to which it identifies with drifters, dreamers, and cosmopolites abroad.[33] For all her official endorsement of the 'underlying wholesome woman' who attains her essence in motherhood, Egerton is exceptional—perhaps unique at the time—in her refusal to root her New Women characters in any particular place. Like their author, these vagabond personae 'would have liked to go in a caravan from hamlet to village, stopping to tell a story with a can for pennies'.[34] Their 'wholeness' has nothing to do with locality, home, or hearth, and is best glimpsed as an oceanic swell or scudding clouds across a cerulean sky. Remarkably, in a mere dozen stories by a woman in the nineteenth century, the word 'sea' appears forty-six times: lexical index of her oceanic imaginary and studied indifference to borders. 'I wish I could offer you my yacht', a man tells the central figure in 'A Cross Line'; 'do you like the sea?' 'I love it; it answers one's moods' (11). What we see 'in her characters' restlessness, in frequent images of unrestrained hybridization, and in the sense of liminality, transition, and

[33] 'Egerton, unlike her male contemporaries, drew attention to the overwhelming importance of gender in the construction of cosmopolitan identities and in determining women's access to international mobility.' Evangelista, *Literary Cosmopolitanisms in the English Fin de Siècle*, 28.

[34] George Egerton, 'A Keynote to *Keynotes*', in John Gawsworth, ed., *Ten Contemporaries: Notes Toward Their Definitive Bibliography* (London: Ernest Benn, 1932), 57 [57–60].

homelessness conveyed by her writing', is an image of the world conceived in terms of migrancy.[35] It is usual to refer here to the life of Mary Chavelita Dunne—born in Melbourne, schooled in Germany, inheriting colonial money from an uncle in Chile, married in Ireland, bigamist in Norway, *littérateur* in London, and so on—who took the name Egerton from her shiftless Irish spouse and turned it to good account. But whatever the association with the life, this rootless insistence in her work nourishes her distinctive characterizations of women. Periodically her personae become centres of spatial dispersion and fantastic orientalisms, as in the most commented-upon passage in her work:

> She fancies herself in Arabia on the back of a swift steed. Flashing eyes set in dark faces surround her, and she can see the clouds of sand swirl, and feel the swing under her of his rushing stride [. . .]. Then she fancies she is on the stage of an ancient theatre out in the open air, with hundreds of faces upturned towards her. She is gauze-clad in a cobweb garment of wondrous tissue. Her arms are clasped by jewelled snakes, and one with quivering diamond fangs coils round her hips. Her hair floats loosely, and her feet are sandal-clad, and the delicate breath of vines and the salt freshness of an incoming sea seems to fill her nostrils.
>
> (8–9)

It is in fantasy that these characters come closest to attaining their putative 'whole womanhood', which we see here through the dense scrim of exotic stereotypes out of *Salomé* and Burton's *Arabian Nights*. Perhaps the best way to conceptualize this dimension of her art of character is to refer to a pseudo-Deleuzian notion of the 'becoming-Gipsy' with which they repeatedly flirt. In his ebullient, affirmative account of the great power of classic Anglo-American literature, Deleuze ascribed it to an affective tendency along what he calls the 'lines of flight' of that tradition: the tendency to become-other. Melville's Ahab is a 'whale-becoming', for example.[36] '*Affects are precisely these nonhuman becomings of man*', he declares apodictically;[37] but they may also be the cross-cultural, dispersive, inverted *becomings of woman* in a transnational space coordinated by imperialism, though not exhausted by it.

It would be churlish to ascribe to Egerton a racism she neither felt nor espoused because of her use of the term 'gipsy' to refer to the Romany people she also names correctly and even quotes in their own language in one of her tales. The word itself recurs eleven times in the stories, and Romany seven times, to underscore

[35] Iveta Jusová, 'George Egerton and the Project of British Colonialism', *Tulsa Studies in Women's Literature* 19.1 (Spring 2000), 29 [27–55].

[36] Gilles Deleuze and Claire Parnet, *Dialogues*, trans. Hugh Tomlinson and Barbara Habberjam (London: Athlone, 1987), 42.

[37] Gilles Deleuze and Félix Guattari, *What Is Philosophy?*, trans. Graham Burchell and Hugh Tomlinson (London: Verso, 1994), 169.

a deep accord with the 'freedom' these travelling people are meant to incarnate in the worlds they traverse. As the old Romany woman says to the protagonist of 'Under Northern Sky': 'A mole on your cheek, and a free Romany heart in your breast, your spirit fights to be free as the Romany chai' (52). The dying barbarian Britisher with whom this young protagonist finds herself in unwed cohabitation in rural Norway is fond of calling her 'witch' and 'gipsy', and idolizes her for those very qualities that disqualify her for a conventional marriage:

> 'Did any Christian man ever have such an atom for a wife? I believe you are a gipsy; your hair curls at the ends like a live thing; and there are red lights in its black, and your eyes have a flash in them at times and a look as if you were off in other lands!'
>
> (52)

The 'tattered healthy Zingari vagabonds' with 'the grace of panthers and the charm of wild untamed natural things' (52) create for this trapped creature a utopian mirror for her inner being, a chance to follow their rootless line of flight:

> 'How strangely my eyes gleam, and what a gipsy I look! No one would know, no one would dream of it. I would soon get brown!' and she looks wistfully out towards the [Romany] camp again. In an hour they will go . . . a heap of fern to lie on, scant fare; but the freedom, ah, the freedom! [. . .] Free to follow the beck of one's spirit, a-ah to dream of it, and the red light glows in her eyes again; they have an inward look; what visions do they see? The small thin face is transformed, the lips are softer, one quick emotion chases the other across it, the eyes glisten and darken deeply, and the copper thread shine in her swart hair.
>
> (53)

This is what happens when the New Woman frame around the 'fallen woman' anecdote falls away, and the two moments are fused into one characterization. In this space of immanence it is no longer an issue of *suffering*, on the one hand, and *observing*, on the other; it is instead entirely a question of *becoming*. The white child of empire turns brown, her hair shimmers and her eyes sparkle, as she immerses her 'inward look' in the ecstasy of a Romany-becoming. The prose has no analytic pretensions here, but adapts itself to the mood at stake: exclamations, questions, semi-colons, as the face 'transforms' under the influence of affects it cannot name—'one quick emotion chases the other across it'.

We are very far indeed from the terror of Harriet Smith at the 'clamorous and impertinent' group of Gypsies in Austen's *Emma* eighty years before; and while there is clearly a significant amount of romantic projection in Egerton's Romany episode, it is also true to say that this kind of 'Gypsy-becoming' marks a significant advance in the characterization of women at the end of the century.[38] In her discussion of New Woman literature, Regenia Gagnier remarks that 'the modern psychological individual that became the subject of psychoanalysis began its self-analysis [in this fiction] through the meticulous calculation of pain and pleasure—affect—aestheticized in the narrative'.[39] What the nameless protagonist of 'Under Northern Sky' does in her long short story is not act, but subject her interiority to a searching 'calculation' of the sufferings and pleasures that define her existence, and then, out of that balance-sheet, effect an imaginary transformation around an errant affect sent from beyond the bounds of civilized society. Her 'primitivism', saturated as it may be with an imperialist *Weltanschauung*, is also a warm sympathy with precapitalist ways of life. As another character says of the missionary activities of her bourgeois peers, the 'poor little niggers in Zanzibar' have no need of flannel petticoats. 'I am sure it's much nicer for them to roll in their little brown bodies in the warm sand; I wouldn't mind doing it myself' (136). When 'Black eyes gleam, and brown skins shine under orange and scarlet kerchiefs' (52), the Egertonian subject is transformed by an empathetic identification with the other. The 'things' belonging to the Slavic workman in 'Her Share' evoke unconscious race memories: 'His things roused the same feeling in me. There was a carved crucifix lying on his pillow, and the first rosary I had ever seen; and on the end of his bed an old violin with sorghum red wood in a carved case. They spoke to me in a strange way; there was an enchanting flavor of mystery about them that spoke of Southern lands and sunshine. I felt vaguely that somewhere in under my pink-and-white English skin there lurked a brown spirit that responded to their influence' (98). Under the brittle white characterology of modernity, a warmer, richer, darker life persists. The return of the repressed has an anthropological, onto-phylogenic logic:

> She seems to live all her life over again. Things she has forgotten completely come vividly back to her. An old Maori man, who used to sell sweet potatoes and quaint ring-shells for napkin rings to the Pakeha lady in Tauranga Bay, floats before her inward vision as tangible as if he were next her; and a soldier servant, she can hear his voice, he used to sing as he pipe-clayed,—
>
> 'But kaipoi te waipero, Kaipoi te waiena;
> For Rangatira Sal, Bob Walker sold his pal,
> But he's now at the bottom o' the harbor!'
>
> Why did the stupid chorus come back to her now; what chink of brain did it lie in all these years?
>
> (59)

[38] See the excellent discussion in Sarah Houghton-Walker, *Representations of the Gypsy in the Romantic Period* (Oxford: Oxford University Press, 2014).
[39] Gagnier, *Individualism, Decadence and Globalization*, 69.

As it is being theorized in Vienna, the unconscious inscribes itself into Anglophone literary history through a 'vivid inward vision' of the South Pacific, a scrambling of imperial racial codes and languages on the ebb tide of a brain permanently in transit. Affect is aestheticized here in the flotsam and jetsam of the forgotten harbours of empire, intimate relics of a cast-off history that haunt the white subject.

When Egerton's women are freed from the burdens of care and sympathy that structurally dominate their lives, they become delicate registering apparatuses for a vast affective vibration insensible to most. These 'souls sensitive to the psychometry of things shiver with the feel of passional atoms vibrating through the atmosphere', as we read in 'Gone Under' (112). Positive or negative, such affective vibrations have a greater power over Egerton's characters than majority moral opinion or convention; they are the medium of true existence. A hotel bed, for instance, is less a physical object than a psychical residue. 'Beds in hotels and places have sometimes disturbed her', the narrator remarks in 'A Psychological Moment at Three Periods', 'so much so that she has started up and rolled herself in her rug and slept in an armchair, because the sense of evil thoughts that never come to her otherwise seem to impregnate her as if the very bed held them; and she, highly sensitive as she is to the psychometrical influence of things, cannot but feel it' (87). It is instructive that the only use of the word 'impregnate' in a series of tales often turning on pregnancy is this one: a kind of psychological rape by the trace traumas of previous hotel guests. Egerton's repeated use of the phrase 'psychometry of things' recalls the 1863 work of William and Elizabeth Denton, *The Soul of Things; Or, Psychometric Researches and Discoveries*, where (like Freud), drawing from researches in hypnotism, dream analysis, and photography, the authors speculate on how the psychometer 'sees without the use of physical eyes,—sees the past as readily as the present, the far-off as easily as the nigh-at hand; hears sounds that are inaudible to physical ears, and travels without the ordinary powers of locomotion'.[40] That is because 'radiant forces' are everywhere and constantly 'passing from all objects to all objects' and 'daguerreotyping the appearances of each upon the other'—'the images thus made, not merely resting upon the surface, but sinking into the interior of them' (30–1), like grief-stains into a mattress. As in Egerton's stories, it only takes an 'inquiring gaze' from a suitably sensitive party to reveal this sunken history of impressions:

> You cannot, then, enter a room by night or day, but you leave on going out your portrait behind you. You cannot lift your hand, or wink your eye, or the wind stir a hair of your head, but each movement is infallibly registered for coming ages. The pane of glass in the window, the brink in the wall, and the paving stone in the street, catch the pictures of all passers-by, and faithfully preserve them.
> (31)

[40] William and Elizabeth M. F. Denton, *The Souls of Things; Or, Psychometric Researches and Discoveries*, 5th ed. (Boston: William Denton, 1871), 306.

It is with some such theoretical basis that Egerton's heroines seem to exist simultaneously in two or more dimensions, why they 'look as if [they] were far off in other lands' (52): radiant forces are embedded in things and are being developed as affection-images by the wet-plate collodion process of these women's gazes. One reason why the character space of her stories seems so restrictive, so tightly delimited to two or three key figures, is that a good deal of the 'actantial' work of character is assumed by inanimate things—intimate objects saturated with nameless feelings that reach into the story with the power of narrative agents. The box carved as a book at the end of 'Her Share' is the most powerful character in the tale. 'All the beauty of my life was on the cover, and my life has been as the empty wooden box with a date in it. [. . .] I have cried so often over it when the loneliness of life has touched me sorely, that the wood is stained and smoothened' (100).

Narrative form matters much less in stories engineered to spring affection-images out of inert phenomena, or in other words to produce *epiphanies*, than in the rapidly dying triple-decker novel. Egerton's form, at its best, is remarkable for its adaptation to the moment and not the incident, the mood and not the matter, the impression and not the fact. Her 'handling of the short-story form relied heavily on the use of ellipsis and fragmentation in order to experiment with the portrayal of psychology, moods, and the emotions'.[41] Her characters hover at the brink of sudden revelations and hallucinatory lyric impressions; but the stories rarely get them anywhere in particular. The tales 'function [. . .] like suggestive photographs, giving precise detail about a single turning point in each woman's lives'.[42] And this has as much to do with their format and material platform as with their aesthetic and moral philosophy. As Hager comments, 'this dedication to giving voice to women's "sensations" requires a radical departure from the Victorian three volume novel'.[43] The short story is a form in which action is demoted, as per Henry James' stipulations, in favour of the affective 'impression, comparatively generalized—simplified, foreshortened, reduced to a single perspective—of a complexity or continuity'.[44] In 1895, Lena Milman, translator of Dostoevsky and Tolstoy into English, lamented 'the contempt for the short story prevalent in England but unknown elsewhere', blaming a national insensitivity to the subtle pleasures, the 'beautiful suggestion' of 'passing emotions, those elusive impressions' that only the short story can deliver.[45] The venue where she published these remarks, in an essay on Henry James, was *The Yellow Book*, a high-brow journal which '[a]ddressing, perhaps even constructing, an elite bohemian readership [. . .], insisted on distinguishing the short story for

[41] Evangelista, *Literary Cosmopolitanism in the English Fin de Siècle*, 121.
[42] Hager, 'A Community of Women', 3.
[43] Hager, 'A Community of Women', 2.
[44] Henry James, 'The Story-Teller at Large' (c.1898), in *The American Essays of Henry James*, ed. Leon Edel (Princeton: Princeton University Press, 1989), 190 [186–96].
[45] Lena Milman, 'Mr Henry James', *The Yellow Book* 7 (October 1895), 72 [71–83].

its sophistication and complexity'.[46] Its reasons for doing so were one part theoretical, two parts commercial. The collapse in fortunes of the long-regnant serialized (then three-decker) novel in England presented an opportunity to a form that, in other national cultures (French, Russian, German, American) had produced masterpieces—Chekhov, Leskov, Maupassant, Kleist, Poe—but which, in England, had stagnated. The late-imperial revolution in attention spans triggered by the photomechanical press, the railroads, and other 'sensations', tended to privilege cultural forms requiring the consumption of less leisure time,[47] and by the 1880s 'short stories had become so popular that even the new illustrated weekly newspapers favoured them over serials'.[48] *The Yellow Book* was published by The Bodley Head, John Lane and Elkin Matthews, which had struck gold with Egerton's *Keynotes* in 1893 and projected ample returns from further investment in the short fictional format. It had no other option: not a monthly, it could scarcely ask readers to maintain interest in a longer format between three-month hiatuses. Egerton was invited to contribute to the inaugural issue, where she was the principal draw alongside James himself, who would say of this remarkable turn of events that *The Yellow Book* had 'offered license that, on the spot, opened up the millennium to the "short story"'.[49] Indeed, the 'periodical freed its contributors from serving structural and plot conventions. Instead, *The Yellow Book* encouraged experimentation and nonconformist short fiction.'[50] Egerton's success with *Keynotes* had convinced Lane and Matthews that the happy conjunction of New Women, aestheticism (the design was by Aubrey Beardsley), and short fiction was more than fortuitous: not only did *The Yellow Book* persist with stories by women and Beardsley's graphics until the Wilde trial, but the book series launched in conjunction—named 'Keynotes' after Egerton's volume—published thirteen further volumes by women, including *Discords*. Most of these privileged the shorter form. This preference for short fiction entailed a growing disregard for the formal necessity to tie up narrative threads and provide satisfying closure. Ann Ardis and Sally Ledger both discuss the *fin-de-siècle* 'feminist's investment in narrative rupture—leaving their stories open-ended because their heroines exceed conventional plotlines'.[51] Open-endedness, indeed, was a striking characteristic of

[46] Winnie Chan, '*The Yellow Book* Circle and the Culture of the Literary Magazine', in Dominic Head, ed., *The Cambridge History of the English Short Story* (Cambridge: Cambridge University Press, 2016), 119 [118–34].

[47] See Stephen Kern, *The Culture of Space and Time, 1880–1918* (Cambridge, MA: Harvard University Press, 1983), 10–35.

[48] Chan, '*The Yellow Book* Circle and the Culture of the Literary Magazine', 120.

[49] Henry James, 'Preface' to *The Lesson of the Master*, in *Literary Criticism: French Writers, Other European Writers, The Prefaces to the New York Edition*, ed. Leon Edel (New York: Library of America, 1984), 1227.

[50] Kate Kreuger Henderson, 'Mobility and Modern Consciousness in George Egerton's and Charlotte Mew's *Yellow Book* Stories', *English Literature in Transition* 54.2 (2011), 188 [185–211].

[51] S. Brooke Cameron, *Critical Alliances: Economics and Feminism in English Women's Writing, 1880–1914* (Toronto: University of Toronto Press, 2020), 131. See Ardis, *New Women, New Novels* and Ledger, *The New Woman*.

women's short fiction at this stage; '[w]hat was new about the *fin de siècle* was that realist stories about white, normative middle-class social life were beginning to end without resolution or clear signs of closure'.[52] Her 'short narratives are [. . .] a perfect medium to focus on causal encounters, separations, rendezvous, and mobility broadly conceived'.[53] And this in turn spawned major changes in the art of characterization.

The quest for affects was one of these. If it was impracticable and implausible to provide satisfying resolutions to stories about women wracked by patriarchal capitalism in ten pages or so, then looking inward, at the unclassified swarm of psychic intensities surging through Freud's 'dark continent',[54] or what Egerton called 'the *terra incognita* of herself, as she knew herself to be', seemed a productive prospect.[55] 'The greatest tragedies I have ever read', avers one of Egerton's characters, 'are child's play to those I have seen acted in the inner life of outwardly commonplace women' (11). Egerton's short fiction particularly attends to this interior theatre, and its formal result is a decoupling of the characters from any motor-sensory chain into which they may have been inserted narratively. Periods of reverie and fantasy, passivity, and sheer psychological attentiveness, usurp the impetus to act, to do, to make. The action-image cedes to the affection-image.[56] In the second part of perhaps her finest tale, 'A Psychological Moment at Three Periods', the present tense narration takes this commitment to the affection-image as far as modulating its point of view from a Dutch 'child-girl [. . .] herding some lean cows' (71) to the passing convent-schoolgirl who slips some money into the cow-girl's hand, and then carries us to the Kermesse at the nearby town, where the cow-girl's transitive desire impels the schoolgirl 'to ride in the carousels and see the dwarfs' and the 'tigers and lions' (71). Siding with the 'half-witted girl, Katrine, the daughter of rich Zeeland peasants' against the 'finer Fraülein' (73), the schoolgirl mounts the carousel with this 'great-hipped clumsy girl' (a clear delegate for the peasant girl in the pasture) and, as the hurdy-gurdy strikes up a haunting polka:

[52] Stephanie Palmer, 'Compromised Conclusions: Market Considerations and the Open Ending in New Woman Short Stories', *Nineteenth-Century Gender Studies* 16.1 (Spring 2020), 1 [1–16].

[53] Evangelista, *Literary Cosmopolitanism in the English Fin de Siècle*, 121–2.

[54] Freud labelled women's sexuality the 'dark continent' of psychoanalysis, explicitly drawing on Henry Morton Stanley's use of the phrase to describe Africa, in 'The Question of Lay Analysis' (1926), *The Standard edition of the Complete Psychological Works of Sigmund Freud*, Volume XX (1925–1926): An Autobiographical Study; Inhibitions, Symptoms and Anxiety; The Question of Lay Analysis; and Other Works, trans. James Strachey (London: Hogarth Press, 1959), 212 [183–250]. See also Ranjana Khanna, *Dark Continents: Psychoanalysis and Colonialism* (Durham, NC: Duke University Press, 2003).

[55] Egerton, 'A Keynote to *Keynotes*', 58.

[56] Deleuze's distinction in relation to early cinema has a clear relevance to *fin-de-siècle* fiction. See Gilles Deleuze, *Cinema 1: The Movement-Image*, trans. Hugh Tomlinson and Barbara Habberjam (London: Athlone, 1986).

> The girl's keen eyes note that at one point in the round the breeze blows aside the trappings of the pagoda; she peeps idly in, but each time after that her eyes seek it with a look of shrinking fascination. Her thin nostrils quiver, and her pupils dilate, and an indignant flush dyes her face in a beautiful way as she gazes—why?
>
> An idiot lad is turning the handle of the hurdy-gurdy; he is fastened by a leathern strap round his middle to the pole in the centre of the tent. His head is abnormally large; the heavy eyelids lie half folded on the prominent eyeballs, so that only the whites show; his damp hair clings to his temples and about his outstanding ears; his mouth gapes, and his long tongue lolls from side to side, the saliva forming little bubbles as the great head wags heavily as he grinds,—indeed, every part of his stunted, sweat-dripping body sways mechanically to the lively air of white-footed Polly.
>
> 'Polly Witfoet, Polly Witfoet, lallallallallala!'
>
> (74)

Here is the quintessence of Egertonian affect: dilating pupils, quivering nostrils, a beautifying flush in the cheeks, all in unconscious sympathetic response to the nearby presence of the social other, the non-integrated 'idiot', whom nobody else notices. The epiphany is vouchsafed to the protagonist alone. 'They don't see, they don't see', she cries to herself. 'I alone see. My God, is that to be my fatal dowry, to go through life and always see?' (74). And what she sees, the nature of her epiphany, is nothing less than the ubiquity of social exploitation and injustice—'some poor idiot turning the organ for all the luckier born to dance' (75).

Though bearers of what we may call 'resting mask-face' ('her face is a mask to the inner woman', 81), these characters' faces can suddenly become barometers of the inchoate moods traversing their interiors. 'The paleness of some strong feeling tinges her face; a slight trembling runs through her frame. Her inner soul-struggle is acting as a strong developing fluid upon a highly sensitized plate; anger, scorn, pity, contempt chase one another like shadows across her face' (41–2). Psychometrical photography develops the inner life of these women as affection-images on the visage, in infinitely richer and more suggestive ways than the governing protocols of physiognomy would allow.[57] It is impossible, in this last example, to say exactly what the woman in question is feeling; rather, we are plunged with her into a quicksilver concatenation of affective states whose complex has no name.

[57] Another view of this states that 'sensuous impressionism borrows naturalism's photographic frankness in order to chart the unseen world of the emotions'. See Simon Joyce, 'Impressionism, Naturalism, Symbolism: Trajectories of Anglo-Irish Fiction at the Fin de Siècle', *Modernism/modernity* 21.3 (September 2014), 797 [787–803].

> It is with her, sitting there, as it is with most men, that when numbed in mind and heart by some great trouble her senses are more alive to outward sounds and scenes. It is as if when one's inner self is working with some emotion, wrestling with some potential moral enemy, crying out under the crucifixion of some soul-passion, eyes and ears, and above all sense of smell, are busy receiving impressions and storing them up, as a phonograph records a sound, to reproduce them with absolute fidelity if any of the senses be touched in the same way by the subtile connection between perfume and memory. [. . .] She is rocking unconsciously to and fro. Her thoughts, and the emotions belonging to them, cross one another rapidly, flash past as the landscape seen from a mail train, so that she cannot fasten any of them. The weary vigils of many months, the details of days and hours, are ticked off as the events on a tape.
>
> (60)

The broader media ecology in which the short story is enmeshed in 1892 inscribes itself into the registration of affect in Egerton's prose. Photograph, phonograph, mail train, ticker-tape, hurdy gurdy: these are the choice metaphors for the New Woman's psychometric sensorium, which receives and stores perceptual and affective data like any of the new storage media in the process of supplanting literature itself.[58] The singling out of smell in this context is particularly interesting, as smell was as incapable of storage/playback in 1900 as it is today. Egerton turns out to have been one of the great writers of the olfactory, her characters exquisitely susceptible to its mercurial powers, best detected at sea. 'The sun distils the scent from the clove carnations and the sweetbrier leaves, and coaxes the pungent resin through the cracks in the bark, until the air is heavy with a smell that would cease to be perfume, were it not filtered through the salt ooze of the incoming sea-breeze' (55). Huysmans would have been proud of an aesthetic period like this, its deft, musical transitions among aromatic tones and keynotes. But Egerton can push in the direction of Proustian nostalgia, too:

> She arranges her few belongings, and goes on deck. The smell of the cattle—for it is hot down there, and the hatchways are open—oozes forth and mingles with the briny smell of the sea, recalling childhood scenes,—stretches of sandy dune melting into the gray-green sea, red-tiled homesteads, and lowing kine going home to be milked; and she realizes that she has been home-sick unawares . . .
>
> (102)

The 'smell of steaming beasts blow[ing] with the wind' (105), 'wine, with its fume of cardamoms and nutmeg, [and] the strong smell of cows and stable from her

[58] See Friedrich Kittler, *Discourse Networks, 1800/1900*, trans. Michael Meteer, with Chris Cullens (Stanford: Stanford University Press, 1990). And my *Multimedia Modernism: Literature and the Anglo-American Avant-Garde* (Cambridge: Cambridge University Press, 2009).

clothes' (159) continue to infuse these stories, and that strikes deep chords in the psychoanalytic record. Freud would relate the repression of the olfactory to the repression of sexuality itself,[59] but it was Adorno and Horkheimer who took the point furthest towards an appreciation of its role here in Egerton, whose *jouissance of the other* has been remarked: 'The multifarious nuances of the sense of smell embody the archetypal longing for the lower forms of existence, for direct unification with circumambient nature, with the earth and mud. Of all the senses, that of smell—which is attracted without objectifying—bears closest witness to the urge to lose oneself in and become the "other". When we see, we remain what we are; but when we smell, we are taken over by otherness. Hence the sense of smell is considered a disgrace in civilisation, the sign of lower social strata, lesser races and base animals.'[60] Indeed, how often, when '[f]leeting images of forgotten scenes cross and clash through her inner vision' (88), does this Egertonian character type 'other' herself via the primitive, the animal, the base? Cow-becomings, dog-becomings, idiot-becomings, Gipsy-becomings, Zanzibarian-becomings, Maori-becomings: odoriferous and sonorous lines of flight from the great centres of civilization to the ecstatic periphery.

It has been remarked that '[Egerton's] narratives have all the characteristics we now think of as distinctly modern: they are impressionistic, compressed, concentrated, elliptical, episodic, and make much use of dream, reverie, and other forms of interiority',[61] and that her 'aesthetic experimentation' in the art of the short story forged 'a new way of expressing women's experience' which predated Woolf and Dorothy Richardson by decades.[62] We have been pressing on these concerns by attending particularly to the rising quotient of affect relative to action in her stories, to the specific 'psychometric' and mediated complexion of 'interiority' at stake here, and to the dynamic of 'becoming-other' that defines her personae's routine slippage off the maps of conventional bourgeois fiction. Formally, we have observed, these precious developments of modern character depend upon the foreclosure of a consistent temptation in her work: to divide the 'New Woman' into two separate persons—sufferer and observer—and lapse into relatively safe sentimental moralizing. But when the two aspects are fused and the woman in question subjects *herself* to the remorseless analytic disquisitions of her intellectual nature ('to analyse myself, to see what was under the form into which custom

[59] 'The conjecture that goes deepest ... is to the effect that, with the assumption of an erect posture by man and with the depreciation of his sense of smell, it was not only his anal erotism which threatened to fall a victim to organic repression, but the whole of his sexuality.' Sigmund Freud, *Civilization and Its Discontents*, trans. James Strachey (New York: W. W. Norton, 1962), 53n3.

[60] Max Horkheimer and Theodor W. Adorno, *Dialectic of Enlightenment*, trans. John Cumming (New York: Continuum, 1989), 184.

[61] Lyn Pykett, *Engendering Fictions: The English Novel in the Early Twentieth Century* (London: Edward Arnold, 1995), 62.

[62] Sally Ledger, 'Introduction: George Egerton, New Woman', in Egerton, *Keynotes and Discords*, xxiv [ix–xxvi].

had fashioned me, of what pith I was made, what spirit, if any, lay under the outer woman', 164–5), the affective othering that triggers thoughts of modernism is set in motion. Few efforts in contemporary fiction go so far in these directions, and Egerton has a strong claim to being the chief inheritor in English of the great Scandinavian transformation of fictional character into 'modern character' that took place in the 1890s.

10
Chopin and Wharton

As distinct from the 'New Women' of Egerton's short fiction, the protagonists of Edith Wharton's and Kate Chopin's breakthrough novels of the early 1900s have little of the masculine about them and are constrained within a more rigid set of textual determinants than the vagabonds who frequent the pages of *Keynotes*.[1] To be sure, the relatively desublimated Creole culture of Chopin's southern Louisiana and the rootless itinerancy of Lily Bart's desperate trajectory in *The House of Mirth* (1905) are neither of them conventionally domesticated circumstances, and there is continuity across all three writers in their concern with modern materialist and evolutionary thought, particularly Darwin and Spenser;[2] but the ideological differences between these more conservative American writers and the bold antipodean trailblazer of the *Discords* are significant. Neither Wharton nor Chopin can be unproblematically associated with the contemporary feminist movement, and each is too entrenched in a specific cultural and class milieu to take the kinds of formal and stylistic risks that Egerton pursued as a matter of course. Yet there remains a broad affinity, a family resemblance, between the characters of Egerton's fiction and both Edna Pontellier and Lily Bart, suggesting some formal common ground.[3] In either case, there is discernible effort towards a disestablishment of the accepted coordinates of a fictional persona, which catches some of the import of Egerton's experiments with personal integrity. What Wharton described as the 'slow disintegration of Lily Bart'[4] matches to some extent the steady vitiation of line, contour, and substance of Edna Pontellier in *The Awakening* (1899), undoing the figures we are presented with at the outset of these fictions. Moreover, this disintegration is not incidental to the novels' plots but their very purpose to promote: the characters' 'rejection of narrative structure' is the narrative structure itself.[5] The shattering implications of some affective upsurge wrenches them so out

[1] Wharton herself remarked of her heroine that she was 'a young girl [...] who rouged, smoked, ran into debt, borrowed money, gambled, and—crowning horror!—went home with a bachelor friend to take tea in his flat'. Edith Wharton, Introduction to 1936 edition of *The House of Mirth*, reprinted in Janet Beer and Elizabeth Nolan, eds., *The House of Mirth*, Broadview Critical Edition (Toronto: Broadview, 2005), 375.

[2] On this, see Sharon Kim, 'The Dark Flask: Epiphany and Heredity in *The House of Mirth*', in *Literary Epiphany and the Novel, 1850–1950* (New York: Palgrave Macmillan, 2012), 87–108.

[3] See Ann Heilmann, '*The Awakening* and New Woman Fiction', in Janet Beer, ed., *The Cambridge Companion to Kate Chopin* (Cambridge: Cambridge University Press, 2008), 87–104.

[4] Wharton, Introduction to 1936 edition of *House of Mirth*, 373.

[5] Mary Cuff, 'Edna's Sense of an Ending', *The Mississippi Quarterly* 69.3 (Summer 2016), 330 [327–46].

Modern Character. Julian Murphet, Oxford University Press. © Julian Murphet (2023).
DOI: 10.1093/oso/9780192863126.003.0011

of true with their assumed plots that there can be no reconciliation. What Wharton and Chopin share with their more eccentric contemporary, Egerton, is a sense that 'woman' is the place where a conspicuous characterological unfitness between role and substance might foment a crisis of identification. Each proposes a character with 'a jumbled, distorted, inappropriate relation to the "social script" or plot designed to contain her legally, economically, and sexually',[6] and resolves the discord with a suicide; but equally, each endeavours to locate, within the bounds of that character, another way through that is neither social nor spiritual, but affective.

Some of the differences here are simply formal. Although it may be generally true that, in Elaine Showalter's words, 'the best work of the [1890s] was in the short story not in the novel', it does not necessarily hold for individual writers.[7] Despite the fact that 'Women writers in the 1890s found the short story a suitable form for the new feminist themes of the decade: the exploration of female sexuality and fantasy, the development of a woman's language, and the critique of male aestheticism' (12), it can't be said that either Chopin or Wharton found the same room to move in the form as Egerton did, for reasons that have principally to do with the market. Chopin and Wharton both commenced their writing careers in the pages of America's thriving periodical and magazine culture, sharply distinct in purpose and policy from Lane's and Matthews' *Yellow Book*. More the forum for the kind of author emblematized by James' Henrietta Stackpole and Susan Shepherd, those quintessential Americans who write for money and reputation, and to leave some small mark of improvement on the vast national ignorance, the *fin-de-siècle* US periodical scene stratified its reading public into bands of 'high' (*The Atlantic Monthly, McClure's, Scribner's, Cosmopolitan*), 'middle' (where regional magazines and newspapers like *The St. Louis Post-Dispatch* throve on large subscriptions), and an ever-expanding base of non-intellectual readerships catered for by the lowest-common denominator.[8] Wharton, by birth a New World aristocrat, gravitated naturally to *Scribner's* and *Harper's*, while Chopin's stories, rejected by all the major periodicals,[9] appeared in the *Post-Dispatch*, the *St. Louis Spectator, New Orleans Times-Democrat, Youth's Companion*, the *Philadelphia Musical Journal*, and ultimately *Vogue*—far from the illustrious heights of her contemporary's outlets. But in neither case is it possible to speak of truly innovative, modernizing editorial initiatives; 'high' and 'middle' were circumscribed alike by conventional

[6] Rachel Blau DuPlessis, 'Endings and Contradictions', in Brian Richardson, ed., *Narrative Dynamics: Essays on Time, Plot, Closure, and Frames* (Columbus: Ohio State University Press, 2002), 295 [282–99].

[7] Elaine Showalter, 'Smoking Room', *Times Literary Supplement* (16 June 1995): 12.

[8] See for instance Scott E. Casper, 'Periodical Studies and Cultural History/Periodical Studies as Cultural History: New Scholarship on American Magazines', *Victorian Periodicals Review* 29.3 (Fall 1996): 261–8.

[9] See Janet Beer, *Kate Chopin, Edith Wharton, and Charlotte Perkins Gilman: Studies in Short Fiction* (Basingstoke: Macmillan, 1997), 3.

moral and political outlooks,[10] and resistant to any significant formal disruption to the prevailing model of the short story. As Hermione Lee puts it, the '1890s world of letters' that Wharton and Chopin appealed to could be characterized by the 'genteel censoriousness of Charles Scribner, known in the trade as an "old Dodo", who would not publish George Moore's *Esther Waters* in 1894 because of its "plainspokenness", or of Richard Gilder at *The Century*, who refused to put the thrilling but dangerous Whitman in his family magazine'.[11] Despite her influence by Maupassant, Chopin's published short stories, qualified by a 'light, brisk and essentially optimistic irony',[12] offer no innovative developments to the art of characterization. There is some unprudish frankness about the flesh, disease, and moral hypocrisy in these stories; but shot through as they are with casual racism and an immitigable class arrogance, they never allow for any formal reappraisal of the function of protagonist or her consistency, which are made to agree with the always 'appropriate endings' assigned to them.[13]

Wharton's short fiction demonstrates some of the formal drive of Gogol, Turgenev, Leskov, and the lesser Tolstoy (as well, in her ghost stories, of Poe and Hawthorne), and she had even translated some of D'Annunzio's early Naturalist tales.[14] She pursued in her stories what she called 'the dramatic rendering of a situation' and 'the impression of vividness, of *presentness*'.[15] Her success with what she called this 'smaller realism' turns on those 'small incidental effects that women have always excelled in, the episodical characterization', which never amount to an epiphany.[16] Her mere 'sketches of character' in this form might occasionally have attained to a 'quick precision of characterization', but never anything more searching.[17] Indeed, her inveterate dread of '*over-psychologizing*' might be said to have kept her back from some of the bolder efforts taking place in Britain concurrently.[18] Barbara White has observed that Wharton was 'too late to pioneer in the [short story] form and too early to participate in the formal experiments of the 1920s', and given that this truncated chronology omits all the remarkable developments in Europe in the 1890s, the 'antimodernistic aesthetic' of her prose seems peculiarly marked against the backdrop of *The Yellow Book*.[19] R. W. B. Lewis concluded

[10] Although, as far as *Vogue* was concerned, things were somewhat more liberal. See Emily Toth, *Kate Chopin* (New York: William Morrow, 1990), 279–81.

[11] Hermione Lee, *Edith Wharton* (London: Pimlico, 2013), 164–5.

[12] Martin Scofield, *The Cambridge Introduction to the American Short Story* (Cambridge: Cambridge University Press, 2012), 99.

[13] Beer, *Kate Chopin, Edith Wharton, and Charlotte Perkins Gilman*, 63.

[14] For a Scribner volume entitled *Stories by Foreign Authors* (1898).

[15] Edith Wharton, *The Writing of Fiction* (c.1924) (New York: Octagon, 1966), 47.

[16] Edith Wharton to Robert Grant, 19 November 1907, in *The Letters of Edith Wharton*, ed. R. W. B. Lewis and Nancy Lewis (New York: Scribner's, 1988), 124.

[17] Edward E. Hale, 'Recent Fiction', *The Dial* 61 (8 December 1916): 586; Brooke Allen, 'The Accomplishment of Edith Wharton', *New Criterion* 20.1 (2001), 39 [33–40].

[18] Wharton, qtd. in Lee, *Edith Wharton*, 161. Emphasis in original.

[19] Barbara White, *Edith Wharton: A Study of the Short Fiction* (New York: Twayne, 1991), xi; Frederick Wegener, 'Form, "Selection," and Ideology in Edith Wharton's Antimodernist Aesthetic', in Clare

from this lack of real innovation that Wharton did not significantly modify the short-story form, and it is hard to disagree.[20]

The Awakening

So it is to their two now canonical novels that we must turn to make sense of whatever it was Chopin and Wharton were doing with the art of characterization in the period under investigation in this volume. Key to grasping the problematic character of Edna Pontellier is the extreme discrepancy between the earliest readers' reactions to her, and her author's understanding.

> According to the majority of 1899 reviews, *The Awakening*'s Edna Pontellier is a selfish wife and mother who not only does not appreciate her good husband, but she also rebels in the worst possible way by taking a lover or two. She is not sympathetic; she is wicked, foolish, or both. As for the ending, the journal *Literature* expressed the common view of 1899: 'the waters of the gulf close appropriately over one who has drifted from all right moorings, and has not the grace to repent.'[21]

For Chopin, on the other hand, Mme Pontellier was above all a useful lens on the inner world of sensations, whose signal advantage over the other characters was her evolved susceptibility to moods. The moral rigidity of the contemporary interpretations tended to miss what we might describe as Chopin's proto-Woolvian interest in evocations of atmospheres, landscapes, flora, and faces; with what Deleuze calls 'becomings': '*Affects are precisely these nonhuman becomings of man*, just as percepts [...] are *nonhuman landscapes of nature*.'[22] It is such becomings that allow Edna finally to make her celebrated 'New Womanish' declaration: 'I am no longer one of Mr. Pontellier's possessions to dispose of or not. I give myself where I choose.'[23] The characterological declaration of independence, her decisive rejection of the marriage in which she is ensnared, proceeds not from intellectual or political convictions, but from the gradual blooming of an affect—cultivated like an orchid of the self in the relative freedom of her husband's long absences

Colquitt, Susan Goodman, and Candace Waid, eds., *A Forward Glance: New Essays on Edith Wharton* (Newark: University of Delaware Press, 1999), 116–38.

[20] R. W. B. Lewis, Introduction in *The Collected Short Stories of Edith Wharton*, Vol. 1 (New York: Scribner's, 1968), vii. See also Garry Totten, 'Critical Reception and Cultural Capital: Edith Wharton as a Short Story Writer', *Pedagogy: Critical Approaches to Teaching Literature, Language, Composition, and Culture* 8.1 (2007): 115–33.

[21] Emily Toth, *Unveiling Kate Chopin* (Jackson: University Press of Mississippi, 1999), 209.

[22] Gilles Deleuze and Félix Guattari, *What Is Philosophy?*, trans. Hugh Tomlinson and Graham Burchell (London: Verso, 1994), 169.

[23] Kate Chopin, *The Awakening*, in *Complete Novels and Stories*, ed. Sandra M. Gilbert (New York: Library of America, 2002), 464.

and the anti-Puritan Creole culture that washes over her like the Gulf Stream.[24] In which case, what is most interesting about the declaration is not its sociological implications (which at any rate have nowhere to go and end in death), but its aesthetic ones: an establishment of the protagonist's prerogatives to be a bearer of *feelings* intense enough to disentangle her from fictional propriety and plot.[25]

The typical reading of the novel ascribes all of this to sexuality and desire.[26] But the truth is that the love-plot between Edna and Robert Lebrun, and the sex-plot between her and Arobin, are equally trite, and their respective sentiments conventional. Edna is exceptional rather as the bearer of an affect she cannot name or master, irreducible to sexuality, which estranges the world around her, enchanting and distorting it in equal measure. We can frame the affect in question according to its two dominant metaphors in the novel: the *oceanic wave*, and the *musical chord*. And we can evince Edna's peculiar susceptibility to it through her capacity to 'color' on short notice at the touch of some well-timed French prose (presumably the Goncourts' *Germinie Lacerteux*, 1864)—'the color mount[ed] into Mrs. Pontellier's face' (530), 'she could not keep the mounting color back from her cheeks' (531)—and thence the application of the same faculty to a wider horizon: 'she was seeing with different eyes and making the acquaintance of new conditions in herself that colored and changed her environment' (566); as opposed to 'that colorless existence which never uplifted its possessor beyond the region of blind contentment' (585). This upsurge of affective coloration, a flush that suffuses the persona and her world, sets those 'new conditions' and 'different eyes' to work, and opens the way for a minor breakthrough in the art of character—at the place where music and the ocean coincide.

We are first made aware of this difference in the way Edna responds to Mademoiselle Reisz's piano performance on the island. Having been used to 'seeing pictures' in conventional imaginary accompaniment to programme music, Edna is suddenly overcome by the 'incipient musical otherness' that rises from the keyboard:[27]

> The very first chords which Mademoiselle Reisz struck upon the piano sent a keen tremor down Mrs. Pontellier's spinal column. [...] She saw no pictures of

[24] 'A characteristic which distinguished them and which impressed Mrs. Pontellier most forcibly was their entire absence of prudery.' Chopin, *Complete Novels and Stories*, 530.

[25] It is worthwhile considering Chopin's celebrated riposte to her critics as evidence of a quasi-experimental approach to protagonist and plot: 'Having a group of people at my disposal, I thought it might be entertaining (to myself) to throw them together and see what would happen. I never dreamed of Mrs. Pontellier making such a mess of things and working out her own damnation as she did. If I had had the slightest intimation of such a thing I would have excluded her from the company. But when I found up what she was up to, the play was half over and it was then too late.' Chopin, *Complete Novels and Stories*, 1052.

[26] As for instance: '*The Awakening* issues an implicit warning to male readers to gain an understanding of and become attentive to their wives' sexual needs.' Heilmann, '*The Awakening* and New Woman Fiction', 91.

[27] John W. Crowley, 'Kate Chopin, Frédéric Chopin, and the Music of the Future', *American Literary Realism* 47.2 (Winter 2015), 99 [95–116].

> solitude, of hope, of longing, or of despair. But the very passions themselves were aroused within her soul, swaying it, lashing it, as the waves daily beat upon her splendid body. She trembled, she was choking, and the tears blinded her.
>
> (549–50)

This is the sure trace in the work of Kate Chopin (like her Polish namesake a 'convinced Wagnerite'[28]) of that constant trope: the shattering musical touch of the 'Tristan' chord or the 'Liebestod', breaking down characterological consistency and rearranging its cardinal terms at 'a spiritual point equivalent to orgasm'.[29] Of course, the music is here both Wagner's ('the quivering love notes of Isolde's song', 594) and Frédéric Chopin's, a fact of the greatest metafictional interest; but the synaesthetic effect is identical to what we have noted in D'Annunzio and corresponds to another Pole's description of Chopin, who 'mixed sounds as paints are mixed on a palette, and produced colors that had not been imagined before'.[30] It is as affects that such sounds are registered in the prose: the tremor down the spinal cord, the lashing of the body with anonymous agitations.

> The music grew strange and fantastic—turbulent, insistent, plaintive and soft with entreaty. The shadows grew deeper. The music filled the room. It floated out upon the night, over the housetops, the crescent of the river, losing itself in the silence of the upper air.
>
> (594–5)

Winged and wavelike, affect lifts the body out of personality, out of character, and into an open becoming.

> [T]he beginning of things, of a world especially, is necessarily vague, tangled, chaotic, and exceedingly disturbing. How few of us ever emerge from such beginning! How many souls perish in its tumult!
>
> The voice of the sea is seductive; never ceasing, whispering, clamoring, murmuring, inviting the soul to wander for a spell in abysses of solitude; to lose itself in mazes of inward contemplation.
>
> The voice of the sea speaks to the soul. The touch of the sea is sensuous, enfolding the body in its soft, close embrace.
>
> (535)[31]

[28] Eulalia Piñero Gil, 'The Pleasures of Music: Kate Chopin's Artistic and Sensorial Synesthesia', in Heather Ostman and Kate O'Donoghue, eds., *Kate Chopin in Context: New Approaches* (New York: Palgrave Macmillan, 2015), 85 [83–100].

[29] Crowley, 'Music of the Future', 101.

[30] Kazimierz Wierzynski, *The Life and Death of Chopin* (New York: Simon & Schuster, 1949), x.

[31] This last sentence will be exactly reprised at the novel's climax, as Edna is borne to her death by that same embrace.

Edna's 'exultation' (551) on learning how to swim these currents is a measure of her new capacity to 'cut like a knife through things' and be cut and disassembled by them in turn. 'A thousand emotions have swept through me to-night. I don't comprehend half of them' (553), she says. To be so swept is to be evacuated of a self. 'She was blindly following whatever impulse moved her, as if she had placed herself in alien hands for direction, and freed her soul of responsibility' (557); for 'she herself—her present self—was in some way different from the other self' for whom she had learned to answer (566). Such is the tremulous interval that affect introduces into modern character, a minimal difference of self from self, a mitosis of the person, which can only spread and dilate from that point on. The phrase that occurs to Edna to describe it is '*life's delirium*', an automated locution that 'crossed her thought like some unsought, extraneous impression' (my emphasis; 586). The 'shock of the unexpected and the unaccustomed' (617) takes root here, in an affect that is never named, never stabilized into anything more than an elusive figure of wave and sound.

All of which is pitched, as it were, against the monotony of what Heidegger would call the *Grundstimmung* of boredom [*Langeweile*]:

> An indescribable oppression, which seemed to generate in some unfamiliar part of her consciousness, filled her whole being with a vague anguish. It was like a shadow, like a mist passing across her soul's summer day. It was strange and unfamiliar; it was a mood.
>
> (527)

The story of *The Awakening*, then, is not a story of personal liberation or anti-patriarchal position-taking, or at least not primarily. Instead, it is the story of how an unanticipated capacity for affect blossoms in the sterile stretches of the *Langeweile* and breaks apart the definitive mood of the modern. To do so, the narrative space occupied by a character is co-opted; but rather than operate as an ethical dynamic within that space, the affect disassembles it. 'Edna Pontellier' is the name that accompanies this disestablishment of the contours and protocols of the self in a fiction that looks to all intents and purposes like a moral plea for greater individual autonomy. Not autonomy but *self-differentiation* is what really answers to the urgent directives of the novel's surging, nameless affect. The 'awakening' in question is not of a character at all, but a depersonalized susceptibility to *life's delirium*—a 'drifting from all right moorings' into oceanic irresponsibility.

But how is it that a character in a broadly realistic fiction is afforded the literary space so to deliquesce, to surf and tumble down the waves of affect? A line of Lawrence Selden's from Wharton's contemporary novel comes to mind: 'a great many dull and ugly people must, in some mysterious way, have been sacrificed to produce her', and still further to permit her 'awakening'.[32] What is the ground against which this figure defines itself and modifies its contours? Who assumes the burden of narrative *work* in this novel, configuring in literary terms the essential division of labour between bourgeois subject and proletarian workforce that Alex Woloch has claimed structures the very space of the nineteenth-century protagonist?[33] It cannot be the various minor characters who populate this fiction that serve this purpose, since it is their role—the role of Mlle Reisz, the ugly spinster; of Alcée Arobin, the bounder; of Lebrun, the fine young man; of Mme Ratignolle, the breeding friend; of Doctor Mandelet, the progressive medic—to mark off the limits of the acceptable on the social map of the text, within which Edna is obliged to move. Rather, there emerges in this novel a far more extensive reservoir of anonymous personae whose literal and figurative labour it is to replenish the characterological salience of Mme Pontellier. These are the Black Americans, who populate the novel in great numbers, and yet dissolve into a mass of unnamed 'Negroes': the 'little negro girl who worked Madame Lebrun's sewing-machine' (557), Mme Ratignolle's 'young black woman' (584), the 'little quadroon boys' who scamper about the place, the numberless 'darkies' and 'mulattoes', and above all 'the quadroon nurse' who relieves Edna of her most demanding function, namely her motherhood. This, finally, is the price to be paid for Chopin's decomposition of her central subject, a racial discrimination between fixed orders of characterological being, one of which toils namelessly in order that the other should have the wherewithal to embrace life's delirium.

The House of Mirth

Edith Wharton's plans for what would become her masterpiece—which started as a sketch entitled 'A Moment's Ornament'—are plainly glimpsed in her contemporary drafts of an unfinished novel with a telling working title: 'Disintegration'. A character named Henry Clephane plots a novel:

> It's to be a study of the new privileged class—a study of the effects of wealth without responsibility. [...] The inherent vice of democracy is the creation of a powerful class of which it can make no use—a kind of Frankenstein monster, an engine of social disintegration. [...] The place to study [this] is here and now—here in this huge breeding-place of inequalities that we call a republic,

[32] Edith Wharton, *The House of Mirth*, in *Collected Novels*, ed. R. W. B. Lewis (New York: Library of America, 1985), 5.

[33] Alex Woloch, *The One vs. the Many: Minor Characters and the Space of the Protagonist in the Novel* (Princeton: Princeton University Press, 2003), esp. 12–42.

> where class-distinctions, instead of growing out of the inherent needs of the social organism, are arbitrarily established by a force that works against it![34]

The case is plainly stated: a novel offered as a critical analysis of the 'new privileged class' whose 'engine' is 'social disintegration'. But it is a plan with significant formal problems. The novel as a form was not engineered to map the asphyxiating and frigid moral stratosphere of a tiny ruling class. Cervantes' rogues and peasants, Defoe's outcasts and isolates, Fielding's, Dickens', or Trollope's casts of hundreds: the novel in its 'heroic' phase was inherently expansive and incorporative, and fretted against containment. Yet, as we have seen with D'Annunzio, James, Maeterlinck, Huysmans, and Wilde, it is one of the attractive options of this first moment of literary modernism to recoil from the democratizing world of industrial society into a restrictive aristocracy of property, wealth, and refinement; and the novelists among this group found new possibilities for the art of character within this constriction of the social field. Edith Wharton's *House of Mirth* is less immediately experimental than D'Annunzio's abstract allegories or James' rarefied geometrical games, and far more indebted to the classical form than the airless novellas of high decadence; but therein lies a tension that has been identified this way: 'there is a curious and persistent tension between the novel's form and the aristocratic speech code the book documents', that is, between the *ethos* of its principal characters and the manner of their presentation.[35] This is our first point of entry into a text whose characterological lessons are of a far greater degree of interest than the majority of ethical readings of the novel have allowed.

The House of Mirth first appeals as an inversion of the protocols of Wharton's great contemporary, Theodore Dreiser in *Sister Carrie* (1900): a negative mirror image of that Naturalist fable of unstoppable rise from street to salon, which thereby takes in collateral glimpses at Stephen Crane's *Maggie: A Girl of the Streets* (1893), and Robert Grant's *Unleavened Bread* (1900). Wharton's approach was to turn the telescope around, and consider what social determination, entrapment, and opportunity looked like to one of the elect; albeit one whose membership was compromised enough to allow for the possibility of vertical movement, which is to say, of failure. Presenting herself some thirty years later as an aspiring 'novelist of manners' looking to establish her reputation with a tale of contemporary mores, Wharton cast her Naturalism in the key of fate:

> I wrote about totally insignificant people [the 'shallow and the idle'], and 'dated' them by an elaborate stage-setting of manners, furniture and costume .... Such

[34] Wharton, from the draft of 'Disintegration' at the Beineke Library; qtd. in Lee, *Edith Wharton*, 178.

[35] Michael Tavel Clarke, 'Between Wall Street and Fifth Avenue: Class and Status in Edith Wharton's *The House of Mirth*', *College Literature: A Journal of Critical Literary Studies* 43.2 (Spring 2016), 363 [342–74].

> groups always rest on an underpinning of wasted human possibilities and it seemed to me that the fate of the persons embodying these possibilities ought to redeem my subject from insignificance. This is the key to The House of Mirth, and its meaning; and I believe the book has owed its success, from the first, as much to my picture of the slow disintegration of Lily Bart as to the details of the 'conversation piece' of which she forms the central figure.[36]

Here we recognize the transference and displacement of the leisure class's 'engine of social disintegration' onto a specific figure, in whom the entire dynamic is to be concentrated. The New England aristocracy becomes available for serious, naturalistic fiction by virtue of its ability to represent 'wasted human opportunities'; and the best way to demonstrate that representability is to subject one of them—the protagonist, indeed—to a 'slow disintegration.'[37] Lily Bart's characterological dismantlement will prove to have been the key to her author's formal success with this great novel, as well as its ideological centrepiece.[38]

It is possible so to experiment upon this protagonist due to the emphasis on her disabled agency within the plot.[39] Indeed, Lily Bart, though enjoined to a putative 'quest for identity,'[40] is defined by her inability to do anything at all, and it is one of the perverse satisfactions of this narrative to share in her glacial inertia when faced with all the disagreeable acts she is called upon to perform: to refrain from an indiscrete visit to Selden's apartments; to refrain from cards; to follow through with her seduction of Percy Gryce; to stay on Bertha Dorset's good side; to pursue her desire for Selden; to flatter her Aunt Peniston, or defeat the dull hypocrite Grace Stepney; to accept the terms of Gus Trenor's transaction; to refuse the invitation to board the *Sabrina*; to turn down the Gormers, the Welly Brys, or Mrs. Hatch; to accept Rosedale; to use the correspondence between Bertha and Selden; or to enter satisfactorily into the charitable projects of Gerty Farish.

[36] Wharton's preface to the 1936 edition, reproduced in Beer and Nolan, eds., *The House of Mirth*, 373.

[37] Lawrence Buell presents this, in a very strained ethical reading, as Lily's 'choice': 'Lily Bart in her own irregular way does, in fact, choose downward mobility for conscience sake', as a way of avoiding the pitfalls of immoral wealth; 'self-privation trumps conscienceless affluence'. See Lawrence Buell, 'Downwardly Mobile for Conscience's Sake: Voluntary Simplicity from Thoreau to Lily Bart', *American Literary History* 17.4 (Winter, 2005), 662 [653–65].

[38] In an excellent discussion, Jesús Blanco Hidalga analyses 'the tension that can be perceived between, on the one hand, Wharton's reliance on a specific series of rhetorical procedures for the production of the individual subject in literature and, on the other hand, her particular vision of a social configuration, namely that of industrial capitalism, which seems to dissolve that rhetorical product'. See Jesús Blanco Hidalga, 'The Produced Self: Conflicts of Depersonalization in Edith Wharton's *The House of Mirth*', *Complutense Journal of English Studies* 27 (2019), 259 [259–74].

[39] A lack of agency that must immediately be referred to 'the contemporary woman's condition as part of a patriarchy, dramatizing the lack of choices available to women who either follow or break patriarchal roles'. Karin Garlepp Burns, 'The Paradox of Objectivity in the Realist Fiction of Edith Wharton and Kate Chopin', *Journal of Narrative Theory* 29.1 (Winter 1999), 38 [27–61].

[40] Joan Lidoff, 'Another Sleeping Beauty: Narcissism in *The House of Mirth*', in Carol J. Singley, ed., *Edith Wharton's The House of Mirth: A Casebook* (New York: Oxford University Press, 2003), 184–207.

There is not a moral choice that she doesn't 'fail', simply as a result of preferring not to change course. Lily is a character who, in effect, does nothing. She is suggestible and agreeable, always ravishingly beautiful, but signally fails: to marry (Rosedale, Dorset, Gryce, Selden), to have an affair, to inherit a fortune, to exact her revenge on Bertha, to hold down any job, to be consistently charitable; and so forth. Drifting from situation to situation like social tumbleweed, she dwells, as Alan Bourassa says, in the unactualized, the *virtual*; that is her element.[41] Wharton exhausts every possible alternative in order to demonstrate how fully detached Lily Bart is from the mechanics of the plot which will grind her, irresistibly, into atoms.[42]

Any represented 'disintegration' of a character in this period, whatever its social or political relevance, is simultaneously an autoreferential meditation on the protocols of characterization itself. The social decline of Lily Bart, her ejection into labour and insalubrious accommodation, is also the 'motivation of the device' for Wharton to experiment with some of the fundamental terms of novelistic personhood: figural salience, contour, line, shading, and the like, in relation to a background of indefinite anonymity. 'Who wants a dingy woman?' (12) is the question that hovers over the text, and it speaks simultaneously to the official 'ethical' theme of the narrative (Lily's decline from wealth and youthful beauty into indistinct and unmarriageable poverty) and to the formal preoccupations of its construction—to the perverse undertaking of abrading and degrading the crisp, cartoon contours that set Lily apart at the outset of this fiction, and seeing what might happen to readerly attention and sympathy once the outline gives way to a general 'dinginess'. It is a term that recurs: the 'dinginess' (36) of Lily's early life mirrored in its 'dingy houses' (32) sprinkled with 'dingy volumes' (36), and her mother's defining credo ('She had hated dinginess, and it was her fate to be dingy', 37); her aunt Mrs Peniston's dwelling, 'at least not externally dingy. But dinginess is a quality which assumes all manner of disguises' (38); the reality of Gerty Farish, 'being fatally poor and dingy' (93), her small apartment festooned with 'a coil of dingy pipes' (177), which prompts Lily's reflection, 'She was quite aware that she was of interest to dingy people, but she assumed that there is only one form of dinginess, and that admiration for brilliancy is the natural expression of its inferior state' (128); down to 'the dingy communal existence of the boarding-house' (336) where she ends her days, which Selden duly appraises as a 'dingy scene' (342).

[41] Alan Bourassa, 'Wharton's Aesthetics and the Ethics of Affect', *CLA Journal* 50.1 (September 2006): 84–106.

[42] Even the contemporary reviews tended to remark this effect of disintegration: 'And this is the tragedy—that a creature so morally sane should be subjected to a process sure to prove disintegrating.' *Independent*, 20 July 1905, reprinted in Beer and Nolan, eds., *The House of Mirth*, 388.

It is Selden himself who repeatedly cajoles us to perceive Lily Bart as the radiant figure which emerges, like Venus from the foam, out of this sordid anonymity:

> He led her through the throng of returning holiday-makers, past sallow-faced girls in preposterous hats, and flat-chested women struggling with paper bundles and palm-leaf fans. Was it possible that she belonged to the same race? The dinginess, the crudity of this average section of womanhood made him feel how highly specialized she was.
>
> (5)

If it is her mother's 'last adjuration to her daughter [...] to escape from dinginess if she could' (37), then by the novel's opening scene, she would appear to have succeeded in this if nothing else. Accreting the membrane that separates such a 'specialized' creature from the looming fatality of her own congenital dinginess is the settled purpose of her biography to date, the form taken by her 'angry rebellion against fate': 'She knew that she hated dinginess as much as her mother had hated it, and to her last breath she meant to fight against it, dragging herself up again and again above its flood till she gained the bright pinnacles of success which presented such a slippery surface to her clutch' (40).

The novel is structured by this animus of the protagonist against her ground, a ground into which she is destined to be resolved, thanks to a progressive 'breaking down of the bounds of self' (282), as Gerty Farish puts it, which grinds her salience back into the dreadful category of the dingy, the dull (the word recurs thirty-four times), the indistinct. Like Beckett's 'grey-black', the dull or dingy in *The House of Mirth* is a kind of ontological zero-degree of being, a void against which the event of character must delineate itself.[43] Lily Bart, who has emerged only recently from this domain, and struggled gamely for definition, is haunted by its constant proximity and the evidence it gives of the merely generic dimension of social personhood. On a visit to Gerty's drab domicile, we read: 'Dull stairs destined to be mounted by dull people: how many thousands of insignificant figures were going up and down such stairs all over the world at that very moment—figures as shabby and uninteresting as that of the middle-aged lady in limp black who descended Gerty's flight as Lily climbed to it!' (276–7). Here we discern the deepest lesson that Wharton is adapting from the Naturalists at a formal level: the insistence of the insignificant, the uninteresting, the shabby and dull, in the vicinity of what the narrative machinery cannot help but render significant—its protagonist. It is the 'highly specialized' function of protagonicity to define itself against the insignificant, and never to surrender to it; and the business of characterization is to ensure that this blurring never takes place.

[43] For a thoroughgoing discussion of this, see Alain Badiou, *On Beckett*, ed. and trans. Alberto Toscano and Nina Power (Manchester: Clinamen, 2003), 5–10.

Again, it is Selden who works hardest to confirm this effect of salience, outline, and form. In an oft-quoted early passage, what mostly goes unremarked is this sheer rhetorical insistence on the labour of contour:

> Selden was conscious of taking a luxurious pleasure in her nearness: in the modelling of her little ear, the crisp upward wave of her hair—was it ever so slightly brightened by art?—and the thick planting of her straight black lashes. Everything about her was at once vigorous and exquisite, at once strong and fine. He had a confused sense that she must have cost a great deal to make, that a great many dull and ugly people must, in some mysterious way, have been sacrificed to produce her. He was aware that the qualities distinguishing her from the herd of her sex were chiefly external: as though a fine glaze of beauty and fastidiousness had been applied to vulgar clay.
>
> (5)

Lawrence Selden, a major persona who does little but observe, exists to certify what Lily Bart *is* in Wharton's text: namely, an effect of distinction created by all the emphatic outlines of 'art'—crisp waves, straight lashes, fine glazes, and so on—against a 'dull ugly herd' of nameless others. In the discursive echo chamber created by Wharton and Selden, her aesthetic delegate if not her moral one, Lily's refined character is drawn as a 'vigorous and exquisite' cartoon.[44] Narratively, this effect is referred to Lily's 'immense social facility, her long habit of adapting herself to others without suffering her own outline to be blurred, the skilled manipulation of all the polished implements of her craft' (248)—that is to say, to her powers of defining and maintaining her contour through group adaptation. She wields metaphorical 'polished implements' with which to touch up any blurring. The group itself is defined by what it excludes, and contour is the necessary badge of admittance to a collective that recognizes only individuals. Yet if the group senses that an individual is, despite all the resources of her art, too sharply defined and, worse still, hails from the world of the 'minor', dull, and dingy, the effect is radical; it is to '[swing] unsphered in a void of social non-existence' (275).

> Lily stood apart from the general movement, feeling herself for the first time utterly alone. No one looked at her, no one seemed aware of her presence; she was

[44] While one takes the point of Dianne Chambers' critique of Selden—'The discrepancy between Selden's perspective as primary reader of Lily Bart and his repeated misunderstandings of events becomes an invitation for the reader to consider how conventional narrative structures can distort female experience'—it does not really account for the obvious aesthetic symmetry between this reader and his novelist; a symmetry which does not gainsay the moral friction of its deployment. See Dianne L. Chambers, *Feminist Readings of Edith Wharton: From Silence to Speech* (New York: Palgrave Macmillan, 2009), 54.

> probing the very depths of insignificance. And under her sense of the collective indifference came the acuter pang of hopes deceived. Disinherited—she had been disinherited—
>
> (233)

The ratification of insignificance through literal disinheritance is the point beyond which the aesthetic play of salience can no longer work its charms. Prior to this moment, and even in the teeth of her greatest social risk at the Riviera, Selden can remark yet again the astonishing power of Lily's distinction—measurable against the muddier figures of members of her own class. In a major passage we find the narrator turning over in Selden's free indirect discourse the dazzling dialectics to which Wharton has given voice in the semiotic elaboration of her text:

> But what especially struck him was the way in which she detached herself, by a hundred undefinable shades, from the persons who most abounded in her own style. It was in just such company, the fine flower and complete expression of the state she aspired to, that the differences came out with special poignancy, her grace cheapening the other women's smartness as her finely-discriminated silences made their chatter dull. The strain of the last hours had restored to her face the deeper eloquence which Selden had lately missed in it, and the bravery of her words to him still fluttered in her voice and eyes. Yes, she was matchless—it was the one word for her; and he could give his admiration the freer play because so little personal feeling remained in it. His real detachment from her had taken place, not at the lurid moment of disenchantment, but now, in the sober after-light of discrimination, where he saw her definitely divided from him by the crudeness of a choice which seemed to deny the very differences he felt in her. It was before him again in its completeness—the choice in which she was content to rest: in the stupid costliness of the food and the showy dulness of the talk, in the freedom of speech which never arrived at wit and the freedom of act which never made for romance. The strident setting of the restaurant, in which their table seemed set apart in a special glare of publicity, and the presence at it of little Dabham of the 'Riviera Notes,' emphasized the ideals of a world where conspicuousness passed for distinction, and the society column had become the roll of fame.
>
> (225)

Here one half of *The House of Mirth*'s pitiless semiological architecture is laid bare (Fig. 10.1); the narrative's spring coiled in the spiral of an aesthetic judgement. We see the degree to which Lily is only ever a relational by-product of figural detachment, difference, distinction, discrimination, and matchlessness, amidst the closed group—a powerful aesthetic effect which comes home to Selden in the access of Kantian disinterest that follows his own libidinal 'disenchantment'. His 'definite division' from her, which permits this perception of the full play of her incalculable

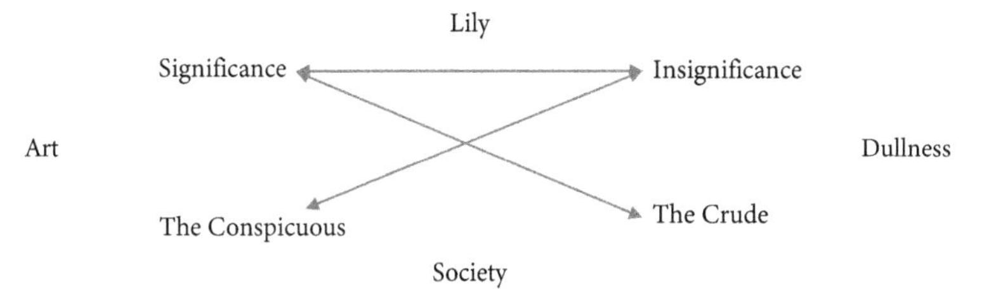

Fig. 10.1 Semiotics of character value in *The House of Mirth*

'differences', is prompted by his melancholy acceptance of her 'crudeness of choice' in displaying her radiant figure in this setting to begin with. A vital categorical difference is clinched here, between mere conspicuousness and true distinction, which provides Selden with the grounds of his judgement, and allows us to grasp the nature of Lily's 'significance' in relation to the ultimately 'insignificant' group she graces with her presence. As we recall her writing later, Wharton's purpose in composing *House of Mirth* was to expose the socially pernicious effects of these 'totally insignificant people', the 'shallow and the idle'—realized in their destruction of the one truly 'significant' person in their midst. It is Lily's function to show them up for being merely 'conspicuous' (Veblen[45]), buoyed by 'stupid costliness' and 'showy dullness' in a 'special glare of publicity', without once attaining the outline of a true character; to be the solitary character their circle both admires and annihilates.

It is telling in this sense that the moment when the greatest proportion of the novel's population embraces her as an ornament of the ruling tribe is the moment of her vivid embodiment of Reynolds' painting 'Mrs. Lloyd' in the *tableau vivant*. As a recreation of a painterly figure, itself sharply defined against a plain woodland setting and engaged in the direct inscription of her new name in the bark of an elm, Lily—in the height of artifice and self-display—becomes through 'the long dryad-like curves that swept upward from her poised foot to her lifted arm' nothing less than 'the real Lily' (142–3). Having long since learned to engrave her own outline on the social medium, 'detached from all that cheapened and vulgarized it' (142), Lily becomes most 'real' at the moment of her grandest artifice. Wharton seems here to be reflecting on one of the tenets of literary realism: that there is no body, no character, that has not always and already been represented in what Barthes called 'the code of the arts', a code he insisted was circular:

> Once the infinite circularity of codes is posited, the body itself cannot escape it: the real body (fictionally given as such) is the replication of a model set forth by

[45] On the importance of Veblen for Wharton at this time, see Wisam Chaleila, 'The Collapse of the American Upper-Class Collective Identity: Capitalism and the Nouveaux Riches in Wharton's *The House of Mirth*', *Cogent Arts & Humanities* 6 (2019): 1–14.

> that code of the arts, so that the most 'natural' of bodies [...] is always only the promise of the artistic code from which it has previously issued.[46]

To be 'real' is to copy and paste oneself into a code of the arts that can be disinterestedly admired by an aesthete like Selden. It is to become 'brilliant' and 'significant' as only a work of art can, at the antipode of the cheap and the vulgar, but at the cost of narrative possibility.

Still, there is an ambivalence in the totemic adjective 'insignificant', which creates seismic effects across the text. We recall that Lily 'assumed that there is only one form of dinginess, and that admiration for brilliancy is the natural expression of its inferior state' (128)—but the novel has awful surprises in store for this view. For there are at least two, competing forms of dinginess at stake, and Lily's tragic flaw is simply to have conflated them. As the narrator puts it in the context of her sojourn with the Welly Brys, 'the sense of being of importance among the insignificant was enough to restore to Miss Bart the gratifying consciousness of power. If these people paid court to her it proved that she was still conspicuous in the world to which they aspired; and she was not above a certain enjoyment in dazzling them by her fineness, in developing their puzzled perception of her superiorities' (117–18). But we are already some distance here from the 'insignificance' of the Dorsets and Trenors, the Gryces and Silvertons, amongst whom Lily has crafted those 'superiorities': the Wellington Brys are an orbit or two removed from that hallowed inner circle; and there is much further for our protagonist to go. The problem with the concept of insignificance is that it tends to conflate an aesthetic with a sociological purview, a conflation evident even in Wharton's own comments on the 'insignificance' of her 'shallow and idle' primary targets. But very different degrees of insignificance are now pressing upon our heroine, the deepest shades of which give onto a scarcely imaginable exteriority—unimaginable because, simply put, the 'other-regarding sentiments had not been cultivated in Lily' (117).

In his powerful analysis of the nineteenth-century realist novel, Alex Woloch demonstrates how the interplay between the teeming space of minor characters and the relatively exclusive space of the protagonist tends to reveal 'a character with more and more depth' at the core of the narrative, but is progressively challenged in doing so by the ever-increasing number of people it is called upon to distribute across its complex topography.[47] In many ways, we should be surprised if this happened in *The House of Mirth*, with its cleanly organized character spaces, populated by fewer and fewer named individuals as it steps away from the blessed heights: the initial gathering at the Trenor's country residence can stand as the novel's privileged character space, where everyone, major or minor, is named,

[46] Roland Barthes, *S/Z*, trans. Richard Miller (Oxford: Blackwell, 1990), 55.
[47] Woloch, *The One vs. the Many*, 78.

described, and organized rigidly into sets, alliances, and intrigues. It is here that Lily is designed to 'show', her figure exquisitely adapted to the highly restrictive 'other-regarding sentiments' that knit together this company of named persons of high social rank. As we are pulled further and further away from this happy centre, through the agency of Carry Fisher, to the less distinct spaces of the various aspirants to the inner sanctum, we also enter a strangely less populated zone, with only a few named personages and very little detail to flesh out the space. Finally, with the figure of Gerty Farish we get a glimpse of the vertiginous abyss where only one name resounds, and the Dantean multitudes blur and overlap in terrifying generic forms. In direct proportion to this steadily diminishing roster of names and known figures, so too the 'depth' of Lily herself, which is calibrated to its sensitive introjection of a viable community, empties out into the barren space of anonymity and dingy half-light.

The space of the protagonist, then, increasingly draws its sustenance from that unnavigable space where 'a great many dull and ugly people' churn the Lethean waters of otherness. It is the purpose of Gerty Farish to induct the protagonist into some 'other-regarding' consciousness, which is also an acknowledgement of this multi-dimensional spatiality, and a shocking revisitation—in the first-person—of those narratological ethics explored only in the third by George Eliot: 'why always Dorothea?' It is an issue raised already by Hamsun in *Hunger*, that gnawing anxiety of the protagonist with regard to his own centrality, his own 'brilliancy' within the narrative space: 'But why exactly me? Why not just as well some person in South America, for that matter?'[48] In *The House of Mirth*, 'the fact that such existences as [Lily's] were pedestalled on foundations of obscure humanity' (159) is initially accepted as a given, as much a function of social distinction as it is of formal laws rooted in narrative itself. 'The dreary limbo of dinginess lay all around and beneath that little illuminated circle in which life reached its finest efflorescence, as the mud and sleet of a winter night enclose a hot-house filled with tropical flowers. All this was in the natural order of things' (159). But before long, as the sphere of the 'insignificant' swells and encroaches, the protagonist is brought face to face with what it means to have been sequestered within 'that little illuminated circle', her salience defined only in relation to those lights. 'Lily, for all her dissatisfied dreaming, had never really conceived the possibility of revolving about a different centre' (275). Now, however, the impersonal process of decentring is the *primum mobile* of the plot. Lily's nascent 'paralyzing sense of insignificance' (178) is fostered by her instruction in the existence of the poor:

> But it is one thing to live comfortably with the abstract conception of poverty, another to be brought in contact with its human embodiments. Lily had never conceived of these victims of fate otherwise than in the mass. That the mass was

[48] Knut Hamsun, *Hunger*, trans. Sverre Lyngstad (Melbourne: Text, 2006), 28.

> composed of individual lives, innumerable separate centres of sensation, with her own eager reachings for pleasure, her own fierce revulsions from pain—that some of these bundles of feeling were clothed in shapes not so unlike her own, with eyes meant to look on gladness, and young lips shaped for love—this discovery gave Lily one of those sudden shocks of pity that sometimes decentralize a life.
>
> (159)

The novel's plot is designed to accelerate this process, to overcome the protagonist's inherently narcissistic self-centredness.[49] Wharton is exact in her formal summation of the problem: it is numerical and geometrical (masses, shapes, and centres); but she misjudges the affective arena to which it should be referred. For pity (along with the unconvincing topic of the 'two selves', one true, one false[50]) is a sentimental residue of the very melodrama such a perspective might be thought to have transcended, and Wharton's recourse to it is surely an avoidance of some more properly political structure of feeling—perhaps something like the reverse of *ressentiment*, whatever that might be. As it is, at least in Lily's own consciousness of the problem, sympathy comes initially as a spasm—'She pictured herself leading such a life as theirs—a life in which achievement seemed as squalid as failure—and the vision made her shudder sympathetically' (117)—and finally as a tragic accommodation. Along the way, it clarifies her own exposure to the multiple. As Sharon Kim points out, her early years have consisted in this above all: 'she adapts to mutability of character instead of developing an inner core that will last over time.'[51] In Bourassa's reading, she becomes progressively aware of her own powers of decomposition and rearrangement. 'Lily's power, the power that lies beyond her personality, beyond her humanity, beyond her worth as an individual, is the power to break her social circle down into the affects that make it up.'[52] Meanwhile, in the language of the novel, her very sense of society

> had been checked by the disintegrating influences of the life about her. All the men and women she knew were like atoms whirling away from each other in some wild centrifugal dance: her first glimpse of the continuity of life had come to her that evening in Nettie Struther's kitchen.
>
> (337)

To be sure, the episode of Mrs. Struther is as bad as anything in Dickens, but it is at least an effort to reset the perimeters of a text that had seemingly made every

[49] 'But as she descends into a world where privacy is no longer possible or valued, she makes faltering efforts to open up to other people.' See Clarke, 'Between Wall Street and Fifth Avenue', 360.

[50] See, on this, Hidalga, 'The Produced Self', 270; and Carol Baker Sapora, 'Female Doubling: The Other Lily Bart in Edith Wharton's *The House of Mirth*', *Papers on Language & Literature* 29.4 (Fall 1993): 371–94.

[51] Kim, 'The Dark Flask', 100.

[52] Bourassa, 'Wharton's Aesthetics and the Ethics of Affect', 102.

effort to suppress the fact and the space of her existence—to follow the path of centrifugal expansion out to the limits of representability.[53] And this is an artistic stroke, in line with any number of other contributions to the emergent 'aesthetic regime', which engenders a reconsideration of the very work we have been reading, since it wrenches us rudely out of the confined orbit of the novel of manners and plunges us into the Naturalist social novel.[54]

Such generic dissonance sparks the sudden realization that, from the moment we first meet her to the moment she takes her life, Lily has been only one thing: *dependent*. This is the characteristic that fatally contaminates her alluring distinction, her fascinating significance, with an ineluctable quotient of the dinginess, the characterological minority, that drives it. It is a characteristic shared by most female protagonists in the history of the novel hitherto;[55] but rarely has this quality been matched with an almost completely disabled sense of narrative agency. Lily's dependency is absolute, in content and in form, since apart from some intuitive reticence predicated on taste and civility, she exerts no real influence on the world around her that isn't simply aesthetic. Her progress from the position of protagonist to a precarious member of the minority, is assured. In a letter to Robert Graves, written as she was completing *House of Mirth*, Wharton demonstrated a striking insensitivity to the logic of her own labour; writing 'Every piece of fiction is an anecdote that exemplifies something, an instance. The lives of your characters are bound to touch at all points other lives irrelevant to the special anecdote you are telling about them, & part of the process of art is to discard these irrelevances, however interesting they are in themselves.'[56] Yet it was precisely her innovation to circumvent this stricture; indeed, to turn it into a formal problem resolvable only through the 'becoming-minor' of her protagonist. It is Lily's fate, and her function, to have her protagonicity pulverized through the very effort to translate her structural dependency into a characterological superiority, within the ethos of a world defined entirely by its determination to shut out the 'dreary world of dinginess' that surrounds it. It is due to Lily's emanation from this engulfing sphere that she can

[53] Wai-Chee Dimock's assessment of Nettie Struther is still apt; see Wai-Chee Dimock, 'Debasing Exchange: Edith Wharton's *The House of Mirth*', *PMLA* 100.5 (Oct. 1985), 790 [783–92].

[54] See Donald Pizer, 'The Naturalism of Edith Wharton's *The House of Mirth*', *Twentieth Century Literature* 41.2 (Summer 1995): 241–8; Bonnie Lynn Gerard, 'From Tea to Chloral: Raising the Dead Lily Bart', *Twentieth Century Literature* 44.4 (Winter, 1998): 409–27; and Myrto Drizou, 'The Undecidable Miss Bart: Edith Wharton's Naturalism in *The House of Mirth*', *49th Parallel* 38 (2016): 21–49. Elaine Showalter espies a different set of generic dissonances, arguing that *House of Mirth* reprises the familiar scenario in late Victorian women's fiction of the orphaned protagonist dependent upon the good will of a tyrannical aunt, but transforms it into a tragic naturalist plot where the heroine goes down to defeat and death. See Elaine Showalter, 'The Death of the Lady (Novelist): Wharton's *House of Mirth*', *Representations* 9 (1985): 133–49.

[55] Such dependency is virtually a condition of many female protagonists' peculiar allegorical density as *bearers* rather than *doers*. '*The House of Mirth* focuses attention specifically on how novels use the figure of woman as a carrier or code of value—that is, as a sign.' Margot Norris, 'Death by Speculation: Deconstructing *The House of Mirth*', in Shari Benstock, ed., *Edith Wharton's The House of Mirth* (New York: St. Martin's Press, 1994), 433 [431–46].

[56] Wharton to Robert Grant, 5 December 1904, Houghton Library; qtd. in Lee, *Edith Wharton*, 164.

shine so brightly within the 'little illuminated circle'. The inhabitants of the circle themselves see nothing of the characterological darkness around them; but they recognize in Lily the incontestable brilliancy of an emissary from without, bringing her hard-won lessons of salience and form to bear on the only remaining place where a 'character' might still mean something, amid the languid decadence of the idle rich. The one certain thing is that it means nothing at all to the infinitely larger domain of the insignificant, where like a brief candle it must immediately be extinguished. The shattering question, 'how many thousands of insignificant figures were going up and down such stairs all over the world at that very moment' (276), will not allow for the possibility of any named individual capable of representing them all, for they are legion.

11
Conrad

As with some other initiatives in the art of modern character, Conrad's too begins with a clearing of the feminine element: 'the book is entirely free of that eternal feminine'; 'there is no heroine in the plot—for the excellent reason that there is no woman in the ship's company'; '[t]here is not a petticoat in all Mr Conrad's pages'; and the 'only female in the book is the ship herself'.[1] An ocean-going vessel is its own kind of bachelor-machine, as *Nostromo*'s Captain Mitchell reflects upon his incarceration in the strong room of Sulaco's Custom House.[2] So many of Conrad's chief characters—Marlow, Jim, Nostromo, James Wait, Kurtz—are bachelors by avocation (the occasional Intended or shore-side lover notwithstanding) because they are seamen or men who seek their advantage by imperial waterways. The merchant marine, profoundly homosocial and often enough homoerotic in practical ethos, constitutes a privileged space, however distantly removed from the exclusive salons and decadent retreats of the idle rich in Wilde, Huysmans, and D'Annunzio, conducive like those to the hothouse forcing of a literary subspecies of modern character. The subtraction of significant female figures and the obsolescence of the marriage plot obliges Conradian narration to stall and in its paralysis to shift its energies towards the functions of description and inventory; and the characters trapped in this entropic system must find other wellsprings of motive, will, and style to etch their salience upon the circumambient mist.[3]

The Nigger of the 'Narcissus'

We begin with his book about a routine passage from Bombay to London, around the Cape of Good Hope, a narrative characterized by a notable suspension of plot and an experiment in collective agency. Given the absence of 'the feminine' and of

[1] Reviews of *The Nigger of the 'Narcissus'* in, respectively, the *Daily Chronicle*, 22 December 1897, *Spectator*, 25 December 1897, the *Glasgow Herald*, 9 December 1897, and the *Daily Mail*, 7 December 1897; all reprinted in Norman Sherry, ed., *Joseph Conrad: The Critical Heritage* (London: Routledge, 1973), 69, 70, 66, 62.

[2] Joseph Conrad, *Nostromo: A Tale of the Seaboard*, ed. Véronique Pauly (London: Penguin, 2007), 148.

[3] The word occurs twenty-three times in *Lord Jim* alone, frequently to suggest uncertainty as to the salience, motive, and style of the central figure. As for example, 'I see well enough now that I hoped for the impossible—for the laying of what is the most obstinate ghost of man's creation, of the uneasy doubt uprising like a mist, secret and gnawing like a worm, and more chilling than the certitude of death—the doubt of the sovereign power enthroned in a fixed standard of conduct.' Joseph Conrad, *Lord Jim: A Tale*, ed. Allan H. Simmons (London: Penguin, 2007), 41.

Modern Character. Julian Murphet, Oxford University Press. © Julian Murphet (2023).
DOI: 10.1093/oso/9780192863126.003.0012

human intrigue on board the *Narcissus* (with the exception of Donkin's treachery), we are given over to a characterology predicated on a working situation: all roles are assigned within the division of labour vouchsafed by the merchant marine. As per Conrad's description of his tale as 'an unrestful episode in the obscure lives of a few individuals out of all the disregarded multitude of the bewildered, the simple and the voiceless', these men are humble, constitutively minor characters.[4] None can claim eminence, since even the captain and mates (Allistoun, Baker, and Creighton) are presented from the outside by the mobile, polymorphous narrative voice. What compels is their integrity as a unit, their corporate character. Some of them are named—Charley (youth), Belfast (loyal friend), Singleton (ancient mariner), Archie (blue-eyed), Knowles (lame), Donkin (traitor), Wamibo (Norwegian), and Wait himself ('nigger')—but many are not: sailmaker, cook (who spends 80 per cent of the journey anonymously, then is named Podmore by the Captain), Scandinavians, boatswain, carpenter, washerman, and so forth. There is no 'space of the protagonist' as set against a protean space of minority; rather, all are knotted together, like Hauptmann's weavers, in a state of bundled protagonicity.[5] It is a notable instance of what Deleuze called 'dividuality' in relation to Eisenstein's cinema (and especially the collective naval protagonist of *Potemkin*): 'What theatre and especially opera had unsuccessfully attempted, cinema achieves *(Battleship Potemkin, October)*: to reach the Dividual, that is, to individuate a mass as such, instead of leaving it in a qualitative homogeneity or reducing it to a quantitive [sic] divisibility.'[6]

The ethic is one of indiscriminate confraternity:

> Night and day the head and shoulders of a seaman could be seen aft by the wheel, outlined high against sunshine or starlight, very steady above the stir of revolving spokes. The faces changed, passing in rotation. Youthful faces, bearded faces, dark faces: faces serene, or faces moody, but all akin with the brotherhood of the sea; all with the same attentive expression of eyes, carefully watching the compass or the sails.
>
> (21)

Modulating between named characters and anonymous functions, the crew can be narrated in the first or third person, depending upon the context: if there is an event to react to, it becomes 'we', while in moments of inactivity, the third-person

[4] Joseph Conrad, *The Nigger of the 'Narcissus'*, ed. Cedric Watts (London: Penguin, 1989), xlviii.

[5] Ian Watt writes that 'the book's real protagonist [is] the ship and its crew. So protean a protagonist could be fully observed only from a shifting point of view.' *Essays on Conrad* (Cambridge: Cambridge University Press, 2004), 67.

[6] Gilles Deleuze, *Cinema 2: The Time-Image*, trans. Hugh Tomlinson and Robert Galeta (Minneapolis: University of Minnesota Press, 1989), 162.

suffices—typically ticking off a number of them in sequence, as if to establish always their interdependence and equality before the bar of grammar. The narrator is 'undramatized' in Werner Senn's sense, but not depersonalized; he morphs into whatever shape is required by the circumstances; 'display[ing] both the detachment, the moralizing attitude of an observer [. . .] and the involvement of a man bound to others by [the merchant marine's] "feeling of fellowship"'.[7] There is one character, however, not incorporated in this protean voice. Note in the following how 'James Wait', the name of the eccentric member, appears as a gothic tremor within the egalitarian montage-composition of nameless functions:

> Something like a weak rattle was heard through the forecastle door. It became a murmur; it ended in a sighing groan. The washerman plunged both his arms into the tub abruptly; the cook became more crestfallen than an exposed backslider; the boatswain moved his shoulders uneasily; the carpenter got up with a spring and walked away—while the sailmaker seemed mentally to give his story up, and began to puff at his pipe with sombre determination. In the blackness of the doorway a pair of eyes glimmered white, and big and staring. Then James Wait's head protruding, became visible, as if suspended between the two hands that grasped a doorpost on each side of the face.
>
> (24)

From this apparition, it is clear that Wait exists to trouble the unselfconscious dividuality of the crew.

The fundamental situation at stake in this novella can be summarized as follows. James Wait boards the *Narcissus* as a 'sick man pretending to be a well man pretending to be sick'. Some of the crew, because of their simplicity, take him directly for a sick man (Singleton is the leader of this faction); keener, more cynical members take him for a shammer, a fraud, and a rebel (Donkin leads this party); Jimmy feeds both hypotheses. At the critical moment, the Captain, the only man who sees Jimmy for what he is—a sick man pretending to be a well man pretending to be sick—adds a critical ingredient to the reception of this complex masquerade: out of what he calls sympathy and kindness, he pretends to treat Wait as a well man shamming sick, while knowing that he is truly ill. This is all the crew needs to come apart at the seams and threaten mutiny, for it is a layer of bad faith and deception of which it is incapable. It is this element, the acting *as if* when *knowing full well*, that inserts the gap or abyss of 'modern character' into the situation of a working vessel, where it cannot be tolerated. The mutiny shimmers around this gap, where dividuality cedes to errant individualism.

[7] Werner Senn, *Conrad's Narrative Voice: Stylistic Aspects of His Fiction* (Leiden: Brill, 2017), 27, 42.

It is an existential abyss, of the kind explored by Sartre in his *Being and Nothingness* half a century later.

> In irony a man annihilates what he posits, within one and the same act; he leads us to believe in order not to be believed; he affirms to deny and denies to affirm; he creates a positive object but it has no being other than its nothingness.[8]

The character of James Wait is the exemplary instance of this irony. 'Ironically' is the adverb best associated with him: 'He said ironically, with gasps between the words:—"Thank you . . . chaps. You . . . are nice . . . and . . . quiet . . . you are! Yelling so . . . before . . . the door . . ."' (25); 'His eyes gleamed ironically, and in a weak voice he reproached us with our cowardice' (104). It is *in* irony that James Wait has his whole existence: a vast, muscular man who does no work; the sole Black man in an all-white crew; the piercing affection-image whose 'face was indistinguishable' (12); the titular character who scarcely appears; the man whose name in the ship's ledger is 'all a smudge' (11). But it is *as* irony that he exerts his most critical power over the world of the text, and many subsequent ones across the following century.

For James Wait is posited within the dividual protagonist of the crew as the negation, the counter-instance of that anachronistic example of characterological simplicity and sincerity, old Singleton. Singleton, singly, just is what he is, 'untouched by human emotions' (347), 'monumental, indistinct' (95), 'the archetype of the simple and reliable seaman',[9] with 'his unreflecting, single-minded [. . .] devotion to an outmoded heroic ideal',[10] in a manner we are given to understand is archaic, even chthonic, preserved against decay by the unaltering laws of the sea. It is over and against this salient archetype that Wait is sketched, more as an absence than a presence, a blur within the composition that troubles its consistency and scrambles its coordinates. The 'hypnotic unaccountable pathos' he instils in his comrades proceeds from his multifoliate ironies of being.[11] What Sartre calls the 'nihilating ambiguity of these temporal ekstases' (58)—Wait's maintaining at one and the same time that *I am what I have been* (a gallant sailor) and *I am not what I have been*—pries open a void within the corporate identity of the group. 'He fascinated us. He would never let doubt die. He overshadowed the ship. Invulnerable in his promise of speedy corruption he trampled on our self-respect, he demonstrated to us daily our want of moral courage; he tainted our lives' (34). The divisions that appear around Jimmy ('All our certitudes were going [. . .]. We suspected Jimmy, one another, and even our very selves', 31), are then tentatively

[8] Jean-Paul Sartre, *Being and Nothingness*, trans. Hazel E. Barnes (London: Methuen, 1957), 47.

[9] Ludwig Schnauder, *Free Will and Determinism in Joseph Conrad's Major Novels* (Amsterdam: Rodopi, 2009), 86.

[10] Senn, *Conrad's Narrative Voice*, 153.

[11] Unsigned review, *Glasgow Herald* (9 December 1897), 10; reprinted in Sherry, *Critical Heritage*, 66.

sealed over by the solder of action after the storm, as an offshoot of the crew traverses the semi-submerged deck to rescue him from his sick bed on the other side of the carpenter's shop. But even this will not hold.

> And we hated James Wait. We could not get rid of the monstrous suspicion that this astounding black-man was shamming sick, had been malingering heartlessly in the face of our toil, of our scorn, of our patience—and now was malingering in the face of our devotion—in the face of death. Our vague and imperfect morality rose with disgust at his unmanly lie. But he stuck to it manfully—amazingly. No! It couldn't be.
>
> (53)

James Wait cannot be drawn; he is the incarnate principle of ironic uncertainty—representing himself, to others and to himself, as a thing he is not.

The 'proper' corporate bond around the feminine ship has been usurped by this impossible bond around an ironic, hollow, Black St Kitts sailor.

> We stood up surrounding Jimmy. We begged him to hold up, to hold on, at least. He glared with his bulging eyes, mute as a fish, and with all the stiffness knocked out of him. He wouldn't stand; he wouldn't even as much as clutch at our necks; he was only a cold black skin loosely stuffed with soft cotton wool; his arms and legs swung jointless and pliable; his head rolled about; the lower lip hung down, enormous and heavy.
>
> (52)

The bond around this *nothing* is secured, certified and sanctioned, by the Captain himself.

> 'I've been sick . . . now—better,' mumbled Wait glaring in the light.—'You have been shamming sick,' retorted Captain Allistoun with severity: 'Why...' he hesitated for less than half a second. 'Why, anybody can see that. There's nothing the matter with you, but you choose to lie-up to please yourself—and now you shall lie-up to please me. Mr. Baker, my orders are that this man is not to be allowed on deck to the end of the passage.'
>
> (88)

With this, the immutable law of the sea itself has given way to the figure of nothingness (*nothing is the matter* of him) to accede to its infamous modernity, its irony, its bottomless reserves of bad faith; and the crew descends into the tumult of a prospective mutiny. The Captain's unexampled fit of sympathy, playing along with Wait's own self-delusion, is owned: '"the notion came to me all at once, before I could think. Sorry for him—like you would be for a sick brute. If ever a creature was in a mortal funk to die! . . . I thought I would let him go out in his own way. Kind of impulse"' (93). And so, one aspect of modern character is hatched out of the radical damage done to the corporate ethos of the nautical fraternity by an unmanageable access of bad faith: 'He was demoralising. Through him we were becoming highly humanised, tender, complex, excessively decadent' (103). Or in other words, *feminine.*

Lord Jim

The 'all-male, quasi-family of the Mercantile Marine'[12] has the additional advantage to Conrad of enshrining perhaps the last institutionalized bastion of feudal romance in the rapidly modernizing world of new technology and increasing political representation. An early review of *Lord Jim* writes: 'The romance of the merchant service is not a whit less enthralling, and is many times more curious, than that of the Navy, and Mr. Conrad knows it all.'[13] That romance is, first and foremost, a function of the archaic seaman's code of conduct submitting sailors to a form of absolute autocracy at sea while upholding standards of self-sacrifice, valour, and *esprit de corps* that are steadily disappearing from the bourgeois lifeworld.[14] 'The nineteenth century, indeed, may be characterized as the era of the triumph of everyday life, and of the hegemony of its categories everywhere, over the rarer and more exceptional moments of heroic deeds and "extreme situations".'[15] Modernity, defined as capitalism's resistless process of disenchantment and rationalization, is the eclipse of romance and the proliferation of the ordinary.

> One is reminded of the antithesis evoked in the Protestant Ethic between 'adventure capitalism'—impulsive, violent, confiding in fortune, and present in almost every epoch, like those narratives that in English are called 'romances'—and the sober, predictable, repressed ethos of bureaucratic-rational capitalism, which is instead, like the 'novel,' a recent European invention.[16]

[12] Katherine V. Snyder, *Bachelors, Manhood, and the Novel, 1850–1925* (Cambridge: Cambridge University Press, 1999), 181.

[13] Unsigned review of *Lord Jim, Academy* 10 (November 1900), 443; reproduced in Sherry, *Critical Heritage*, 87.

[14] And from the service itself, which saw a steep decline in sailing ships (in preference to steam) over the years of Conrad's service. 'Between 1875 and 1894 the total tonnage of British shipping had risen from 6,153,000 to 8,956,000; but in the same period the number of vessels registered with the British Merchant Navy had diminished from 25,461 to 21,206; and of the sailing ships in this number, there had been a steep decline from 21,291 to 12,943.' Cedric Watts, *Joseph Conrad: A Literary Life* (Basingstoke: Macmillan, 1989), 20.

[15] Fredric Jameson, *The Antinomies of Realism* (London: Verso, 2013), 109.

[16] Franco Moretti, 'Serious Century', in Moretti, ed., *The Novel, Vol. 1: History, Geography, and Culture* (Princeton: Princeton University Press, 2006), 384.

The literary novel, a major instrument of modernization, is complicit in the extinction of adventure and romance, categories it is in the business of overcoming from within.[17] Conrad's choice of form is steeped in these interminable ironies. What Fredric Jameson calls 'the problematics of a social value from a quite different mode of production [than ours]—the feudal ideology of honor', is implicit in Conrad's frequent use of the merchant marine as a lens on the world of high imperialism.[18] This 'obscure body of men held together by a community of inglorious toil and by fidelity to a certain standard of conduct' is, like the Arthurian knights of yore, a corporate image of selfless courage and unquestioning fealty to a vanishing order of things.[19] The 'uneven development' implicit in the imperial nexus of metropole and colony, rising democratic standards at home and violent despotisms abroad and at sea, is gathered up into the typical form-problems of Conrad's work—which subsumes romance and modernistic elements in its own formal unevenness. And if, as Ian Watt once observed, 'we can hardly make Conrad responsible for the fact that no ship was ever successfully sailed democratically',[20] neither can we ignore the reactionary aspects of an 'ideology of honour' predicated on this archaic residue of an older dispensation.

Conrad's attitude to 'adventure' was equivocal. In a 1898 review of Marryat's sea yarns, he confessed 'to having been "enslaved", not only by the formulaic heroes, but also by the idealizing power of the work—both characteristics of adventure fiction', and there are good reasons for thinking that his own 'Quixotic' impulse to go to sea against his family's wishes was at least partially inspired by his youthful readings of Cooper, Hugo, and Marryat, as well as stirring accounts in his father's library of the voyages of Cook and Sir John Franklin.[21] Yet, of the kind of person shaped by this sort of preparation for the world, he could be scornful. 'The mere love of adventure is no saving grace. It is no grace at all. It lays a man under no obligation of faithfulness to an idea and even to his own self. [. . .] I have noticed that the majority of mere lovers of adventure are mightily careful of their skins; and the proof of it is that so many of them manage to keep it whole to an advanced age.'[22] Critical to Conrad's ethical attitude towards 'adventure' is a need to transcend its terms in the arena of worldly engagement: one can endorse its power to move youth towards action, but ultimately it is the world that sets

[17] See the discussion in Julian Murphet, *Faulkner's Media Romance* (Oxford: Oxford University Press, 2017).

[18] Fredric Jameson, *The Political Unconscious: Narrative as a Socially Symbolic Act* (Ithaca: Cornell University Press, 1981), 217. 'Conrad tended to idealise the traditional and professional morality of the British Merchant Navy; the courage and integrity that he celebrated were often real enough, but were not racial prerogatives of Englishmen; and he was inclined to elide the historic instances of irresponsibility, baseness and brutality.' Watts, *Joseph Conrad*, 73.

[19] Conrad, *Lord Jim*, 41.

[20] Watt, *Essays on Conrad*, 82.

[21] Andrea White, *Joseph Conrad and the Adventure Tradition: Constructing and Deconstructing the Imperial Subject* (Cambridge: Cambridge University Press, 1993), 100–1.

[22] Joseph Conrad, *Notes on Life and Letters* (London: Dent, 1949), 190.

the terms in which individual capacity will be tested. Implicit in this dialectical conviction is something like a proto-*Bildungsroman* form, in which youthful idealism becomes mature wisdom through the catalyst of romance—the vanishing mediator necessary to attaining rounded subjectivity.

All of which has clear and pressing implications for the technical business of characterization in Conrad's fiction. To be situated as so many of his personae are on the cusp between a broader world of modernity, empire, trade, and novels, and a much narrower, residual world—without which the broader could not function—of caste, discipline, honour, and oral storytelling, is to be sprung with the coils of a formal contradiction, an uneven development of represented personhood. This is further ramified in the imbalance between an exhausted romance characterology comprising that 'good, stupid kind' of man of whom Jim wishes he might be one, and the unmapped modern character of whom 'there remains nothing but the surrender to one's impulses, the fidelity to passing emotions [...] "ever becoming—never being"'.[23] Conrad's privileged bachelor figures are palimpsests of two overlapping literary regimes: the imperial romance in which older tropes and functions are plausibly resuscitated for a market in sensations;[24] and something that will be called 'modernism', or Rancière's aesthetic regime, where entirely new sensations and affects are instantiated in prose that flies under the radar of character altogether.[25]

So young Jim—'unflinching as a hero in a book'[26]—daydreams aboard the *Patna*,

> full of valorous deeds: he loved these dreams and the success of his imaginary achievements. They were the best parts of life, its secret truth, its hidden reality. They had a gorgeous virility, the charm of vagueness, they passed before him with a heroic tread; they carried his soul away with them and made it drunk with the divine philtre of an unbounded confidence in itself.
>
> (18)

Yet the fact that he becomes chief mate 'of a fine ship, without ever having been tested by those events of the sea that show in the light of day the inner worth of a man, the edge of his temper, and the fibre of his stuff' (10), betrays the source of these heroic 'dreams'. '[H]e would forget himself, and beforehand live in his mind the sealife of light literature. He saw himself saving people from sinking ships, cutting away masts in a hurricane, swimming through a surf with a line; or

[23] Edward Garnett, ed., *Letters from Joseph Conrad, 1895–1924* (Indianapolis: Bobbs-Merrill, 1928), 46.
[24] Linda Dryden, *Joseph Conrad and the Imperial Romance* (Basingstoke: Macmillan, 2000).
[25] See for example Jacques Rancière, *The Politics of Aesthetics*, trans. Gabriel Rockhill (London: Continuum, 2004), 53–6.
[26] Conrad, *Lord Jim*, 7.

as a lonely castaway, barefooted and half naked, walking on uncovered reefs in search of shellfish to stave off starvation' (7). Jim is fatally infected by the literary bacillus, joining a long line of the afflicted. From the first pages of the *Quixote*, through Catherine Morland's confusions in *Northanger Abbey*, down to Flaubert's quintessential treatment of Emma Bovary, what Gaultier called *Bovarysme* is coeval with the novel itself and crystallizes Western literature's strategy of self-distancing from the lures of romance.[27] The peculiar status of Jim rests on this tradition, which it uses as a metafictional crowbar into the problem of modern character. For what is *Lord Jim* but an extensive examination of this constitutive gap between 'character' and character, feudal ethos and modern complexity, enslavement to a literary paradigm and transcendence of all models?[28]

The *Patna* section is an astonishing exercise in the new art of characterological impressionism—a spectrum of free-floating and diversely sourced aspects from which our narrator, Marlow (himself as it were conjured into being by the power of Jim's gaze in the courtroom), will want to fashion a character, 'Jim', worthy of asking the question: 'is he *one of us*?' So much hinges on this last phrase that it is worth observing at once how ambivalent it is; grouping Jim simultaneously with the anachronistic confraternity of British gentleman sailors, and with the modern, Western, white subjectivity his eastward trajectory will attempt to reverse engineer. But the novel begins on the horns of an 'essence/appearance' dilemma over the young chief mate's claims to membership of that 'obscure body of men' with its 'certain standard of conduct', that would never countenance the act of which Jim stands accused: the sudden abandonment of his post at the moment of maximum peril to human life. Like Billy Budd before him, nothing could be more certain than Jim's ability to signify the *handsome sailor*, and, on his own terms, to incarnate the 'good, stupid kind' of man he has already proven himself not to be by the time Marlow first claps eyes on him.[29] Jim would seem to be such a type, but he is not:

> There he stood, clean-limbed, clean-faced, firm on his feet, as promising a boy as the sun ever shone on; and, looking at him, knowing all he knew and a little

[27] Jules de Gaultier, *Le Bovarysme, la psychologie dans l'œuvre de Flaubert* (Paris, 1892).

[28] It is arguable that another bachelor fiction already considered in this study, Wilde's *Picture of Dorian Gray*, is also an entry in the annals of *Bovarysme*, albeit a diabolical instance where the pliable young man's susceptibility to the charms of a degenerate French novella leads him irreversibly astray—despite one powerful moment's conviction that, if only he could put the temptations of that literary model behind him, he might escape his moral damnation. One way of looking at *Lord Jim* is as an illustration of how a bachelor might escape his *Bovarysme* not by breaking the hold of literary romance on his world but by obliging his world to conform itself to the romance he cannot relinquish. Patusan is the name of that obligation.

[29] 'Jim is seen as the heroic type of young man, the type Marlow and the mercantile marine depend upon, the type the writers of romantic adventure fiction hand adventures upon and the type, like Rajah James Brooke of Arawak, who in real life act out the fictional adventures. [. . .] There is no question, I think, that Conrad was attempting to take the typical character (Jim) and the typical sea adventure of light literature (man rescues from the perils of the deep) in order to transform the convention.' Norman Sherry, 'Introduction' to *Lord Jim* (New York: Knopf/Everyman, 1992), xiii.

> more too, I was as angry as though I had detected him trying to get something out of me by false pretences. He had no business to look so sound.
>
> (33)

In face, in figure, in speech, Jim is nothing less than what his course in light literature would make of him; he is as if sprung from the pages of a book by Marryat, Cooper, or Sue. And there is enough of an unquestioned continuity between this two-dimensional type and the corporate vanity of the merchant marine to trigger the faith Marlow spontaneously holds for him: 'I liked his appearance; I knew his appearance; he came from the right place; he was one of us. He stood there for all the parentage of his kind, for men and women by no means clever or amusing, but whose very existence is based upon honest faith, and upon the instinct of courage' (35). Due to the narrative precedence of the Act, however ('I had jumped, it seems', 103), over this appearance, the shattering of Marlow's expectations—'I would have trusted the deck to that youngster on the strength of a single glance, and gone to sleep with both eyes' (37)—has always already taken place.[30] The grounds of effective characterization have been compromised so radically that there is nothing for it but to regroup, become the detective, retrace one's steps, circle back to the beginning, and seek help from the others whose sense of Jim's appearance may differ from Marlow's. 'In the novel's first half, these include the *Patna*'s European crew, Captain Brierly, the Malay helmsman, Bob Stanton of the Sephora, the French Lieutenant, Chester, Mr Denver and a host of minor characters, before Marlow calls upon Stein to ask his advice.'[31] Those 'minor characters'—a Parsee Dubash, stray acquaintances, 'complete strangers' (29), Archie Ruthvel, Archie's 'half-caste' Portuguese clerk, old Father Elliot, the rascal Antonio Mariani, Mr Jones, the villagers with the dog, ad infinitum—are numerous and diverse enough to unsettle any rested conviction about Jim's character. Indeed, so fractal and polycentric has the medium of his perception become by the end of the *Patna* section that 'Jim' has seceded from the domain of the objectively knowable,[32] making a nonsense of Marlow's faith, which reverts back to the novelistic reading habits from which Jim seems projected: 'these blue, boyish eyes looking straight into mine, this young face, these capable shoulders, the open bronzed forehead with a white line under the roots of clustering fair hair, this appearance appealing at sight to all my sympathies: this frank aspect, the artless smile, the youthful seriousness. He was of the right sort; he was one of us' (61).

Rather, he is none of us, or all of us, because by this point 'Jim' is merely a moment of nominal convergence in a swarm of overlapping speech-zones, a node

[30] The discussion in Tony E. Jackson, 'Turning into Modernism: *Lord Jim* and the Alteration of the Narrative Subject', *Literature and Psychology* 39.4 (1993): 65–85, is of the highest interest in this regard.

[31] Simmons, 'Introduction' to Conrad, *Lord Jim*, xxiv.

[32] See the discussion in John G. Peters, *Conrad and Impressionism* (Cambridge: Cambridge University Press, 2001), 61–85.

or quilting point in an extremely complex weave of transitions between different language-games, all of them rooted in narrative space and time, but none especially privileged or sound. Marlow observes that the 'affair' of Jim 'seemed to live, with a sort of uncanny vitality, in the minds of men, on the tips of their tongues. I've had the questionable pleasure of meeting it often, years afterwards, thousands of miles away, emerging from the remotest possible talk, coming to the surface of the most distant allusions' (106). Jim is the occasion for a limitless game of Chinese whispers, a game of which the text gives us ample illustration; 'the novel could almost be described as a collage of verdicts'.[33] '[W]hat was secondary and inessential in one moment becomes the center and the dominant, the figure against the ground, in the next. [. . . E]ach new detail, each new perspective on the anecdote, brings into being, as the very center of its whirlpool, another new speaker, himself for the moment the transitory center of a narrative interest which will quickly sweep him away again.'[34] Here indeed we have arrived at the true originality of Conrad's art of character in this novel, which, looking for the secret kernel of a 'self' always just maddeningly out of reach on the other side of a face or figure, discovers something completely different in the complex diffractions and chromatic bridging passages where the frustrated quest for essence must find compensatory rewards among a babel of conflicting accounts. 'It is when we try to grapple with another man's intimate need that we perceive how incomprehensible, wavering, and misty are the beings that share with us the sight of the stars and the warmth of the sun', Marlow muses (138). And of Marlow himself it had elsewhere been written that:

> to him the meaning of an episode was not inside like a kernel but outside, enveloping the tale which brought it out only as a glow brings out a haze, in the likeness of one of these misty halos that sometimes are made visible by the spectral illumination of moonshine.[35]

So it is, too, with Jim's spectral persona in *Lord Jim*, which shimmers just so in the doubtful space where a person should be, because there is finally no kernel, no 'last word' with which to dissipate the mist in an apocalypse of presence, even after the departure to Patusan:

> I ask myself whether his rush had really carried him out of that mist in which he loomed interesting if not very big, with floating outlines—a straggler yearning inconsolably for his humble place in the ranks. And besides, the last word is not said—probably shall never be said. Are not our lives too short for that full

[33] Jacques Berthoud, *Joseph Conrad: The Major Phase* (Cambridge: Cambridge University Press, 1978), 66.
[34] Jameson, *Political Unconscious*, 223–4.
[35] Joseph Conrad, *Heart of Darkness and Other Tales*, ed. Cedric Watts (Oxford: Oxford University Press, 2002), 105.

> utterance which through all our stammerings is of course our only and abiding intention? I have given up expecting those last words, whose ring, if they could only be pronounced, would shake both heaven and earth.
>
> (172)

Even 'in all his brilliance' (134) Jim lacks distinctness; 'He was not clear' (135), 'I cannot say I had ever seen him distinctly' (169)—'At the moment of greatest brilliance the darkness leaped back with a culminating crash, and he vanished before my dazzled eyes as utterly as though he had been blown to atoms' (136). In place of omniscience and clear judgement, we have this radical decomposition, the multiplicity and relativism of 'all the stammerings' of minor characters who would speak of Jim and exhale the mist through which he is glimpsed, less as a character than a looming portent of the failure of all our categories of personhood. It is the multiplicity and minority that matter most here, this sense of Jim's 'exquisite corpse' being drawn by too many hands reaching out from a vast hinterland of narrative space, names and persons we cannot finally keep stable, but who dissolve into a principle of composition, of the flickering on and off of candles in a fog.

Such multiplicity, such minority, have something to do with Jim's most ardent wish, to be re-absorbed into 'the ranks of an insignificant multitude' (255) from which he has defected through his Act, and with the ethical dilemma of that Act itself: the question of 'the pious multitude' (67), those eight hundred pilgrims making the hajj from the Malay peninsula to Mecca, the 'human cargo' (15) who never congeal into anything capable of character, but remain suspended in a kind of primordial impressionistic impersonality: 'a chin upturned, two closed eyelids, a dark hand with silver rings, a meagre limb draped in a torn covering, a head bent back, a naked foot, a throat bared and stretched as if offering itself to the knife' (17). At stake is whether these pilgrims, 'dese cattle' (14), can be considered human at all, their sheer number and homogeneity baffling the novel's characterological machinery with a nameless, sublime pressure that is explicitly numerated at the text's obscure navel: the little engineer's *delirium tremens* nightmare of 'millions of pink toads' (42–3) realized in Marlow's world of 'twelve hundred millions of other more or less human beings' (46). Novelistic characterology was not designed to withstand this demographic pressure, and *Lord Jim* is perhaps the first literary text to think 'character' through the scrim of these unimaginable numbers—'more or less human' because *the human* is a category stabilized by a relation to what it is not. Let Captain Brierly make clear the ethical vacuum in which this multitude resides: 'Frankly, I don't care a snap for all the pilgrims that ever came out of Asia, but a decent man would not have behaved like this to a full cargo of old rags in bales' (54). Experiencing Jim's defection before this multitude as 'a radical disturbance of the notion of the unified self', Brierly embraces the destructive element and kills himself.[36]

[36] Jackson, 'Turning into Modernism', 75.

The long romance section of *Lord Jim*, in which Jim, faithful to his *Bovarysme*, tries to transcend his misty, molecular being as a modern character through the detour of a formally reactionary adventure narrative, is fatally afflicted by this sense of the not-quite-human multitude which peoples its setting.[37] This 'more or less human' demography is the foil that sets off the brilliance and lustre of Jim's now isolated personality.

> In the midst of these dark-faced men, his stalwart figure in white apparel, the gleaming clusters of his fair hair, seemed to catch all the sunshine that trickled through the cracks in the closed shutters of that dim hall, with its walls of mats and a roof of thatch. He appeared like a creature not only of another kind but of another essence.
>
> (175)

But this dialectic, this sudden exceptionalism and ease of definition, is cheaply bought, according to Marlow, who cannot finally accept (as the book cannot) that this is any fitting place in which to redeem a character. Marlow first hints at this cheapness, nominated as the cheapness of the *symbol*:

> [Jim] dominated the forest, the secular gloom, the old mankind. He was like a figure set up on a pedestal, to represent in his persistent youth the power, and perhaps the virtues, of races that never grow old, that have emerged from the gloom. I don't know why he should always have appeared to me symbolic.
>
> (202)

Jim's whiteness, his gleaming young English body, is 'captive' (200) to the darker 'races that never grow old' in Patusan, who bind 'the fetters of that strange freedom' (200) in which he now moves. The adjective 'white' recurs so frequently in the Patusan section, in relation to Jim and the girl he loves, as to clinch the 'essence' they embody in no uncertain terms; and this leaves in profound doubt the quality of Jim's redemption through Romance. Marlow's letter to the 'privileged man' makes this point explicitly, displacing the responsibility for articulating it onto an evident apologist for empire:

> You said also—I call to mind—that 'giving your life up to them' (them meaning all of mankind with skins brown, yellow, or black in colour) 'was like selling your soul to a brute'. You contended that 'that kind of thing' was only endurable and enduring when based on a firm conviction in the truth of ideas racially our own, in whose name are established the order, the morality of an ethical progress.
>
> (258)

[37] Even in Patusan, where named indigenous characters like Dain Waris assume some agency and salience, 'the native is denuded of humanity, and therefore easily dismissed as he would be in a boy's adventure book'. See Sherry, 'Introduction', *Lord Jim*, xv.

In other words, imperial romance jeopardizes its capacity for subjective synthesis by mortgaging it to an 'otherness' it despises, implicitly or explicitly: at the level of the symbol or of the racist Real. Characterological salience, brilliance, clarity, and distinction, purchased via existential immersion in the 'destructive element' of dark multitudes of 'other more or less human beings', is artificial salience at best. This is where the ambivalence of the totemic phrase 'one of us' comes full circle; for if being 'one of us' means 'not being one of them', then that negation is fatefully inscribed in the very heart of civilization itself.

Indeed, reading back the other way, Conrad's striking emphasis on the swarming 'otherness' that engulfs the fragile isthmus of modern subjectivity shows this latter to have been the unstable product of a contingent and carefully patrolled organization of social forms. Conrad was acutely aware of the contribution he wished to make with regard to the growing demographic pressure on the achieved contours of European character. But what is most telling about his attention to it is that what is being 'pressurized' by the outside (the more-or-less human otherness) is already a fully artificial, bureaucratized function of social forms. In an early story, 'An Outpost of Progress' (1897), what would subsequently be left latent in the material is broached explicitly:

> [Kayerts and Carlier] were two perfectly insignificant and incapable individuals, whose existence is only rendered possible through the high organization of civilized crowds. Few men realize that their life, the very essence of their character, their capabilities and their audacities, are only the expression of their belief in the safety of their surroundings. The courage, the composure, the confidence; the emotions and principles; every great and every insignificant thought belongs not to the individual but to the crowd: to the crowd that believes blindly in the irresistible force of its institutions and of its morals, in the power of its police and of its opinion. But the contact with pure unmitigated savagery, with primitive nature and primitive man, brings sudden and profound trouble into the heart. To the sentiment of being alone of one's kind, to the clear perception of the loneliness of one's thoughts, of one's sensations—to the negation of the habitual, which is safe, there is added the affirmation of the unusual, which is dangerous; a suggestion of things vague, uncontrollable, and repulsive, whose discomposing intrusion excites the imagination and tries the civilized nerves of the foolish and the wise alike.[38]

Perhaps only Melville before had so openly sought to separate his characters from their embeddedness in contemporary social substance—the habitual 'crowds' and institutions of the metropolis—and plunge them into 'unmitigated savagery', to ironize and defamiliarize the 'very essence of their character' as alienated outposts

[38] Joseph Conrad, *Tales of Unrest*, public domain, 139–40.

of civilization. It is only that, as Michael Levenson has remarked, this attention to atavism and devolution is another way of thinking about Weberian modernity; about capitalism's dismantlement of character into functions, forms, and institutions—'the extension of the collective will into the intimacies of an individual life' having reached such lengths in modern bureaucracy that no instinctual, affective, or irrational residue is suffered to remain intact.[39] For Conrad, what crystallizes the concept of modern character is this doubly valent pressure, from the inside (society's bureaucratic colonization of the individual psyche) and the outside (from the actually colonized world with all its darker-skinned peoples), which exposes the threadbare consistency of the 'individual' and its absence of any stable kernel. But what comes in 'An Outpost of Progress' as a kind of thesis statement and programme had to be comprehensively recalibrated as a *technique* if it was to affect the arts of character and narrative.[40] It was in *Heart of Darkness* that the greatest strides were made.

Heart of Darkness

In order to make those strides, it was first of all necessary to persist with the ingenious breakthrough of a dramatized narrator, Marlow, for whom the residual ethos of the merchant marine automatically trumps the breaking apart of character into anonymous bureaucratic functions. It will be Marlow's critical eye that transports us upriver, past all the outposts of progress where *homo bureaucratus* can be witnessed in his most absurd and pestilential guises, equally alienated from his native habitat (in the winding metropolitan corridors of the Company) and from all around him in Africa. It is once again as a characterological impressionist that Marlow serves as our guide, charting, as it were laterally, the 'criminality of inefficiency and pure selfishness' of 'the civilizing work in Africa' as manifest in those personages—the accountant, the first-class agent, the manager—who appear as the bearers of that idea.[41] Impressionism is a method of presentation suited to the threadbare remnants of character left by the 'machinery' of bureaucratic rationalization along the snaking river. 'His starched collars and got-up shirt-fronts

[39] Michael Levenson, *Modernism and the Fate of Individuality: Character and Novelistic Form from Conrad to Woolf* (Cambridge: Cambridge University Press, 1991), 45. The quotations there are taken from Max Weber, *Economy and Society*, ed. Guenther Roth and Claus Wittich (New York: Bedminster Press, 1968), 988; and Max Weber, *Max Weber on Law in Economy and Society*, ed. Max Rheinstein (Cambridge, MA: Harvard University Press, 1954), 351.

[40] This story left scarcely any mark on contemporary literary history; its form fell far behind the implications of its content, leaving Conrad with the task of designing *Heart of Darkness*. See the discussion in Cedric Watts, *Conrad's Heart of Darkness: A Critical and Contextual Discussion* (Amsterdam: Rodopi, 2012), 28–31.

[41] Conrad, letter to William Blackwood, 31 December 1898, in *Letters to William Blackwood and David S. Meldrum*, ed. William Blackburn (Durham, NC: Duke University Press, 1958), 36.

were achievements of character', we read of one of them;[42] another is 'young, gentlemanly, a bit reserved, with a forked little beard and a hooked nose' (126); the third is 'commonplace in complexion, in feature, in manners, and in voice. He was of middle size and of ordinary build' (123): a full spectrum from the synecdochic through the clichéd to the utterly unremarkable. But this impressionism rapidly turns over on itself and attains to a higher formal principle, namely the idea that these two-dimensional figures cut from flimsy metropolitan cloth are themselves nothing more than media of the diffusion of another idea, another name, on to which Marlow will rapidly fasten as an imaginary corrective to the flagrant characterological dehiscence of the 'Civil Servant' as a type: Kurtz the Atavist, saturated with charisma and pointing in another direction entirely from the bleached bones of personality glimpsed under the outrageous costume of the accountant—'a high starched collar, white cuffs, a light alpaca jacket, snowy trousers, a clear necktie, and varnished boots' (119). As Levenson has remarked, 'the Civil Servant and the Atavist have served as cautionary instances, competing extremes for the modern temperament. The one surrenders character, the other accumulates too much.'[43]

The ingenuity of Conrad's method in *Heart of Darkness*, then, consists in his avoidance, through the alibi of Marlow's long approach to the Inner Station, of any too robust confrontation with character as such, since Kurtz is notably absent as a figure from much of the tale, and when he does appear, is already scooped-out of substance, 'hollow at the core' (164). This throws us, and Marlow, back upon impressionism per se, since just as it was for Jim, so too Kurtz is less an agent and figure in this fiction than he is the quilting point of a host of competing stories and impressions supplied by minor voices along the way. As David Galef has written, 'it is the fully realized minor characters who are left to eke out Kurtz's existence: through their voices, he lives; through their praise, he grows in stature. If Kurtz is hollow, his essence simply lies elsewhere; the displaced center of *Heart of Darkness* rests with the supporting cast.'[44] The great *figura* of this hypnotic tale, then, is (like Jim Wait before him and Lord Jim after) nothing in himself but a palimpsestic aura built up around a name by interested participant-agents, minor dramatized client-narrators, who, out of the dearth and nullity of their own pretensions to character, collaborate in the effort to create from rumour and hearsay a personality so enthralling and so charismatic as to make a story worth telling.[45]

[42] Conrad, *Heart of Darkness and Other Tales*, 119.

[43] Levenson, *Modernism and the Fate of Individuality*, 48.

[44] David Galef, 'On the Margin: The Peripheral Characters in Conrad's "Heart of Darkness"', *Journal of Modern Literature* 17.1 (Summer, 1990), 117 [117–38].

[45] In other words, Kurtz is the third of Conrad's great early sequence of meditations on 'modern character'. If James Wait is the allegorical precipitant of a fall from the corporate ethos into the bad faith of serialized subjectivity; and 'Lord Jim' is the allegorical precipitant of a defection from the corporate ethos into a *Bovarysme* under the sign of the multiple; then Kurtz is the transfiguration of bureaucratic rationalization into its atavistic other in the mouths of the displaced white-collar professional class.

Kurtz is declared to be 'a higher intelligence', 'a singleness of purpose', 'a special being', 'a genius': a long series of vague reports supplied by a string of self-interested eccentrics, whose obsessions mirror some aspect of Kurtz's personality, gradually congealing into something that will pass for an outline of a person. Only one vestige of character remains to do the work of suturing the fragments together, and that is a voice—'a voice! A voice!'—speaking in the wilderness of nothing at all.

> The point was in his being a gifted creature, and that of all his gifts the one that stood out preeminently, that carried with it a sense of real presence, was his ability to talk, his words—the gift of expression, the bewildering, the illuminating, the most exalted and the most contemptible, the pulsating stream of light, or the deceitful flow from the heart of an impenetrable darkness.
>
> (152)

This notion of a pulsating voice as the suture between an exhausted body and a language without content makes a minimal demand of all that is left of 'Kurtz'—neither an agent nor a character, Kurtz is rather a pure cry of the mute word in the desert of sense. 'He was very little more than a voice. And I heard—him—it—this voice—other voices—all of them were so little more than voices—and the memory of that time itself lingers around me, impalpable, like a dying vibration of one immense jabber, silly, atrocious, sordid, savage, or simply mean, without any kind of sense. Voices, voices . . .' (153). This space where languages dissolve into a babel of primordial being is the site of a derangement of categories, above all categories of character; partly educated in England, with a half-English mother and a half-French father, '[a]ll Europe contributed to the making of Kurtz', and all Africa to his unmaking (154). Bakhtin once remarked of the novel form that, in it, characters spoke not a single, homogeneous language, but partook of the extraordinary proliferation of dialects, speech genres, idioms, jargons, that constituted the complex heteroglossia of any single national language. What we are seeing in the 'immense jabber' of Kurtz in the jungle is something else again: an impossible cohabitation of languages with no organic relation to one another beside the imperial relation itself.[46]

All of which is really to say that Kurtz himself is finally nothing but another imaginary projection of a much more fundamental principle. This is the characterological premise of an ontological barrier between two completely different classes of being, having in this case been breached in such a way as to imbue the diligent bureaucrat with an energy incompatible with his fashioning. It starts as another species of impressionism, this uncomfortable registration of a background, not-quite-human presence: 'two more bundles of acute angles sat with

[46] Mikhail M. Bakhtin, *The Dialogic Imagination: Four Essays*, trans. Caryl Emerson and Michael Holquist (Austin: University of Texas Press, 1981).

their legs drawn up' (118); 'I made out, deep in the tangled gloom, naked breasts, arms, legs, glaring eyes,—the bush was swarming with human limbs in movement, glistening, of bronze colour' (149). But it builds to a statement of principle:

> It was unearthly, and the men were No, they were not inhuman. Well, you know, that was the worst of it—this suspicion of their not being inhuman. It would come slowly to one. They howled, and leaped, and spun, and made horrid faces; but what thrilled you was just the thought of their humanity—like yours—the thought of your remote kinship with this wild and passionate uproar. Ugly. Yes, it was ugly enough; but if you were man enough you would admit to yourself that there was in you just the faintest trace of a response to the terrible frankness of that noise, a dim suspicion of there being a meaning in it which you—you so remote from the night of first ages—could comprehend. And why not? The mind of man is capable of anything—because everything is in it, all the past as well as all the future.
>
> (139)

Heart of Darkness is another effort to wrestle with the great fact of demographic otherness as an affront to the categories of character as we understand it. The 'two-character' of Marlow-Kurtz is generated by the energy required to think the problem at all, let alone give it characterological shape. One pole of this dyad retreats into mild, self-effacing irony, while the other is magnified into that inordinate scale of what Deleuze calls the 'Original'.[47]

Nostromo

The opening chapters of *Nostromo* (1904) appear, in part, to confirm the pattern established by *Heart of Darkness* and developed by *Lord Jim*, of approaching its enigmatic central figure through partial accounts and impressions, as the eponymous character, with nothing much to do in this first section, is variously composited out of Captain Mitchell's unstinting praise of him, Teresa Viola's obsessive distrust, and a range of other less emphatic opinions, all contributing to a masterful impressionism: 'the compositional art with which he is handled is exceptional', as Watt observes.[48] The character, moreover, is significantly over-nominated, each nickname contributing yet another note to the pot-pourri of his character bouquet: 'Gian' Battista' for the Violas (but finally 'Giovanni' for Giselle); 'Nostromo' ('boatswain' for the Italian sailors; 'our man' for Mitchell, Monygham, and the other Europeans); 'Capataz de Cargadores' to the working poor of Sulaco; and

[47] Gilles Deleuze, 'Bartleby; or the Formula' (1993), in *Essays Critical and Clinical*, trans. Daniel W. Smith and Michael A. Greco (Minneapolis: University of Minnesota Press, 1997), 82.
[48] Ian Watt, *Conrad: Nostromo* (Cambridge: Cambridge University Press, 1988), 65.

'Captain Fidenza' after he gets his schooner and amasses his fortune.[49] But all of this is soon enough shown to have little to do with any one figure among the bewildering heterogeneity of dramatis personae now on view and is instead justified according to a quite distinct aesthetic criterion, namely as the 'motivation of the device' that propels this novel's 'extreme mobility of viewpoint'[50]—having transcended the captivation by any particular character, and launched into the unprecedented 'any-space-whatever' of Deleuze's 'gaseous perception'.[51]

No previous novel had so thoroughly deranged the agreed norms of character identification in this way:

> The first part of Nostromo invites and then frustrates the normal objectives of readers to an astonishing degree. A reader's first objective may be to identify with one figure and then use him as a post of observation. But each opportunity—Captain Mitchell, Giorgio Viola, Nostromo, Sir John, Mrs Gould, Charles Gould—is withdrawn almost as soon as offered [. . .]. The common reader's notorious general aim—to enter into the book and become one of its characters—is carefully and austerely baffled.[52]

Nostromo cedes his rightful position as protagonist of the novel to a dynamic of deterritorialization and decentralization, which the novel now claims as its major formal conquest (it is arguably the world's first 'network fiction'[53]), and which appears to have turned the tables on conventional characterology altogether—with its centre and periphery, primary and secondary agents, protagonists and minor characters, flat and rounded personae. For with the place of the protagonist now not simply shared by two complementary bachelor figures but radically evacuated and socialized (the novel has been described as a book with over twenty protagonists[54]), the very notion of a stable character space is compromised and we are tumbled into multiplicity—'perhaps seventy or so named or unnamed persons [. . .] rich in variety—of ages, sexes, races, religions, educations, and moral

[49] See the excellent discussion in Senn, *Conrad's Narrative Voice*, 159–61.

[50] Cedric Watts, *'Janiform Novels' and other Literary Essays*, Kindle Edition (New York: PublishNation, 2016), 82.

[51] 'In the final analysis, we would have to speak of a perception which was no longer liquid but gaseous. For, if we start out from a solid state, where molecules are not free to move about (molar or human perception), we move next to a liquid state, where the molecules move about and merge into one another, but we finally reach a gaseous state, defined by the free movement of each molecule.' Gilles Deleuze, *Cinema 1: The Movement-Image*, trans. Hugh Tomlinson and Barbara Habberjam (London: Athlone 1986), 84.

[52] Albert Guerard, *Conrad the Novelist* (Cambridge, MA: Harvard University Press, 1958), 215.

[53] 'Network fiction makes use of hypertext technology in order to create emergent and recombinatory narratives', as David Ciccoricco argues in *Reading Network Fiction* (Tuscaloosa: University of Alabama Press, 2007), 4. But perhaps it also made use of international trade routes, railway lines, ports, newspapers, telegraphs, telephones, and roadways, as Conrad's novel does.

[54] See Joseph Conrad, *Conrad's Polish Background: Letters to and from Polish Friends*, ed. Zdzisław Najder, trans. Halina Carroll (New York: Oxford University Press, 1964), 289.

attitudes';[55] its two-score 'foreground' figures, equally prominent, 'are not only presented in relation to one another but also in relation to a middle-ground of subordinate figures of great variety, and to the background of an entire population'.[56] Convinced after several unrelenting chapters, as various in temporal location as they are in characterological aspect, that no privileged or stable vantage point is forthcoming, the reader has no option but to accede to the new formal principle at work—the *multiplication of protagonicity*.

> We are now no longer granted unimpeded access to the inner life of a privileged individual; instead we are obliged, even on those occasions when we are invited to share the desires and intentions of a particular character, to retain a vigilant sense of his relativity to the desires and intentions of his fellow-citizens. To a far more immediate degree than in *Lord Jim* we are made to see [. . .] that an individual exists not only in relation to himself but also in relation with others—that each and every member of a group is at once subject and object, observer and observed.[57]

And with that, the early adventure of modern character in literary fiction reaches a kind of culminating apex that only subsequent writers will be able to develop. Conrad achieves an aesthetic innovation in the art of character comparable only with Chekhov in this period, while exploring a formal territory distinct from Wilde's, D'Annunzio's, and Hamsun's affect-riven solitaries, James' geometrical groups, and Egerton's 'becoming' vagabonds, still remarkable a century or more later for the sheer exhilaration of its transcendence of the very problem the others had merely been wrestling with.

With Conrad, and particularly with *Nostromo*, the question of modern character is posed in such a way as finally to obviate the lingering machinery of the realist and Naturalist novel—not by probing and anatomizing the *stultus* of 'modern man', but by socializing his representability in the language of form.[58] The novel turns around on its reader the compulsive literary appetite for a protagonist with whom to identify and lays bare the implicit political logic of that ethical demand. As Edward Said wrote, 'the action at the beginning of the novel seems to wind its confused way forward until a hero appears who can dominate it in order to give it intention and method, whereas it eventually becomes apparent that the action has merely been searching for a hero (Nostromo or Gould) to own, to use, to enslave'.[59]

[55] Watt, *Conrad: Nostromo*, 48.
[56] Berthoud, *Joseph Conrad*, 94.
[57] Berthoud, *Joseph Conrad*, 96.
[58] On the *stultus*, see Michel Foucault, *Discourse and Truth and Parrhesia*, ed. Daniele Lorenzini, Henri-Paul Fruchaud, and Nancy Luxton, trans. Nancy Luxton (Chicago: University of Chicago Press, 2019), 29; and Michel Foucault, *Hermeneutics of the Subject: Lectures at the Collège de France, 1981–1982*, ed. Frédéric Gros, trans. Graham Burchell (New York: Palgrave Macmillan, 2005), 133.
[59] Edward Said, *Beginnings: Intention and Method* (New York: Basic Books, 1975), 133.

It has been one of the defining purposes of 'modern character' that it should resist this logic of domination and exploitation hard-wired into classical characterology, this quest for a hero 'to own, to use' via the structures of empathy and identification (and its corollary quest for a lordly will in relation to a tempestuous upsurge of drives and affects). Conrad had arrived at a creative bourn from which the very notion of individuals, with their exemplary destinies and motivations, seemed an absurd postulate unworthy of serious aesthetic effort—given the unsparing vision he had had of the clockwork universe: 'It knits us in and it knits us out. It has knitted time, space, pain, death, corruption, despair and all the illusions,—and nothing matters. I'll admit however that to look at the remorseless process is sometimes amusing.'[60] The individual in this kind of space is a *non sequitur*, and in his final word on that insupportable category Conrad leads his dashing young journalist, one of his protagonists *manqués*, Martin Decoud out to the Isabellas to confront and come to terms with whatever might remain of his character. 'The brilliant "Son Decoud", the spoiled darling of the family, the lover of Antonia and journalist of Sulaco, was not fit to grapple with himself single-handed' (217): all the stirring epithets collapse around the empty vessel of his name, denuded of its semes.

> After three days of waiting for the sight of some human face, Decoud caught himself entertaining a doubt of his own individuality. It had merged into the world of cloud and water, of natural forces and forms of nature. In our activity alone do we find the sustaining illusion of an independent existence as against the whole scheme of things of which we form a helpless part. Decoud lost all belief in the reality of his action past and to come.
>
> (217)

In these searing moments, Conrad's relentless mission to undermine, afflict, and relativize the bourgeois individual and replace it with a more honest effort at seeing through that 'sustaining illusion' to the busy flux of becoming, comes to a tympanic crescendo. Nowhere in literature to this date has a literary character been so programmatically robbed of its coordinates, dissolved into the unified field of an inhuman cosmos, 'swallowed up in the immense indifference of things' (219). Identify with *that*, the novel seems to dare us; and if we do, then we have ceased to behave as if characters were 'objects of identification, sources of emotional response, or agents of moral vision and behavior', because we have learned that before they are any of that, they are bundled semiotic constructions, fragile representations, that fall apart with the merest touch of a word.[61] By this stage of the proceedings, I should not need to rehearse the metafictional application

[60] Joseph Conrad, *Letters to Cunninghame Graham*, ed. Cedric T. Watts (Cambridge: Cambridge University Press, 1969), 57.

[61] Amanda Anderson, Rita Felski, and Toril Moi, *Character: Three Inquiries in Literary Studies* (Chicago: University of Chicago Press, 2019), 4.

of Conrad's observations on his own personality to the literary history of modern character, which can now, having been systematically prepared by the artists treated in this book, begin in earnest.

> When once the truth is grasped that one's own personality is only a ridiculous and aimless masquerade of something hopelessly unknown the attainment of serenity is not very far off. Then there remains nothing but the surrender to one's impulses, the fidelity to passing emotions which is perhaps a nearer approach to truth than any other philosophy of life. And why not? If we are 'ever becoming—never being' then I would be a fool if I tried to become this thing rather than that; for I know well that I will never be anything.[62]

[62] Letter to Edward Garnett, c.1895, qtd. in Ian Watt, *Conrad in the Nineteenth Century* (Berkeley: University of California Press, 1981), 71.

Select Bibliography

Adorno, Theodor, *Aesthetic Theory*, ed. Gretel Adorno and Rolf Tiedemann, trans. Robert Hullot-Kentor (London: Continuum, 2004).

Adorno, Theodor, *Minima Moralia: Reflections from Damaged Life*, trans. E. F. N. Jephcott (London: Verso, 2005).

Adorno, Theodor, *Philosophical Elements of a Theory of Society*, ed. Tobias ten Brink and Marc Phillip Nogueira, trans. Wieland Hoban (Cambridge: Polity, 2019).

Adorno, Theodor, and Horkheimer, Max, *Dialectic of Enlightenment: Philosophical Fragments*, ed. Gunzelin Schmid Noerr, trans. Edmund Jephcott (Stanford: Stanford University Press, 2002).

Adorno, Theodor, and Sohn-Rethel, Alfred, *Carteggio 1936/1969* (Rome: manifestolibri, 2000).

Ahluwalia, Pal, 'Specificities: Citizens and Subjects—Citizenship, Subjectivity and the Crisis of Modernity', *Social Identities* 5.3 (1999): 313–29.

Albanese, Mary Grace, 'Experimental *Maisie*: Zolien Naturalism and the Compulsion to Convert', *The Henry James Review* 38.1 (Winter 2017): 53–70.

Anderson, Amanda, *The Way We Argue Now: A Study in the Cultures of Theory* (Princeton: Princeton University Press, 2006).

Anderson, Amanda, Felski, Rita, and Moi, Toril, *Character: Three Inquiries in Literary Studies* (Chicago: University of Chicago Press, 2019).

Ardis, Ann, *New Women, New Novels: Feminism and Early Modernism* (New Brunswick: Rutgers University Press, 1990).

Aristotle, *The Complete Works of Aristotle*, Vol. 2, ed. and trans. Jonathan Barnes, Bollingen Series LXXI: 2 (Princeton: Princeton University Press, 1984).

Aristotle, *Prior Analytics*, trans. A. J. Jenkinson, http://classics.mit.edu/Aristotle/prior.mb.txt

Armstrong, Nancy, *Desire and Domestic Fiction* (New York: Oxford University Press, 1987).

Armstrong, Nancy, *How Novels Think: The Limits of Individualism from 1719–1900* (New York: Columbia University Press, 2005).

Artaud, Antonin, *Selected Writings*, ed. Susan Sontag, trans. Helen Weaver (New York: Farrar, Straus & Giroux, 1976).

Badiou, Alain, *On Beckett*, ed. and trans. Alberto Toscano and Nina Power (Manchester: Clinamen, 2003).

Badiou, Alain, *Being and Event*, trans. Oliver Feltham (London: Continuum, 2005).

Bakhtin, Mikhail M., *The Dialogic Imagination: Four Essays*, trans. Caryl Emerson and Michael Holquist (Austin: University of Texas Press, 1981).

Barilli, Renato, *D'Annunzio in prosa* (Milan: Mursia Editore, 1993).

Barricelli, Jean-Pierre, ed., *Chekhov's Great Plays: A Critical Anthology* (New York and London: New York University Press, 1981).

Barthes, Roland, *S/Z*, trans. Richard Miller (Oxford: Blackwell, 1990).

Beer, Janet, *Kate Chopin, Edith Wharton, and Charlotte Perkins Gilman: Studies in Short Fiction* (Basingstoke: Macmillan, 1997).

Bell, Millicent, '"Type" in *The Wings of the Dove* and the Invention of Kate Croy', *Cambridge Quarterly* 37.1 (March 2008): 90–7.

Bell, Nigel, 'The "Woman Question", the "New Woman", and Some Late Victorian Fiction', *English Academy Review* 30.2 (2013): 79–97.

Bely, Andrey, 'The Cherry Orchard', in Laurence P. Senelick, ed. and trans., *Russian Dramatic Theory from Pushkin to the Symbolists* (Austin: University of Texas Press, 1981), 89–92.

Benjamin, Walter, *Selected Writings, Vol. 3: 1935–1938*, ed. Howard Eiland and Michael W. Jennings (Cambridge, MA: Belknap Press of Harvard University Press, 2002).

Bennett, Benjamin K., 'Strindberg and Ibsen: Toward a Cubism of Time in Drama', in Frederick J. Marker and Christopher Innes, eds., *Modernism in European Drama: Ibsen, Strindberg, Pirandello, Beckett* (Toronto: University of Toronto Press, 1998), 69–91.

Bersani, Leo, *A Future for Astyanax: Character and Desire in Literature* (Boston: Little, Brown & Co., 1976).

Berthoud, Jacques, *Joseph Conrad: The Major Phase* (Cambridge: Cambridge University Press, 1978).

Boumelha, Penny, *Thomas Hardy and Women: Sexual Ideology and Narrative Form* (Brighton: Harvest, 1982).

Bourassa, Alan, 'Wharton's Aesthetics and the Ethics of Affect', *CLA Journal* 50.1 (September 2006): 84–106.

Brandt, George W., ed., *Modern Theories of Drama: A Selection of Writings on Drama and Theatre, 1840–1990* (Oxford and New York: Clarendon Press, 1998).

Brecht, Bertolt, '[Notizen über] Individuum und Masse' (1929), in *Gesammelte Werke* (Frankfurt am Main: Suhrkamp, 1967).

Brecht, Bertolt, *Collected Plays: Two*, ed. John Willett and Ralph Mannheim (London: Methuen, 1979).

Brecht, Bertolt, *Große kommentierte Berliner und Frankfurter Ausgabe* (Berlin-Weimar-Frankfurt am Main: Suhrkamp, 1989–2000).

Briusov, Valery, 'Realism and Convention on the Stage' (1908), trans. Laurence Senelick in Bert Cardullo, ed., *Theories of the Avant-Garde Theatre: A Casebook from Kleist to Camus* (Lanham: Scarecrow Press, 2013), 69–80.

Buell, Lawrence, 'Downwardly Mobile for Conscience's Sake: Voluntary Simplicity from Thoreau to Lily Bart', *American Literary History* 17.4 (Winter, 2005): 653–65.

Burns, Karin Garlepp, 'The Paradox of Objectivity in the Realist Fiction of Edith Wharton and Kate Chopin', *Journal of Narrative Theory* 29.1 (Winter 1999): 27–61.

Cameron, S. Brooke, *Critical Alliances: Economics and Feminism in English Women's Writing, 1880–1914* (Toronto: University of Toronto Press, 2020).

Cameron, Sharon, *Thinking in Henry James* (Chicago: University of Chicago Press, 1989).

Caracciolo, Marco, *Strange Narrators in Contemporary Fiction: Explorations in Readers' Engagement with Characters* (Lincoln: University of Nebraska Press, 2016).

Cardullo, Bert, ed., *Theories of the Avant-Garde Theatre: A Casebook from Kleist to Camus* (Lanham: Scarecrow Press, 2013).

Carlson, Harry G., *Strindberg and the Poetry of Myth* (Berkeley: University of California Press, 1982).

Carlson, Marvin, *Theories of the Theatre: A Historical and Critical Survey, from the Greeks to the Present* (Ithaca: Cornell University Press, 1984).

Carlyle, Thomas, *On Heroes, Hero-Worship, and the Heroic in History*, ed. David R. Sorenson and Brent E. Kinser (New Haven: Yale University Press, 2013).

Carroll, Joseph, 'Aestheticism, Homoeroticism, and Guilt', *Philosophy and Literature* 29.2 (October 2005): 285–304.
Chambers, Dianne L., *Feminist Readings of Edith Wharton: From Silence to Speech* (New York: Palgrave Macmillan, 2009).
Chan, Winnie, '*The Yellow Book* Circle and the Culture of the Literary Magazine', in Dominic Head, ed., *The Cambridge History of the English Short Story* (Cambridge: Cambridge University Press, 2016), 118–34.
Chekhov, Anton, *Five Plays*, trans. Ronald Hingley (Oxford: Oxford University Press, 1998).
Chekhov, Anton, *Stories*, trans. Richard Pevear and Larissa Volokhonsky (New York: Bantam Books, 2000).
Chekhov, Anton, *Plays*, trans. Peter Carson (London: Penguin, 2002).
Chevrillon, André, 'Les Principes Critiques de Taine: II: La Faculté Maîtresse', *La Revue des Deux Mondes, Septième Période* 46.1 (July 1928): 116–44.
Chopin, Kate, *Complete Novels and Stories*, ed. Sandra M. Gilbert (New York: Library of America, 2002).
Ciccoricco, David, *Reading Network Fiction* (Tuscaloosa: University of Alabama Press, 2007).
Cixous, Hélène, 'The Character of "Character"', *New Literary History* 5 (1974): 383–402.
Cogsdill, Emily J., Todorov, Alexander T., Spelke, Elizabeth S., and Banaji, Mahzarin R., 'Inferring Character from Faces: A Developmental Study', *Psychological Science* 24.5 (2014): 1132–9.
Conrad, Joseph, *Tales of Unrest* (Garden City: Doubleday, 1925).
Conrad, Joseph, *Notes on Life and Letters* (London: Dent, 1949).
Conrad, Joseph, *Letters to William Blackwood and David S. Meldrum*, ed. William Blackburn (Durham, NC: Duke University Press, 1958).
Conrad, Joseph, *Conrad's Polish Background: Letters to and from Polish Friends*, ed. Zdzisław Najder, trans. Halina Carroll (New York: Oxford University Press, 1964).
Conrad, Joseph, *Letters to Cunninghame Graham*, ed. Cedric T. Watts (Cambridge: Cambridge University Press, 1969).
Conrad, Joseph, *The Nigger of the 'Narcissus'*, ed. Cedric Watts (London: Penguin, 1989).
Conrad, Joseph, *Lord Jim*, with an Introduction by Norman Sherry (New York: Knopf/Everyman, 1992).
Conrad, Joseph, *Heart of Darkness and Other Tales*, ed. Cedric Watts (Oxford: Oxford University Press, 2002).
Conrad, Joseph, *Lord Jim: A Tale*, ed. Allan H. Simmons (London: Penguin, 2007).
Conrad, Joseph, *Nostromo: A Tale of the Seaboard*, ed. Véronique Pauly (London: Penguin, 2007).
Cope, Jonas, *The Dissolution of Character in Late Romanticism, 1820–1839* (Edinburgh: Edinburgh University Press, 2018).
Culler, Jonathan, *Structuralist Poetics: Structuralism, Linguistics, and the Study of Literature* (Ithaca: Cornell University Press, 1975).
D'Annunzio, Gabriele, *Trionfo della morte* (Milan: Fratelli Treves, 1894).
D'Annunzio, Gabriele, *The Intruder* [*L'Innocente*], trans. Arthur Hornblow (Boston: L. C. Page, 1897).
D'Annunzio, Gabriele, *The Flame* [*Il fuoco*] (London: The National Alumni, 1906).
D'Annunzio, Gabriele, *Il piacere*, a cura di Giansiro Ferrata (Rome: Arnoldo Mondadori, 1974).

D'Annunzio, Gabriele, *Pleasure* [*Il Piacere*], trans. Lara Gochin Raffaelli (London: Penguin Classics, 2013).

D'hoker, Elke, '"Half-Man" or "Half-Doll": George Egerton's Response to Friedrich Nietzsche', *Women's Writing* 18.4 (October 2011): 524–46.

da Silva, M. Helena Gonçalves, *Character, Ideology, and Symbolism in the Plays of Wedekind, Sternheim, Kaiser, Toller, and Brecht* (London: Modern Humanities Research Association, 1985).

de Figueiredo, Ivo, *Henrik Ibsen: The Man and the Mask*, trans. Robert Ferguson (New Haven: Yale University Press, 2019).

de Gaultier, Jules, *Le Bovarysme, la psychologie dans l'œuvre de Flaubert* (Paris, 1892).

Delaporte, François, *Anatomy of the Passions* (Stanford: Stanford University Press, 2008).

Deleuze, Gilles, *Cinema 1: The Movement-Image*, trans. Hugh Tomlinson and Barbara Habberjam (London: Athlone, 1986).

Deleuze, Gilles, *Cinema 2: The Time-Image*, trans. Hugh Tomlinson and Robert Galeta (Minneapolis: University of Minnesota Press, 1989).

Deleuze, Gilles, *Essays Critical and Clinical*, trans. Daniel W. Smith and Michael A. Greco (Minneapolis: University of Minnesota Press, 1997).

Deleuze, Gilles, *Empiricism and Subjectivity: An Essay on Hume's Theory of Human Nature* (New York: Columbia University Press, 2001).

Deleuze, Gilles, and Guattari, Félix, *Anti-Oedipus: Capitalism and Schizophrenia*, trans. Robert Hurley, Mark Seem, and Helen R. Lane (Minneapolis: University of Minnesota Press, 1983).

Deleuze, Gilles, and Guattari, Félix, *What is Philosophy?*, trans. Hugh Tomlinson and Graham Burchell (London: Verso, 1994).

Deleuze, Gilles, and Parnet, Claire, *Dialogues*, trans. Hugh Tomlinson and Barbara Habberjam (London: Athlone, 1987).

Denton, William, and Denton, Elizabeth M. F., *The Souls of Things; Or, Psychometric Researches and Discoveries*, 5th ed. (Boston: William Denton, 1871).

Derrida, Jacques, *Acts of Literature*, ed. and trans. Derek Attridge (New York: Routledge, 1992).

Docherty, Thomas, *Reading (Absent) Character: Towards a Theory of Characterization in Fiction* (Oxford: Clarendon Press, 1983).

Dorra, Henri, ed., *Symbolist Art Theories: A Critical Anthology* (Berkeley: University of California Press, 1994).

Dryden, Linda, *Joseph Conrad and the Imperial Romance* (Basingstoke: Macmillan, 2000).

Dube, Saurabh, *Subjects of Modernity* (Manchester: Manchester University Press, 2017).

Durbach, Errol, *Ibsen the Romantic: Analogues of Paradise in the Later Plays* (London: Macmillan, 1982).

Eagleton, Terry, *Criticism and Ideology: A Study in Marxist Literary Theory* (London: Verso, 1978).

Eagleton, Terry, *Sweet Violence: The Idea of the Tragic* (Oxford: Blackwell, 2003).

Eagleton, Terry, *After Theory* (New York: Basic Books, 2004).

Eekman, Thomas, *Anton Čechov, 1860–1960: Some Essays* (Leiden: E. J. Brill, 1960).

Egan, Michael, *Henrik Ibsen: The Critical Heritage* (London: Routledge, 1972).

Egerton, George, 'A Keynote to *Keynotes*', in John Gawsworth, ed., *Ten Contemporaries: Notes Toward Their Definitive Bibliography* (London: Ernest Benn, 1932), 57–60.

Egerton, George, *A Leaf from the Yellow Book: The Correspondence of George Egerton*, ed. Terence de Vere White (London: Richards, 1958).

Egerton, George, *Keynotes and Discords*, ed. Sally Ledger (London: Continuum, 2006).

Ellis, Havelock, *Views and Reviews: A Selection of Uncollected Articles 1884–1932* (Boston: Houghton Mifflin, 1932).
Ellmann, Maud, *The Hunger Artists: Starving, Writing and Imprisonment* (London: Virago, 1993).
Ellmann, Richard, *James Joyce*, new and revised ed. (Oxford: Oxford University Press, 1982).
Ellmann, Richard, *Oscar Wilde* (New York: Vintage Books/Random House, 1988).
Erickson, Jon, 'The *Mise en Scène* of the Non-Euclidean Character: Wellman, Jenkin and Strindberg', *Modern Drama* 41.3 (Fall 1998): 355–70.
Esposito, Fernando, *Fascism, Aviation and Mythical Modernity* (Basingstoke: Palgrave Macmillan, 2015).
Esslin, Martin, *The Field of Drama: How the Signs of Drama Create Meaning on Stage and Screen* (London: Methuen, 1987).
Evangelista, Stefano, *Literary Cosmopolitanism in the English Fin de Siècle: Citizens of Nowhere* (Oxford: Oxford University Press, 2021).
Felski, Rita, 'The Counterdiscourse of the Feminine in Three Texts by Wilde, Huysmans, and Sacher-Masoch', *PMLA* 106.5 (October 1991): 1094–105.
Ferguson, Robert, *Enigma: The Life of Knut Hamsun* (London: Faber, 2011).
Figlerowicz, Marta, *Flat Protagonists: A Theory of Novel Character* (Oxford: Oxford University Press, 2016).
Foster, John, *Essay on Decision of Character* (New York: Printed for booksellers, 1830).
Foucault, Michel, *Language, Counter-Memory, Practice: Selected Essays and Interviews*, ed. Donald F. Bouchard (Ithaca: Cornell University Press, 1977).
Foucault, Michel, *Hermeneutics of the Subject: Lectures at the Collège de France, 1981–1982,* ed. Frédéric Gros, trans. Graham Burchell (New York: Palgrave Macmillan, 2005).
Foucault, Michel, *Discourse and Truth and Parrhesia*, ed. Daniele Lorenzini, Henri-Paul Fruchaud, and Nancy Luxton, trans. Nancy Luxton (Chicago: University of Chicago Press, 2019).
Fowler, Elizabeth, *Literary Character: The Human Figure in Early English Writing* (Ithaca: Cornell University Press, 2003).
Freud, Sigmund, *The Standard Edition of the Complete Psychological Works of Sigmund Freud, Volume VII (1901–1905): A Case of Hysteria, Three Essays on Sexuality and Other Works*, trans. James Strachey (London: Hogarth Press, 1953).
Freud, Sigmund, *The Standard Edition of the Complete Psychological Works of Sigmund Freud, Volume X: Two Case Histories (1909)*, trans. James Strachey (London: Hogarth Press, 1955).
Freud, Sigmund, *The Standard edition of the Complete Psychological Works of Sigmund Freud*, Volume XX (1925-1926): An Autobiographical Study; Inhibitions, Symptoms and Anxiety; The Question of Lay Analysis; and Other Works, trans. James Strachey (London: Hogarth Press, 1959)
Freud, Sigmund, *Civilization and Its Discontents*, trans. James Strachey (New York: W. W. Norton, 1962).
Freud, Sigmund, *The Standard Edition of the Complete Psychological Works of Sigmund Freud, Volume I, 1886–1899: Pre-Psychoanalytic Publications and Unpublished Drafts*, trans. James Strachey (London: Vintage, 2001).
Frow, John, *Character and Person* (Oxford: Oxford University Press, 2014).
Fuchs, Elinor, *The Death of Character: Perspectives on Theater after Modernism* (Bloomington: Indiana University Press, 1996).

Gagnier, Regenia, *Individualism, Decadence and Globalization: On the Relation of Part to Whole, 1859–1920* (Basingstoke: Palgrave Macmillan, 2010).
Gallagher, Catherine, 'The Rise of Fictionality', in Franco Moretti, ed., *The Novel: Volume 1, History, Geography, and Culture* (Princeton: Princeton University Press, 2006), 336–63.
Garber, Marjorie, *Character: The History of a Cultural Obsession* (New York: Farrar, Straus & Giroux, 2020).
Garnett, Edward, ed., *Letters from Joseph Conrad, 1895–1924* (Indianapolis: Bobbs-Merrill, 1928).
Gaskell, Ronald, *Drama and Reality: The European Theatre since Ibsen* (London: Routledge & Kegan Paul, 1972).
Gilman, Richard, *The Making of Modern Drama: A Study of Büchner, Ibsen, Strindberg, Chekhov, Pirandello, Brecht, Beckett, Handke* (New Haven: Yale University Press, 1999).
Goffman, Erving, *The Presentation of Self in Everyday Life* (New York: Doubleday, 1959).
Goode, John, '"Character" and Henry James', *New Left Review* I/40 (December 1966): 55–75.
Goode, John, ed., *The Air of Reality: New Essays on Henry James* (London: Methuen, 1972).
Green, Michael, 'The Russian Symbolist Theater: Some Connections', *Pacific Coast Philology* 12 (1977): 5–14.
Greimas, A. J., *On Meaning: Selected Writings in Semiotic Theory*, trans. Paul J. Perron and Frank H. Collins (Minneapolis: University of Minnesota Press, 1987).
Grimley, Daniel M., *Carl Nielsen and the Idea of Modernism* (Woodbridge: Boydell, 2010).
Guerard, Albert, *Conrad the Novelist* (Cambridge, MA: Harvard University Press, 1958).
Hagberg, Garry L., ed., *Fictional Characters, Real Problems: The Search for Ethical Content in Literature* (Oxford: Oxford University Press, 2016).
Hamilton, Clayton, *The Theory of the Theatre* (New York: Henry Holt, 1913).
Hamsun, Knut, *Sult* (Copenhagen: P. G. Philipsens Forlag, 1890).
Hamsun, Knut, *Selected Letters, Vol. 1: 1879–1898*, ed. Harald Næss and James McFarlane (Norwich: Norvik Press, 1990).
Hamsun, Knut, 'From the Unconscious Life of the Mind', trans. Marie Skramstad de Forest, in *Two Essays*, Heaven Chapbook Series #48 (Louisville, KY: White Fields Press, 1994).
Hamsun, Knut, *Mysteries*, trans. Gerry Bothner (New York: Farrar, Straus & Giroux, 1999).
Hamsun, Knut, *Hunger*, trans. Sverre Lyngstad (Melbourne: Text, 2006).
Hamsun, Tore, ed., *Knut Hamsun som han var* (Oslo: Gyldendal, 1956).
Hardy, Barbara, *The Appropriate Form: An Essay on the Novel* (London: Athlone, 1964).
Härmänmaa, Marja, 'Anatomy of the Superman: Gabriele D'Annunzio's Response to Nietzsche', *The European Legacy: Toward New Paradigms* 24.1 (2019): 59–75.
Härmänmaa, Marja, and Nissen, Christopher, eds., *Decadence, Degeneration, and the End: Studies in the European Fin de Siècle* (Basingstoke: Palgrave Macmillan, 2014).
Harrison, Thomas, ed., *Nietzsche in Italy* (Saratoga: Anma Libri, 1988).
Harvey, W. J., *Character and the Novel* (Ithaca: Cornell University Press, 1965).
Haug, Wolfgang, 'Philosophizing with Marx, Gramsci and Brecht', *boundary* 2 34.3 (Fall 2007): 143–60.
Haworth, David R., *Poststructuralism and After: Structure, Subjectivity and Power* (Basingstoke: Palgrave Macmillan, 2013).
Hawthorne, Julian, 'The Romance of the Impossible' (c.1908), at https://www.gutenberg.org/files/33689/33689-h/33689-h.htm
Hayman, Ronald, *Artaud and After* (Oxford: Oxford University Press, 1977).
Helland, Frode, and Holledge, Julie, eds., *Ibsen on Theatre* (London: Nick Hern Books, 2018).

Hochman, Baruch, *Character in Literature* (Ithaca: Cornell University Press, 1985).
Hughes-Hallett, Lucy, *The Pike, Gabriele D'Annunzio: Poet, Seducer and Preacher of War* (London: Fourth Estate, 2013).
Huysmans, Joris-Karl, *Against Nature*, trans. Margaret Mauldon (Oxford: Oxford World's Classics, 1998).
Ibsen, Henrik, *Letters and Speeches*, ed. and trans. Evert Sprinchorn (New York: Hill & Wang, 1964).
Ibsen, Henrik, *The Oxford Ibsen, Volume VII: The Lady from the Sea, Hedda Gabler, The Master Builder*, ed. James McFarlane (Oxford: Oxford University Press, 1966).
Ibsen, Henrik, *The Oxford Ibsen, Volume VIII: Little Eyolf, John Gabriel Borkman, When We Dead Awaken*, ed. James McFarlane (Oxford: Oxford University Press, 1977).
Ibsen, Henrik, *Ibsen: The Complete Major Prose Plays*, trans. Rolf Fjelde (New York: Plume, 1978).
James, Henry, *The Notebooks of Henry James*, ed. F. O. Matthiessen and Kenneth B. Murdock (New York: Oxford University Press, 1947).
James, Henry, *Theory of Fiction: Henry James*, ed. James E., Miller Jr. (Lincoln: University of Nebraska Press, 1972).
James, Henry, *The Letters of Henry James, Vol. 4: 1895–1916*, ed. Leon Edel (Cambridge, MA: Harvard University Press, 1984).
James, Henry, *Literary Criticism: Essays on Literature, American Writers, English Writers*, ed. Leon Edel (New York: Library of America, 1984).
James, Henry, *Literary Criticism: French Writers, Other European Writers, The Prefaces to the New York Edition*, ed. Leon Edel (New York: Library of America, 1984).
James, Henry, *The Complete Notebooks of Henry James*, ed. Leon Edel and Lyall H. Powers (Oxford: Oxford University Press, 1987).
James, Henry, *The American Essays of Henry James*, ed. Leon Edel (Princeton: Princeton University Press, 1989).
James, Henry, *Novels 1896–1899*, ed. Myra Jehlen (New York: Library of America, 2003).
James, Henry, *Novels 1901–1902*, ed. Leo Bersani (New York: Library of America, 2006).
James, Henry, *Novels 1903–1911*, ed. Ross Posnock (New York: Library of America, 2010).
Jameson, Fredric, *The Political Unconscious: Narrative as a Socially Symbolic Act* (Ithaca: Cornell University Press, 1981).
Jameson, Fredric, 'The Realist Floor-Plan', in Marshall Blonsky, ed., *On Signs* (Baltimore: Johns Hopkins University Press, 1985), 373–83.
Jameson, Fredric, *Brecht and Method* (London: Verso, 1998).
Jameson, Fredric, *The Cultural Turn: Selected Writings on the Postmodern, 1983–1998* (London: Verso, 1998).
Jameson, Fredric, *The Modernist Papers* (London: Verso, 2007).
Jameson, Fredric, *The Ideologies of Theory* (London: Verso, 2008).
Jameson, Fredric, *The Antinomies of Realism* (London: Verso, 2013).
Jameson, Fredric, *Allegory and Ideology* (London: Verso, 2019).
Jannidis, Fotis, *Figur und Person: Beitrag zu einer historischen Narratologie* (Berlin: De Gruyter, 2004).
Jauß, Hans Robert, 'Levels of Identification of Hero and Audience', *New Literary History* 5.2 (1974): 283–317.
Jehlen, Myra, *Five Fictions in Search of Truth* (Princeton: Princeton University Press, 2008).
Jonsson, Stefan, *Crowds and Democracy: The Idea and Image of the Masses from Revolution to Fascism* (New York: Columbia University Press, 2013).
Jullian, Philippe, *D'Annunzio*, trans. Stephen Hardman (New York: Viking Press, 1973).

Jusová, Iveta, *The New Woman and the Empire* (Columbus: Ohio State University Press, 2005).

Kandinsky, Wassily, *Concerning the Spiritual in Art*, trans. Michael Sadler (London: Constable and Co., 1914).

Kern, Stephen, *The Culture of Space and Time, 1880–1918* (Cambridge, MA: Harvard University Press, 1983).

Khanna, Ranjana, *Dark Continents: Psychoanalysis and Colonialism* (Durham, NC: Duke University Press, 2003).

Klein, Michael L., *Music and the Crises of the Modern Subject* (Bloomington: Indiana University Press, 2015).

Kolloen, Ingar Sletten, *Knut Hamsun: Dreamer and Dissenter*, trans. Deborah Dawkin and Erik Skuggevik (New Haven: Yale University Press, 2009).

Krasner, David, *A History of Modern Drama*, Vol. 1 (Oxford: Wiley-Blackwell, 2012).

Krutch, Joseph Wood, *Modernism in Modern Drama: A Definition and an Estimate* (Ithaca: Cornell University Press, 1953).

Kuhn, Tom, and Giles, Steve, eds., *Brecht on Art and Politics*, trans. Laura Bradley, Steve Giles, and Tom Kuhn (London: Bloomsbury, 2003).

Kvam, Kela, *Max Reinhardt og Strindbergs visionaere dramatik* (Copenhagen: Akademisk Forlag, 1974).

Lacan, Jacques, *The Seminar of Jacques Lacan, Book VII: The Ethics of Psychoanalysis, 1959–1960*, ed. Jacques-Alain Miller, trans. Dennis Porter (New York: Norton, 1992).

Lacan, Jacques, *The Sinthome: The Seminar of Jacques Lacan Book XXIII*, ed. Jacques-Alain Miller, trans. A. R. Price (Cambridge: Polity, 2016).

Lacey, Nicola, *Women, Crime, and Character: From Moll Flanders to Tess of the D'Urbervilles* (Oxford and New York: Oxford University Press, 2008).

LaRocque, Monique Marie, 'Decadent Desire: The Dream of Disembodiment in *À rebours*, *The Picture of Dorian Gray*, and *L'Eve future*' (PhD dissertation, Dept. of Comparative Literature, Indiana University, 2001).

Larsen, Hanna Astrup, *Knut Hamsun* (London: Gyldendal, 1922).

Ledger, Sally, *The New Woman: Fiction and Feminism at the Fin de Siècle* (Manchester: Manchester University Press, 1997).

Lee, Hermione, *Edith Wharton* (London: Pimlico, 2013).

Levenson, Michael, *Modernism and the Fate of Individuality: Character and Novelistic Form from Conrad to Woolf* (Cambridge: Cambridge University Press, 1991).

Lewis, R. W. B., ed., *The Collected Short Stories of Edith Wharton*, Vol. 1 (New York: Scribner's, 1968).

Lindenberger, Herbert, *The Historical Drama: The Relation of Literature and Reality* (Chicago: University of Chicago Press, 1975).

Lissi, Leonardo, *Marginal Modernity: The Aesthetics of Dependency from Kierkegaard to Joyce* (New York: Fordham University Press, 2012).

Lucas, F. L., *The Drama of Chekhov, Synge, Yeats, and Pirandello* (London: Cassell, 1963).

Lukács, Georg, *Writer and Critic and Other Essays*, ed. and trans. Arthur D. Kahn (New York: Grosset & Dunlap, 1970).

Lukács, Georg, *History and Class Consciousness: Studies in Marxist Dialectics*, trans. Rodney Livingstone (Cambridge, MA: MIT Press, 1971).

Lukács, Georg, *Theory of the Novel*, trans. Anna Bostock (London: Merlin, 1971).

Lukács, Georg, *Studies in European Realism: A Sociological Survey of the Writings of Balzac, Stendhal, Zola, Tolstoy, Gorki, and Others*, trans. Edith Bone (London: Merlin Press, 1972).

Lukács, Georg, *Essays on Realism*, ed. Rodney Livingstone, trans. David Fernbach (Cambridge, MA: MIT Press, 1981).
Lukasik, Christopher J., *Discerning Characters: The Culture of Appearance in Early America* (Philadelphia: University of Pennsylvania Press, 2010).
Lutterbie, John Harry, *Hearing Voices: Modern Drama and the Problem of Subjectivity* (Ann Arbor: University of Michigan Press, 1997).
Lynch, Deidre Shauna, *The Economy of Character: Novels, Market Culture, and the Business of Inner Meaning* (Chicago: University of Chicago Press, 1998).
McFarlane, James, *Ibsen and Meaning: Studies, Essays, & Prefaces* (Norwich: Norvik Press, 1989).
McFarlane, J. W., 'The Whisper of the Blood: A Study of Knut Hamsun's Early Novels', *PMLA* 71.4 (September 1956): 563–94.
McGuinness, Patrick, *Maurice Maeterlinck and the Making of Modern Theatre* (Oxford: Oxford University Press, 2000).
Maddox, Jr., James H., *Joyce's Ulysses and the Assault upon Character* (New Brunswick: Rutgers University Press, 1978).
Maeterlinck, Maurice, *Three Little Dramas* (London: Duckworth & Co., 1899).
Maeterlinck, Maurice, *The Treasure of the Humble*, trans. Alfred Sutro (New York: Dodd, Mead & Co., 1902).
Maeterlinck, Maurice, *The Double Garden*, trans. Alfred Sutro (New York: Dodd, Mead & Co., 1904).
Maeterlinck, Maurice, *A Maeterlinck Reader: Plays, Poems, Short Fiction, Aphorisms, and Essays*, Belgian Francophone Library, ed. and trans. David Willinger and Daniel Gerould (New York: Peter Lang, 2011).
Malabou, Catherine, *What Should We Do with Our Brain?*, trans. Sebastian Rand (New York: Fordham University Press, 2008).
Mallarmé, Stéphane, 'Hamlet', in *Divagations*, trans. Barbara Johnson (Cambridge, MA: Belknap Press of Harvard University Press, 2007), 124–8.
Manning, Susan, *Poetics of Character: Transatlantic Encounters 1700–1900* (Cambridge: Cambridge University Press, 2013).
Marx, Karl, *Capital, Vol. 1*, trans. Ben Fowkes (London: Penguin, 1990).
Maudsley, Henry, *The Physiology and Pathology of the Mind* (1867), qtd. in *The Westminster Review* (January and April 1868): 37–64.
Meizoz, Jérôme, *Postures littéraires. Mises en scène modernes de l'auteur. Essai* (Genève: Slatkine Érudition, 2007).
Meyer, Michael, *Ibsen: A Biography* (Garden City, NY: Doubleday, 1971).
Meyerhold, Vsevolod, *Meyerhold on Theatre*, ed. and trans. Edward Braun, 4th ed. (London: Bloomsbury, 2016).
Moi, Toril, *Henrik Ibsen and the Birth of Modernism* (Oxford: Oxford University Press, 2006).
Moody, Alys, and Ross, Stephen J., eds., *Global Modernists on Modernism: An Anthology* (London: Bloomsbury, 2020).
Moretti, Franco, ed., *The Novel, Vol. 1: History, Geography, and Culture* (Princeton: Princeton University Press, 2006).
Moretti, Franco, *The Bourgeois: Between History and Literature* (London: Verso, 2013).
Murphet, Julian, 'Character and Event', *SubStance* 36.3 (113) (September 2007): 106–25.
Murphet, Julian, *Multimedia Modernism: Literature and the Anglo-American Avant-Garde* (Cambridge: Cambridge University Press, 2009).

Murphet, Julian, 'On the Market and Uneven Development', *Affirmations* 1.1 (Autumn 2013): 1–20.

Murphet, Julian, *Faulkner's Media Romance* (Oxford: Oxford University Press, 2017).

Næss, Harald, *Knut Hamsun* (Boston: Twayne, 1984).

Nancy, Jean-Luc, ed., 'Who Comes after the Subject?', Special Issue, *Topoi* 7.2 (September 1988).

Naremore, James, *The World without a Self: Virginia Woolf and the Novel* (New Haven: Yale University Press, 1973).

Nietzsche, Friedrich, *Selected Letters of Friedrich Nietzsche*, trans. Christopher Middleton (Chicago: University of Chicago Press, 1969).

Nietzsche, Friedrich, *Human, All Too Human: A Book for Free Spirits*, trans. R. J. Hollingdale (Cambridge: Cambridge University Press, 1996).

Nietzsche, Friedrich, *Daybreak: Thoughts on the Prejudices of Morality*, ed. Maudemarie Clark and Brian Leiter, trans. R. J. Hollingdale (Cambridge: Cambridge University Press, 1997).

Nietzsche, Friedrich, *The Birth of Tragedy and Other Writings*, ed. Raymond Geuss and Ronald Speirs, trans. Ronald Speirs (Cambridge: Cambridge University Press, 1999).

Nietzsche, Friedrich, *The Gay Science*, ed. Bernard Williams, trans. Josefine Nauckhoff (Cambridge: Cambridge University Press, 2001).

Nietzsche, Friedrich, *Beyond Good and Evil*, ed. Rolf-Peter Horstmann and Judith Norman, trans. Judith Norman (Cambridge: Cambridge University Press, 2002).

Nietzsche, Friedrich, *Writings from the Late Notebooks*, ed. Rüdiger Bittner, trans Kate Sturge (Cambridge: Cambridge University Press, 2003).

Nietzsche, Friedrich, *On the Genealogy of Morality*, ed. Keith Ansell-Pearson, trans. Carol Diethe (Cambridge: Cambridge University Press, 2006).

Nilsson, Nils Åke, 'Intonation and Rhythm in Chekhov's Plays', in Robert Louis Jackson, ed., *Chekhov: A Collection of Critical Essays* (Englewood Cliffs, NJ: Prentice-Hall 1967), 161–74.

Opperud, I. M., ed., 'Ibsen och Strindberg: Giganternas kamp', Special Issue, *Parnass* 16.2 (2009): 3–33.

Orr, John, *Tragic Drama and Modern Society: A Sociology of Dramatic Form from 1800 to the Present*, 2nd ed. (Basingstoke: Macmillan, 1989).

Oxfeldt, Elisabeth, *Nordic Orientalism: Paris and the Cosmopolitan Imagination* (Copenhagen: Musuem Tusculanum Press, 2005).

Palmer, Alan. *Fictional Minds* (Lincoln: University of Nebraska Press, 2004).

Panthel, Hans W., *Rainer Maria Rilke und Maurice Maeterlinck* (Berlin: Erik Schmidt, 1973).

Paraschas, Sotirios, *Reappearing Characters in Nineteenth-Century French Literature: Authorship, Originality, and Intellectual Property* (London: Palgrave Macmillan, 2018).

Peter, John, *Vladimir's Carrot: Modern Drama and the Modern Imagination* (London: Methuen, 1988).

Peters, John G., *Conrad and Impressionism* (Cambridge: Cambridge University Press, 2001).

Phelan, James, *Living to Tell about It: A Rhetoric and Ethics of Character Narration* (Ithaca and London: Cornell University Press, 2005).

Phillips, Michelle H., 'The "Partagé Child" and the Emergence of the Modernist Novel in *What Maisie Knew*', *The Henry James Review* 31.2 (Spring 2010): 95–110.

Pitcher, Harvey, *The Chekhov Play: A New Interpretation* (Berkeley: University of California Press, 1985).

Pizer, Donald, 'The Naturalism of Edith Wharton's *The House of Mirth*', *Twentieth Century Literature* 41.2 (Summer 1995): 241–8.
Plato, *Complete Works*, ed. John M. Cooper (Indianapolis: Hackett, 1997).
Porter, Laurence M., 'Huysmans' *À rebours*: The Psychodynamics of Regression', *American Imago* 44.1 (Spring 1987): 51–65.
Pound, Ezra, *Literary Essays of Ezra Pound*, ed. T. S. Eliot (London: Faber & Faber, 1960).
Pound, Ezra, *The Spirit of Romance* (New York: New Directions, 1968).
Powers, Richard, *The Echo Maker* (London: Vintage, 2007).
Price, Martin, *Forms of Life: Character and Moral Imagination in the Novel* (New Haven: Yale University Press, 1983).
Prideaux, Sue, *Strindberg: A Life* (New Haven: Yale University Press, 2012).
Pykett, Lyn, *The 'Improper' Feminine: The Women's Sensation Novel and the New Woman Writing* (New York: Routledge, 1992).
Pykett, Lyn, *Engendering Fictions: The English Novel in the Early Twentieth Century* (London: Edward Arnold, 1995).
Ram, Harsha, *The Imperial Sublime: A Russian Poetics of Empire* (Madison: University of Wisconsin Press, 2006).
Rancière, Jacques, *The Politics of Aesthetics: The Distribution of the Sensible*, trans. Gabriel Rockhill (London: Continuum, 2004).
Rancière, Jacques, *The Aesthetic Unconscious*, trans. Debra Keates and James Swenson (Cambridge: Polity, 2009).
Rancière, Jacques, *The Politics of Literature*, trans. Julie Rose (Cambridge: Polity, 2011).
Rancière, Jacques, *Aisthesis*, trans. Zakir Paul (London and New York: Verso, 2013).
Rancière, Jacques, *Figures of History*, trans. Julie Rose (Cambridge: Polity, 2014).
Raunig, Gerald, *Dividuum: Machinic Capitalism and Molecular Revolution*, trans. Aileen Derieg (Pasadena: Semiotext(e), 2016).
Rees, Daniel, *Hunger and Modern Writing: Melville, Kafka, Hamsun, and Wright* (Köln: Modern Academic Publishing, 2016).
Rhodes, Anthony, *The Poet as Superman: A Life of Gabriele D'Annunzio* (London: Weidenfeld & Nicolson, 1959).
Ribot, Théodule, *Les maladies de la personnalité* (Paris: Alcan, 1885).
Ribot, Théodule, *Diseases of the Will*, trans. Merwin-Marie Snell (Chicago: Open Court, 1894).
Rilke, Rainer Maria, 'Das Theater des Maeterlinck' (1901), in *Sämtliche Werke*, vol. 5 (Frankfurt: Insel Verlag, 1965), 479–82.
Rilke, Rainer Maria, *Diaries of a Young Poet*, trans. Edward Snow and Michael Winkler (New York: Norton, 1997).
Rilke, Rainer Maria, *The Notebooks of Malte Laurids Brigge*, trans. Michael Hulse (London: Penguin, 2009).
Robinson, Michael, *Studies in Strindberg* (London: Ubiquity Press, 1998).
Rose, Margaret, *The Symbolist Tradition from Maeterlinck and Yeats to Beckett and Pinter* (Milan: Edizione Unicopli, 1989).
Rosen, Jeremy, *Minor Characters Have Their Day: Genre and the Contemporary Literary Marketplace* (New York: Columbia University Press, 2016).
Said, Edward, *Beginnings: Intention and Method* (New York: Basic Books, 1975).
Said, Edward, *On Late Style* (London: Bloomsbury, 2006).
Sartre, Jean-Paul, *Being and Nothingness*, trans. Hazel E. Barnes (London: Methuen, 1957).
Schönberg, Arnold, *Theory of Harmony*, trans. Roy E. Carter (Berkeley: University of California Press, 1978).

Schoolfield, George C., *A Baedeker of Decadence: Charting a Literary Fashion, 1884–1927* (New Haven: Yale University Press, 2003).

Sedgwick, Eve Kosofsky, *Between Men: English Literature and Male Homosocial Desire*, 30th anniversary ed. (New York: Columbia University Press, 2016).

Seigel, Jerrold E., *The Idea of the Self: Thought and Experience in Western Europe since the Seventeenth Century* (Cambridge: Cambridge University Press, 2005).

Senelick, Laurence, ed., *Russian Dramatic Theory from Pushkin to the Symbolists* (Austin: University of Texas Press, 1981).

Senn, Werner, *Conrad's Narrative Voice: Stylistic Aspects of His Fiction* (Leiden: Brill, 2017).

Sennett, Richard, *The Corrosion of Character: The Personal Consequences of Work in the New Capitalism* (New York and London: W. W. Norton, 1998).

Seys, Madeleine, *Fashion and Narrative in Victorian Popular Literature: Double Threads* (London: Routledge, 2017).

Shaw, George Bernard, 'Against the Well-Made Play', in George W. Brandt, ed., *Modern Theories of Drama: A Selection of Writings on Drama and Theatre, 1840–1990* (Oxford: Oxford University Press, 1998), 99–105.

Sherry, Norman, ed., *Joseph Conrad: The Critical Heritage* (London: Routledge, 1973).

Showalter, Elaine, *A Literature of Their Own: From Charlotte Brontë to Doris Lessing*, rev. ed. (London: Virago, 1999).

Shtutin, Leo, *Spatiality and Subjecthood in Mallarmé, Appolinaire, Maeterlinck, and Jarry: Between Page and Stage* (Oxford: Oxford University Press, 2019).

Simmel, Georg, *Georg Simmel, 1858–1918: A Collection of Essays*, ed. Kurt H. Wolff, trans. Lore Ferguson (Columbus: Ohio State University Press, 1959).

Smith, Murray, *Engaging Characters: Fiction, Emotion, and the Cinema* (Oxford: Clarendon Press, 1995).

Snyder, Katherine, *Bachelors, Manhood, and the Novel, 1850–1925* (Cambridge: Cambridge University Press, 1999).

Sprinchorn, Evert, *Strindberg as Dramatist* (New Haven: Yale University Press, 1982).

Sprinchorn, Evert, 'Strindberg and the Superman', in Göran Stockenström, ed., *Strindberg's Dramaturgy* (Minneapolis: University of Minnesota Press, 1988), 14–26.

Steiner, George, *The Death of Tragedy* (New York: Alfred A. Knopf, 1961).

Stevenson, Robert Louis, *The Strange Case of Dr Jekyll and Mr Hyde and Other Tales of Terror*, ed. Robert Mighall (London: Penguin, 2002).

Storm, William, *Dramaturgy and Dramatic Character: A Long View* (Cambridge: Cambridge University Press, 2016).

Strindberg, August, *Son of a Servant*, trans. Claud Field (New York: G. P. Putnam's Sons, 1913).

Strindberg, August, *Inferno, Alone, and Other Writings*, ed. and trans. Evert Sprinchorn (Garden City, NY: Anchor Books Doubleday, 1968).

Strindberg, August, *The Plays*, Vol. 2, trans. Michael Meyer (London: Secker & Warburg, 1975).

Strindberg, August, *Selected Letters*, Vol. 2, ed. and trans. Michael Robinson (Chicago: University of Chicago Press, 1992).

Strindberg, August, *Selected Essays*, ed. and trans. Michael Robinson (Cambridge: Cambridge University Press, 1996).

Strindberg, August, *Miss Julie and Other Plays*, ed. and trans. Michael Robinson (Oxford: Oxford University Press, 1998).

Strindberg, August, *Strindberg on Drama and Theatre: A Source Book*, ed. and trans. Egil Törnqvist and Birgitta Steene (Amsterdam: Amsterdam University Press, 2007).

Styan, J. L., *Modern Drama in Theory and Practice*, Vol. 1 (Cambridge: Cambridge University Press, 1981).
Symons, Arthur, *The Symbolist Movement in Literature* (New York: E. P. Dutton & Co., 1919).
Symons, Arthur, *Dramatis Personae* (London: Faber and Gwyer, 1925).
Szondi, Peter, *Theory of the Modern Drama*, Critical Edition, ed. and trans. Michael Hays, Theory and History of Literature 29 (Minneapolis: University of Minnesota Press, 1987).
Taine, Hippolyte, *On Intelligence*, trans. T. D. Haye, Kindle edition (New York: Holt & Williams, 1872).
Taylor, Charles, *Sources of the Self: The Making of the Modern Identity* (Cambridge, MA: Harvard University Press, 1989).
Thomas, David, *Henrik Ibsen*, Macmillan Modern Dramatists (London: Macmillan, 1983).
Törnqvist, Egil, *Strindbergian Drama: Themes and Structure* (Stockholm: Almqvist & Wiksell International, 1982).
Toth, Emily, *Unveiling Kate Chopin* (Jackson, MI: University Press of Mississippi, 1999).
Trotter, David, *Literature in the First Media Age: Britain Between the Wars* (Cambridge, MA: Harvard University Press, 2013).
Valency, Maurice, *The Flower and the Castle: An Introduction to Modern Drama* (New York: Macmillan, 1963).
Vermeule, Blakey, *Why Do We Care about Literary Characters?* (Baltimore: Johns Hopkins University Press, 2009).
Vernon, John, *Money and Fiction: Literary Realism in the Nineteenth and Early Twentieth Centuries* (Ithaca: Cornell University Press, 1984).
Watt, Ian, *Conrad in the Nineteenth Century* (Berkeley: University of California Press, 1981).
Watt, Ian, *Essays on Conrad* (Cambridge: Cambridge University Press, 2004).
Watts, Cedric, *Joseph Conrad: A Literary Life* (Basingstoke: Macmillan, 1989).
Weinstein, Arnold, *Fictions of the Self: 1550–1800* (Princeton: Princeton University Press, 1981).
Weinstein, Arnold, *Northern Arts: The Breakthrough of Scandinavian Literature and Art, from Ibsen to Bergman* (Princeton: Princeton University Press, 2008).
Wharton, Edith, *The Writing of Fiction* (New York: Octagon Books, 1966).
Wharton, Edith, *Collected Novels*, ed. R. W. B. Lewis (New York: Library of America, 1985).
Wharton, Edith, *The Letters of Edith Wharton*, ed. R. W. B. Lewis and Nancy Lewis (New York: Scribner's, 1988).
White, Andrea, *Joseph Conrad and the Adventure Tradition: Constructing and Deconstructing the Imperial Subject* (Cambridge: Cambridge University Press, 1993).
White, Brandon, 'Artless: Ignorance in the Novel and the Making of Modern Character' (PhD dissertation, University of California, Berkeley, 2017).
Wientzen, Timothy, 'The Aesthetics of Hunger: Knut Hamsun, Modernism, and Starvation's Global Frame', *NOVEL: A Forum on Fiction* 48.2 (August 2015): 208–23.
Wilde, Oscar, *The Soul of Man under Socialism and Selected Critical Prose*, ed. Linda Dowling (London: Penguin, 2001).
Wilde, Oscar, *The Picture of Dorian Gray* (London: Penguin, 2012).
Williams, Raymond, *Drama from Ibsen to Brecht* (New York: Oxford University Press, 1969).
Williams, Raymond, *Modern Tragedy*, ed. Pamela McCallum (Toronto: Broadview, 2006).
Woloch, Alex, *The One vs. the Many: Minor Characters and the Space of the Protagonist in the Novel* (Princeton: Princeton University Press, 2003).

Woodhouse, John, *Gabriele D'Annunzio: Defiant Archangel* (Oxford: Oxford University Press, 1998).

Worth, Katharine, *The Irish Drama of Europe from Yeats to Beckett* (London: Athlone, 1986).

Zola, Émile, *Le Naturalisme au théâtre*, trans. George Brandt, excerpted in Brandt, ed., *Modern Theories of Drama:* A Selection of Writings on Drama and Theatre, 1840–1990 (Oxford: Oxford University Press, 1998), 80–8.

Index